Russian Officialdom in Crisis

Autocracy and Local Self-Government, 1861–1900

THOMAS S. PEARSON

Monmouth College

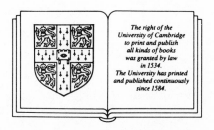

CAMBRIDGE UNIVERSITY PRESS

CAMBRIDGE

NEW YORK   NEW ROCHELLE   MELBOURNE   SYDNEY

Published by the Press Syndicate of the University of Cambridge
The Pitt Building, Trumpington Street, Cambridge CB2 1RP
32 East 57th Street, New York, NY 10022, USA
10 Stamford Road, Oakleigh, Melbourne 3166, Australia

First published 1989,

Printed in Canada

Library of Congress Cataloging-in-Publication Data
Pearson, Thomas S.
Russian officialdom in crisis : autocracy and local self-
government, 1861–1900 / Thomas S. Pearson.

p.   cm.
Bibliography: p.
Includes index.
ISBN 0-521-36127-3
1. Local government – Soviet Union – History – 19th century.
2. Civil service – Soviet Union – History – 19th century.   3. Soviet
Union – Politics and government – 19th century.   I. Title.
JS6057.P43   1989
352.047–dc19   88-17658

British Library Cataloguing in Publication Data
Pearson, Thomas S.
Russian officialdom in crisis : autocracy
and local self-government, 1861–1900

1. Russia.   Local government, 1861–1900
I. Title
352.047

ISBN 0 521 36127 3

Contents

v

TABLES

Preface

Of the four great European empires that met their demise in World War I, the Russian empire surely had the most traumatic initiation into the twentieth century. Beleaguered by famine, workers' strikes, student unrest, and military defeat, the old regime stumbled into the revolution of 1905 and came perilously close to losing its power. Although many causes lay behind this event, the administrative shortcomings of tsarism in the late nineteenth century were undoubtedly among the most important. These failings were particularly noticeable in the government's policy on local self-government, for here Russia's rulers confronted the centuries-old problem of governing a uniquely huge, underdeveloped empire with inadequate human and economic resources and with largely uneducated social classes who, for various reasons, regarded self-government with indifference.

Russian officialdom from the Petrine era on had grappled with the task of devising an effective system of central control over the Russian countryside without stifling all local development, and this dilemma continues to preoccupy Soviet leaders. Time and time again, they have reorganized the local Communist Party apparatus and government agencies to achieve a balance between party control and local economic initiative. Like their tsarist predecessors, Soviet leaders introducing reform have had to steer an unpredictable course designed to overcome official inertia without arousing overly sanguine expectations among officials and the population concerning the scope and tempo of the reform program.[1] In a broader vein, the problems of Russian

---

[1] Such reorganizations occurred in 1918, 1957–62, and 1972. Most recently, the dilemmas of reform at the local level have surfaced in the intense party discussions over the program of the Twenty-Seventh Party Congress (1986) and General Secretary Gorbachev's call for "restructuring" (*perestroika*). For discussions of previous reorganization at the local level, see Mervyn Matthews, ed., *Soviet Government: A Selection of Official Documents on Internal Policies* (New York, 1974), pp. 22–9, 93–102, 112–16; and Jerry F. Hough, *The Soviet Prefects: The Local Party Organs in Industrial Decisionmaking* (Cambridge, Mass., 1969), which concentrates on the post–World War II era. For one recent example of the party's effort to educate Soviet people on the limits of reform, see Bill Keller, "Soviet Youth Unit Seeks to Rein In

local administration discussed in this work have parallels in developing nations undergoing rapid social and economic change. Although the late tsarist regime did not have to deal with the legacy of colonial occupation or to integrate its population into a new national state, it did experience many of the same problems of local administrative development that have haunted developing nations. The Russian government, like other developing states, needed local self-government because the state bureaucracy lacked sufficient personnel and fiscal resources of its own to provide basic services (education, medical facilities, food relief, road construction) to modernize rural areas. Yet, paradoxically, the tsarist state found that illiteracy, poverty, and the lack of an adequate tax base in the countryside were large obstacles to the development of effective local self-government. Caught in this predicament, the Russian government encountered great difficulty in moving beyond its traditional rural functions of maintaining law and order and collecting taxes to a more dynamic role in tapping economic resources, meeting human needs, and mobilizing grass roots support.[2] Indeed, as with later developing countries, the evolution of local self-government in Russia provided a source of conflict within all levels of officialdom and between the state and public institutions of self-government.[3]

The problem of local self-government in tsarist Russia nevertheless warrants special attention because postreform Russia came under unusual pressures as a great power and a developing state, and because self-government provided a critical link between autocracy and Russian society. Faced with unprecedented demographic growth and the need for economic change in his realm, Tsar Alexander II abolished serfdom and in 1861–4 introduced a series of Great Reforms, among them a system of elected self-government that was to become the most significant local administrative reform in Russian history between the Petrine era and 1905. Although these changes put Russia in the ranks of European states that had established a decentralized system

Political Groups – Internal Report by Komsomol Reflects Wariness on Call for Democratic Moves," *New York Times*, 8 November 1987, pp. 1, 15.

[2]Fred W. Riggs, *Administration in Developing Countries: The Theory of Prismatic Society* (Boston, 1964), pp. 365–9, 372–4. On Russia as a model for developing nations see Teodor Shanin, *The Roots of Otherness: Russia's Turn of Century* (2 vols.; New Haven, 1985), vol. 1: *Russia as a "Developing Society."* This is not to suggest that the late tsarist experience with modernization on the local level was identical with that of decolonizing developing nations; indeed, late nineteenth-century Russian officials introduced social and economic change much more reluctantly (and political "modernization" did not really begin in Russia until after the 1905 revolution), whereas many developing nations embarked on a program of modernization explicitly to cultivate political support for the new states. Hence, the programs of rural administrative reform in such states were much more hurried. For the differences in the modernization of Russia and developing nations, see C. E. Black, *The Dynamics of Modernization: A Study in Comparative History* (New York, 1967), pp. 119–28. The term "modernization," as used here, refers not only to industrialization but also to a variety of other developments (population growth, urbanization, increases in mass literacy, professionalization and specialization of the government, administrative centralization, the formation of social classes) as defined by Black, pp. 7, 13–15, 46–7.

[3]For instance, see Douglas E. Ashford, *National Development and Local Reform: Political Participation in Morocco, Tunisia, and Pakistan* (Princeton, 1967), pp. 12–14, 24–5, 28, 39; Richard P. Taub, *Bureaucrats under Stress: Administrators and Administration in an Indian State* (Berkeley, 1969), pp. 114–16; and Riggs, pp. 382–91, who focuses on the problems of Philippine development.

of public self-government at midcentury to harness new social forces and perpetuate monarchical rule, the Russian experiment with self-government proved exceptional in two respects.[4] On the one hand, the creation of elected peasant and zemstvo self-government compounded tensions in the tsarist government – for instance, between central and local concerns and between local public and state officials – that were unmatched in their extent and gravity elsewhere in Europe. This was largely because a strong and active system of public self-government in Russia potentially provided the basis for the development of civil liberties, constitutional government, and religious and national freedom – forces antithetical to the tsarist order.[5] On the other hand, the Russian experience with local self-government stands out because the tsarist empire was the only European state to reverse its course of decentralization so abruptly in the late nineteenth century, with the same purpose of perpetuating imperial rule and consolidating its social support.

This book focuses on the Russian government's efforts to direct local self-government and its reform from its introduction in 1861 to its bureaucratization under the land captains and zemstvo counterreforms of 1889 and 1890. It seeks to answer two interrelated questions: Why did the Russian government introduce these counterreforms in local self-government? and What does our case study of the administrative reasons for these counterreforms and the bureaucratic politics surrounding them tell us about the nature and viability of the imperial government on the eve of the twentieth century? The origin and elaboration of these counterreforms suggest themselves as a case study of Russian officialdom in crisis on several counts. First, these measures, traditionally overshadowed by the Great Reforms of the 1860s and the revolution of 1905, were the legislative cornerstones of Alexander III's reign (1881–94) and were autocracy's foremost attempt in the postreform era to renovate its rural institutions without relinquishing political authority. A study of local self-government reform under Alexander II and Alexander III provides insight into the Russian government's authority and ability to adapt to changing social, economic, and political conditions – clearly a vital consideration in any assessment of the late imperial regime and its standing among nineteenth-century European powers.

Second, as an issue that involved many state ministries and all estates of the realm (*sosloviia*) and that molded public opinion about tsarism, local self-government linked central and local concerns in a unique way. It repeatedly raised questions about the structure and performance of autocracy at the

---

[4]For the European setting, see Robert C. Binkley, *Realism and Nationalism: 1852–1871* (New York, 1935); Brigitte Basdevant-Gaudemet, *La Commission de décentralisation de 1870: Contribution à l'étude de la décentralisation en France au XIXe siècle* (Paris, 1973); A. D. Gradovskii, *Sobranie sochinenii* (9 vols.; St. Petersburg, 1899–1904), especially vol. 5; and N. M. Korkunov, *Russkoe gosudarstvennoe pravo* (2 vols.; St. Petersburg, 1903), vol. 2. The importance of local government in the development of the well-ordered police state in Imperial Russia is discussed in Marc Raeff, *Understanding Imperial Russia: State and Society under the Old Regime*, trans. Arthur Goldhammer (New York, 1984), pp. 58–60, 64, 82.

[5]Paul Vinogradoff, *Self-Government in Russia* (London, 1915), p. 4.

grass roots level; its potential, by Western standards, for evolving into a more modern, activist government that could provide the local population with essential services as well as order; the applicability of Western political theories on local self-government in Russia; the relationship of autocracy to the traditional social structure in Russia and the future of both; and the direction and pace of socioeconomic change in the Russian countryside at a time when, compared with the turn of the century, tsarism was relatively free from war and diplomatic entanglements and could concentrate on domestic reform.[6]

Beyond these general concerns about rural development and the autocratic order, the reform of peasant and zemstvo self-government raised unique political issues. This stemmed from the fact that in postreform Russia local government consisted of state, corporate (estate), and public institutions. Contemporary officials and writers concurred that the legal separation of the peasantry and the establishment of peasant self-government in 1861 were a necessary alternative to the serfowner's authority in providing the state with administrative and fiscal control over the village. They rightly emphasized that the abolition of serfdom necessitated other reforms in local administration, the judiciary, the universities and school system, and the military. Beyond that, however, they disagreed on nearly everything else regarding elected peasant administration, its relationship to the peasant land commune (*obshchina*) and state authorities, and its impact on village society and economy. Significantly, these issues were at the heart of later land reform discussions during the Stolypin era and the early Soviet period.[7] In the period under study, top officials were most concerned with the ramifications of peasant self-government reform for the landed gentry and the state. One faction envisioned the inclusion of peasant self-government in a comprehensive system of public self-government and the eventual eradication of all estate distinctions, whereas their opponents (including pro-gentry journalists M. N. Katkov and Prince V. P. Meshcherskii) defended separate peasant self-government under gentry tutelage as the raison d'être of the postreform gentry and fitting compensation for their losses in the peasant emancipation.

By contrast, the debate over zemstvo self-government (established in 1864) between the local public and bureacracy and within those two groups centered on broader political issues. The main question from the Great Reforms era on was whether the zemstvos, as elected institutions of self-government,

[6]Theodore S. Hamerow, *The Birth of a New Europe: State and Society in the Nineteenth Century* (Chapel Hill, N.C., 1983), pp. 261–2. On the connection between international pressures and the tsarist government's structural weakness and growing rigidity after 1890, see Theda Skocpol, *States and Social Revolutions: A Comparative Analysis of France, Russia, and China* (Cambridge, 1979), pp. 90–4; and Dietrich Geyer, *Russian Imperialism: The Interaction of Domestic and Foreign Policy, 1860–1914*, trans. Bruce Little (New Haven, 1987), pp. 126–7.

[7]See, for instance, David A. J. Macey, *Government and Peasant in Russia, 1861–1906: The Prehistory of the Stolypin Reforms* (DeKalb, Ill., 1987); Dorothy Atkinson, *The End of the Russian Land Commune 1905–1930* (Stanford, 1983); Graeme J. Gill, *Peasants and Government in the Russian Revolution* (New York, 1979); and Moshe Lewin, *Russian Peasants and Soviet Power: A Study of Collectivization* (London, 1968).

constituted part of the state bureaucracy. One school of thought held that the zemstvos were public institutions that handled local administrative functions such as fire prevention and public health, which had no connection to the tasks of the state bureaucracy. Contrary to the "social" theory of self-government, the "state" theory viewed the zemstvos as adjuncts of the state discharging only those functions that the government, for want of personnel and fiscal resources, delegated to them. Consequently, another question in the minds of officials was whether an autonomous zemstvo might become the nucleus of a public constitutional movement.[8] Nevertheless, they recognized, as did many others, that peasant and zemstvo self-government were the keys to systematic state administration and control in Russia at the district (*uezd*) level and below. Accordingly, local self-government reform was the litmus issue in domestic politics because it forced tsarism to delineate its administrative priorities, its policy toward the various estates, and its own political future. More than a reorganization of the state bureaucracy, local self-government reform raised or dampened public expectations and required Russian officials to evaluate autocracy's course vis à vis Western administrative development.

Given these considerations, it is no surprise that scholars to date, almost without exception, have treated the land captains and zemstvo counterreforms as part of a growing conflict between an "all-powerful autocracy" and "oppressed society" (*obshchestvo*) and have concentrated on the political aspects of the legislation. These works depict the counterreforms as part of the government's reaction to Alexander II's assassination in 1881 and resulting political pressures, while paying little heed to the concrete activity of peasant and zemstvo institutions. Prerevolutionary "liberal" historians writing circa the 1905 Revolution dismissed the counterreforms and Alexander III's "new pro-gentry course" in general as an unfortunate step backward in Russia's constitutional development from 1861 to 1905. In their view the zemstvos were emasculated in 1890 because of their political activism (which these historians exaggerated), not their administrative record (which, with the noteworthy exception of B. B. Veselovskii, they overlooked).[9] Although Soviet historians in recent years have produced more sophisticated studies of Russia's "crisis of autocracy" of the late 1870s and early 1880s, they, too, ritualistically emphasize the reactionary political character of the counterreforms, introduced in the wake of the "revolutionary situation of 1878–82" that culminated with Alexander II's death. Using the paradigm of class conflict, these historians criticize prerevolutionary historians for not emphasizing the gentry "class" nature of the counterreforms. They maintain that

---

[8]For a good synopsis of the debate, see Neil B. Weissman, *Reform in Tsarist Russia: The State Bureaucracy and Local Government, 1900–1914* (New Brunswick, N.J., 1981), pp. 15–16.

[9]Classic "liberal" works on the subject include I. P. Belokonskii, *Zemstvo i konstitutsiia* (Moscow, 1910); A. A. Kornilov, *Krest'ianskaia reforma* (St. Petersburg, 1905); V. M. Gessen, *Voprosy mestnogo upravleniia* (St. Petersburg, 1904); G. A. Dzhanshiev, *Epokha velikikh reform; istoricheskie ocherki* (8th ed., Moscow, 1900); and B. B. Veselovskii, *Istoriia zemstva za sorok let* (4 vols.; St. Petersburg, 1911), vol. 3.

the "bourgeois-capitalist" reforms of the 1860s, in precipitating the political and economic decline of the landed gentry, deprived autocracy of its social support and plunged the government into a crisis marked by revolutionary terrorist attacks and peasant unrest. Consequently the counterreforms and general bureaucratic arbitrariness (*proizvol*) of the 1880s and 1890s, according to Soviet accounts, answered the needs of the government and landed gentry in the countryside and reforged the social alliance between them.[10]

Recent Western studies of the elite bureaucracy under Alexander II and Alexander III dispute the view that the government was the landed gentry's instrument and that the counterreforms were mainly gentry legislation. They contend that elite officials of both reigns, as represented in the various ministries and the State Council, were socially and professionally isolated from the landed gentry and polarized into opposing ideological groups over the relationship of law to autocracy, as defined by Western bureaucratic theory set to Russian political conditions.[11] These studies are of particular

[10]See Iu. B. Solov'ev, *Samoderzhavie i dvorianstvo v kontse XIX veka* (Leningrad, 1973), pp. 3–5, 28–65, 84–92, 106–11, 165ff.; B. S. Itenberg, "Krizis samoderzhavnoi vlasti," *Rossiia v revoliutsionnoi situatsii na rubezhe 1870–1880-kh godov: Kollektivnaia monografiia*, ed. B. S. Itenberg and others (Moscow, 1983), pp. 91ff.; and, more generally, P. A. Zaionchkovskii, *Rossiiskoe samoderzhavie v kontse XIX stoletiia* (Moscow, 1970); S. N. Valk, "Vnutrenniaia politika tsarizma v 80–90-kh godakh," *Istoriia SSSR*, vol. 2: *1861–1917 gg. Period kapitalizma*, ed. L. M. Ivanov, A. L. Sidorov, and V. K. Iatsunskii (Moscow, 1959); L. G. Zakharova, *Zemskaia kontrreforma 1890 g. (Moscow, 1968)*; A. P. Korelin, *Dvorianstvo v poreformennoi Rossii 1861–1904 gg.: Sostav, chislennost', korporativnaia organizatsiia* (Moscow, 1979); N. M. Pirumova, *Zemskoe liberal'noe dvizhenie: Sotsial'nye korni i evoliutsiia do nachala XX veka* (Moscow, 1977); and V. A. Tvardovskaia, *Ideologiia poreformennogo samoderzhaviia (M. N. Katkov i ego izdaniia)* (Moscow, 1978). The recent work of P. N. Zyrianov offers some interesting variations on this argument. True, in stereotypical fashion he asserts that the autocracy sought to perpetuate its archaic control and gentry influence by establishing a separate peasant village and *volost'* administration under gentry control and by granting the gentry primary authority in district administration (as opposed to provincial administration where the state bureaucracy dominated). This policy served to counter the penetration of capitalism and the control of the bourgeoisie (kulaks) in the countryside. But more than other Soviet historians, Zyrianov suggests that the land captains counterreform was introduced not so much to prop up the gentry as to improve the *efficiency* of *volost'* administration and to give gentry supervisors the authority to protect the mass of petty and middle peasants from the village bourgeoisie. P. N. Zyrianov, "Sotsial'naia struktura mestnogo upravleniia kapitalisticheskoi Rossii (1861–1914 gg.)," *Istoricheskie zapiski*, vol. 107 (Moscow, 1982), pp. 237–8, 251–2, 262–5, 267, 271, 273–4.

[11]Daniel T. Orlovsky, *The Limits of Reform: The Ministry of Internal Affairs in Imperial Russia, 1802–1881* (Cambridge, Mass., 1981); and Heide W. Whelan, *Alexander III and the State Council: Bureaucracy and Counter-Reform in Late Imperial Russia* (New Brunswick, N.J., 1982). The development of bureaucracy in Russia is discussed in Daniel T. Orlovsky, "Recent Studies on the Russian Bureaucracy," *Russian Review* 34 (October 1976): 448–67; Marc Raeff, "The Bureaucratic Phenomena of Imperial Russia, 1700–1905," *American Historical Review* 84 (April 1979): 399–411; Walter M. Pintner and Don Karl Rowney, eds., *Russian Officialdom: The Bureaucratization of Russian Society from the Seventeenth to the Twentieth Century* (Chapel Hill, N.C., 1980); and P. A. Zaionchkovskii, *Pravitel'stvennyi apparat samoderzhavnoi Rossii v XIX v.* (Moscow, 1979). See also the following specialized studies: W. Bruce Lincoln, "Russia's Enlightened Bureaucrats and the Problem of State Reform, 1848–1866," *Cahiérs du monde russe et soviétique* 12 (October-December 1971), 410–21; Walter M. Pintner, "Russian Civil Service on the Eve of the Great Reforms," *Journal of Social History* 8 (Spring 1975): 55–65; Daniel Field, *The End of Serfdom: Nobility and Bureaucracy in Russia, 1855–1861* (Cambridge, Mass., 1976); Richard S. Wortman, *The Development of a Russian Legal Consciousness* (Chicago, 1976); and two unpublished dissertations: Theodore Taranovski, "The Politics of Counter-Reform: Autocracy and Bureaucracy in the Reign of Alexander III 1881–1894" (Harvard University, 1976); and Helju A. Bennett, "The *Chin* System and the Raznochintsy in the Government of Alexander III" (University of California, 1971).

value in showing that the principles behind the Great Reforms provided an ideological context for later debates over local government reform. Likewise, they show that the German concepts of *Rechtsstaat* (rule of law) and *Polizeistaat* (well-ordered police state) were tailored in postreform Russia to ensure that the autocrat maintained his personal authority. Within this framework the tsar used the law and institutions to regulate and coopt society (*Reglaments-staat*) rather than prepare society to play the dynamic role in local development that it did in the West.[12] According to these works, Alexander III, following the lead of his minister of internal affairs, abandoned the legal principles behind the Great Reforms and advocated a return to the personal, discretionary authority that characterized the Russian *Polizeistaat* of the pre-reform period. Yet the tsar and his minister D. A. Tolstoi were thwarted in part by the old reformers in the State Council, who had enough power in the 1880s to water down the counterreform proposals.[13]

Although these writings shed light on the ethos of elite officials in the nineteenth century and bureaucratic politics surrounding the counterreforms, they are similar to Soviet studies in two respects – they draw virtually no connection between the record of local self-government and the counterreforms (as if to prove the isolation of the elite bureaucracy from rural Russia) and they suggest that the late imperial government was doomed by divisions and dysfunctioning at the highest levels.[14] Whereas Soviet scholars attribute the demise of autocracy to its "crisis of support," Western scholars have tended to emphasize the ideological sterility and conflict of the late imperial regime. In marked contrast, George Yaney treats the land captain counter-reform as part of a process of bureaucratic interaction with the peasantry that represented a vast improvement over elected peasant officials in supervising the village and provided a means for government mobilization of rural society. At last the state was bringing law and order to replace the confusion and custom of the peasant world and was enlisting the landed gentry in the

---

[12]On this theme, see Raeff, "Bureaucratic Phenomena," pp. 408–9; and the following works by him: *The Well-Ordered Police State: Social and Institutional Change through the Law in the Germanies and Russia, 1600–1800* (New Haven, 1983), pp. 178, 181–8, 198, 214–16; and "The Well-Ordered Police State and the Development of Modernity in Seventeenth- and Eighteenth-Century Europe: An Attempt at a Comparative Approach," *American Historical Review* 80 (December 1975): 1234–9. The differences between Russia and the Germanies showed up in the concept of *Rechtsstaat* as well; whereas in German territories *Rechtsstaat* in the early nineteenth century became an antonym of the *Polizeistaat* and a doctrine meaning "rule by law" – with some protection of individual freedom – in Russia it served more as a means for "rule through the law and institutions." In official debates over the counterreforms, the opponents of the legislation advocated a *Rechtsstaat* in this limited sense. On this point, compare Leonard Krieger, *The German Idea of Freedom: History of a Political Tradition* (Chicago, 1957), pp. 252–61; and Whelan, pp. 87–92. See also V. V. Leontovich, *Istoriia liberalizma v Rossii 1762–1914*. Trans. from German by Irina Ilovaiskaia (Paris, 1980), pp. 8–9.

[13]For the clearest statement of this argument see Taranovski, "The Politics of Counter-Reform," chap. 3.

[14]Combining the interpretations of recent Soviet and Western specialists, Becker attributes the counterreforms to the autocracy's desire to restore traditional paternalistic gentry tutelage in the countryside, as advocated in the 1880s by the *soslovniki* (the gentry in favor of reorganizing local administration along estate lines) and their journalistic champions, Katkov and Meshcherskii. Seymour Becker, *Nobility and Privilege in Late Imperial Russia* (DeKalb, Ill., 1985), pp. 55–62, 130–2.

process. Yet Yaney's comprehensive studies on rural agrarian and institutional change tend to overlook the interministerial politics that impeded the government's ability to perceive and respond to rural needs.[15]

By focusing on elite bureaucratic politics and ideologies or the evolution of the gentry from a social order to a class, recent scholarship has told us more about *how* the land captain and zemstvo counterreforms were enacted, rather than *why*. All of these accounts (including Yaney's) view the arrival of A. D. Pazukhin, the gentry marshal from Alatyr' district (Simbirsk Province), in St. Petersburg in 1884–5 as the beginning of the counterreform process, thereby drawing little continuity between the official discussions of local self-government reform at the end of Alexander II's reign and those that dominated his successor's rule. Nor do they fully explain why it took the government almost a decade to introduce counterreforms that, in their view, were triggered by the assassination of Alexander II (1881) and his son's desire to eradicate self-government in Russia. Similarly, the view of the counterreforms as primarily a means of arresting the landed gentry's political and economic decline raises serious questions. If tsarist officials were guided by reasons of state in establishing public self-government in the 1860s, as most Soviet and Western historians concur, why would the government overhaul it in the 1880s owing to pressure from a splintered, politically weaker gentry? Moreover, even if we assume that the government introduced these counterreforms to promote the interests of the traditional landed gentry as its rural social support, why did these gentry overnight become the leading critics of the legislation?[16] The institutional studies of Whelan and Taranovski are not particularly helpful in answering this question in that they do not address the administrative and social context of the legislation. They do not explain why the tsar's bureaucracy, factionalized and inert, persisted and introduced the land captain and zemstvo counterreforms nearly a decade after Alexander II's assassination.

This study aims to redress the balance and show the interplay of administrative, institutional, and ideological factors, in the provinces and the capital, that led to the land captains and zemstvo counterreforms.[17] By analyzing the interaction of ministerial politics and the grass-roots devel-

[15]George L. Yaney, *The Systematization of Russian Government: Social Evolution in the Domestic Administration of Imperial Russia, 1711–1905* (Urbana, Ill., 1973); and idem, *The Urge to Mobilize: Agrarian Reform in Russia, 1861–1930* (Urbana, Ill., 1982). Several articles in a recent collection on the zemstvo focus on zemstvo activity, yet none of them explore the connection between its shortcomings and the enactment of the zemstvo counterreform. The articles focus largely on the post–1890 period. See Terence Emmons and Wayne Vucinich, eds., *The Zemstvo in Russia: An Experiment in Local Self-Government* (Cambridge, 1982).

[16]Becker, pp. 133–4.

[17]A similar administrative approach has been used for other periods of Russian history: For 1830–70, see S. Frederick Starr, *Decentralization and Self-Government in Russia, 1830–1870* (Princeton, 1972); and for 1900–14, Weissman. For a valuable forthcoming study of the provincial governors and their crucial role in local administration see Richard G. Robbins, Jr., "The Tsar's Viceroys: Provincial Governors and Governance in the Last Years of the Empire."

opment of local self-government as the state perceived it, we get a fuller picture of the administrative crisis that faced tsarism and of the practical limits of autocracy in Russia at the end of the nineteenth century. By and large, historians agree that the autocracy was in crisis in the late 1870s and early 1880s, as illustrated by terrorist attacks on its officials and its reliance on extralegal means to suppress opposition. The 1890s have also been called a period of crisis because of the outbreak of famine and cholera in the provinces and burgeoning strike activity in the cities. However, the term "crisis" is also warranted in a wider sense, as used here, to characterize the government's increasing futility at managing rural administrative development with its paternalistic bureaucracy and traditional corporate institutions, and its inability to renovate local government with its ministerial apparatus. In this sense, Russian officialdom experienced what some scholars have called a crisis of "penetration," which entailed the extension of government control over its territories and social groups and the development of bureaucratic efficiency.[18] To be sure, bureaucratic inefficiency alone does not constitute a crisis. Yet in autocratic Russia, as perhaps nowhere else in Europe, state attempts at rural control through the Great Reforms bred public disillusionment and administrative and economic problems for Russian officials far beyond the routine type. When an activist state (such as Russia following the Crimean defeat) is unsuccessful in managing its broader, more complex responsibilities effectively, the result is often social alienation and bureaucratic rigidity – especially when there is no basis for meaningful public participation in government. These conditions make the regime more vulnerable to political challenges of its legitimacy, such as occurred in Russia during the revolutionary years 1905 and 1917.[19]

Along these lines I contend that the land captain and zemstvo counterreforms, like the local self-government established in the 1860s, were designed to meet specific rural needs and were a product of a ministerial system of government that Alexander II developed with his Great Reforms. This compartmentalized arrangement promoted more professional administration and bureaucratic penetration in the provinces and left the tsar's personal power intact by allowing the autocrat to choose from different ministerial approaches and ideologies of local development. Unfortunately, it also produced ministerial fragmentation and confusion at all levels and helped put

---

[18]On the crisis of "penetration," see Raymond Grew, "The Crises and Their Sequences," *Crises of Political Development in Europe and the United States*, ed. Raymond Grew (Princeton, 1978), pp. 7, 10–13, 22–5; and Walter M. Pintner, "Russia," in the above-mentioned volume, pp. 366–8. In a similar vein, see Yaney, *Urge to Mobilize*, pp. 7–8. This type of broad administrative crisis characterized by structural breakdown has been investigated for other periods; for instance, see H. R. Trevor-Roper, "The General Crisis of the Seventeenth Century," *Crisis in Europe 1560–1660*, ed. Trevor Aston (Anchor Book ed.; Garden City, N.Y., 1967), pp. 67–8, 77–102; and Riggs, pp. 378–9. For a description of the general crisis in Russia's autocratic system in the late nineteenth century, see Solov'ev, pp. 3–7; and *Krizis samoderzhaviia v Rossii 1895–1917*, ed. B. V. Anan'ich and R. Sh. Ganelin (Leningrad, 1984).

[19]Grew, pp. 20, 26, 30; Pintner, "Russia," pp. 371–5.

state institutions into conflict with the new zemstvo and peasant institutions. Besides generating reverberations in the provincial bureaucracy,[20] these conflicts impeded the work of local self-government and complicated state efforts to modify, not to mention overhaul, the legislation of the 1860s.

Nonetheless, Russian officialdom pressed on and devised the counterreforms for practical statist reasons. I maintain that the government did so following the autocratic crisis of the late 1870s because it was convinced that elected peasant and zemstvo institutions, as established in the 1860s, were mismanaged, insolvent, and politically troublesome to autocracy. Indeed, that crisis revealed that the administrative and fiscal order of the state ultimately hinged on the work of elected institutions outside the government's strict control. Put another way, the state's efforts to control the provinces in the Great Reform era were shown to be inadequate by the political crisis of 1878–82. Yet in the 1880s, as two decades earlier, the state had few options for overhauling local administration owing to shortages of personnel and funds, its distrust of elected officials, and sporadic tensions between local state and public institutions.[21]

Viewed against this backdrop, the counterreform proposals of Minister of Internal Affairs Dmitrii Andreevich Tolstoi and his role in their enactment merit reevaluation. We shall show how throughout the 1880s he insisted that local self-government be depoliticized and bureaucratized in order to fulfill its administrative functions. However, the prospect of all local self-government concentrated under his ministry challenged the ministerial power equilibrium established under Alexander II and violated the principles of Alexander II's reform officials who sat in the State Council. Tolstoi's peers recognized that the balance of power between the capital and localities was a key to state security, administrative order, and their own political status, and thus most of them joined forces and employed various strategies, with some success, to blunt the counterreform measures. By the end of the nineteenth century, as elaborated in the following chapters, public self-government had been repudiated but not fully bureaucratized, leaving a tangled, confused local administration and divided ministerial hierarchy that would come under attack at the turn of the century.

Owing to limitations of the topic, I have passed over or treated briefly certain themes of local self-government. Municipal institutions clearly com-

---

[20]Zyrianov, pp. 289–90.

[21]From 1858 to 1897 the population of the Russian empire rose from 59.2 million to 116 million (excluding Finland and the Caucasus). Although the ratio of tsarist officials to population increased from 1:929 in 1851 to 1:335 in 1897, the tsarist empire remained seriously undergoverned at the end of the nineteenth century in comparison with other European states. For instance, at the turn of the century Russia had only 6.2 administrators per thousand inhabitants as opposed to 17.7/1,000 and 12.6/1,000 for France and Germany, respectively. Weissman, p. 111. As shown in the following chapters, the shortage of state personnel was compounded by the limited number of rural people traditionally involved in local self-government from the 1860s to 1905. For the population data, see Ia. E. Vodarskii, *Naselenie Rossii za 400 let (XVI–nachalo XX v.)* (Moscow, 1973), pp. 113–14; for the figures on the growth of Russian bureaucracy, see Zaionchkovskii, *Pravitel'stvennyi apparat*, p. 221.

prised a part of local self-government, yet a detailed analysis of town administration would raise issues exclusively urban in nature and of little relevance
to the politics of local government reform in the countryside. Moreover, the
guiding concepts of the municipal legislation of 1870 and 1892 (which I
hope to analyze in later work) were taken from the zemstvo legislation of
1864 and 1890, respectively.[22] In addition, I have treated the development
of central and local administration in the 1890s (following the implementation of the counterreforms) in rather summary fashion, in part because a
detailed analysis of the various state commissions dealing with the rural
economy, gentry needs, and local administration would expand this account
immeasurably without substantially altering the interpretation of local administrative problems and political conflicts. These records have proved
especially fruitful to students of gentry politics and the background of the
Stolypin Land Reforms (1906–11), and the reader may turn to several good
accounts of these topics.[23] For similar reasons I have confined this study to
an analysis of local self-government, as opposed to all of the institutions of
local government. State and corporate institutions of local administration
are discussed only insofar as they affected, or were affected by, local self-
government.

The terminology in this type of study creates difficulties because certain
Russian concepts and words (for example, *obshchina*) have no precise English
equivalents on the one hand, and because officials in the debate over local
self-government reform frequently used Western terms (separation of powers,
decentralization) on the other. I have provided a translation to explain terms
of the first type as they appear in the text; the Russian term *dvorianstvo*,
however, requires a special note here. The *dvorianstvo* resembled neither a
nobility (closed corporation, hereditary privileges) nor a gentry (land as
primary source of income) in the true Western sense. I have chosen to render
the term as gentry, however, because the focus here is on the landed segment
of the *dvorianstvo* and their leadership, or lack thereof, in local self-
government and corporate institutions. The Western terms can also be briefly
defined here. The decentralists comprised those officials who advocated a
diffusion and, in some cases, a devolution of decision-making authority;
expanded initiative and autonomy for public self-government; explicit laws
protecting these institutions; and separate administrative and judicial
branches of government. In contrast, the centralists were those who favored
rigid state control over local institutions, the concentration of all authority
over local self-government in one central agency, usually the Ministry of

---

[22]The best of the few surveys of municipal reform and self-government are I. I. Ditiatin, *Ustroistvo i
upravlenie gorodov v Rossii* (2 vols.; Moscow, 1875–1877); D. D. Semenov, *Gorodskoe samoupravlenie:
Ocherki i opyty* (St. Petersburg, 1901); and V. A. Nardova, *Gorodskoe samoupravlenie v Rossii v 60-kh-
nachale 90-kh godov XIX v.: Pravitel'stvennaia politika* (Leningrad, 1984).

[23]Besides Yaney, *Urge to Mobilize*, and Macey (see note 7), see James I. Mandel, "Paternalistic Authority
in the Russian Countryside, 1856–1906" (Unpublished Ph.D. dissertation, Columbia University,
1978). On the zemstvo after 1890, see Emmons and Vucinich, eds., *Zemstvo in Russia*.

Internal Affairs, and a combination of administrative, judicial, and punitive authority in one set of state officials. In addition, I have used the phrase "ministerial circles" in a general context, referring to top officials as a whole (ministers, State Council members, governors), and in a more limited sense when dealing with specific ministers or ministries. The usage in each case is clear from the text.

All Russian names are transliterated according to the Library of Congress system except for those of the tsars, Witte, and Count Pahlen, which are rendered in the anglicized form. First names and patronymics are given for all ministers in this study, with the initials given for other individuals. All dates are based on the Julian calendar, which lagged twelve days behind the Western calendar during the period of this study. The specific citations and titles of archival *dela* used in this study are given in the notes according to the customary Soviet form: archive, *fond* (*f.*) [collection], *god* (*g.*) [year], *opis'* (*op.*) [inventory], *delo* (*d.*) [file], *karton* (*k.*) [box], *papka* (*p.*) [folder], *list/-y* (*l.*, *ll.*) [sheet], *oborot* (*ob.*) [verso]. Citations for *listy*, as for pages, will be given in abbreviated form (for instance, *ll.* 146–7 for *ll.* 146–147) except in cases involving the *oborot* of a *list*, where more detailed citations (*ll.* 146–146 *ob.*) will be used to avoid confusion.

Acknowledgments

This book has been in the works a long time, a point recently impressed on me by my six-year-old son, who asked if the history I was describing had taken as long to happen as the book I was writing. Now that I have reached this juncture, however, it is my pleasant task to thank the institutions and individuals who have assisted me in this endeavor. For financial support I am indebted above all to the International Research and Exchanges Board, who funded a year of research in the Soviet Union. I likewise thank Monmouth College and Eugene Rosi, provost, and Gloria Nemerowicz, dean of humanities and social sciences, for several grants-in-aid for my research and writing. The Russian and East European Research Center at the University of Illinois and the University of North Carolina provided grants for me to do preliminary research on the topic.

I am especially indebted to the directors and archivists of the Central State Historical Archive in Leningrad, the Central State Archive of the October Revolution in Moscow, and the Manuscript Sections of the Lenin Library (Moscow) and Public Library (Leningrad) for invaluable assistance in locating pertinent sources for my work. Without their help this book could never have been written. I also thank the library staffs of the Hoover Institution, Harvard University, Columbia University, Illinois University, the Library of Congress, Monmouth College, Princeton University, Duke University, and the University of North Carolina for much help along the way. I am grateful for permission to use material from my previously published articles: "The Origins of Alexander III's Land Captains: A Reinterpretation," *Slavic Review* 40 (Fall 1981), 384–403; and "Russian Law and Rural Justice: The Activity and Problems of the Russian Justices of the Peace, 1865–1889," *Jahrbücher für Geschichte Osteuropas*, no. 1 (1984), 52–71 (publisher – Franz Steiner Verlag, Wiesbaden GmbH, Stuttgart).

My work has benefited greatly from the encouragement and suggestions of scholars who helped me turn a doctoral dissertation into a book. In the early stages of this study I was fortunate to have the advice of E. Willis Brooks, Sam Baron, David Griffiths, Josef Anderle, and Lamar Cecil. In the Soviet Union I had fruitful consultations with B. V. Anan'ich (my *rukovoditel'*), V. G. Chernukha, Iu. B. Solov'ev, L. G. Zakharova, and the late P. A. Zaionchkovskii, the real pioneer in recent work on nineteenth-century Russian administrative history. I am especially grateful to S. Frederick Starr, Gregory Freeze, Richard Wortman, Marc Raeff, Ken Stunkel, and Tad Swietochowski for reading and commenting on the manuscript at various stages; this book is much better because of their criticisms and those of the readers at Cambridge University Press. Here I must single out Richard Robbins, Jr., for his steady encouragement and constructive suggestions during the years that I have worked on this book and for allowing me to read the manuscript of his forthcoming book "The Tsar's Viceroys: Provincial Governors and Governance in the Last Years of the Empire." I thank George Yaney for his interest in my research over the years, and all at Cambridge University Press who have aided me in the publication of this book. Needless to say, I accept responsibility for any errors in facts or interpretations stated in this work.

Like most authors, I have derived my greatest support from family and friends in and out of the profession. I thank my colleagues in the History Department at Monmouth College for their encouragement as I prepared the manuscript for publication. I owe my two sons, Tim and Mark, my love and thanks for bearing with me when I could not give them the time they deserved. My greatest regret is that my parents, Donn and June Pearson, did not live to see this book published. Words cannot adequately express my love for or debt to them. My greatest debt in preparing this work, however, is to Susie, my wife, friend, editor, and typist for so many years. I have always regarded this book as our work, and for this reason I dedicate it to her.

CHAPTER I

Introduction: old problems, new principles – tsarist government and the Great Reforms

The Crimean War of 1853–6 is invariably regarded as a turning point in modern Russian history and with good reason. Not only did it end the reign of Nicholas I (1825–55) and shatter the ideal of enlightened autocratic rule that he inherited from his predecessors. Even more, it triggered unprecedented levels of peasant unrest in the provinces and left the state bankrupt. Under such circumstances, as so often in the past, the Russian state embarked on a series of reforms that in the 1860s created a new administrative order in rural Russia and solidified a ministerial system of government that remained fatefully intertwined down to 1917. Yet by almost all accounts changes in provincial administration were urgently needed. So ubiquitous was the corruption and inefficiency of rural officials that the description of it in the works of Gogol, Saltykov-Shchedrin, and other contemporary writers amused but did not shock their readers.[1] As for officials themselves, Petr Aleksandrovich Valuev, the governor of Courland Province and later minister of internal affairs (1861–8) was not alone in pointing out that suspicion, ignorance, and incompetence were the most distinguishing shortcomings of Russian bureaucrats, and that provincial administration stood in need of complete overhaul.[2]

The shortcomings of provincial administration noted by Valuev were not new to Russian officials. They had long wrestled with the problem of how to make local government efficient and had faced the dilemma of whether

---

[1] Starr, *Decentralization*, pp. 4–5.

[2] P. A. Valuev, "Duma russkogo vo vtoroi polovine 1855 goda," *Russkaia starina* 24, no. 9 (1893): 509, 514. Slavophile I. S. Aksakov referred to provincial administration in similar terms in a letter sent in 1850 to Nikolai Alekseevich Miliutin, his superior in the Provisional Section of the Economic Department of the Ministry of Internal Affairs. Aksakov claimed that, "out of every hundred minor bureaucrats, one cannot even find two honest ones." Quoted in W. Bruce Lincoln, "N. A. Miliutin and the St. Petersburg Municipal Act of 1846: A Study of Reform under Nicholas I," *Slavic Review* 33, no. 1 (1974): 56. For other criticisms, see Lincoln, *In the Vanguard of Reform: Russia's Enlightened Bureaucrats 1825–1861* (DeKalb, Ill., 1982), pp. 63–5.

to administer local affairs directly from St. Petersburg, an approach consistent with the extension of ministerial power in nineteenth-century Russia, or to turn such matters over to officials elected by the local population. Throughout the period covered in this and the next chapter the government invariably and ineffectively combined both approaches. These efforts to establish effective decentralized administration using peasant and zemstvo self-government, without threatening the autocrat's monopoly on political power or the interests of his ministers, are the subjects of these first two background chapters. Following a brief analysis of prereform local administration in Russia, this chapter looks at the ideology of the Great Reforms as it pertained to government in general and local administration in particular, and at the ministerial system of government effected by Alexander II's reforms. This chapter thus provides a context for our discussion of the new peasant and zemstvo institutions created in the early 1860s and the ministerial conflict over them up to the mid–1870s, the subject of Chapter 2. Together the two chapters provide an introduction to the main topic of this study, the local government crisis of the late 1870s to early 1880s and the key administrative and political concerns that dominated official reform discussions in the 1880s and local administration policy into the next century.

Prereform gentry administration: a legacy of failure

Although it is commonplace to credit Peter I and Catherine II with the creation of prereform local administration in Russia, their contributions were by no means equal. Despite Peter the Great's reforms of 1708–10 and the post-Petrine statute of 1727, which introduced a more rational organization of local bureaucracy on paper, the arbitrary administration that characterized seventeenth-century Muscovite *voevody* (civil governors) continued, with all of its ruinous effects in the provinces. Such was not the case with Catherine II's provincial reform of 1775. It truly decentralized and rationalized local administration by establishing fifty provinces (in place of Peter's eleven), each subdivided into twenty districts with 20,000 to 30,000 male souls apiece. In each province a governor served as chief executive of the provincial administration and was assisted by the provincial directorate and the provincial chambers, although in practice the governors-general, handpicked by the ruler to administer regions of two or more provinces, exercised virtually unlimited authority and made decisions on the most important matters. Notwithstanding some increases in the powers of governors under Nicholas I and the administrative reorganization of Alexander II discussed in the following paragraphs, the provincial reform of 1775 remained largely intact and defined the parameters of rural Russian administration until the end of the old regime.[3]

[3] For details, see Iu. V. Got'e, *Istoriia oblastnogo upravleniia v Rossii ot Petra I do Ekateriny II* (2 vols.; Moscow, 1913), 1:18–20; Zyrianov, p. 286; Robert E. Jones, *The Emancipation of the Russian Nobility 1762–1785* (Princeton, 1973), pp. 221–2; and Raeff, *Understanding Imperial Russia*, pp. 94–7.

In terms of organization and purpose, the provincial government established by Peter I and Catherine II adhered to the Russian version of the well-ordered police state. As it turned out, this would have two lasting consequences for the evolution of local self-government and local self-government reform in Imperial Russia. On the one hand, the Russian state was far more prescriptive and prohibitive in regulating the participation of social groups in local administration than its German counterparts. The German police ordinances left room for more collaboration and initiative on the part of the local population. Over time local society assumed a leading role in German administration and economic development and the state shared in the wealth and benefits.[4] On the other hand, the local administrative reforms of Peter and Catherine showed Russia's tendency to adapt western concepts and institutions to suit the tsars' purposes. This is not to suggest that Imperial Russia was a Western state or that it fit the Weberian model of rational bureaucratic administration; on the contrary, the idiosyncrasies of autocratic Russia were even more striking than its similarities to old regimes in the West.[5] But it is important to emphasize that Russian officials increasingly used Western concepts and criteria to evaluate the government's performance and, when needed, to introduce reform (as would be particularly evident in the midnineteenth century).

Indeed, experience proved that throughout the prereform period the government had far more difficulty finding qualified people to administer local affairs than establishing the organizational structure of local government. Most of the population had no opportunity to participate in local administration because they were enserfed either to the landlords or the state. As late as 1857 seigneurial serfs constituted almost 42 percent of the population, and state peasants and bonded townsmen comprised an additional 48 percent.[6] Consequently, the burden of rural administration fell almost exclusively on the landed gentry, who preferred more personalized, discretionary authority, and the regular provincial bureaucracy, who conversely advocated more regulation and accountability – a conflict of interests that had detrimental influences on rural administration and all participants in it.[7] Historians with diverse views on Catherine's motives for granting the gentry a permanent role in local government generally agree that her edicts of 1771, 1775, and 1785 made them responsible for preserving order in the provinces

---

[4]Raeff, *Well-Ordered Police State*, pp. 204–13, 228–33. Raeff notes that Catherine did seek to involve social groups in local administration much more than Peter I, who limited the gentry to tax collection (pp. 237–8); nonetheless, the Western and Russian *Polizeistaat* were quite different even in Catherine's era.

[5]David Christian, "The Supervisory Function in Russian and Soviet History," *Slavic Review* 41 (Spring 1982): 73, 88–9. Shanin argues that the Russian bureaucracy adhered to the Weberian model (which saw the bureaucracy as a distinct group characterized by its formal employment, functional division of labor, appointment and promotion by merit, and hierarchy), except that the tsarist bureaucracy was much more defenseless against its own superiors and more prone to petty corruption than Western bureaucracies. Shanin, pp. 35–6.

[6]Vodarskii, pp. 56–7.

[7]Raeff, *Understanding Imperial Russia*, pp. 92–3.

and for providing essential local economic services (famine relief, construction of roads, bridges, and the like).[8] Taken as a whole, these three measures provided the framework for gentry participation in elected local administration for the rest of the prereform period. To be sure, other free social estates had their own corporate offices and local self-regulation; but the gentry's local organization was the most extensive and autonomous, far surpassing that of their distant land captain successors, as we shall see.[9] Gentry administration consisted of four components: the provincial gentry assemblies, the district deputies, the gentry marshals, and the local officials elected by the gentry assemblies. Besides electing these officials, the provincial assemblies passed resolutions and appropriated funds for local needs when they convened every three years. They had the right to petition the tsar about local needs but rarely exercised it. The district deputies on their part originally were confined to certifying the status of individuals who acquired gentry status by birth or through service, but later participated in the allocation of taxes and similar functions.[10]

The most important official in local gentry administration was the provincial marshal of the gentry, who ranked second in the province to the governor in terms of authority and jurisdiction. The elected marshals acted as the spokesmen for gentry corporate interests in dealing with the central and local bureaucracy and transmitted the orders of the government to their gentry constituents. They were responsible for preserving and spending gentry funds, for maintaining order in the assemblies, and for participating as voting members in various administrative institutions such as recruiting boards and commissions on public food supply and on the apportionment of local economic duties (*zemskie povinnosti*).[11] However, the government's unwillingness to give the elected gentry full control over these functions or to do away with the offices altogether soon bred gentry dissatisfaction. In saddling the marshals with more and more bureaucratic functions that included assisting the governors, the government, beginning in Alexander I's reign, put gentry officials increasingly in the position of unsalaried state

[8]The motives cited include Catherine's desire to buy gentry support through such concessions and her intention, following the Pugachev Rebellion (1773–5), to maintain domestic security in the provinces by using local gentry as her provincial agents. The first interpretation is found in S. A. Korf, *Dvorianstvo i ego soslovnoe upravlenie za stoletie 1762–1855 gg.* (St. Petersburg, 1906), pp. 110–11, 207; and M. P. Pavlova-Sil'vanskaia, "Sotsial'naia sushchnost' oblastnoi reformy," *Absoliutizm v Rossii*, ed. N. M. Druzhinin, N. I. Pavlenko, and L. V. Cherepnin (Moscow, 1964), pp. 460–1. For the second interpretation, see Jones, *Emancipation of the Russian Nobility*, pp. 121–2, 202–3. Jones also maintains that fiscal considerations played an important part in Catherine's decision to introduce local gentry corporate administration. For a detailed study of how the gentry used local government reforms to consolidate its power, see John LeDonne, *Ruling Russia: Politics and Administration in the Age of Absolutism, 1762–1796* (Princeton, 1984), pp. 79–82; see also Robbins, "Viceroys," chap. 1.

[9]Starr rightly suggests that there was probably more continuity in the actual working of local government before and after Alexander II's reforms than has usually been recognized. S. Frederick Starr, "Local Initiative in Russia before the Zemstvo," *The Zemstvo in Russia: An Experiment in Local Self-Government*, p. 6.

[10]Field, pp. 15–16; Korf, *Dvorianstvo*, p. 122.

[11]Korf, pp. 560–1.

agents rather than spokesmen for their constituents. Although this trend stemmed in large part from the gentry's disinterest in their elected corporate administration and from the need for state intervention in gentry affairs to maintain order and to provide local services in the provinces, such state intervention only reinforced gentry indifference toward elected corporate office.[12]

As a case in point, the landed gentry under the 1775 reform were required to elect a number of local police and judicial officials from among their corporate estate. These included the chairmen and assessors of the criminal and civil courts of arbitration, the judge and assessors of the district courts, the district police chief, and the four to five assessors of the lower land court (the basic police organ that enforced all the orders of the governor, the provincial directorate, and the district police chief).[13] In no other area did the gentry demonstrate so clearly their disdain for serving in elected corporate administration. The absentee rate for gentry at the assemblies called to elect these officials was so high that an edict issued in 1832 conceded that "the best nobles [gentry] refuse to serve or acquiesce indifferently to the election of men who lack the qualities required."[14]

Why did the gentry shun elected office in local administration? The preeminent official of the era, M. M. Speranskii, as well as numerous historians have cited a variety of reasons to explain the gentry's indifference, notably their low level (or often lack) of education, their servile attitude toward government, the absence of a homogeneous gentry estate, and bureaucratic interference in local gentry affairs.[15] In fact, all of these problems derived from the way in which local self-government was established

---

[12]Becker, pp. 20–2. Raeff credits Catherine with expanding administration and moving toward local autonomy, but concludes that her efforts to create a vital corporate gentry administration largely failed. In his view, local gentry initiative was checked by bureaucrats controlling local gentry budgets and by laws of local custom, which impeded the development of local rational administration. In essence, state "paternalism degenerated into bureaucratic arbitrariness." Raeff, *Understanding Imperial Russia*, p. 101. Still, as shown below, local bureaucrats often had reason to take direct, arbitrary measures against local gentry administration.

[13]A. Romanovich-Slavatinskii, *Dvorianstvo v Rossii ot nachala XVIII veka do otmeny krepostnogo prava. Svod materiala i prigotovlennye etiudy dlia istoricheskogo issledovaniia* (St. Petersburg, 1870), p. 490; and A. A. Kizevetter, *Mestnoe samoupravlenie v Rossii, IX–XIX st.; Istoricheskii ocherk* (2d ed.; Petrograd, 1917), p. 96. Local police in the prereform period are analyzed in Robert J. Abbott, "Police Reform in Russia, 1858–1878" (Unpublished Ph.D. dissertation, Princeton University, 1971), pp. 14–16.

[14]Quoted in Field, p. 17.
Wortman and Field have noted that in the reign of Nicholas I the numbers of gentry in the local judiciary increased whereas those in the police diminished, thereby suggesting that the legal profession was becoming more socially respectable. See Wortman, pp. 46–7; and Field, p. 16. Although there was a trend beginning in this direction, it still does not overshadow the fact that the gentry in general avoided elected offices of local administration except the marshal's post, which brought much prestige and power to its holder.

[15]Speranskii's view, which emphasizes the first two factors, is found in Korf, *Dvorianstvo*, p. 375. Field argues persuasively that the gentry were too divided in their interests, goals, and material status to take elected corporate service seriously, whereas A. V. Lokhvitskii stresses bureaucratic interference as the main force paralyzing the activity of locally elected corporate officials. See Field, p. 19; and A. V. Lokhvitskii, *Guberniia, ee zemskie i pravitel'stvennye uchrezhdeniia* (St. Petersburg, 1864), p. 203. Korf cites all four factors in *Dvorianstvo*, pp. 165–6, 173.

by the tsars, and for that reason they recurred no matter what form local self-government took in nineteenth-century Russia. Whereas in many Western European countries public self-government evolved as a political right extracted from the monarchy, in Russia the government imposed self-government on the local population, in this case the gentry, to suit its own purposes, much as a century earlier it had created the gentry corporate estate. This process had important consequences. First, the government regarded the reform of local self-government as its prerogative and constantly opposed attempts on the part of the public to influence the provisions of such reform. Typical of traditional states, the government's resistance to public participation only increased as it faced the challenge of adapting its institutions to modern social and economic conditions. Second, the local population in general and the gentry in particular never embraced self-government with the enthusiasm that the English gentry, for example, had for the concept.[16] Local elected service in Russia meant added administrative burdens and possible disciplinary punishment with little economic compensation and no political rights for the officeholder.

Nor were the gentry a unified pressure group capable of extracting political rights from the throne in the nineteenth century. Baron August von Haxthausen, a German expert on and traveler to Russia in the 1840s, accurately pointed out that the gentry "exists only as a favor to the ideas and intentions of the state" and that it would disband at once and with little resistance if the government issued such an order.[17] There were few ties between wealthy and poor gentry, and the lack of common interests put them in a weak position to defend their current privileges, much less obtain new political rights from the state. Indeed, one of the few characteristics uniting the gentry was their contempt for elected office, and they proved so adept at avoiding such service that in 1832 governors were formally empowered to appoint the district police chief and the personnel of the provincial and district courts in the event the gentry failed to elect these officials.[18]

The artificial nature of local self-government established by imperial fiat did not escape the notice of the gentry, the most ambitious and competent of whom capitalized on the expansion of the central government and pursued careers in the military or upper bureaucracy in accordance with the tsar's wishes.[19] This was an important reason why local elected office found little support among the gentry. Partners with the government in administration and stewards in the provinces, they were in no mood to assume the menial tasks of elected service, despite Nicholas I's manifesto of 1832 proclaiming

[16]Korkunov, *Russkoe gosudarstvennoe pravo*, 2:366; and Elie Halévy, *England in 1815*, trans. E. I. Watkin and D. A. Barker (paperback ed.; New York, 1961), p. 15. On the actions of traditional states, see Black, pp. 31, 64.

[17]August von Haxthausen, *Studies on the Interior of Russia*, trans. Eleanore L. M. Schmidt, ed. and intro. S. Frederick Starr (Chicago, 1972), p. 248.

[18]Korf, *Dvorianstvo*, pp. 566–7; Becker, p. 24.

[19]Zaionchkovskii, *Pravitel'stvennyi apparat*, pp. 152–3, 163, 166, 172.

corporate service to be one of the gentry's most important duties. Count Arsenii Andreevich Zakrevskii, the minister of internal affairs (1828–31), was much closer to reality when he admitted that elected gentry service *"promised nothing more than hard work and responsibility."*[20] Unlike the honor, prestige, and financial security associated with military or state rank, especially in the capitals, the gentry landlord with a corporate administration position suffered the social degradation that came from working side by side with professional bureaucrats of nongentry origins.[21] It is little wonder that the gentry turned a deaf ear to the tsar's appeal and continued to elect inexperienced pensioned army officers and petty landowners who needed the salaries to make ends meet as local officials, or left the offices vacant for the government to fill by appointment – trends that continued even after the reforms of the 1860s.

Local corporate service frequently entailed jurisdictional conflicts with bureaucrats owing to vague laws governing the relations between local corporate administration and the provincial bureaucracy, and this fact also dissuaded landed gentry from such work. No sooner were the gentry marshals installed in 1768 than misunderstandings arose between the government and the new officials over the nature of their duties. Nor did the situation improve significantly during the nineteenth century. In drafting the Code of Laws in 1832, the government, in a manner that anticipated the zemstvo reform three decades later, failed to delineate between the jurisdictions of the provincial bureaucracy and gentry officials. The result was a series of conflicts between them in the 1830s to 1850s over the election of gentry assembly delegates who the government insisted had no right to be elected. The government also reprimanded a number of marshals for allowing their assemblies to discuss state measures, for example, the emancipation of the serfs, which it considered outside their jurisdiction.[22]

The crux of the problem was that autocrats from Catherine II on, who allowed some measure of public participation in local administration, refused to have their powers constrained by precise laws. In their concept of autocratic rule, they insisted that the gentry participate in local administration on the

---

[20]Quoted in Romanovich-Slavatinskii, p. 498. Emphasis in the original.

[21]Starr, *Decentralization*, p. 24; Field, p. 10; Gradovskii, 9:42.

The subordination of gentry-elected officials to the provincial bureaucracy and the ill-defined jurisdiction of each prompted one gentry landlord of the period to comment: "Who wants to serve as district police chief, who according to the law is the head of the district, the censor of morals, and guardian of prosperity and order, when he is ordered about by the governors and even by their clerks and according to their whims races like a whippet from one province to another." This resulted in a situation where, according to another contemporary, "no one is elected [because] everyone declares himself ill; no one is afraid of prosecution, and in fact they request to be turned over to the courts, because they prefer to be on trial and consequently exempt from service." The passages are quoted from S. M. Seredonin, comp., *Istoricheskii obzor deiatel'nosti Komiteta ministrov* (5 vols.; St. Petersburg, 1902), 1:277–8.

[22]Korf, *Dvorianstvo*, pp. 334–40, 580–3; and I. A. Blinov, *Otnosheniia senata k mestnym uchrezhdeniiam v XIX veke* (St. Petersburg, 1911), pp. 95–110. In a number of cases, the governors abused their right to veto the election of marshals and rejected the candidates for personal reasons.

state's terms, and the rural state bureaucracy remained wedded to this view. The tsars' aim in formulating laws was to transmit imperial authority to the population, instruct the bureaucracy in its activity, and curb official arbitrariness and inefficiency. At the same time, the absence of precise laws left open the safety valve of direct autocratic intervention or arbitrary measures by officials that transgressed normal procedures but, in the view of the ruler, were necessary for expedient action (*tselesoobraznost'*) in emergency cases.[23] The autocrats refused to admit publicly (while no doubt realizing privately) that a legally regulated government required the autocrat, the highest official of all, to adhere to the law and circumscribe his authority in order for it to be effective.

Thus, the creation of local self-government in Russia by autocracy, the avoidance of local elected service by the most qualified gentry in favor of military careers, the vague laws on the relations between corporate and state officials, and bureaucratic interference in gentry corporate administration all combined to make gentry administration ineffective. Its shortcomings were evident everywhere. Many willfully avoided the local assemblies and provincial commissions organized to allocate economic duties for peasants (such as the amount of corvée on roads, bridges, and postal stations, and the peasants' share of the conveyance, billeting, and food supply duties).[24] They neglected to protect their serfs from the abusive treatment of the police assigned to collect these duties and to supervise peasant performance of corvée obligations. In the area of public food supply, the gentry displayed little interest in helping the government build the grain warehouses provided for under the Public Food Supply Statute of 1834, or in electing honest officials to guard grain supplies. By the end of the 1850s, the grainhouses were more notorious for filling the pockets of the gentry-elected guardians, who sold the grain they embezzled, than for providing famine relief.[25]

In short, despite Nicholas I's proclamations in favor of a stronger autocracy, the central government during his reign had little control over its provincial administration. By the late 1850s, top officials recognized that local administration contingent on the goodwill and voluntary services of a limited

---

[23]The role of law in autocratic Russia as opposed to the more bureaucratized states of Prussia and France is analyzed in Taranovski, "Politics of Counter-Reform," pp. 289–91, 632–3; and Raeff, *Understanding Imperial Russia*. The government's refusal to give a precise legal definition to the functions of officials in order to maintain autocratic control over the local hierarchy has carried over into the Soviet period, along with the problems of local level jurisdictional conflicts resulting from vague laws. See John A. Armstrong, *The European Administrative Elite* (Princeton, 1973), p. 265; and Hough, pp. 26–32.

[24]The system of local economic duties was established in 1805 to provide essential goods and services for the local population. Several times during the prereform period the government reorganized it, the last time in 1851. Many of these duties were included as mandatory expenses for zemstvo institutions when the latter were introduced. See S. Ia. Tseitlin, "Zemskaia reforma," *Istoriia Rossii v XIX veke* (9 vols.; St. Petersburg, n.d.), 3: 186–8; and B. B. Veselovskii, "Detsentralizatsiia upravleniia i zadachi zemstva," *1864–1914: Iubileinyi zemskii sbornik*, ed. B. B. Veselovskii and Z. G. Frenkel' (St. Petersburg, 1914), p. 37.

[25]Tseitlin, "Zemskaia reforma," pp. 189–90.

number of gentry was completely inefficient and required substantial changes. No longer could the government be the patron and client of the gentry, dependent on and supportive of it, in its efforts to develop an efficient local administration.[26] Hence, the reign of Nicholas I signified the end of the era of exclusive gentry control over elected local government in the nineteenth century. The failure of local corporate administration was all the more critical given the many shortcomings of Nicholas I's provincial bureaucracy and the undergoverned nature of rural Russia. Not only did Russia have far fewer civil servants for its population in 1861 (1.1 to 1.3 + civil servants for every thousand people) than other major European states,[27] but Russia's provincial officialdom was notorious for its corruption, incompetence, formalism, inefficient procedures, and illiteracy — the latter of which the state sought to rectify through the Law of 14 October 1827.[28] Yet, tragically, the tsar's last efforts to improve local administration by increasing the size of provincial staffs resulted merely in more paperwork, red tape, and longer administrative delays. For example, in 1841 the Ministry of Internal Affairs received and sent out a total of 22,326,842 separate documents; a decade later the figure had risen to 31,103,676.[29]

Consequently, by the time of the reform era the government had reason enough to rule out direct government control over all local administration as a remedy to its administrative problems. Not only had such an approach proved futile under Nicholas I, owing to the shortage of bureaucratic personnel and the bureaucratic formalism that stigmatized his reign, but the budgetary deficit of a half billion rubles following the Crimean War precluded the increase in bureaucratic personnel necessary to introduce social and economic reform in Russia. Yet the record of gentry failure in prereform local corporate administration dissuaded the government from delegating these functions exclusively to the gentry as a group. Consequently, new approaches to reform and institutional renovation were required if the autocracy intended to initiate change in the provinces, engage public support and service, and maintain its control over the process. Such approaches found their expression in the ideology of the Great Reforms and in the new doctrines of decen-

---

[26]Field, p. 146. The one exception to the rule was the enthusiastic gentry participation on the Social Welfare Boards, established according to the 1775 legislation, to supervise construction and management of hospitals, orphanages, insane asylums, and schools. Yet, as Starr notes, the gentry tended to pocket government contributions to these projects for their own use, fully aware that the state lacked the resources to hold the gentry accountable for the funds. Starr, "Local Initiative Before the Zemstvo," pp. 13–14.

[27]Starr, *Decentralization*, p. 48.

[28]The law required that all new civil service recruits furnish proof that they could read and write and that they had mastered the basic rules of arithmetic and grammar. The law accelerated the shift from retired military officers of gentry status to career civil officials in the capitals and higher offices in the provinces — clear evidence, according to Walter M. Pintner, of the professionalization of the imperial bureaucracy under Nicholas I. See his essay, "The Evolution of Civil Officialdom, 1755–1855," in *Russian Officialdom*, p. 214.

[29]Lincoln, *Vanguard*, p. 36.

tralization and public self-government prevalent in Western Europe in the 1850s – ideas antithetical to the autocratic system and ministerial authority that constituted the Nicholaevian order.

Architects and ideology of the Great Reforms

If the reign of Nicholas I revealed the limits of the traditional well-ordered police state in Russia, especially with respect to local administration and rural development, his death and Russia's defeat in the Crimea in 1855 offered an unusual opportunity for administrative reform and renewal. It was these two occurrences, along with the problems in nearly all areas of Russian administration and economy and the appearance of a generation of enlightened bureaucrats, that gave impetus to the enactment of the Great Reforms. Although the individual reforms and the climate that spawned them have been studied at length by Soviet and Western scholars, it is appropriate here to discuss briefly the proponents and principles of the Great Reforms, because the ideology of reform was instrumental in the establishment of local self-government in 1861–4 and in the counterreform debates some twenty years later. Moreover, these reform ideas would come into conflict with Alexander II's determination to preserve autocracy and with his ministerial system in the first decade of his reign, thus diminishing the prospects for the successful development of public self-government.

Alexander II's decision to emancipate the serfs and introduce related administrative reforms soon after the Crimean debacle brought to the fore a cadre of "enlightened bureaucrats." Although these officials did not question Russia's need for autocratic authority, which they regarded as sacrosanct, they did reject Nicholas I's version of the well-ordered police state based on Official Nationality in favor of a more activist state responsive to social and economic change. Having a superior, well-rounded education and deriving their livelihood from service rather than land, these officials rose to prominence in the 1840s, especially in the Ministries of Internal Affairs, State Properties, and Justice. A number of them (for instance, N. Miliutin, K. Grot, N. Girs) had experience with and knowledge of provincial conditions, based on work they had done for their ministries. As a group, they received the patronage of the royal family (Grand Duke Konstantin Nikolaevich and Grand Duchess Elena Pavlovna) and were urged to use their knowledge of the provinces to think in terms of broad legislative reform.[30] Consequently, when Alexander II commissioned them to draft the emancipation statutes and other reform legislation, these officials seized the opportunity to propose a new type of state in which the government would not only police the population, but likewise would provide it with vital services. Their view

[30]Ibid., pp. 16–18, 22, 30–3, 64ff., 109–14, 135–8, 169–78; Zaionchkovskii, *Pravitel'stvennyi apparat*, pp. 139–41; and Daniel T. Orlovsky, "High Officials in the Ministry of Internal Affairs, 1855–1881," *Russian Officialdom*, pp. 255–9.

allowed for a somewhat more dynamic role for the local population in rural administration, as we shall see, but it also implied criticism of gentry corporate administration. At the same time, in their main task of abolishing serfdom they refused to tamper with the traditional social structure (*sosloviia*) – at least for the short term – or to permit any group outside the government to assume the dominant role in reform discussions.[31]

In essence, Alexander II had, in the enlightened bureaucrats, a vehicle for introducing change in rural Russia, yet it was one that would not challenge his autocratic control.[32] In looking for the means to refurbish and modernize tsarist administration, Alexander's reformers used some modified political ideas from Western Europe – specifically, publicity (*glasnost'*), legality (*zakonnost'*), decentralization, and self-government (*samoupravlenie*).[33] They argued that public knowledge of the procedures and actions of local officialdom was necessary to uncover the bureaucratic venality and arbitrariness that stigmatized prereform administration, with its police justice and serfowners' capriciousness. Holding themselves up as models of integrity and efficiency (and understandably earning the enmity of other officials and many landowners), the enlightened bureaucrats incongruously contended that *glasnost'* was necessary for legal government, yet it could be limited so as not to open the floodgates of public criticism of the state. As for *zakonnost'*, the reformers envisioned that it, too, would reduce the arbitrariness, corruption, and custom that distinguished the undergoverned provinces; however, it proved far easier to talk about legal order in the countryside than to bring it about, as the rest of the nineteenth century illustrated. Still, *zakonnost'* left a greater mark on the reform legislation than *glasnost'*, given the separation of powers and the independent judiciary that were the foundations of the judicial reforms of 1864. Equally important, the Great Reformers who survived into Alexander III's reign clung to the concept of *zakonnost'* in attacking the counterreforms and espoused views that came close to representing a *Rechtsstaat* theory of government (rule by law).[34]

Generally speaking, these two principles provided the framework for the government's extension into the provinces through administrative decentralization and local self-government. The problem facing the reformers was how to create new institutions of self-government distinct from state and

---

[31]Lincoln, *Vanguard*, p. 177.

[32]Ibid., p. 172.

[33]Ibid., pp. 183–6; Starr, *Decentralization*, pp. 247–9. Lincoln's book provides the best succinct account of the importance of these principles in the reform discussions.

[34]On this point, see Theodore Taranovski, "The Aborted Counter-Reform: Murav'ev Commission and the Judicial Statutes of 1864," *Jahrbücher für Geschichte Osteuropas* 29 (1981): 163–4; and idem, "Politics of Counter-Reform," chaps. 1–3. Taranovski has provided the most thorough study of the ideological conflict within the elite bureaucracy in postreform Russia; he characterizes the supporters of Alexander II's reform principles as "liberals" and their opponents, who adhered to the concept of *polizeistaat*, as "conservatives." I have generally eschewed such categorizations because the ministerial conflict over local self-government reform revealed ideological inconsistencies on the part of individual ministers and because factors other than ideology often determined the political actions of these officials. On this point, see Raeff, "Bureaucratic Phenomena," p. 408.

corporate institutions, given the limited personnel available in the provinces. A second problem was how to introduce local self-government without arousing social (particularly gentry) desires for political power. We shall discuss the specifics of the establishment of peasant and zemstvo self-government in Chapter 2. Suffice it to note here that the official and public debate in the late 1850s to early 1860s focused on defining the Western term "decentralization" and on pinpointing the gentry's role in the new self-government. As soon became clear in the debates, decentralization could mean either delegation (deconcentration) of authority, whereby the state bureaucracy retained central control but assigned specific functions to subordinate personnel, or it could represent the devolution of authority. In the latter case, responsibility for certain areas of administration (for instance, famine relief) would be transferred to elected self-governing institutions distinct from the local bureaucracy. As Fred Riggs has noted in his study of administration in developing nations, the norms of policy action are more likely to be defined in cases of delegation, as opposed to devolution, of authority – a situation that portended future conflicts between the state and public self-government in postreform Russia.[35]

In their efforts to apply Western ideologies of administrative development to the practical reality of Russia's undergoverned provinces, the participants in the reform discussions put forth these two different approaches. Prince V. A. Cherkasskii, called by one historian "Russia's Tocqueville" because of his antipathy toward "bureaucratism,"[36] advocated genuine self-government and the devolution of authority. Prince P. D. Dolgorukov, one of the more radical publicists of his day, went even further and maintained that broader participation in provincial government by rural residents of all classes was a vital way of subjecting the state to *glasnost'* and establishing legal, more responsive government.[37] In contrast, B. N. Chicherin, the noted legal scholar, attacked the devolution of authority as an alien theory that had no place in Russia, where the state bureaucracy historically played the leading role in administrative development. Chicherin instead spoke on behalf of delegation (deconcentration) of power as a means of preserving national unity and social harmony – arguments that would be resurrected in future debates over local government reform.[38]

Complicating the issue further was the problem of the part that the various social estates would play and whether it was possible, in terms of rural self-government, to surmount estate distinctions and create public self-government (*vsesoslovnoe samoupravlenie*). Given the complex task of dismantling serfdom and the illiteracy and customary law that governed the peasants,

[35] See Riggs, pp. 341–4; and S. Iu. Vitte [Witte], *Samoderzhavie i zemstvo: Konfidentsial'naia zapiska Ministra finansov Stats-Sekretaria S. Iu. Vitte (1899 g.)* (2d ed.; Stuttgart, 1903), p. 28.
[36] Starr, *Decentralization*, pp. 71, 75.
[37] Lincoln, *Vanguard*, pp. 184–5; and Starr, *Decentralization*, pp. 69–70.
[38] Starr, pp. 83–8; Gradovskii, 9: 1–18; Leontovich, pp. 186–7.

the reformers decided to separate the peasantry under the law, at least on the village and *volost'* levels. As for the gentry, who maintained their own corporate institutions, their past performance and potential role in local self-government sparked much discussion at the turn of the decade. Cherkasskii, for instance, proposed that local administration be reorganized along federal lines and that the new self-governing institutions include men of all estates, who through their property ties would develop a common bond in public self-government. M. N. Katkov instead advocated that local self-government be placed under the gentry's control. Like Cherkasskii, he attacked the bureaucracy's interference in local corporate life, but unlike the renowned landowner Katkov believed that the gentry, by virtue of their previous experience and their noble qualities, were best suited to play the leading role in the new institutions. He maintained that autocratic order was based on the traditional estates organization, which in the 1850s included distinct social corporations for the gentry, clergy, honorary citizens, merchants, town dwellers, and the peasantry. In fact, by the mid-nineteenth century each of these social categories had a number of subdivisions and there were other groups, for instance, certain professional people, who did not fit easily into the *soslovie* structure. Still, Katkov argued in favor of the traditional distinctions and claimed that, in view of the peasant emancipation, the gentry needed a new purpose to protect their dominant position in the countryside.[39]

In short, in the ideological debates that preceded and coincided with the Great Reforms, some of the critical problems that would influence the development of local self-government for the rest of the century were first brought to light. For instance, what role in local administration would the new public institutions have vis à vis the state bureaucracy and gentry corporate officials? Would these institutions enjoy autonomy protected by law, or would they be controlled by state agencies? Indeed, what was to be the tie, if any, between these three branches (state, corporate, public) of local government?[40] And were the new institutions to provide the embryo for new class relations in the countryside, or were they to be dominated by the gentry as compensation for the loss of their serfs? These were vitally important issues that governed the reform discussions and shaped the views of the enlightened bureaucrats during the early 1860s. Yet, equally important, the discussions were to be influenced by the ministerial system of

---

[39]Starr, *Decentralization*, pp. 75–83. On the estates order (*sosloviia*) see Gregory Freeze, "The *Soslovie* (Estate) Paradigm and Russian Social History," *American Historical Review* 91 (February 1986): 18ff. It should be noted that the enlightened bureaucrats and certain publicists saw local self-government as a means of involving a "minority of lords who expressed a clear sense of political responsibility" without bringing in the majority embittered by the emancipation and anxious to regain their former economic and social power. Lincoln, *Vanguard*, p. 179. The flaw in this line of reasoning was that the state needed too much assistance on the local level to count on simply the "minority of lords," yet its determination to have elected officials serve on its terms would lead quickly to public disillusionment with local self-government.

[40]Gradovskii, 9: 55.

government that Alexander II introduced in the reform era as part of his aim to keep the reform process and the proposals for a more open, legal-based government under his control.

The ministerial system of Alexander II

The decade of reform in Russia that brought forth changes in nearly all aspects of Russian life was also instrumental in the reorganization of min-isterial power in St. Petersburg and the extension of ministerial authority in the provinces. Both processes would have important ramifications for the work of local self-governing institutions as well as for later state efforts to reform them. In introducing the Great Reforms, Alexander II organized a ministerial system of government that tapped the professional expertise in the ministries for reform work without compromising his own leverage as autocrat. Yet his parceling out of political power among the ministries during the first decade of his reign, without any institutional reorganization to coordinate them, jeopardized the prospects for effective peasant and zemstvo administration; even worse, the resulting division of power in the provinces among the ministries competing for the tsar's favor (and in some cases against the enlightened bureaucrats) produced paralyzing bureaucratic conflicts for decades to come over proposals to reform local self-government and con-tributed to a crisis of the autocratic system twenty years later.

Alexander II's ministerial reorganization was in response to the impressive growth of ministerial power and the professionalization of the elite Russian bureaucracy during the first half of the nineteenth century. Although the period was notorious for the dominance of the secret police in many European countries, it also marked the beginning of ministerial centralization and the participation of various ministries in provincial life.[41] This was especially true in Russia under Nicholas I; contrary to the atrophy and apathy that stigmatized the lowest echelons of the provincial bureaucracy, his reign saw the number of ministries increase from eight (created in 1802) to thirteen, and their power grew accordingly while such traditional institutions as the Senate and the State Council were often bypassed by the tsar in the decision-making process.[42] As a whole, these processes underlined a maxim of tsarist politics that applied throughout the nineteenth century and dictated the activity of ministers, namely that tsarist institutions had political significance only as long as the autocrat patronized them (fuller details are provided elsewhere).[43] The proximity of an official to the tsar was far more important

---

[41]Binkley, pp. 140–1.

[42]N. P. Eroshkin and others, *Istoriia gosudarstvennykh uchrezhdenii Rossii do velikoi oktiabr'skoi sotsialisticheskoi revoliutsii* (2d ed.; Moscow, 1965), pp. 185, 281; Korkunov, 2: 235–8; and Yaney, *Systematization*, p. 196.

[43]In particular, see Orlovsky, *Limits of Reform*, pp. 18–30; Yaney, *Systematization*, pp. 207–21; Lincoln, *Vanguard*, pp. 39–45; and Raeff, *Understanding Imperial Russia*, pp. 116–19.

than his title in terms of the power he wielded.[44] And Nicholas indeed patronized the ministers, as is evident from the fact that they exercised their right of direct access to the tsar, the most important privilege that an official could have. In contrast, during his reign senate members lost this right in practice and the senate itself was subordinated to the minister of justice.[45]

The effects of increasing ministerial authority were particularly noticeable in the provinces. The imperial instructions to the governors in 1837 abolished the governors-general in many areas and gave more responsibility to the ministers, who were to exercise it through their provincial agents and governors. For this reason, the 1837 edict has been called "a decisive turning point in favor of a ministerial bureaucracy."[46] In fact, the 1837 Provincial Reform, while making the governor accountable to all ministries, in practice subordinated him to the Ministry of Internal Affairs – a development of critical importance to the evolution of local administration and to the status of the governor in postreform Russia.[47] For the latter, these changes in effect reduced his personal authority and added to his already overwhelming, diverse responsibilities. Significantly, unlike some of his prefectural counterparts in Europe, the Russian governor in the nineteenth century was losing his power to coordinate and control provincial administration, without enjoying the full protection of the Ministry of Internal Affairs either.[48] That ministry after 1837 claimed for itself the leading role in local affairs and, to prove the point, carried out the first in-depth studies of social, economic, and administrative conditions in provincial towns in 1842–6. Many of its most talented and promising young officials were assigned to provincial posts; their work provided the government with much of the raw data and expertise to undertake the emancipation of the serfs and the various reforms in local self-government and justice in the following decade.[49] Even in the area of personnel, the responsibility for provincial appointments devolved more and more to the ministers.[50]

Thus, Alexander II inherited a ministerial bureaucracy that already had made inroads into the provinces and that, contrary to the ideal of interministerial coordination, had shown signs of compartmentalization and fragmentation in the capital and the localities. In this situation, bureaucratic conflict, which was endemic in the tsarist system, could be paralyzing; and

---

[44] A. F. Koni, *Sobranie sochinenii v vos'mi tomakh*, ed. V. G. Bazanov, A. N. Smirnov, and K. I. Chukovskii (8 vols.; Moscow, 1966–9), 5: 285.

[45] Wortman, pp. 36–7; Korkunov, 2: 246.

[46] Yaney, *Systematization*, p. 218.

[47] Starr, *Decentralization*, pp. 33–4; Lokhvitskii, pp. 204–25.

[48] Robbins, "Viceroys," chaps. 1, 4; Robert C. Fried, *The Italian Prefects: A Study in Administrative Politics* (New Haven, 1969), pp. 86–119, 301–10.

[49] The two commissions studying these problems for the Ministry of Internal Affairs were the Provisional Section for the Reorganization of Municipal Government and Economy, headed by Nikolai Miliutin, and the Provisional Statistical Committee. Statistical studies were also undertaken at this time by the Department of Rural Economy and the Academic Committee of the Ministry of State Properties, under the supervision of Andrei Parfenovich Zablotskii-Desiatovskii. Lincoln, *Vanguard*, pp. 49, 109–25.

[50] Wortman, p. 44; Yaney, *Systematization*, p. 206.

yet, paradoxically and contrary to the western states, *formalized conflict* in the political system (or even in the ruling class in general) was suppressed.[51] The Tsar-Liberator's contribution to the ministerial system was to exacerbate the problem of disunity. On the one hand, once the Great Reforms advanced beyond the drawing board and entered the implementation phase, Alexander II increased and diffused his ministers' power. The main casualties in this process were the enlightened bureaucrats who sat on the reform commissions established by Alexander II and who, for reasons discussed in Chapter 2, lost the support of their institutional patron, the minister of internal affairs.[52] The latter soon realized that in the reforms the emperor had further diffused responsibility for local government among numerous ministries, rather than centralizing it in one agency. In addition, however, Alexander II exploited the situation by refusing to introduce institutions for interministerial co-ordination at the center, thereby maintaining his own power during the implementation of the reforms, much to the detriment of tsarist adminis-tration in general and the new self-government in particular.

In other European countries, rulers faced with the problems of intermin-isterial disunity had been forced to create a cabinetlike institution or share political power with the public (usually the gentry) by establishing a par-liamentary body. There is evidence that Alexander II considered the first option, for in 1857 (apparently to initiate work on peasant reform) he established a Council of Ministers, modeled on a similar institution in the British Parliament, to reduce the paperwork he received from his ministers and to coordinate their activities.[53] But having established this body, he refused to give it authority and, in keeping with his view of undiluted imperial power, prescribed that the autocrat preside over the council in order to dispel any notions about a prime minister. The council met only in emergencies and Alexander II followed tradition and dealt with his ministers on an individual basis.[54] Similarly, from 1861 to 1865 he vetoed numerous ministerial proposals, several coming from his Minister of Internal Affairs Valuev, to create interministerial unity through a cabinet and/or a prime minister. Although the tsar was the main opponent of such institutional reform, these proposals, significantly enough, encountered opposition from other ministers, who feared that such a reform would upset the ministerial

[51]Ibid., pp. 212–14; and Christian, 81.

[52]Lincoln, *Vanguard*, pp. 202–4.

[53]See Seredonin, 3, pt. 1: 8, 10–14; and Chapter 2 of the V. G. Chernukha, *Vnutrenniaia politika tsarizma s serediny 50-kh do nachala 80-kh gg. XIX v.* (Leningrad, 1978), pp. 144–55.

[54]P. A. Zaionchkovskii, *Krizis samoderzhaviia na rubezhe 1870–1880-kh godov* (Moscow, 1964), pp. 21–2; and Chernukha, *Vnutrenniaia politika tsarizma*, p. 170. Zaionchkovskii points out that the archival *fond* of the Council of Ministers contains only 96 cases (*dela*) for 1861–1905. For all intents and purposes, it ceased to exist after 1881. Chernukha argues that Alexander II was the real obstacle to any ministerial unity, yet provides evidence to show that a number of ministers preferred to deal individually with their sovereign, regardless of the problems this caused for domestic policy making. Ibid., pp. 154, 170–2, 177–9. On this theme and Valuev's political and administrative philosophy, especially as it concerned the relevance of Western institutions to Russian reforms, see Orlovsky, *Limits of Reform*, pp. 6–7, 70–4.

16

power balance that Alexander II was establishing through reforms in local administration (including self-government) and other areas.

Thus, as Alfred J. Rieber rightly notes, Alexander II passed up a real opportunity to make the bureaucracy an efficient and rational instrument of reform by not using the Council of Ministers.[55] Rather, Alexander's goal was to give his ministers even greater responsibilities in diverse areas of Russian administration and to distribute this authority among ministries that pursued different goals at the local level and consisted of officials who spent their careers in the provinces working for one central ministry.[56] The tsar meanwhile maintained absolute control over state activity by playing off various ministers against each other, toying with them at times, and supporting their separate programs without giving control to any one of them.[57] In fairness to Alexander, it should be noted that he wished to create a systematized bureaucracy by instilling in officials the notion of administrative law and by going through the State Council to enact legislation. But War Minister Dmitrii Miliutin contended that Alexander's methods in dealing with his ministers made them reluctant to propose decisive measures that might induce their colleagues to complain to the autocrat.[58] Indeed, the tsar was the indispensable element in a ministerial system given to impulsive activity, bureaucratic intrigue, and confusion, when efficiency and speed were prerequisites for autocratic control over reform in the countryside. As we shall see later, the only exceptions to this pattern of ministerial politics occurred in crisis situations, such as that in 1880–1, when one minister was able to take the lead in central policy making with the complete backing of the tsar.

Viewed against this backdrop, any institutional reform, particularly one as extensive as the decentralization of government and the establishment of local self-government, had critical consequences for Alexander II's ministerial power balance at the court and in the countryside. His diffusion of power among ministers in St. Petersburg curbed the nominal control of the minister of internal affairs in the provinces, and it is not surprising that from the early 1860s on the heads of that agency sought to assert their exclusive control over local self-government. The main beneficiaries of the decentralization and diffusion of ministerial authority and the development of self-government in the countryside were the Ministries of Justice and of Finance. Besides their increased budgetary appropriations in the late 1850s and early 1860s, they were given authority over new local institutions. Autonomous

---

[55] Alfred J. Rieber, ed., *The Politics of Autocracy: Letters of Alexander II to Prince A. I. Bariatinskii*, with a historical essay by Alfred J. Rieber (The Hague, 1966), p. 40.

[56] Raeff, *Understanding Imperial Russia*, p. 156.

[57] Alexander II's tendency to toy with ministers can be seen in his policy on the reform of the Council of Ministers (as noted in this chapter) and of the State Council (as noted in Chapter 2). In both cases, Valuev was encouraged by the tsar to draft reform projects only to find Alexander lose interest in them – a tactic that Nicholas I rarely employed. Valuev was not the only official thwarted by the tsar's impulsiveness. Chernukha, *Vnutrenniaia politika tsarizma*, pp. 162, 165.

[58] Rieber, *Politics of Autocracy*, p. 56.

justices of the peace and circuit courts introduced by the Judicial Reform of 1864 replaced the prereform system of police justice, proof of Alexander's desire to inculcate a sense of administrative law and justice in local officials.[59] New agencies under the Ministry of Finance – for instance, the provincial commissions on taxes and duties and the district (*okruzhnyi*) excise inspectors (1861) – were organized to assist the district treasuries and provincial fiscal chambers in providing a more reliable flow of revenue to St. Petersburg. Coming on the heels of a measure (1845) that replaced the vice-governor with a Finance Ministry official to head the provincial fiscal chamber, the legislation of 1861 further eroded the provincial authority of the minister of internal affairs. Officials regarded the collection of taxes by the local police as the most inefficient aspect of prereform local administration, and finance ministers exploited this concern to increase their leverage in matters of local government reform.[60]

Moreover, as it turned out, the tsar's new ministerial system in local affairs was not especially conducive to effective government nor to more efficient tax collection. The reasons were many. First of all, the reliance of ministries on decentralization and on elected peasant and zemstvo officials to assist in tax collection, famine relief, and similar functions after 1861 would provide new headaches for the central government and produce ministerial battles over local institutions until the end of the old regime. As in other "developing states," in tsarist Russia the rural agencies competed with each other, carried out overlapping and duplicating functions, failed to cooperate with one another in executing local projects, and required the higher authorities to intervene to resolve minor conflicts among provincial ministerial officials. Where policy objectives are not defined, decentralization is likely to exacerbate, rather than resolve, local administrative problems.[61]

Even worse, just as there was no means to provide interministerial unity and coordination at court outside of the tsar himself, in the provinces no effective institutions existed to coordinate policy or even to see that local officialdom adhered to the new concepts of legality. This resulted in frequent ministerial conflicts outside the capital. For example, the minister of internal affairs concerned himself with preserving order in the provinces, sometimes by expedient methods that local judicial officials, as guardians of the law, considered illegal. Finance officials, preoccupied with economizing and maintaining the cash flow from the countryside, rarely hesitated to blame the understaffed local police (under the Ministry of Internal Affairs) for tax losses or for ruining the peasant economy in collecting tax arrears.[62] Such interministerial friction was not new, of course; but it took on greater significance in the postreform period, as the government sought to introduce a new legal-

[59]Wortman, pp. 250–1, 260; and Starr, *Decentralization*, p. 341.
[60]Starr, p. 278; Eroshkin, pp. 235, 246; and Zyrianov, p. 275.
[61]For comparison with administrative problems in the Philippines, see Riggs, pp. 340–1, 370.
[62]On this point, see Weissman, pp. 10, 43–6; and Yaney, *Systematization*, pp. 305–18.

administrative order that embodied the process of bureaucratic penetration in rural Russia. In these conditions, the traditional institutions for provincial administrative unity were wholly inadequate. In theory, the provincial governors were to serve the interests of all ministries, and not simply the Ministry of Internal Affairs; yet, in actuality, the governors were overburdened by their executive duties, not to mention supervisory functions that included presiding over nearly twenty provincial collegial bodies (that rarely produced a consensus on policy).[63] Like their police subordinates, the governors were a target of rivalry between the ministers of internal affairs and of finance. Thus, contrary to the objectives of *zakonnost'* and *glasnost'* that were at the heart of the Great Reforms, tsarist administration in the capital and the provinces in practice took its cue from the traditional personal power of the tsar and his agents, and would continue to do so until the end of the old regime.

To sum up, this introductory chapter has outlined the main problem that Alexander II's government faced in the Great Reform era: It needed to renovate local administration and involve the rural population in the process without relinquishing political authority or reducing the tsar's political power. To be sure, the Crimean defeat and the economic backwardness associated with serfdom served notice that the traditional well-ordered police state was outmoded, even if its legacy lived on. It revealed that the tsarist state, to catch up and compete with the great powers of Europe, would have to create a more dynamic government based on legal administrative procedures and broader social participation, and employing more effective means of administrative coordination. Even more, the West provided the ideology of administrative reform, as adapted to Russian conditions by enlightened bureaucrats and other political theorists. In place of the undergoverned yet paradoxically "overcentralized" regime of Nicholas I, these reformers proposed a new administration based on decentralization, separation of powers, legality, public input, and self-government − ideas designed to introduce effective and responsive government at the grass roots level.

Unfortunately, these ideas were distilled and distorted in the debates over all the Great Reforms, in part because of the ministerial bureaucracy that had extended its influence into the countryside, a vital precondition itself in the development of modern states. Their involvement and diverse viewpoints underscored the importance of the autocrat and his personal authority in all reform discussions and routine administration. Between Peter the Great's reign and the Great Reform era, autocratic power was the one unmistakable reality of Russian political life. It could be an imposing barrier to successful administrative reform, as shown in the case of preform gentry administration, where imperial authority sharply circumscribed gentry initiative; or it could be a force that brought about dramatic and far-reaching changes in administrative life, as our discussion of the new institutions of

[63]Christian, pp. 74, 76.

19

rural self-government will reveal in Chapter 2. Equally important, the events of the Great Reform era would illustrate that the tsar's view on reform, and that of his ministers, could shift markedly between the preparation and implementation phases of reform.[64]

[64]Chernukha, *Vnutrenniaia politika tsarizma*, p. 180.

The birth of a new rural order: the state and local self-government, 1861–75

The reign of Alexander II is understandably remembered more for the emancipation of the serfs than for the reorganization of ministerial power, because the peasant reform in Russia was unique in nineteenth-century Europe in its scope and complexity. Fittingly enough, it is commonly regarded as the beginning of the modern era in Russian history. With the stroke of a pen, Alexander II signed into law measures that in 1862–6 liberated nearly 90 percent of his subjects, although getting the peasants, landed gentry, and various officials to abide by its provisions proved far more nettlesome. Yet, in the same period the tsar contemplated a far-reaching comprehensive reform of local administration that would have affected all levels and nearly all elements (police, judiciary, municipal, and rural self-government). The boldness of the vision reflected the government's desire in the mid-1850s to eradicate much of the Nicholaevian order; as fate would have it, the failure of the reformers to enact such a comprehensive plan, owing to resistance from gentry conservatives led by Mikhail Nikolaevich Murav'ev, the minister of state properties (1857–62), revealed even more about elite bureaucratic politics in the Great Reform era. By separating the economic functions of the police from their security role (1858), the state committed itself to a process of piecemeal administrative reform that compounded the fragmented nature of local administration and made local self-government reform the focus of bitter ministerial conflict throughout the postreform era.[1]

The development of peasant self-government

In calling for the abolition of serfdom in his 30 March 1856 speech to the Moscow gentry, Alexander II initiated a reform program of staggering proportions and complexity. Indeed, in all likelihood the emperor and his

---

[1]Starr, *Decentralization*, pp. 141–51, 213–15.

enlightened bureaucrats did not fully appreciate the ramifications of peasant emancipation until they began the tedious work of drafting the reform legislation in the late 1850s. This was so because serfdom not only provided an economic way of life for the landed gentry and their peasants, but it also constituted a system of rural control in the form of the landlord's police powers over his serfs, a means for levying state taxes, and a system of famine relief and other services that were the landlord's responsibility. In abolishing serfdom, the government had to ensure that order would be maintained in the countryside and taxes collected on time, and in this regard it had three choices: (1) to allow landlords to retain personal control over all peasant institutions and functions (an approach favored by the majority of the provincial gentry); (2) to create a system of administrative and judicial control over peasants in the form of a district commandant similar to the officials created for state peasants in 1839;[2] or (3) to establish a system of peasant self-government that would save the state the expense of providing bureaucratic supervisors for peasant communities while eliminating the abuses of landlord control. The government eventually chose the third option on the assumption that separate peasant self-government would last only for the transition period of temporary obligations, whereupon the peasants would be integrated into a system of all-estate local self-government (*vsesoslovnoe samoupravlenie*).[3] In the meantime, peasants were to be placed under their own self-government and courts, were to be governed largely as in the past by their customs, and were to be responsible for taxes and other local economic duties.

Left to their own devices, state officials would probably have made little effort to prepare comprehensive peasant reform legislation for Alexander II's ratification, especially by February 1861. The bureaucracy was split on the emancipation issue, and reform proposals in general evoked widespread opposition among the traditionalist gentry. Within the Editing Commissions that drafted the legislation there were fundamental differences of opinion, even over the nomenclature for the new institutions of peasant self-government, and these disagreements bogged down the discussions. The State Council that debated the proposed emancipation legislation consisted largely of opponents of the reform who loyally deferred to the tsar's wishes on this subject. It is indeed a testimony to Alexander's personal power, persistence, and skill in using subordinates such as Ia. I. Rostovtsev, the

---

[2]A. A. Kornilov, "Krest'ianskoe samoupravlenie po Polozheniiu 19 fevralia," *Velikaia reforma. Russkoe obshchestvo i krest'ianskii vopros v proshlom i nastoiashchem. Iubileinoe izdanie*, ed. A. K. Dzhivelegov, S. P. Mel'gunov, and V. I. Picheta (6 vols.; Moscow, 1911), 6: 137–8.

On the reform of the state peasants' administration in 1839, see A. Vorms and A. Parenago, "Krest'ianskii sud i sudebno-administrativnye uchrezhdeniia," *Sudebnaia reforma 1864–1914*, ed. N. V. Davydov and N. N. Polianskii (2 vols.; Moscow, 1915), 2: 84–6.

[3]Kornilov, "Krest'ianskoe samoupravlenie," pp. 139–40; and I. M. Strakhovskii, "Krest'ianskii vopros v zakonodatel'stve i zakonosoveshchatel'nykh komissiiakh posle 1861 g.," *Krest'ianskii stroi: Sbornik statei*, vol. 1: *Istoricheskaia chast'*, ed. P. D. Dolgorukov and S. L. Tolstoi (St. Petersburg, 1905), pp. 376–7.

chairman of the Editing Commissions, that a reform that at times aroused the sovereign's own apprehensions was elaborated within four years.[4] In this respect, the emancipation truly was Alexander's reform.

The provisions of the Emancipation Statutes concerning peasant self-government adhered to the blueprint devised in 1859 by N. A. Miliutin, deputy minister of internal affairs and a member of the Editing Commissions. The ratified legislation divided the functions of peasant administration between the village community (sel'skoe obshchestvo), the economic-administrative unit, and the volost', the police-administrative unit. Although Russia's legislators were spared some of the obstacles that have plagued village reorganization in other traditional nations – for instance, mountainous terrain and deep tribal divisions[5] – they met frustration during the postreform period in their efforts to mesh village administration with existing peasant communities, their local customs, and diverse economic resources. According to the emancipation legislation, the village community was to consist of no more than twenty taxable male souls who lived in a settlement belonging to one or more landlords. Blocs of adjacent communities comprising 300 to 2,000 male souls each in the same district were formed into a volost'. In establishing such a mathematically symmetrical system of self-government, the tsarist administration overlooked practical, historical considerations and joined peasants from different obshchiny (landed communes) with different economic interests, religions, and even languages into the same village community. Such an organization truly compounded the problems of self-government that peasants faced for the first time in 1861.[6]

The village administration comprised the village assembly and village elder, although the village was allowed to elect its own tax collectors, clerks, and guards for breadstores, hospitals, and forests. All heads of households in the community took part in the assembly and elected the village executive authorities. One of these authorities, the elder (starosta), convoked and presided over the assembly. Although the assembly could discuss a wide range of subjects, including the repartitioning of communal lands and the admission to or expulsion of harmful or "depraved" (porochnye) members from the community, the government had no intention of allowing it free rein in its considerations. If the assembly made a

---

[4]Rieber, Politics of Autocracy, pp. 53–4. Field attributes Alexander's determination not to breadth of vision or strength of will, but to his passive tendency and skill at being a deft autocrat who capitalized on the initiatives of others. Such comments suggest that the tsar was committed not only to autocratic rule but to reform and governing through his ministerial system. See Field, p. 95.

On discussions of the Editing Commissions concerning peasant self-government, see N. P. Semenov, Osvobozhdenie krest'ian v tsarstvovanie imperatora Aleksandra II: Khronika deiatel'nosti komissii po krest'ianskomu delu (3 vols. plus index; St. Petersburg, 1889–94), 3: pt. 1; and Peter A. Czap, Jr., "The Influence of Slavophile Ideology on the Formation of the Volost' Court of 1861 and the Practice of Peasant Self-Justice between 1861 and 1889" (Unpublished Ph.D. dissertation, Cornell University, 1959), pp. 23–52.

[5]See Ashford, pp. 41–5, 108–10; and Marion J. Levy, Jr., Modernization and the Structure of Societies: A Setting for International Affairs (Princeton, 1968), pp. 277–9.

[6]S. M. Bleklov, "Krest'ianskoe obshchestvennoe upravlenie," Istoriia Rossii v XIX veke, 5: 144.

decision on an issue outside its jurisdiction, the resolution by law would be invalid and those who took part in adopting it, along with the elder, would be subject to trial or disciplined by the peace arbitrator, a gentry official established in part to supervise peasant self-government.[7] The burden of responsibility rested above all on the elder because, as assembly chairman, he was required to prevent discussion of forbidden issues. This was a heavy responsibility to impose on peasants who with rare exceptions were illiterate, ignorant of the law, and inexperienced in governing their own affairs. Such obligations were a factor in the peasants' disillusionment with self-government soon after 1861.

The village elder performed police and executive functions as well. Besides convoking the village assembly, he presented matters concerning the needs of the village community to the assembly for its consideration and enforced the decisions of the village assembly, the *volost'* courts, the peace arbitrators and, after 1864, the zemstvos and the justices of the peace. The *volost'* administration and the peace arbitrators held the elder strictly accountable if the peasants did not discharge their temporary obligations to the landlords or pay taxes to the state. The elder also served as custodian of communal revenues and supervised the maintenance of roads, bridges, and breadstores in the community. On top of all this, he had to do his share of the communal agricultural work. In short, heavily burdened with responsibilities, subject to diverse public and local state officials (representing the Ministries of Internal Affairs, Justice, and Finance especially), and grossly underpaid, the elder who wished to do his job conscientiously was in an unenviable position. Little wonder that within two years of the emancipation the most qualified peasants, much like the prereform gentry with their corporate posts, used any means to avoid being elected, and the peasants who were elected did not hesitate to supplement their income with bribes.[8]

A parallel set of peasant institutions existed at the *volost'* level. A particularly important official was the *volost'* elder (*starshina*), who performed police and administrative functions similar to those of the village elder and on tax collection matters specifically dealt with a variety of state officials.[9] The *volost'* administrative board (*volostnoe pravlenie*) and *volost'* court established by the Peasant Reform had no counterparts at the village level. The *volost'* elder, all the village elders or their assistants, and all peasant tax collectors in the *volost'* sat on the *volost'* administrative board, which rendered decisions in the disposal of *volost'* funds and the private property of peasants in order to pay individual debts. In practice, however, the *volost'* elder decided these matters himself or, if necessary, consulted with the *volost'* scribe (*pisar'*), who was often the only literate person in the territory. The scribe interpreted the

[7]*Polnoe sobranie zakonov Rossiiskoi imperii* [hereafter cited as PSZ], 2d ser., vol. 36, no. 36657, 19 February 1861.
[8]See A. A. Polovtsov, "Dnevnik mirovogo posrednika Aleksandra Andreevicha Polovtsova (Peterburgskoi gubernii, Luzhskogo uezda)," *Russkaia starina*, no. 1 (1914): 98.
[9]Zyrianov, pp. 249–50.

laws for the *volost'* elder and illiterate judges on the *volost'* court, where he served as a secretary.[10] Notorious for his lack of moral scruples, the scribe invariably took advantage of his role as interpreter of the laws in order to influence the judges in their decisions. Not surprisingly, a lucrative bribe was often the price for the scribe's influence in attaining a favorable verdict.

Thus, the basic shortcomings of peasant self-government in the 1860s and 1870s – the corruption of peasant officials, bureaucratic interference, and peasant apathy toward self-government – had their roots in the legislation of 1861. Still, the magnitude of these problems and the government's commitment to rectify them were apparent only in the late 1870s and early 1880s, particularly after the senatorial inspections of 1880–1. Before then, peasant institutions themselves, the inadequacies of which were well documented by several commissions,[11] were not the source of much official concern or ministerial conflict, for several reasons. On the one hand, in creating a modest system of peasant self-government, the architects of the Peasant Reform were too idealistic about the capabilities of the peasants to govern themselves, just as they were naive to think that within a matter of years the peasants would be prepared to participate as equals with the privileged estates of the realm in a common system of public self-government. On the other hand, so exhausting was the process of enacting the Peasant Reform that top officials were willing to dismiss the initial disorders in peasant self-government as temporary phenomena connected with its implementation. Even Valuev, one of the few high-level officials who recognized the shortcomings of peasant self-government throughout the 1860s, did not acknowledge these problems until 1863, two years after he became minister of internal affairs.[12] With the outbreak of the Polish Revolt (1863) and the sporadic political disturbances in St. Petersburg in mind, he concluded that the disinterest of the peasants in elected office, the incompetence of peasants who held these offices, and the arbitrary disciplinary punishments imposed on peasant officials by the police, landlords, and peace arbitrators were all circumstances that might touch off peasant discontent. Accordingly, he demanded that his ministry be given control over peasant affairs throughout the 1860s because he considered peasant self-government in its current form a threat to domestic security and welfare. As proof, he cited the food shortage of 1867–8, which he attributed to peasants' inability to manage their own bread reserves. Because the minister of internal affairs was ultimately accountable to the tsar for famine relief operations, Valuev no doubt made the accusation to deflect the criticism of other officials against him.[13] Never-

---

[10]Kornilov, "Krest'ianskoe samoupravlenie," pp. 150, 155.

[11]Yaney, *Urge to Mobilize*, especially pp. 22–32.

[12]Shortly after his appointment as minister of internal affairs, Valuev had praised the enthusiasm and industriousness of peasant officials. See his 15 September 1861 memorandum to Alexander II in P. A. Valuev, "Zapiska P. A. Valueva Aleksandru II o provedenii reformy 1861 g. (Publikatsiia i predislovie O. N. Shepelevoi)," *Istoricheskii arkhiv*, no. 1 (1961): 70–1.

[13]Passage for 2 February 1868 in P. A. Valuev, *Dnevnik P. A. Valueva, ministra vnutrennikh del 1861–1876 gg.*, ed. P. A. Zaionchkovskii (2 vols.; Moscow, 1961), 2: 244–5.

theless, his explanation of the famine situation revealed a knowledge of and concern for the problems of peasant self-government and their impact on rural agrarian distress that few officials had at the time. His work in 1872 as the head of an interministerial commission to investigate the state of agriculture and rural productivity (he was then minister of state properties) confirmed his belief that peasant self-government as established in 1861 was completely inadequate and was one of the primary causes for the depressed state of peasant agriculture.[14]

Similarly, the government's policy toward the *volost'* courts shows that prior to the late 1870s neither the minister of internal affairs nor his ministerial counterparts seriously contemplated further reform of peasant self-government, despite the fact that preliminary government investigations attested to the inefficiency and corruption of peasant justice. The government introduced the *volost'* court in 1861 because the regular judicial apparatus was in a state of disarray and unable to handle the additional burden of petty litigation. In addition, owing to their formal judicial procedures, which were based on written proof and statutory law, the regular courts were not suited for deciding cases on the basis of peasant custom, which at times varied even within individual districts. As a rule, peasant customary law attached far greater importance to peasant offenses against the family and communal neighbors than against state authorities (or nonpeasants); and peasants at times skipped the hearings altogether and carried out *samosud*, or brutal punishment of an offender, for particularly serious offenses in the village such as horse theft.[15] For the more "formal" peasant justice, the *volost'* assembly was required to elect from four to twelve bench judges for one-year terms, with at least three sitting on the bench at any time. Along with petty lawsuits between peasants (up to 100 rubles in value), the *volost'* courts decided all lawsuits regardless of value if both the contesting parties (including peasants and nonpeasants) agreed to abide by its decision. The court had the right to sentence the convicted party to a maximum of six days of public labor, a three-ruble fine, seven days of detention, or twenty strokes with a birch.

The Emancipation Statutes provided for the separation of administrative

Valuev's criticism of peasant self-government, which he made in a memorandum to the tsar on 15 February 1868, had some validity, in view of the fact that the peasants and zemstvos were largely responsible for famine relief. When the famine came in 1868, many of the bread stores were empty and peasant and zemstvo officials had no records available on the existing reserves, a situation that added to the chaos surrounding relief operations. In his memorandum, Valuev pointed out other problems in peasant self-government such as the losses and wasteful expenditure of village funds by peasant officials, the tendency of wealthy peasants to pay bribes in order to avoid elected service, and the harmful effect of the mutual guarantee and communal land tenure on the peasant economy. However, he made no concrete reform proposals to correct these problems. The episode was an important factor in Valuev's removal as minister in March 1868. See ibid., p. 498; and Veselovskii, *Istoriia zemstva*, 3: 161.

[14] Yaney, *Urge to Mobilize*, p. 38.

[15] Cathy Frierson, "Crime and Punishment in the Russian Village: Rural Concepts of Criminality at the End of the Nineteenth Century," *Slavic Review* 46 (Spring 1987): 55, 64–5.

and judicial authority, a principle that was reaffirmed in the Judicial Statutes of 1864. But the records of a commission appointed in 1871 to investigate the *volost'* courts showed that nearly everywhere peasant officials ignored this concept, and the *volost'* elders and scribes interfered at will in the deliberations of peasant judges. In fact, peasants questioned by members of Senator M. N. Liuboshchinskii's commission were frequently quoted as replying: "What the scribe says goes."[16] *Volost'* elders prompted peasant judges to render decisions favorable to their wishes, and there were almost unlimited opportunities for bribes and graft. The prospect of receiving bribes was the one inducement for peasants to serve on the *volost'* courts, and the offices of peasant judges invariably had an abundance of willing candidates, unlike other peasant-elected positions. Decisions were customarily rendered in favor of the party offering the larger bribe, in most cases in the form of wine and vodka. If a defendant was convicted, he could later bribe judges to reverse their decision or he could bribe the scribe, in writing up the verdict, to insert extenuating circumstances that the district assembly of peace arbitrators would not overlook in their review of the case. Finally, if all else failed, the guilty party could persuade the *volost'* elder not to enforce the court's decision with a bribe.[17]

Despite all the accumulated evidence on the shortcomings of the *volost'* court, the Liuboshchinskii Commission made no formal reform recommendations, contending that such proposals constituted the work of a subsequent commission.[18] Like the aforementioned commission organized in 1872 under Valuev, it concluded that the depressed state of the peasant economy caused the problems in peasant administration and justice. Unlike the Valuev Commission, however, it argued that peasant self-government might yet improve if agricultural conditions improved. Very few members on either commission recognized that peasant officials were a force in helping to ruin the village economy or insisted, as did Valuev, that the government could not wait indefinitely for the peasants to accustom themselves to the routines and ethics of public service.[19] As shown in Chapter 3, it took the autocratic crisis of the late 1870s – with its collapse of rural authority and precipitous increase in tax and redemption arrears – to rouse these officials to legislative action. Equally important, however, the reform of any aspect of local administration was a protracted process that usually evoked much ministerial conflict; and

[16]Czap, "Influence of Slavophile Ideology on the Formation of the *Volost'* Court," pp. 72–6; Vorms and Parenago, pp. 94–5.

[17]Vorms and Parenago, p. 101. According to Zyrianov, the scribe was especially susceptible to pressure from the local kulaks (*miroedy*), who determined the amount of his salary and authority. Naturally, they were the people who could afford to bribe the *volost'* scribe and elder. Zyrianov, pp. 257–8.

[18]Yaney credits these commissions with collecting valuable data and evaluating peasant institutions in peasant terms. In his view, this represented a first step in government mobilization in the countryside. Yet, in criticizing these commissions for not doing more, Yaney fails to pinpoint the institutional and political resistance to such reform (revealed even within these interministerial commissions). Yaney, *Urge to Mobilize*, pp. 33–4, 43.

[19]Strakhovskii, "Krest'ianskii vopros v zakonodatel'stve," pp. 407–11.

neither Count Konstantin Ivanovich Pahlen, the minister of justice, nor Valuev himself felt secure enough in his position to begin this arduous work. After all, as Valuev learned by his failure to abolish the peace arbitrators, until ministers as a whole found it in their interests to support a reform in peasant self-government – that is, until the ramifications of disorderly peasant self-government forced ministers to look beyond their particularistic concerns – the prospects for reform were minimal whereas the personal risks for its official sponsor were great.

Ministerial conflict over the peace arbitrators, 1861–74

The organism of the state either develops or weakens: there is no middle course.
– P. A. Valuev (1866)[20]

Unlike the peasant institutions themselves, the peace arbitrators were the object of several important ministerial clashes from 1861 to 1874. This point is rarely made by historians, who usually emphasize the arbitrators' work in mediating land settlements between peasants and landlords according to the Emancipation Statutes or draw analogies between the peace arbitrators and the later land captains in their use of discretionary powers.[21] Yet, in supervising newly created peasant self-government, the arbitrators were a key element in maintaining provincial order as well as a vehicle for official influence over the peasant villages. That is why the minister of internal affairs desired exclusive control over their appointment, removal, and activities. But the efforts of Valuev and Aleksandr Egorovich Timashev, Valuev's successor as minister of internal affairs (1868–78), to attain such controls were frustrated continuously by several ministers, above all the ministers of justice and finance. Although they spoke in terms of the honorary, public status of peace arbitrators and of the need to maintain the conditions for attracting the most qualified gentry to the office, these ministers also defended the autonomy of arbitrators because it was in their interest in terms of their authority in the provinces and leverage in central policy making. The arbitrators were, in theory, responsible to the ministers of justice and finance, respectively, in overseeing the peasant courts and supervising tax collection in their territories, and these ministers intended to keep it that way at all costs.

The legislation establishing the peace arbitrators was drafted in the Commission for Provincial and District Institutions organized in 1859 under N. A. Miliutin. Since the bureaucracy lacked the personnel and money to implement the emancipation in the provinces, the government decided that the provincial governor, with the consent of the district gentry marshal, would appoint arbitrators from among local gentry landlords for the first three-year period. Their selection required the approval of the senate, which

---

[20]Quoted from passage for 15 August 1866 in Valuev, *Dnevnik*, 2: 143.
[21]The latter claim is made particularly in Yaney, *Systematization*, pp. 366–7, and idem, *Urge to Mobilize*, pp. 62–3, 72–3.

alone had the authority to dismiss them.[22] The Emancipation Statutes established a peace arbitator in each section consisting of three to five *volosti*. Directly above the arbitrators in the administrative hierarchy were the district assemblies of peace arbitrators, which included all the peace arbitrators of the district and a government-appointed member under the chairmanship of the district gentry marshal.[23] This body had the authority to review all decisions of the arbitrators in the district (especially regarding land settlements between landlords and temporarily obligated peasants) and the complaints of arbitrators against peasant officials. It was directly subordinate to the provincial bureau for peasant affairs, an institution presided over by the governor and, unlike the arbitrators and their district assemblies, a part of the administrative hierarchy of the Ministry of Internal Affairs.

Given the diverse and important functions of the arbitrators, the government set high requirements in order to guarantee that the most qualified people sympathetic to the peasant emancipation would hold these offices. Only hereditary landed gentry who qualified for elected gentry service were eligible for appointment, provided they satisfied one of the following criteria: (1) ownership of at least 500 *desiatiny* (approximately 546 hectares) of land either under their direct management or allotted for the use of peasants; (2) ownership of at least 100 *desiatiny* and a graduation certificate in a science curriculum from an academic institution that carried with it the right to enter state service at the twelfth rank; or (3) voting rights in the provincial gentry assembly. Although arbitrators were supposed to receive no salary by law, they each received 1,500 rubles per annum as an expense allowance. In March 1861 Count Stepan Stepanovich Lanskoi, the minister of internal affairs and a spokesman for the "enlightened bureaucrats," reminded the governors that Alexander II attached utmost importance to the selection of arbitrators who supported the reform because they would enjoy independence from the regular provincial bureaucracy:

The moral qualities required of the office of peace arbitrator are demonstrated by its very name. His main task is to be a conciliator and judge of the interests of both classes [peasants and landlords]. Such an exalted mission cannot be carried out successfully either by persons who, by their previous public activity or way of thought in general, declare themselves to be biased and exclusively supporters of the interests of one class alone, or even less by habitual seekers of staff positions who pursue only their own personal ambitions and frequently selfish gains in service.[24]

---

[22]A. A. Kornilov, "Deiatel'nost' mirovykh posrednikov," *Velikaia reforma*, 5: 237; and Vorms and Parenago, p. 89.

Contrary to Yaney's claim (*Urge to Mobilize*, p. 62), the arbitrators were not appointed by the minister of internal affairs. Selection was left to local governors and gentry marshals on the grounds that they were better able to pick gentry familiar with local agrarian conditions and sympathetic to the peasant reform. On the autonomy of peace arbitrators vis à vis the local bureaucracy and gentry (especially in comparison with the later land captains), see Zyrianov, p. 252.

[23]*PSZ*, 2d ser., vol. 36, no. 36660, 19 February 1861.

In areas in which gentry elections were not held, an arbitrator in the district would preside over the meetings of the district assembly of peace arbitrators. See Mandel, chap. 2.

[24]Quoted from *PSZ*, 2d ser., vol. 36, no. 36700, 22 March 1861.

As both prereform and postreform experience revealed, the quality of personnel holding these positions – and specifically the prospect of "careerists" flooding the ranks – proved a constant, valid concern for the government. To drive home this point to the governors, Lanskoi bluntly ordered them to select reform-minded gentry who were on good terms with the peasantry, because harmonious relations between the peasant and arbitrator would be the surest guarantee of order and tranquility in the provinces.

The timely fulfillment of these instructions by the governors was neither enough to save Lanskoi as minister nor a source of comfort to his successor Valuev. Replacing Lanskoi as minister on 20 April 1861, Valuev found that his policy of maintaining order in the provinces depended to a large extent on peace arbitrators who were already appointed and over whom he had no direct control. This situation disturbed him particularly because of the circumstances surrounding his appointment (a topic of considerable controversy that need not be detailed here).[25] Suffice it to say that Valuev, as shown by his attitude toward local self-governing officials, was a bureaucrat who advocated state control over the reform process and shared Alexander II's concept of autocracy, even though he listened patiently to complaints from gentry landlords over the terms of the emancipation. According to Valuev, all power resided in the autocrat and no political authority was to devolve to the local public. Like his colleagues under Alexander's system of ministerial government, he regarded his ministry as the most important executor of the sovereign's authority and complained about local officials who were outside his control. Because the peace arbitrators were subordinated to the Senate, which in turn was under the nominal jurisdiction of the Ministry of Justice, their autonomy enjoyed the protection of the law and the judicial authorities.

At the same time, Valuev stressed the practical need for local self-governing institutions to handle certain functions, thereby relieving the state of the fiscal and administrative burdens connected with local petty affairs. He contended that, for local self-government to be useful yet politically harmless, the minister of internal affairs required control over self-governing institutions, a position that brought him into conflict with several ministers and other top officials who in some cases were determined to defend the

---

[25]In brief, prerevolutionary historians regard Valuev's appointment as a turning point between periods of reform and reaction, whereas Soviet historians consider him a tool of the reactionary gentry. According to Soviet historians, the tsar appointed Valuev to quiet gentry dissatisfaction with the emancipation. The first interpretation, which idealizes Lanskoi and N. Miliutin as liberal reformers who were victims of a gentry reaction, is found in Dzhanshiev, pp. 297–300; A. A. Kizevetter, "Nikolai Alekseevich Miliutin," *Istoricheskie otkliki* (Moscow, 1915), p. 250; Kornilov, "Deiatel'nost' mirovykh posrednikov," pp. 236, 240; Kornilov, *Obshchestvennoe dvizhenie pri Aleksandre II; istoricheskie ocherki* (Moscow, 1909), pp. 107–8; and Strakhovskii, "Krest'ianskii vopros v zakonodatel'stve," p. 382. In contrast, Tseitlin argues more perceptively that Valuev's views differed little from Miliutin's and that both were first and foremost bureaucrats. Tseitlin, "Zemskaia reforma," pp. 199–200.

For the Soviet argument that Valuev's political ideology was predicated on gentry class interests, see N. M. Druzhinin, "Senatorskie revizii 1860–1870-kh godov (K voprosu o realizatsii reformy 1861 g.)," *Istoricheskie zapiski*, vol. 79 (1966), p. 158; and V. G. Chernukha, *Krest'ianskii vopros v pravitel'-stvennoi politike Rossii (60–70 gody XIX v.)* (Leningrad, 1972), p. 34.

reform ideology of decentralization and separation of powers. Valuev, however, aimed to supervise local life through a network of governors and peace arbitrators answerable to him alone. This is what he had in mind when he spoke about the development of the state organism and when he stressed that "the autocracy must remain inviolable, but its apparatus must be revitalized."[26] Thus, like his distant successor Tolstoi (whom he personally detested), Valuev was an official who favored delegating administrative functions to self-governing institutions without relinquishing political authority, a viewpoint by no means unusual among officials in underdeveloped nations undergoing rapid social and economic change.[27]

Initially, as in his 15 September 1861 memorandum to the tsar, Valuev had much praise for the peace arbitrators, who included such renowned public figures as Prince Cherkasskii, the Slavophile Iu. F. Samarin, the novelist L. N. Tolstoi, and the physician and pedagogue N. I. Pirogov. He applauded the arbitrators for enlightening the newly emancipated peasants about their status and dismissed landlord complaints against their work in the provinces of Pskov, Tver', St. Petersburg, Moscow, Iaroslavl', Kaluga, and Simbirsk as both unjust and rash. The emperor penned his agreement with this statement on the memorandum.[28] But in the same document Valuev confessed worry that arbitrators might abuse their independent status with respect to the administrative authorities, especially if the wrong sort of people held this post. In fact, Valuev used this memorandum to appeal for imperial support in his conflict with the Senate, Grand Duke Konstantin Nikolaevich, and other officials on the Main Committee for Rural Welfare concerning control over the peace arbitrators. In late July 1861 he had challenged the Senate and judicial officials by submitting a proposal to the Main Committee to give the minister of internal affairs the right to dismiss peace arbitrators on the grounds that certain arbitrators were exceeding their legal authority. In view of Valuev's claims about the arbitrators' activities two months later, this argument appears to have been little more than pretext for asserting his control. But the minister lost his battle with the Senate. The Main Committee rejected his proposal, claiming that its implementation would undermine the honor attached to the office of peace arbitrator and would discourage eminent local gentry from accepting the post. This was an argument advanced frequently on behalf of autonomous local self-government during the next three decades. More important, Valuev's defeat can be attributed to the fact that other officials led by the committee chairman Grand Duke Konstantin Nikolaevich and Deputy Finance Minister Mikhail

---

[26] Passage for 15 August 1866 in Valuev, *Dnevnik*, 2: 143.

[27] Levy, p. 55. Orlovsky points to a similarity between Valuev and Tolstoi in noting that "his [Valuev's] advocacy of unbridled administrative and police authority survived Alexander's reign and was carried on by D. A. Tolstoi, V. K. Plehve, I. L. Goremykin, and P. N. Durnovo, later ministers." Orlovsky, *Limits of Reform*, pp. 75, 77–8.

[28] Valuev, "Zapiska Valueva Aleksandru II," p. 71. See also Valuev's report of 1 September 1861 in *Otmena krepostnogo prava: Doklady ministrov vnutrennikh del o provedenii krest'ianskoi reformy 1861–1862*, ed. S. N. Valk (Moscow-Leningrad, 1950), p. 67.

Khristoforovich Reutern teamed up against him, and Alexander II, convinced by the Main Committee's arguments, refused to intervene on his behalf.[29] Thus, several months after his appointment, Valuev, the minister appointed ostensibly to pacify the gentry, had antagonized a vocal and influential segment of them and a majority of top officials by his unsuccessful attempt to impose bureaucratic control over the peace arbitrators.

No sooner had Valuev sustained this defeat than two events occurred that prompted him again to seek control over the peace arbitrators and, more generally, over reform-minded officials impatient with the implementation of peasant reform and outspoken on behalf of local initiative. The political demonstration of thirteen arbitrators in Tver' province in February 1862 against provisions of the peasant emancipation and his clash with Governor V. A. Artsimovich of Kaluga (1862) over the selection of peace arbitrators underscored the ineffectiveness of Senate control as a means of preserving order in the provinces. The episodes convinced Valuev that, contrary to his views five months earlier, a significant number of politically unreliable gentry served as arbitrators and that their irresponsible actions and demands might well touch off peasant unrest. Although he had the thirteen Tver' arbitrators removed from office (and incarcerated temporarily in the Peter and Paul Fortress) and arranged Artsimovich's "promotion" to the Senate, these were temporary solutions that failed to establish regular ministerial control over the arbitrators.[30]

Unable to bring the arbitrators under his regimentation, Valuev proposed to abolish them in 1864–5 and to subordinate the newly created justices of the peace to his authority in the form of the provincial bureau for peasant affairs. In addition, he recommended giving the justices both administrative and judicial powers. Not surprisingly, these proposals shocked Minister of Justice Dmitrii Nikolaevich Zamiatnin, who had just campaigned success-

[29]V. G. Chernukha, "Pravitel'stvennaia politika i institut mirovykh posrednikov," *Vnutrenniaia politika tsarizma (seredina XVI-nachalo XX v.)*, ed. B. V. Anan'ich, S. N. Valk, and R. Sh. Ganelin (Leningrad, 1967), pp. 214–15; and N. M. Druzhinin, "Glavnyi komitet ob ustroistve sel'skogo sostoianiia," *Issledovaniia po sotsial'no- politicheskoi istorii Rossii: Sbornik statei pamiati Borisa Aleksandrovicha Romanova* (Leningrad, 1971), pp. 270–1, 275–6.

An imperial statute on 14 April 1861 gave the first department of the Senate the exclusive right to approve the selection of peace arbitrators. See *PSZ*, 2d ser., vol. 36, no. 36884, 14 April 1861. Later in the year, another statute stipulated that peace arbitrators could be removed only by senate decision. See ibid., no. 37311.

[30]On the episodes, see the entries for 10, 12, 13, and 16 February and 16 June 1862 in Valuev, *Dnevnik*, 1: 145–7, 157–8; the passages for 16 and 20 February 1862 and the editor's notes in A. V. Nikitenko, *Dnevnik v trekh tomakh*, ed. N. L. Brodskii (3 vols.; Leningrad, 1955), 2: 258–9, 606; and Terence Emmons, *The Russian Landed Gentry and the Peasant Emancipation of 1861* (Cambridge, 1968), pp. 330–49.

Valuev's efforts to establish state control over peasant administration were not limited to the peace arbitrators. In 1862 and 1864, he attempted unsuccessfully to establish a *vyt'* administration in which a government-appointed gentry landlord, a definite precursor of the land captain, would serve as *vyt'* chief and deal directly with the landowners and the village elder. However, Valuev's projects were rejected by the Main Committee for Rural Welfare as untimely and contrary to the principles of the 1861 reform. See Peter A. Czap, Jr., "P. A. Valuev's Proposal for a Vyt' Administration, 1864," *Slavonic and East European Review* 45, no. 105 (1967): 391–410.

fully in the State Council for justices of the peace under his exclusive juris-diction and independent of the regular administrative authorities. As a protégé of the eminent jurist A. P. Kuritsyn and an official who received his first practical legal training under Speranskii, Zamiatnin was a firm believer in legality (*zakonnost'*).[31] The officials that Valuev wanted to estab-lish, he argued, would vitiate the separation of powers concept that lay at the heart of all the reform legislation.

The two ministers followed different strategies in this conflict, which lasted almost eighteen months and was one of several between them from 1862 to 1867. Their various intrigues were indicative of the nature of interministerial politics in Russia under Alexander II. They showed how ideology and institutional interests often dovetailed in the reform era, indeed more so than in the ministerial debate over the counterreforms a quarter century later; in that period among Alexander III's ministers (but not in the State Council) the ideology of state control went largely unchallenged. On this occasion, Valuev pleaded his case with other ministers and the emperor, only to receive the support of Finance Minister Reutern and Adjutant General Aleksandr Alekseevich Zelenoi, the minister of state properties (1862–72), who saw in it a means of cutting local expenses.[32] Immediate self-interest apparently dulled the savings-obsessed Reutern to the prospect that Valuev, having asserted his control over the justices of the peace, might well make the local fiscal officials his next target. In contrast, Zamiatnin, long aware of Valuev's ideas on this issue (which he had expressed as early as 1862), produced a counterproposal in March 1865 that reaffirmed the Senate's su-pervisory role over all ministers, a power that it enjoyed by law but rarely exercised in practice. He proposed to require prior Senate approval for all circulars sent by ministers to their subordinates containing instructions and interpretations on the enforcement of certain laws.[33] There can be little doubt that Zamiatnin's bold stroke was an oppositional maneuver and not a serious effort to reestablish the rapidly declining supervisory authority of the Senate. After all, if the latter were his intention, he would have encountered the opposition of nearly every minister in St. Petersburg, as Zamiatnin himself realized.

Zamiatnin's counterproposal, a diversionary and delaying tactic often em-ployed by ministerial critics in order to allow them to muster forces, helped block Valuev's efforts to impose his control over the justices of the peace. Yet ultimately neither minister scored a complete victory. Valuev managed to defeat Zamiatnin's counterproposal by throwing the latter's criticism of the Valuev project back at him and arguing that it would violate the sep-aration of powers by subordinating the administration to a primarily judicial institution (the Senate). The State Council decision of 20 October 1865

---

[31]Lincoln, *Vanguard*, p. 200.
[32]Passage for 12 July 1865 in Valuev, *Dnevnik*, 2: 57.
[33]Wortman, p. 271.

represented a limited victory for Zamiatnin. It transferred nearly all the judicial functions of the peace arbitrators to the justices of the peace, yet ruled against the abolition of the arbitrators because they performed administrative functions incompatible with the office of justice of the peace.[34] The episode illustrated how individual ministers adhered to the fundamentals of the Great Reforms and at the same time, as in Zamiatnin's case, refused to give up newly acquired authority in local affairs.

After 1865, Valuev, convinced that abolishing the peace arbitrators was out of the question, turned to more circuitous methods to impose his ministerial control over them. A change in strategy from a comprehensive measure to a series of piecemeal reforms, he reasoned, might be more expedient in averting ministerial opposition to his policies. In any event, practical needs took priority in Valuev's mind over the political risks. From governors and zemstvos everywhere he received complaints about the laziness and incompetence of the current arbitrators who had replaced the original group in 1864 when the latter assumed the new offices of justices of the peace and zemstvo delegates. In 1867, twenty-five of twenty-eight governors declared that with the main work of implementing the peasant reform completed, the arbitrators regarded their responsibilities with indifference and failed to supervise peasant institutions.[35] In other reports, the governors blamed the rise in peasant arrears in *obrok* (dues in cash and kind) and tax payments on the inactivity of the arbitrators, and Valuev endorsed their recommendations that the police be granted complete control over the collection of arrears.[36] As for the zemstvos, beginning in 1866 they regularly complained about footing the bill for both the arbitrators and justices of the peace and petitioned for relief from supporting the peace arbitrators.

Ultimately, these fiscal considerations were the main reason why the government abolished the peace arbitrators in the heartland of the empire in 1874, following two previous measures in 1866 and 1871 that reduced their numbers by increasing the size of their sections.[37] However, Valuev did not reap the success. In early 1866 he had sought to grant the governors-general in borderland provinces the right, with the consent of the minister of internal affairs and the chief of gendarmes, to dismiss arbitrators suspected of political unreliability, provided that they inform the Senate of the reasons for their action. Yet, on 15 November 1866, the Committee of Ministers, reluctant to change the procedure for removing the peace arbitrators, authorized the governors-general and the minister of internal affairs only to remove them from office temporarily, with the Senate retaining the last word on the matter. In short, despite the tension in St. Petersburg following

[34]Cf. Chernukha, "Pravitel'stvennaia politika," p. 218; and *PSZ*, 2d ser., vol. 37, no. 42603, 25 October 1865.

[35]*Ministerstvo vnutrennikh del. Istoricheskii ocherk* (St. Petersburg, 1901), p. 721; and Chernukha, *Krest'ianskii vopros*, p. 56.

[36]Chernukha, pp. 50–2; and Strakhovskii, "Krest'ianskii vopros," pp. 403–4, 413–14.

[37]*PSZ*, 2d ser., vol. 41, no. 43145, 25 March 1866; and ibid., vol. 46, no. 49664.

Karakozov's attempt on Alexander II's life on 4 April 1866, the ministers refused to give Valuev unlimited control over local officials such as the arbitrators and justices of the peace because they saw it as a measure that would upset the balance of ministerial authority in the provinces.[38] In fact, his brazen attempt to turn political circumstances to his advantage merely hardened Ministers D. A. Miliutin, Reutern, and Zamiatnin in their opposition to his policies. Their complaints to Alexander II against Valuev's heavy-handed actions against the peace arbitrators, the zemstvos, the judiciary, and the press helped hasten his downfall a year and a half later.[39]

The appointment of the second-rate Timashev as Valuev's successor in 1868 provided proof that Alexander II's ministerial power equilibrium was firmly in place and that a police ethos prevailed in the Ministry of Internal Affairs. Still, there were some striking differences between Valuev and Timashev regarding the ministry's use of peace arbitrators and general policy on local self-government. Lacking Valuev's administrative experience and vision, General Timashev, a throwback to the military officials of Nicholas I's reign, sought to maintain rural order through the personal supervision of his agents; Valuev by contrast saw the arbitrators under his control as a vehicle for directing administrative and economic development in the village, all of which would help renovate autocracy from below. Moreover, whereas Valuev used his considerable political skills in bidding for control over the arbitrators, Timashev deferred to more powerful allies such as Count Petr Andreevich Shuvalov, the chief of gendarmes, to outmaneuver the ministerial opposition. The contrast in personality and politics was obvious to all. As State Secretary D. M. Sol'skii quipped in a letter to Valuev in 1869: "Your chair, as happens, is occupied by another. But from him the former spirited discourse does not resound. To put it better, nothing resounds."[40]

[38]Soviet historians, who stress the impact of external factors such as peasant unrest and revolutionary movements on government policy, contend that the increase of ministerial control over the arbitrators on 15 November 1866 stemmed from the panic in official circles following the Karakozov affair. See Zaionchkovskii's commentary in Valuev, *Dnevnik*, 2: 476; and Chernukha, *Krest'ianskii vopros*, pp. 58–9. However, it would seem that the decision of 15 November 1866 was more noteworthy for the limitations on the powers granted to the governors-general.

[39]Nikitenko, *Dnevnik*, 3: 117; and Valuev, *Dnevnik*, 1: 43.

The ministerial conflict took its toll in other quarters. Zamiatnin was relieved as minister of justice because he defended the autonomy of the courts against the attacks of Valuev and quarreled with the latter over what measures to take concerning violations of the 1865 Censorship Law. Valuev repeatedly attacked Zamiatnin in his conversations with the tsar. The principal incident leading to Zamiatnin's dismissal occurred in February 1867. Alexander II ordered him to remove M. N. Liuboshchinskii from the first department of the Senate in connection with Liuboshchinskii's participation in the St. Petersburg zemstvo demonstration of January 1867 (discussed in Chapter 2). Zamiatnin reminded the tsar that judges were irremovable, thus prompting Alexander II to assert that he was above the law. Although the tsar allowed Liuboshchinskii to retain his post, he replaced Zamiatnin with Count Pahlen within two months. Wortman, p. 276.

[40]Quoted in Orlovsky, *Limits of Reform*, p. 86. On the differences in background and policies of Valuev and Timashev see ibid., pp. 88–9, 93. Orlovsky regards Valuev's tenure as minister as pivotal in two respects. First, after 1861 the Ministry of Internal Affairs, in deference to Alexander II's intentions and in accord with its security function, ceased to advocate reform and focused on the defense of autocracy, the traditional estates of the realm, and police authority in the countryside. The adminis-

In any case, in November 1868 Timashev proposed to replace the arbitrators with local district commandants under his personal control to supervise peasant institutions. Immediately, Reutern and Zelenoi balked at the proposal and argued that the subordination of the proposed officials to the minister of internal affairs was no guarantee that they would function properly. Zelenoi pointed out that such a measure, by restoring government tutelage over the peasants, would violate the provisions of the Emancipation and Judicial Reforms, which delineated the boundaries between executive and judicial authority and laid the foundations for peasant self-government.[41] Faced with unexpectedly stiff opposition, Timashev and Shuvalov withdrew the proposal. A second plan that recommended the appointment of the arbitrators by the minister of internal affairs was rejected in 1869, although the Main Committee did grant the provincial bureaus for peasant affairs the right to remove arbitrators temporarily.[42]

Whatever their arguments for repudiating these measures, it is clear that many ministers opposed them because they would alter the diffusion of ministerial authority in the provinces that resulted from the reforms of the early 1860s; and they adhered to this position in the late 1860s despite some sporadic incidents of revolutionary unrest that provided a political climate favorable to a policy of centralization. The fact that they successfully opposed such proposals shows that in the late 1860s Shuvalov and Timashev did not have the extraordinary influence over Alexander II that Soviet historians particularly attribute to them (and that Shuvalov enjoyed briefly in the early 1870s). There is no question that had they enjoyed such favor with the tsar, the ministerial opposition would have crumbled because top officials frequently took their stand on issues according to what they perceived to be the tsar's wishes.[43] For example, Zamiatnin was especially vigorous in defending the autonomy of the courts not only because he believed in an independent judiciary, but also because in the 1860s he rightly concluded that Alexander still wanted a government based on law. By contrast, his successor Count Pahlen reflected his sovereign's apprehension over increasing revolutionary unrest in the early 1870s and concerned himself more with making the prosecuting authority an effective arm of the administration than

---

tration of Loris-Melikov (1880–1) provided the only exception to this pattern. Second, the Ministry of Internal Affairs became the leading ministry – "virtually a state within the state" – during the years 1861–81. Although Orlovsky's point about the importance of political factors in the ministry's policies, especially from the mid-1860s on, is well taken, his study minimizes the role of grass-roots administrative problems in its reform (and later counterreform) proposals. Moreover, the actions and motives of other ministers in foiling such reform proposals, a point overlooked by Orlovsky, was part of the traditional ministerial power ethos that he attributes mainly to the Ministry of Internal Affairs.

[41] Strakhovskii, "Krest'ianskii vopros," pp. 395–6.

[42] Chernukha, *Krest'ianskii vopros*, pp. 62–4.

[43] Most of the governors and other top officials likewise formulated their views in accordance with those of their direct superiors. See Armstrong, *European Administrative Elite*, p. 265; and Orlovsky, *Limits of Reform*, pp. 100–1.

with protecting the independent status of judicial officials.[44] The complicating factor in such a system was Alexander II, who often concealed his own wishes and allowed his ministers to fight it out, and only then declared publicly his support for a particular legislative program.

By the late 1860s, the prospects for abolishing the peace arbitrators indeed appeared bleak. But two factors changed this situation and led to an unprecedented consensus among ministers on the issue. First, the agrarian and fiscal crisis of 1869–70 triggered many more zemstvo complaints against the inactivity of the arbitrators and the burden of paying for them. Second, and most important, Alexander II, distressed by these complaints, growing tax arrears, and Count Shuvalov's warning about possible peasant unrest due to these conditions, made it clear that he favored the abolition of the arbitrators. Through the Committee of Ministers he authorized Timashev to draft a new project in November 1872 that would abolish the office of peace arbitrator. Owing to imperial intervention the proposal was on the table of the Main Committee by March 1873. The debate in the committee centered on whether or not to create a new institution – the district bureau for peasant affairs (*uezdnoe po krest'ianskim delam prisutstvie*) – to take over the functions of the arbitrators, or to turn them over to the provincial bureau, which would include up to six temporary members assigned by the government for this purpose. Timashev favored the latter alternative, which would have allowed his ministry direct supervision of the temporary members, but in later discussions Count Shuvalov and Grand Duke Konstantin Nikolaevich prevailed upon the committee to replace the proposed temporary members of the provincial bureaus with district bureaus.[45]

Unlike its predecessors, the Shuvalov plan received the support of other ministers because it had the backing of the tsar, as evidenced by the fact that Shuvalov and Grand Duke Konstantin, poles apart ideologically, sponsored the legislation. Few officials were inclined to challenge Count Shuvalov, whom they regarded as the tsar's favorite, and the chief of gendarmes was indeed the most powerful official in the government outside the royal family during the early 1870s. Yet Shuvalov in 1873 was destined for a downfall

---

[44]Under Count Pahlen, the activity and authority of the justices of the peace were not curbed, a fact that distinguished them from all other local self-governing organs during the period 1866–76. Scholars traditionally attribute this to the popularity of the justices of the peace with the public because they rendered quick and fair decisions of petty litigation at the local level. See Dzhanshiev, p. 439. In fact, the justices retained their autonomy because of Zamiatnin's spirited defense of their powers and because Count Pahlen generally did not concern himself with petty justice; and after 1874, the issue of combining the powers of the arbitrators and justices of the peace became moot.

[45]See the passage for 18 March 1874 in Valuev, *Dnevnik*, 2: 304–5; Strakhovskii, "Krest'ianskii vopros," pp. 398–401; and Orlovsky, *Limits of Reform*, pp. 137–9. The latter focuses exclusively on the structural problems of the Ministry of Internal Affairs as opposed to the administrative shortcomings of the arbitrators that led to the 1874 statute. The omission is puzzling inasmuch as he recognizes the importance of administrative matters in emphasizing that the problem of creating effective state authority at the *volost'* and district levels remained "at the heart of efforts by the Old Regime to stabilize the government right through the Stolypin era and World War I." Orlovsky, *Limits of Reform*, p. 139.

in the near future. In the aftermath of the debate over the abolition of the peace arbitrators, he boasted so much about his ability to manipulate the tsar and his government that Alexander II, for this and other reasons, reassigned him to the Court of St. James in November 1874.[46]

No less important, the Shuvalov plan did not encroach upon the jurisdiction of other ministers like previous proposals. It removed the unreliable and ineffective peace arbitrators as supervisors of peasant administration without establishing an omnipotent agent of the minister of internal affairs with combined administrative and judicial functions. Indeed, the organization of the district bureaus flowed logically from the collegial principles and structure of provincial administration developed under the reforms of the 1860s. The district bureaus posed no additional fiscal obligations for the state and, with a larger territory to supervise than the peace arbitrators, they were not as expensive for the zemstvos to maintain. Reutern, who was well aware of the financial difficulties of the zemstvos through his consultations with them in 1871–2 over tax reform, endorsed the reform and agreed that the district police chief (*ispravnik*) should have exclusive control over the collection of taxes. With the support of Reutern and Count Pahlen already ensured, the Shuvalov plan sailed through the State Council.

However, the Statute of 27 June 1874 did not provide Timashev with the control over local administration that he desired, nor did it signify the replacement of the peace arbitrators with police supervision.[47] The zemstvo-elected permanent members of the district bureaus created to inspect peasant institutions were further removed from district control than the arbitrators. Whereas by 1870 each arbitrator had to cover from six to ten *volosti*, the permanent member had to work an entire district (with as many as thirteen *volosti*). According to data for European Russia in 1875 (excluding the Don and Baltic regions), 10,080 *volosti* came under the supervision of roughly 500 permanent members and the peace arbitrators who remained in effect in a few borderland provinces.[48] Thus, the permanent members were usually less familiar with local peasant custom and had less time to supervise all the peasant villages under their jurisdiction.[49] By the same token, the district police chief, a district bureau member, concentrated mainly on tax and arrears collection in the village, thereby ignoring general peasant administration and welfare – a key to the health of the state and gentry economies as well. In this sense, the reform backfired on Timashev and failed to provide any real supervision over peasant administration, a fact that was quickly and amply documented. It was rather a victory for decentralization and the diffusion of ministerial power over the centralization plans of the Ministry

[46]See the entry for 8 July 1874 in *Dnevnik D. A. Miliutina*, ed. P. A. Zaionchkovskii (4 vols.; Moscow, 1947–50), I: 159; and Koni, *Sobranie sochinenii*, 5: 281.

[47]Such a claim is made in I. M. Strakhovskii, *Krest'ianskie prava i uchrezhdeniia* (St. Petersburg, 1903), pp. 72, 80–2, 163–77; and Zyrianov, p. 251.

[48]Ibid., p. 246.

[49]*PSZ*, 2d ser., vol. 49, no. 53678, 24 June 1874; and Yaney, *Systematization*, p. 369.

of Internal Affairs. Rather than replace gentry supervision with paternalistic bureaucratic control over the village peasantry, the 1874 legislation would make local administration even more fragmented and unmanageable.

Autocracy's dilemma: state control versus local initiative in the zemstvo reform

As is evident from the four years of debate that preceded it, the zemstvo reform was of even greater concern to top officials anxious to preserve Alexander II's ministerial equilibrium than was reform of peasant self-government. Such concern was certainly warranted. Not only did the zemstvo reform introduce a new system of public self-government that had to compete with the state bureaucracy and corporate institutions in rural Russia for revenues and jurisdiction, but as institutions with an important role in administrative and economic management at the district and provincial levels, the zemstvos discharged functions in school construction, land surveys, and maintenance of roads and bridges that vitally affected many ministries besides Internal Affairs, Justice, and Finance. This fact alone necessitates a brief analysis of the preparation and implementation of the zemstvo reform. Yet this episode is no less pertinent as an example of how some, but certainly not all, ministers used an ideology of administration (public self-government) for consolidating and extending their authority in the provinces. This tendency in tsarist bureaucratic politics was not as prevalent in the 1860s as in the 1880s and 1890s. There were ministers in the Great Reform era, for instance Dmitrii Miliutin and Minister of Education Aleksandr Vasil'evich Golovnin (1861–6) who pressed for *glasnost'* and *zakonnost'* in government and advocated theories of decentralization and self-government, because they truly believed that Russia should follow a Western path of administrative development.[50] But in the heated atmosphere of official debate, ideologies and self-interests frequently merged to render potent opposition to reform proposals that favored a particular interest group or an official agency, with the result that zemstvos in the 1860s and 1870s were left to contend with enemies on two fronts – public apathy and bureaucratic interference.

Unhappy compromise: ministerial conflict and zemstvo reform. Just as with the Peasant Reform, Alexander II provided the impetus and defined the guidelines for the reform of local government. In his decree of 25 March 1859, the tsar committed himself to the principle of all-estate local self-government in economic affairs and two days later set the bureaucratic machinery in motion by establishing the Commission for District and Provincial Institutions, under Nikolai Miliutin, then deputy minister of internal affairs. Alexander announced: "It is necessary to grant greater unity, independence and trust to the economic administration in the district. In view of this,

---

[50]Lincoln, *Vanguard*, p. 203.

the degree of participation by each social estate in the economic administration of the district must be defined."[51] The emperor went well beyond
these specific goals in directing the commission to draft projects to reform
the local police and police justice, to determine the procedure for resolving
disputes between the landowners and peasants, and to increase the governor's
authority in extraordinary cases.

The bureaucratic nature of the commission's initial projects (1859–62)
and their similarity with Valuev's later ideas have been discussed at length
elsewhere and need not concern us here.[52] In brief, the commission's work
can be divided into two stages with the March 1862 memorandum of Ia. A.
Solov'ev, Miliutin's deputy in the commission, providing the dividing line.
Unlike earlier projects that called for local bureaus with government and
public representatives to manage public food supply and local economic
duties, Solov'ev's draft explicitly recommended more public autonomy and
elected public zemstvo institutions to handle these functions.[53] There were
several reasons for the changes. The commission, on further study, realized
that the government lacked the personnel and money to take such an active
part in administering local economic affairs throughout Russia. More important, Alexander's dismissal in April 1861 of Lanskoi and Miliutin, the
targets of the gentry's antibureaucratic attacks, meant that the bureaucratic
nature of the original proposals would have to be toned down considerably,
and the public given a wider sphere of autonomy and jurisdiction in local
economic affairs in order to curry gentry support for the reform. For the
gentry, this was to be compensation for their lost authority as serfowners.
Valuev, whom contemporaries and some later historians criticized for en-
hancing the gentry's role in the zemstvo at the expense of other social groups,
had almost no part in this revision of the zemstvo project.[54]

Although gentry interests were a consideration in the commission's revision of the original project, the resolutions passed by gentry assemblies in

[51]Quoted in MVD, Istoricheskii ocherk, p. 125.
[52]For a detailed review of the commission's work from 1859 to 1862 and a comparison of the views of
N. Miliutin and Valuev, see note 25 above and specifically Kizevetter, Mestnoe samoupravlenie, pp. 104–
5; V. V. Garmiza, Podgotovka zemskoi reformy 1864 goda (Moscow, 1957), pp. 154–7, 164–5, 203–5;
Starr, Decentralization, pp. 242–4; Orlovsky, Limits of Reform, pp. 151–2; and Lincoln, Vanguard, pp.
185–7. On Miliutin's political views, see also Anatole Leroy-Beaulieu, Un Homme d'état russe (Nicolas
Miliutine): d'après sa correspondance inédité (Paris, 1884), pp. 68–9. Orlovsky makes a good point (p.
150) in maintaining that the celebrated conflicts between government and zemstvos have tended to
obscure the more usual harmony and cooperation between them; however, he provides few details on
the administrative rationale for the zemstvo reform or cases of actual cooperation between government
and zemstvo officials. His view that the zemstvo reform was a "controlled but timely political concession"
and an effort to broaden the social support of the autocracy addresses an important consideration but
not the most important one (judging by Valuev's defense of the zemstvo legislation) in the government's
reform plans. Zyrianov claims that the government intentionally turned over district administration
and the zemstvo to the landed gentry, although, as shown in Chapters 3–6, this argument exaggerates
the extent of gentry participation in district administration and confuses class interest with the public
service ideals of many of those gentry active in zemstvo affairs. Zyrianov, pp. 273–5.
[53]N. N. Avinov, "Graf Korf i zemskaia reforma 1864 goda (Iz istorii sostavleniia polozheniia o zemskikh
uchrezhdeniiakh 1864 g.)," Russkaia mysl', no. 2 (1904): 96–7.
[54]Starr, Decentralization, p. 243; and Valuev, Dnevnik, 1: 152.

1861–2 were by no means the major determinant of Valuev's zemstvo reform.[55] The commission bureaucrats seldom looked beyond raisons d'état in devising reform projects because of their bureaucratic backgrounds and sense of duty. Conversely, during the late 1850s and early 1860s, as illustrated by the differences between the democratic proposals of the Tver' and St. Petersburg gentry assemblies and the oligarchical programs of the Tula and Moscow assemblies, the gentry were too divided among themselves to act as a strong pressure group against the government. Valuev expressed a typically bureaucratic view of public participation in government when he emphasized in 1861 that gentry assembly discussions, and presumably the zemstvos in the future, were useful because they provided the autocracy with needed information on local conditions. Having furnished this information, they were no longer needed in the reform process, and in fact bureaucrats resented further public discussion of these issues.[56] *As a rule*, public opinion did not pressure state officials into making political concessions under duress. On the contrary, it helped the government to gauge the practicality of its reform measures in light of local conditions.

Instead, Valuev's program for local self-government under state control consisted of the following elements: governors with broad powers, especially in supervising zemstvo affairs; state officials (the *vyt'* chiefs) under his authority to supervise peasant administration; zemstvo institutions dominated by conservative gentry land magnates and with a precisely defined jurisdiction; and the limited participation of zemstvo representatives in the State Council in a consultative capacity. Valuev emphasized the integrity of his state control system; the repudiation of one or several of its components would undermine the order in his program and in fact might trigger public discontent with other aspects. The success of this system depended largely on his ability to control the governors, and in 1863 he felt enough confidence in them to boast, "I do not have governors; they are my agents."[57] But his desire to decentralize the provincial agencies of the ministers of finance and of state properties and to establish the governors' control over them involved him in a series of confrontations with Reutern that opened the floodgates for ministerial attack on the zemstvo projects. In 1861, Reutern argued that governors had no right to interfere in the internal decisions of the local treasuries, which were the domain of the Finance Ministry alone.[58] This clash was significant because it established Reutern as one of the three

---

[55]Many historians regard these resolutions as the most significant factor in the reform process; see Tseitlin, "Zemskaia reforma," pp. 193–5; Veselovskii, *Istoriia zemstva*, 3: 3–30; N. I. Iordanskii, *Konstitutsionnoe dvizhenie 60-kh godov* (St. Petersburg, 1906), pp. 33–60, 82–113, 132–43, 151–5; S. G. Svatikov, *Obshchestvennoe dvizhenie v Rossii* (2 pts.; Rostov-on-the-Don, 1905), pp. 15–34, 53–66; Kornilov, *Obshchestvennoe dvizhenie*, pp. 112–21; Garmiza, *Podgotovka zemskoi reformy*, pp. 51–129; Emmons, *Russian Landed Gentry*, pp. 240–2, 340–60, 367–97; and Starr, *Decentralization*, pp. 202–18.

[56]Michel Crozier, *The Bureaucratic Phenomenon* (Chicago, 1964), p. 165. Valuev made this point in 1861 as noted in Garmiza, *Podgotovka zemskoi reformy*, p. 65.

[57]Quoted from the entry of 18 October 1863 in Nikitenko, *Dnevnik*, 2: 372.

[58]Starr, *Decentralization*, pp. 180–1.

ministers (Zamiatnin and Dmitrii Miliutin being the others) who attacked virtually all aspects of Valuev's policy toward local government in the 1860s. It also sowed a personal antipathy between the two men that surfaced in their conflicts over ministerial jurisdiction, taxation, and the authority of the governors.

Besides reducing state expenses on civil administration and establishing a more efficient local administration, Valuev advocated a limited degree of public self-government in local economic affairs because it would provide the gentry with a new raison d'être. According to the minister, local zemstvo self-government within these limits constituted no challenge to the state's authority. He saw no opposition between state and zemstvo interests, as he explained in 1863:

The zemstvo administration is only a special organ of one and the same state authority and from the state it receives its rights and powers; zemstvo institutions, having their place in the state organism, cannot exist outside it and, together with other institutions, are subject to the general conditions and that common guidance which is established by the central state authority.[59]

However, Valuev himself did not always define the zemstvo–state relationship in such terms and his inconsistency on this point, along with the revisions in the zemstvo project made by the State Council, obscured the status and role of the zemstvos and led to zemstvo–state conflicts after 1864. For instance, in the final draft of the project Valuev left untouched Solov'ev's definition of the zemstvos as public institutions outside the state hierarchy in order to distinguish them from state officials who received salaries and service privileges and to drum up public enthusiasm for zemstvo administrative service. Yet in the State Council debate he referred to them as state organs in order to justify establishing his control over them. Thus, Valuev's efforts to impose his authority on the zemstvos without paying for them, besides arousing the confusion of the public and bureaucracy over their status, put them in the category of second-class institutions dependent on state officials to carry out their programs. These circumstances would have a deleterious effect on zemstvo activity in the 1860s and even more so in the 1870s. Not long after the zemstvos were implemented, a renowned zemstvo leader observed accurately that antagonism between police and zemstvo officials rather than cooperation was the practical effect of this ambiguous and at times contradictory legislation.[60]

Valuev proposed to establish state control within the zemstvo assembly by introducing a system of representation based on property ownership weighted heavily in favor of the prominent gentry landlords. He maintained that they were the most competent to manage local affairs by virtue of their superior education and previous experience in local corporate administra-

[59]Quoted in *Trudy kommisii o gubernskikh i uezdnykh uchrezhdeniiakh*, pt. 1, bk. 1: *Proekty i obiasnitel'naia zapiska* (St. Petersburg, 1860–3), p. 26.
[60]A. A. Golovachev, *Desiat' let reform, 1861–1871* (St. Petersburg, 1872), p. 199.

tion.[61] In fact, Valuev's proposal stemmed not so much from admiration for the gentry's past record in local administration as from his belief, expressed in 1859, that the gentry should be transformed "from a caste into a state *soslovie* in a rational sense."[62] In essence, Valuev, like Tolstoi later in the Ministry of Internal Affairs, aimed to "bureaucratize" the landed gentry, to harness them once again in state service. He realized that many of the prominent gentry landlords lacked sufficient education and local corporate experience. But this reality did not discourage Valuev, who, for political reasons, preferred their leadership. In his opinion, landlord-dominated zemstvo institutions promised the greatest assurance of order in the assemblies and adherence to state instructions. He also defended the commission's assumption that the degree of participation of each group in zemstvo affairs should be in proportion to its interest in the local economy, as measured by the relative amount of property owned by each group, and not by *soslovie* affiliation, as many conservative gentry landlowners preferred.

To guarantee the predominance of the landed gentry, Valuev proposed to divide the district population into three electoral curiae – the private landowners, the municipal property holders, and the peasants. Although private landlords could participate in their electoral assemblies directly or indirectly, the minister made certain that those gentry landlords with at least 100 maximum allotments (200–800 *desiatiny* in various areas) would have overwhelming majorities in these assemblies. A relatively small number of petty landlords owning one-twentieth the minimal requirement would represent their constituents. Urban residents who owned merchants' certificates or property with factories or commercial institutions yielding an annual turnover of at least 6,000 rubles were eligible to participate in the urban electoral assemblies. This requirement, according to Valuev, would exclude the politically unreliable petty bourgeoisie and urban intelligentsia from zemstvo affairs. Because peasants held their property in communal tenure, they were to elect their zemstvo delegates from among the village and *volost'* elders – the very peasant officials who were subject to district officials and police. Thus, even the peasants in the zemstvo would be under the firm control of the minister of internal affairs through his local agents. The district assemblies would elect the members of the provincial assembly; both the provincial and district assemblies elected from their membership an executive board. In most cases, Valuev anticipated, the board members would be landed gentry.[63]

In Valuev's system of state-controlled self-government, the zemstvo assemblies and executive boards would have jurisdiction only over matters that

[61]Avinov, "Graf Korf i zemskaia reforma," p. 98.

[62]Passage from Valuev, "Dnevnik," *Russkaia starina* 72, no. 10 (1891): 146, as quoted in Freeze, "*Soslovie* (Estate) Paradigm," p. 19.

[63]See *Trudy kommisii o gubernskikh i uezdnykh uchrezhdeniiakh*, pt. 1, bk. 1: 39–48; and Dorothy Atkinson, "The Zemstvo and the Peasantry," *The Zemstvo in Russia*, pp. 80–5, who emphasizes that the 1864 statute was introduced to establish a new bond between gentry and peasants.

the government could not carry out alone. There would be no devolution of political power or public institutions rivaling the state for local control. Repudiating the broad categorization of zemstvo jurisdiction as "economic matters involving local interests" proposed earlier by the commission, he argued for a precise definition of zemstvo affairs. Thus, restricted by these two guidelines, the zemstvos, on the basis of Valuev's program, would have virtually the same jurisdiction in local economic affairs as the prereform commissions that had administered local economic duties, food supply, and public charity. Reflecting the concerns of his ministry as well as an ethos of police control, his proposals indeed were more noteworthy for the areas excluded from zemstvo management, for example, public education, public health, and public apportionment of national taxes at the local level.[64] He even opposed giving these institutions exclusive control over public food supply affairs because he distrusted the ability of zemstvo and peasant officials to maintain sufficient reserves for famine relief.[65] In short, although Valuev was fully aware that a lack of gentry initiative was responsible in part for the inefficient prereform local administration, he opposed autonomy and broad competence for the zemstvos because such a reform might be interpreted as a bold step toward a federalist, democratized form of government. Such fears induced Valuev on 9 October 1862, for instance, to attack Reutern's proposal to allow zemstvo participation in the apportionment of national taxes.[66]

Valuev conferred on the governors the awesome burden of ensuring that the zemstvos remained within their jurisdiction. To give them latitude in this area, he allowed them to suspend any zemstvo resolution contrary to the law or "the general state welfare," and the vagueness of the latter phrase enabled the governors to interfere almost at will in zemstvo activity. It was indeed inconsistent with Valuev's efforts to define zemstvo affairs precisely. However, bureaucratic control over local self-government and the political neutralization of the zemstvos were his goal, not theoretical consistency. To prove that he meant business, he granted the governor the right, with the permission of the minister of internal affairs, to discharge local economic duties at zemstvo expense when he determined that the latter had not fulfilled its obligations.[67] Thus, the commission's final project introduced bureaucratic controls over the jurisdiction and activity of the zemstvos that, contrary

---

[64]See the entries for 14 November, 25 November, and 19 December 1863 in Valuev, *Dnevnik*, 1: 255, 261–2, 409. In early sessions of the State Council debate on the zemstvo proposal in July 1863, Valuev made a case for exclusive state control over tax apportionment by claiming that the zemstvos were closer in nature to private organizations than government agencies. This was another example of Valuev's contradictory statements on zemstvo institutions that perplexed his ministerial colleagues. See Tseitlin, "Zemskaia reforma," p. 212.

[65]Garmiza, *Podgotovka zemskoi reformy*, pp. 197–8.

[66]Ibid., p. 196; and Starr, *Decentralization*, p. 279.

[67]James A. Malloy, Jr., "The Zemstvo Reform of 1864: Its Historical Background and Significance in Russia" (Unpublished Ph.D. dissertation, Ohio State University, 1965), pp. 149–51; and Garmiza, *Podgotovka zemskoi reformy*, pp. 201–2. See also Robbins, "Viceroys," chap. 7.

to Valuev's intentions, fettered the public initiative necessary for effective local self-government, while creating many opportunities for bureaucratic interference in zemstvo affairs.

For all these constraints on zemstvo activity, Valuev did not consider his state control program complete without the addition of approximately fifteen zemstvo representatives to the State Council as advisors. In making this proposal three times (June 1862, April 1863, and November 1863), he emphasized that this reform would pose no threat to the autocracy. On the contrary, public participation in the State Council on the government's terms would undermine demands for a federal zemstvo assembly that, Valuev expected, would arise with the introduction of the zemstvo. It would allow the zemstvo delegates in the State Council to transmit government directives to the local zemstvo as well as provide information on local needs.[68] In one stroke, Valuev intended to neutralize the zemstvo as a potential nucleus of a constitutionalist movement while assuring educated society that the government was listening to their opinions and employing their talents. Hence in its objectives and its limited scope, the reform of the State Council was at the heart of Valuev's program to use public services for the benefit of the state without compromising the political authority of the government.

The politics of opposition. More than any other aspect of Valuev's program, the reform of the State Council, at least in the judgment of Alexander II, had dangerous political implications. Convinced that its implementation at the very minimum would complicate state policy making by making public opinion a factor and that it could be construed as a limitation on autocracy, the tsar never gave it serious consideration. His hesitation to reject the

---

[68]K. L. Bermanskii, "Konstitutsionnye proekty tsarstvovaniia Aleksandra II," *Vestnik prava* 35, bk. 9 (1905): 229–30.

According to Garmiza, Valuev contemplated such a reform of the State Council as early as 1859, long before the wave of gentry "constitutional" addresses. Thus, his proposal for State Council reform cannot be dismissed simply as a concession to the gentry movement of 1861–3, which historians have generally done. See note 55 above. For information on his State Council reform projects and the official debate over them, see Garmiza, *Podgotovka zemskoi reformy*, p. 158; idem, "Predlozheniia i proekty P. A. Valueva po voprosam vnutrennei politiki (1862–1866 gg.)," *Istoricheskii arkhiv*, vol. 1 (1958), pp. 141, 143, 144; and Valuev, *Dnevnik*, 1: 181, 185, 193, 210, 217–19, 261.

In 1866, Grand Duke Konstantin Nikolaevich submitted a similar plan to reform the State Council by creating a congress of zemstvo deputies and a congress of gentry deputies (the latter of which was not in Valuev's projects). Like Valuev's proposals, the Grand Duke's project was rejected. See Bermanskii, "Konstitutsionnye proekty," pp. 270–83; Valuev, *Dnevnik*, 2: 113–14, 116, 150, 166–7; and "Perepiska ministra vnutrennikh del P. A. Valueva i gosudarstvennogo sekretaria S. N. Urusova v 1866 godu," *Istoriia SSSR*, no. 2 (1973): 115–27.

In the early 1870s even Count Shuvalov proposed a similar political reform whereby gentry and zemstvo representatives would participate in a commission to discuss domestic affairs. But the Committee of Ministers, led by Dmitrii Miliutin, Reutern, and Chairman P. N. Ignat'ev, repudiated the project because of the tsar's opposition to similar projects in the past, and because of fears that Shuvalov would use a commission of public representatives to strengthen his control over domestic policy making. This project in fact provided them with an excellent opportunity to discredit Shuvalov. V. G. Chernukha, "Problema politicheskoi reformy v pravitel'stvennykh krugakh Rossii nachale 70-kh godov XIX v.," *Problemy krest'ianskogo zemlevladeniia i vnutrennei politiki Rossii: Dooktiabr'skii period*, ed. S. N. Valk and V. S. D'iakin (Leningrad, 1972), pp. 158–64.

proposal outright prompted Valuev to think that the emperor was seriously considering it. But, in fact, Alexander merely wished to spare Valuev's feelings in repudiating the project. Sensitive in his personal relations with his ministers, the tsar was adept at using his ministers to do his dirty work and scuttle reform proposals that he did not support. With the Polish Revolt escalating in the spring of 1863, he was in no mood for experiments with public participation in the State Council and consequently arranged for Valuev's project to be reviewed by a hand-picked group of officials. Alexander was fully aware that this group of traditionalists would attack the proposal for its "constitutional overtones," and Count V. N. Panin, a former minister of justice, and Prince V. A. Dolgorukov, the chief of gendarmes, did not disappoint him. Using the outcome of the debates as a pretext, Alexander II decided in December 1863 to reject the project because of its constitutional implications. The tsar's decision undermined a foundation of Valuev's system of state-controlled self-government and the minister understandably took the defeat with much bitterness, especially because the tsar, in his opinion, had been less than frank with him.[69]

The ministerial debate over the zemstvo reform project in 1862–3 likewise sheds light on other aspects of ministerial politics under Alexander II – the substantial opposition and the various tactics used by ministerial adversaries to undermine Valuev's project, their reliance on nonministers to attack it, and their ability to use the tsar for their purposes at a critical moment. Valuev's ideas of state-controlled local self-government stirred up the opposition of Reutern and Golovnin, among others, even before the project was submitted to the State Council. These two ministers, who feared that the adoption of Valuev's control program might well preclude zemstvo participation in rural economic development, mobilized the ministerial opposition in an ad hoc commission established in March 1862 under Grand Duke Konstantin Nikolaevich in order to review the zemstvo project.

How could the bureaucratic controls inherent in this project be minimized to protect the autonomy of zemstvo institutions and enlist enthusiastic public participation in local self-government? This was the question that preoccupied Valuev's opponents in the spring of 1862, insofar as their ministerial jurisdictions in local economic and educational development were affected. Past experience suggested three possible alternatives: procrastination in reviewing the project in the ad hoc commission; a ministerial intrigue against Valuev; and the presentation of a counterplan for zemstvo reform. They ruled out procrastination because the tsar had already expressed his impatience over the slow progress of the reform to Valuev in February 1862. A ministerial intrigue against the minister likewise was considered too severe and hasty a maneuver at this point of the debate. Consequently, Valuev's opponents relied on a counterproject drafted by Nikolai Miliutin in Paris. The appearance of this brief in St. Petersburg in May 1862, as the Grand Duke's

[69]See Valuev's diary entry for 13 December 1863 in *Dnevnik*, 1: 261.

commission sat down to review the Valuev commission project, was no coincidence. Reutern, Grand Duke Konstantin, and other top officials at odds with Valuev had corresponded with Miliutin during the previous winter and had invited him to submit a counterproposal highly critical of the Valuev commission's draft. For Miliutin, it represented a chance to become involved again in state affairs and the possibility of being recalled to service in St. Petersburg. Moreover, the proposals in the counterplan concerning broad zemstvo autonomy at the district as well as provincial level differed so markedly from his earlier views that he may well have received instructions on what to recommend. Not surprisingly, the arguments to free the zemstvos from the close supervision of the Ministry of Internal Affairs, to allow them to build and maintain all local public buildings, roads (except turnpikes), and postal facilities, and to assist in the apportionment of national taxes received the enthusiastic support of Reutern, Golovnin, and Adjutant-General Konstantin Vladimirovich Chevkin, the director of the Department of Transportation and Communication.[70]

The use of Miliutin's memorandum by Valuev's ministerial opponents was an effective tactic (and one used later again) because it prevented Valuev from directly accusing his ministerial adversaries of opposing the tsar's wishes for zemstvo reform while simultaneously it gave them the basis for rejecting the gubernatorial control provisions of the Valuev commission draft. In addition, the submission of a counterplan by his predecessor was embarrassing as well as frustrating to Valuev. He realized the absurdity of polemicizing with an official in Paris, yet the ad hoc commission's action clearly required a response. Hence, the ploy of the ministerial opposition worked. On 2 June 1862, they persuaded Alexander II to approve their own guidelines for autonomous public self-government based on the Miliutin plan and sent the zemstvo reform back to Valuev for revisions.[71] Thus, the opposition stalled Valuev's measure while appearing to act responsibly in the reform process. Little did they anticipate, however, that in the revisions Valuev would *strengthen* the governors' control over the zemstvo and further curtail zemstvo jurisdiction, and would take his chances on the project in the State Council debate.

As with Nikolai Miliutin in 1862, Valuev's ministerial adversaries found a nonminister to do their bidding in the State Council debate of July 1863. By his background, Baron Modest Andreevich Korf seemed an unlikely figure to defend public self-government. True, he had assisted Speranskii in codifying the laws in the 1830s. But this Baltic German also had presided over the censorship committee during the years of "censorship terror" following the 1848 revolutions, and under Nicholas I had warned against any modi-

---

[70]Seredonin, 3: pt. 2, pp. 71–2; Garmiza, *Podgotovka zemskoi reformy*, pp. 146–50; and Starr, *Decentralization*, pp. 250–2.
[71]*Trudy o gubernskikh i uezdnykh uchrezhdeniiakh*, pt. 2, bk. 2, pp. 1–20.
    Thinking that the zemstvo reform was imminent, Alexander ordered the Valuev commission to compile a final draft on the legislation and in October 1862 he had the revised document published.

fications in the serf system.[72] A loyal servant of the tsars, he surely must have observed Alexander's growing suspicion of local autonomy in light of the Polish insurrection. Yet Korf was a good choice to speak for the ministerial opposition and public self-government because of Alexander II's confidence in him and because, as head of the Codification Section of His Majesty's Chancellery, he was responsible for ensuring that all reform legislation was drafted in accordance with existing law; and Korf was indeed disturbed by the broad, undefined control over the zemstvo that Valuev proposed to give the governors. When the emperor urged Korf to review the revised Valuev project in the spring of 1863, Valuev's opponents seized the advantage and put the minister of internal affairs on the defensive.

Ironically, with Reutern's collaboration, Korf used his tsar to launch a full-scale attack on Valuev's program. By authorizing Korf to suggest a few changes in the Valuev draft, Alexander appeared to sanction the 150-page commentary that Korf subsequently produced. At least, that is how it appeared to Valuev. The memorandum attacked all areas of Valuev's project and recommended that it be completely rewritten in order to expand public initiative in zemstvo affairs. Only those local affairs that exceeded the capabilities of the zemstvo, Korf insisted, should remain under state control.[73] He noted that whereas administrative centralization was feasible in a small ethnically homogenous country like France, in Russia a system of autonomous local self-government protected by administrative law was the practical solution, given its size, the remoteness of many areas from St. Petersburg, and the diverse nationalities in the empire with their various religions, languages, and ethnic traditions.[74] That these same factors would be the rationale for central control and Russification in the 1880s shows that concepts in Western administrative theory were frequently contorted to support a political ideology or a minister's self-interest in provincial administrative reform.

Korf had many allies in the State Council's attack against Valuev's proposals. War Minister Dmitrii Miliutin and Prince G. A. Shcherbatov, marshal of the St. Petersburg gentry, charged that the curial system of zemstvo representation would sow class divisions in the zemstvo. But Shcherbatov's plan for an all-estate zemstvo of delegates elected at large by the population was voted down by the State Council in favor of Valuev's system.[75] It is difficult to see self-interest motives in the arguments of Miliutin and Korf in the debate over the zemstvo reform: neither of them had jurisdiction over areas to be administered by the zemstvos. Rather their arguments reflected their belief that the state alone could not govern the provinces effectively, and that public participation would be useful to the government only if the

[72]Field, p. 52.
[73]Starr, *Decentralization*, p. 281.
[74]Malloy, p. 180.
[75]Tseitlin, "Zemskaia reforma," p. 228; Garmiza, *Podgotovka zemskoi reformy*, p. 234; and *Dnevnik D. A. Miliutina*, 1: 32.

local population had the freedom to elect their representatives, the autonomy to manage their affairs without bureaucratic interference, and the enthusiasm to take public service seriously. The State Council did approve Korf's recommendation to allow peasants in the *volost'* assemblies to elect their own delegates, who could be either peasants or local landlords.[76]

Nevertheless, the real beneficiaries of this attack were Valuev's ministerial rivals. They were most effective on the matter of zemstvo jurisdiction, owing to the efforts of Reutern, State Council member N. I. Bakhtin, and E. P. Kovalevskii, a former minister of education. Springing upon Valuev the demand that the zemstvo be given control over local public health, public education, and the jails, they backed him into a corner and provoked several weeks of heated debate. When Valuev refused to budge on the issue, Reutern and Kovalevskii proposed to poll the provincial gentry on whether or not the zemstvos should administer these matters. Fully aware of what their answer would be, Valuev grudgingly backed down and revised the project accordingly. He recognized that the appearance of an alliance between the landed gentry and his bureaucratic opponents might well bring down his administration, just as it had his predecessor's. But no tactics or threats could force him to alter his proposals on the governors' supervisory authority over the zemstvo. The majority of the council and the tsar supported him on the grounds that the zemstvo dealt with matters of vital state interest including taxes, public health, education, and transportation.[77]

On the whole, Valuev's adversaries were so successful in watering down and delaying the reform that on 1 November 1863 Alexander II ordered that the project be ready for ratification by 1 January 1864. Although this ultimatum broke the bureaucratic deadlocks, it did not countermand the concessions already made. Consequently, Valuev confessed disappointment with the 1 January statute, even though most of its provisions came directly from his pen.[78] In fact, the statute's provisions on the broad jurisdiction of the zemstvo − without specific gubernatorial controls − signified another defeat for Valuev's policy of state-controlled local self-government. By their collaboration, their presentation of counterplans and their delaying tactics, his opponents had protected their own authority in the provinces while preventing the centralization of local government under the minister of internal affairs. Their resistance to Valuev's proposals on the zemstvos and peace arbitrators provided convincing proof of the government's unwillingness to deviate from the basic principles of the Great Reforms and the ministerial system effected by them, notwithstanding the efforts of the most

[76]Garmiza, *Podgotovka zemskoi reformy*, pp. 218–20, 236–8.

    Korf was less successful in his efforts to legislate the election of the zemstvo assembly chairmen. The State Council ultimately voted in favor of the ex officio appointment of the gentry marshals. See Dzhanshiev, p. 307.

[77]Garmiza, *Podgotovka zemskoi reformy*, pp. 222–4; and N. N. Avinov, "Glavnye cherty v istorii zakonodatel'stva o zemskikh uchrezhdeniiakh," *1864–1914: Iubileinyi zemskii sbornik*, p. 13.

[78]Passage for 1 January 1864 in Valuev, *Dnevnik*, 1: 264.

powerful ministry in Russia and exogenous political pressures in the early 1860s.

Unfortunately, the political compromises worked out in the State Council debate left the zemstvo with the status of a hybrid institution, containing some characteristics of state institutions and certain qualities of public organs. Unlike the *Landräte* in Prussia, the zemstvos were not incorporated into the hierarchy of state institutions but rather were established alongside government organs as separate bodies with no organic tie to the state administration.[79] Nor were they identical to the gentry corporate institutions of the prereform period, even though the gentry were favored to play the leading role in the zemstvo. Rather, the contradictions in the status of the zemstvo were a direct cause of their conflict with the governors, especially in the late 1860s, as both sides sought to take advantage of the vague regulations on zemstvo jurisdiction. Consequently, rather than free the minister of internal affairs from concern about local petty matters, as they were designed to do, the new zemstvos entangled him in a series of jurisdictional conflicts in the provinces during the 1860s and 1870s.

Uneasy partners: government and zemstvo, 1864–76

The decade following the promulgation of the zemstvo reform in 1864 was of critical importance in two ways. First, this period of mutual distrust and periodic outbursts of hostility between zemstvo reformists and tradition-minded bureaucrats, who sought to reorganize local administration on the basis of the zemstvo legislation, set the tone of zemstvo–state relations for the rest of the century. This is not to suggest that zemstvo and state officials were constantly at loggerheads in postreform Russia. On the contrary, co-operation between the two, even in specific periods of political crisis, was more often the rule, despite the occasional zemstvo–government conflicts that became causes célèbres in both quarters. In this sense, the claims of some zemstvo leaders and liberal historians concerning the struggle of "virtuous" zemstvos against a capricious bureaucracy must be regarded with skepticism.[80] Second, during these years the proposals of Valuev and Timashev to prevent this friction by strengthening the governors' control over the zemstvo met with stiff resistance from other ministers who feared that such measures might lead to similar controls over their own provincial agents – apprehensions that were well-founded, as borne out by events a decade later.

Certainly, the Karakozov affair (1866) provided Valuev with a timely argument for administrative centralization, and some of Valuev's ministerial opponents indeed blamed the political climate of 1866 for his subsequent

---

[79]V. P. Bezobrazov, "Zemskie uchrezhdeniia i samoupravlenie," *Russkii vestnik*, no. 4 (1874): 556.
[80]Pirumova, pp. 51–2; Thomas Fallows, "Zemstvo and Bureaucracy," *Zemstvo in Russia*, pp. 178–9.

efforts to control the zemstvos.[81] But actually Valuev had called for state control over the zemstvo long before Karakozov's unsuccessful attempt on Alexander II's life. Unlike Gendarmes Chief Shuvalov, who intended to emasculate the zemstvo, Valuev recognized the need to defend these institutions, which, under the government's direction and with limited competence, could provide valuable economic services at no cost to the central government. Perhaps no other episode so clearly reveals Valuev as the "enlightened official" he was – a perspicacious minister responsible for adapting reform principles to rural administrative conditions and convinced that the Ministry of Internal Affairs should spearhead the process of bureaucratic development of the countryside. However, because Reutern, Zamiatnin, and Dmitrii Miliutin did not distinguish any differences in the ideas of Valuev and Shuvalov concerning the zemstvo, historians generally assume that the two officials had identical views on the topic.[82] In fact, Reutern and Zamiatnin saw both men as a potential threat to their authority in provincial affairs and in central policy making.

Despite his opposition to zemstvo activity in such areas as public education and public health, Valuev pledged to uphold the provisions of the zemstvo statute in his official policy statement in *The Northern Post* on 1 January 1864.[83] But, within two years, he was issuing warnings that the minister of internal affairs would vigorously oppose zemstvo attempts to exceed their jurisdiction and politicize their activities. Given the contradictions and ambiguities of the legislation on zemstvo jurisdiction, adherence to the law was no easy task. During the 1860s and 1870s, some zemstvos clashed with the governors over their jurisdictional rights; both groups believed that they were adhering to the law. In the second half of the 1860s, the Senate and Committee of Ministers issued clarifications on nearly every subject that fell under zemstvo purview, most frequently in the areas of public education, management of highways, railroads, post offices, and the taxation powers of the zemstvo.[84] Such conflicts discouraged many industrious and independently minded gentry from remaining in zemstvo service. In addition, they created a situation in which many zemstvos became more concerned about staying within their legally defined powers than about doing their work,

---

[81]Gosudarstvennaia biblioteka SSSR imeni V. I. Lenina, otdel rukopisei [hereafter cited as ORGBL], *fond* D. A. Miliutin, *karton* 15, *delo* 3, *ll.* 106, 109. I am indebted to E. W. Brooks for the use of this document from the Miliutin archive.

[82]See, for instance, Veselovskii, *Istoriia zemstva*, 3: 120; Kornilov, *Obshchestvennoe dvizhenie*, pp. 178–82.

[83]John G. Gantvoort, "Relations between Government and Zemstvos under Valuev and Timashev, 1864–1876" (Unpublished Ph.D. dissertation, University of Illinois, 1971), p. 16.

[84]For details on these zemstvo-state conflicts and their resolution, see *Sbornik pravitel'stvennykh rasporiazhenii po delam do zemskikh uchrezhdenii otnosiashchimsia* (2d ed.; 4 vols.; St. Petersburg, 1868–76), 1: 40–2, 45–9, 148–9, 297–8, 331–2 (hereafter cited as *SPRDZ*); *Sbornik uzakonenii otnosiashchikhsia do zemskikh uchrezhdenii (po Svodu zakonov i prodolzheniiam izdaniia 1876 goda) s vkliucheniem reshenii Pravitel'stvuiushchego senata i pravitel'stvennykh raziasnenii i s prilozheniem gorodovogo polozheniia* (Novgorod, 1879), pp. 4–6, 14–15, 62–6 (hereafter *Sbornik uzakonenii*); Seredonin, 3: pt. 2, pp. 73–6; and Blinov, *Otnosheniia senata k mestnym uchrezhdeniiam*, pp. 216–17.

with the result that they either limited their activity to small deeds reformism or completely avoided taking measures to improve local conditions.[85]

Valuev's trust in the governors to act judiciously in supervising zemstvo affairs was a shortcoming of his system because governors, as illustrated by the Zelenyi case in Kherson province, at times clearly overstepped their legal authority in this respect. In October 1865, the Elizavetgrad district zemstvo, one of several district zemstvos already at odds with the provincial administration, elected P. I. Zelenyi, a landowner who had attracted police attention earlier in the year for his defense of peasant rights, as chairman of its district board. Governor P. N. Kliushin responded by vetoing Zelenyi's election, as was his prerogative according to the 1864 statute. After making several attempts to find out the reasons for Kliushin's action and going without a board chairman for six months, the Elizavetgrad assembly reelected Zelenyi to this post in June 1866. At this point, Kliushin disclosed that he had rejected Zelenyi's candidacy because, in accordance with the regulations on gentry in state service, the governor had the right to reject elected candidates he considered untrustworthy. Zelenyi's protest that these regulations did not apply to elected zemstvo officials who were public representatives for all social estates did not impress Valuev. He replied that the articles cited by Kliushin were established to ensure that governors would approve suitable candidates as board chairmen.[86] In essence, the controversy boiled down to whether the zemstvo was a public, corporate, or state institution. In 1866, the State Council, after observing that the law in this case was not clear, ruled against Kliushin and Valuev and declared that the Minister of Internal Affairs did not have the same authority over zemstvo officials as over gentry corporate officials.[87]

The Kherson episode was by no means an isolated case. Jurisdictional conflicts stemming from the ambiguity of the zemstvo legislation, the authoritarian attitudes of some governors and quite frequently the rashness of zemstvo delegates occurred in Viatka, Ekaterinoslav, Tavrik, Samara, Vladimir, Kostroma, Nizhnii-Novgorod, and Riazan' provinces over the next half decade.[88] In the light of these circumstances, Valuev's purpose in persuading the tsar to issue the 22 July 1866 rescript is clear. Recent zemstvo political demands and stirrings of revolutionary unrest clearly played into his hands for increasing the governors' control over administrative and corporate institutions. The rescript allowed the governors to conduct general and unannounced inspections of these bodies (*including the judiciary*) at any time, to suspend the instructions of local officials, and to summon them at their discretion. It aimed at restoring some of their prestige and local police powers that the establishment of separate judicial and zemstvo institutions

[85]This observation was made by A. I. Koshelev, a contemporary publicist and delegate in the Riazan' provincial zemstvo assembly. Starr, *Decentralization*, p. 301.

[86]Gantvoort, pp. 79–81; and Veselovskii, *Istoriia zemstva*, 3: 106–7.

[87]Gantvoort, pp. 82–4.

[88]Veselovskii, *Istoriia zemstva*, 3: 110–15.

had diminished.[89] As for the zemstvos, the rescript made no direct reference to them, but the governors rightly interpreted it as a directive to step up their supervision over these institutions without worrying about legal jurisdiction or judicial interference.

As expected, the Valuev–Shuvalov rescript proposal evoked sharp rejoinders from other ministers. Judicial Minister Zamiatnin defended the separation of powers and the role of an independent judiciary in local life. Reutern, Valuev's perennial foe on local government matters, complained that the measure was drafted too hastily and without consideration of existing laws. But no minister was more critical than Dmitrii Miliutin, who added insult to injury by asserting that governors already possessed sufficient powers, and that instead legislation designed to curb the arbitrary governors was needed.[90] Here in a nutshell were the two official views of the significance of the Great Reforms and their subsequent development – devolution versus delegation of power (the latter implying "recentralization" in 1866) – that polarized top officialdom for the rest of the century. This time, however, the emperor sided with Valuev because, as he announced, "all the information reaching me from the provinces confirms the necessity to take the proposed measures without further delay."[91] This information dealt with the conflicts between various local officials, both state and public, that paralyzed administrative activity and added significantly to the politically tense atmosphere in the summer of 1866. On the other hand, in 1869 and 1875 Alexander rejected proposals by Timashev to increase the governors' authority and to organize a rural police force under the minister of internal affairs mainly because the incidents of confrontations between the governors and zemstvos had declined noticeably from 1869–70 on.[92] Senate clarifications on the zemstvo legislation and the reluctance of many zemstvo officials to undertake initiatives in public health and public education reduced the bases for confrontations from 1870 to 1877.

The inevitable early confrontations between the zemstvo and government resulted primarily from differences between zemstvo and state officials in interpreting zemstvo legislation, unlike the later conflicts arising largely from zemstvo administrative activity and fiscal mismanagement. If the arbitrariness of some governors occasionally entangled Valuev in petty local disputes, the control of certain gentry landlords over the zemstvo assemblies turned out to be a constant source of trouble for him. His hopes in 1862–3 that a curial system of representation would provide the gentry with the largest share of zemstvo delegates were fulfilled in the elections of 1864. Of the 11,915 delegates who participated in the district assemblies of twenty-

[89]See William G. Wagner, "Tsarist Legal Policies at the End of the Nineteenth Century: A Study in Inconsistencies," *Slavonic and East European Review* 54, no. 3 (1976): 386; the entry for 14 June 1866 in Valuev, *Dnevnik*, 2: 131–2, 467–8; and Seredonin, 3: pt. 1, pp. 130–8.

[90]ORGBL, f. D. A. Miliutin, k. 15, d. 3, l. 107.

[91]Quoted in Wortman, p. 272.

[92]*Dnevnik D. A. Miliutina*, 1: 55–6.

nine provinces from 1865 to 1867, 4,962 (41.7 percent) came from the landowners' curia, 4,581 (38.4 percent) were from the peasants', and 1,296 (10.9 percent) were merchants and *meshchane* (broadly defined as the lower middle class). At the provincial level, the landlords dominated even more. Of the 2,055 delegates in the provincial assemblies, 1,524 (74.2 percent) were gentry landlords, 217 (10.6 percent) were peasant representatives, and 236 (11.4 percent) were merchants and *meshchane*.[93]

Little did Valuev foresee the undesirable consequences of the landlords' domination nor anticipate that gentry landlords would take seriously their role as public servants and become the most outspoken zemstvo critics of the government and its zemstvo policy. With their advantage in numbers, education, and experience, the landed gentry had little difficulty directing zemstvo activities in their interests, often at the expense of merchants and peasants, who were indifferent toward elected representation and deferred to the gentry delegates.[94] This, too, aroused Valuev's concern. In fact, the gentry's manipulation of the zemstvo in their interests provoked the most serious clash between the state and zemstvos in the 1860s, proof that the Ministry of Internal Affairs, although sensitive to gentry opinion, was not governed by it. To augment zemstvo revenues for their projects and to hold down their own taxes, gentry landlords in most provinces imposed a surtax on the zemstvo taxes for merchant landlords and factory owners in 1866. They contended that the zemstvo legislation allowed them to tax the income as well as the property of factory owners, entrepreneurs, and the like. Finance Minister Reutern, while opposed to gentry schemes to milk the merchants by surtaxes and mortgage banks, conceded that the zemstvo laws were so vague on this subject that zemstvo leaders could easily make the erroneous assumption that they had the authority to tax income.[95] But Valuev claimed that there was no basis for confusion. He pointed out that in January and May 1866 he had issued circulars to clarify zemstvo taxation rights and to curb zemstvo tax violations. Still, the steady increase in complaints from merchants and manufacturers forced him to issue a new law on 21 November 1866 that allowed the zemstvo to tax only immovable property within districts and towns, commercial and manufacturing certificates, and patents for winemaking plants and stores that sold alcohol.[96]

The new law on zemstvo taxation rights unleashed a storm of protest from zemstvos everywhere, who accused Valuev of introducing a punitive measure to hamper their activities and of protecting the interests of the merchants

[93]Veselovskii, *Istoriia zemstva*, 3: 40–1, 43–4, 49–50.

[94]Ibid., 53; Starr, *Decentralization*, pp. 294–8; and Atkinson, "Zemstvo and the Peasantry," pp. 111–12.

The government became so concerned about peasant apathy toward zemstvo affairs that in the 26 January 1866 decree it gave village communities the right to decide whether or not to exempt deputies elected to the village community electoral assemblies from corvée duties during their period of service. The measure was introduced in response to a district zemstvo petition. See *SPRDZ*, 1: 248.

[95]*PSZ*, 2d ser., vol. 39, no. 40458, 1 January 1864.

[96]Ibid., vol. 41, no. 43874, 22 November 1866.

and industrialists at the expense of the landlords. Their accusations had little basis in fact. The 21 November law was the third and most important in a series of laws issued in 1866 to delineate between areas subject to zemstvo taxes, namely property, and those subject to state taxation, such as the income and inventories of merchants and industrialists.[97] But the curtailment of sources of tax revenues available to the zemstvo and the bad timing of the law, which required the district zemstvos to revise their budgets for 1867 in accordance with the new regulations, convinced landlords that Valuev concerned himself solely with the interests of the merchants and industrialists. Thus, these landed gentry decided to put heavy pressure on Valuev by publicizing their discontent and hopefully persuading Alexander II to rescind the measure.

The showdown between the zemstvos and Valuev, who on this occasion had Finance Minister Reutern's support,[98] occurred in January 1867 over a resolution of the St. Petersburg provincial assembly. Although this was the most dramatic confrontation between the zemstvo and government, similar conflicts occurred on a smaller scale elsewhere in the decade. The St. Petersburg assembly, long outspoken in its support for the ideas on public initiative outlined by Baron Korf in 1863, had been a thorn in Valuev's side since its first session in 1865.[99] At its January 1867 sessions, the assembly leaders refused to apply the provisions of the 21 November law to tax estimates and appropriations for 1867, insulted the governor (and by implication Valuev), and made inflammatory appeals in favor of a completely autonomous zemstvo subject to no authority. Faced with opposition that had the earmarks of a gentry fronde, the government shut down the St. Petersburg provincial assembly, punished the board members (one of whom was Senator Liuboshchinskii), and suspended all zemstvo activity in that province for an indefinite period.[100]

Although zemstvo institutions in St. Petersburg Province were reopened six months later, the closure of the St. Petersburg provincial assembly was a crushing defeat for ministerial and public partisans of zemstvo autonomy

[97]SPRZD, 1: 193–7, 199.

In his diary entry for 24 December 1866, Valuev admitted that the law would help protect trade and industry from arbitrary taxes levied by certain zemstvo assemblies. See Valuev, Dnevnik, 2: 170. Historians Veselovskii and Yaney maintain that the measure was introduced primarily to protect the merchantry, an argument that Valuev denied in his 17 February 1867 circular. Cf. Veselovskii, Istoriia zemstva, 3: 202–3; and Yaney, Systematization, p. 348. As an official responsible for maintaining order in the countryside, it hardly suited Valuev's purpose to antagonize the influential gentry landowners by protecting the interests of the merchantry; moreover, zemstvo tax violations, in his opinion, might well lead to unnecessary conflicts in the provinces that could be avoided by issuing precise legislation on this issue. In fact, the law of 21 November 1866 was not the last word on zemstvo taxation rights, as the zemstvos continued to assess taxes in areas that the government considered outside their jurisdiction. The government issued the decrees and circulars of 3 July 1867, 10 January 1868, 15 January 1868, and 8 May 1869 to eliminate zemstvo taxation abuses. See SPRDZ, 1: 69; 2: 111, 254–8; and 3: 40–3.

[98]Starr, Decentralization, p. 307.

[99]Ibid., p. 331.

[100]PSZ, 2d ser., vol. 42, no. 44114, 16 January 1867.

that had ominous implications for the future of local self-government in Russia.[101] The events in St. Petersburg, like those involving the Tver' peace arbitrators, demonstrated how easily administrative differences could spill over into political opposition, and confirmed Valuev in his belief that self-governing institutions free from his ministry would act irresponsibly and ineffectively. Although he consistently pursued a policy of state control over the zemstvos, the zemstvo response to the 21 November 1866 law and especially the St. Petersburg episode convinced him that more stringent controls over the subjects discussed in the zemstvo assemblies were necessary. The upshot was the legislation of 13 June 1867 which, in outlining the procedure for conducting business in zemstvo and corporate assemblies, transformed their chairmen into government policemen. It gave them the discretionary powers to convoke and adjourn meetings, set the agenda, issue warnings, silence delegates discussing taboo issues, and expel nondelegates from the assembly hall. Chairmen who did not heed these regulations were subject to removal from office, administrative punishment, and even prosecution, depending on the gravity of their offense.[102] Gendarmes Chief Shuvalov, however, went even further in warning that zemstvos were a greater and more tangible threat to autocracy than either the nihilists or Poles. Beginning in January 1867 he played an increasingly prominent part in zemstvo policy making, particularly after Timashev replaced Valuev, and alluded to connections between the zemstvos and revolutionary circles. The willingness of Alexander II and some top officials to accept this allegation, and politicize zemstvo work, is illustrated by the government's severe response in the St. Petersburg episode.[103]

Still, the laws of 13 June, even if they challenged the status of zemstvo delegates as public representatives, failed to deliver a mortal blow to zemstvo work. In fact, they were the last of the stringent government controls imposed on the zemstvo until the late 1870s. Aside from the two attempts described above to increase the governor's authority over the zemstvo that were blocked by the ministerial opposition, Timashev confined his zemstvo policy to reviewing zemstvo petitions, which he rejected in an overwhelming number of cases.[104] On the other hand, he spearheaded the opposition to Reutern's plan that would have allowed the zemstvos to participate in a systematic manner in the discussion of tax reform in the early 1870s. Reutern empha-

---

[101]See Nikitenko's passage for 27 January 1867 in *Dnevnik*, 3: 71.

[102]*SPRDZ*, 1: 62–6; and *PSZ*, 2d ser., vol. 42, no. 44690, 13 June 1867. A second law of 13 June 1867 allowed the printing of reports, speeches, debates, and resolutions of the zemstvo assemblies only with the government's approval.

[103]Starr, *Decentralization*, p. 332.

[104]Mention should be made of Timashev's circular of 19 September 1869, which was an important measure. It revoked the right of zemstvos to free postage on the grounds that they were public and not state institutions. As a result, this legislation provided a new source of confusion among zemstvo leaders and state officials over the status of zemstvo institutions. The previous laws of 13 June 1867 and earlier legislation on the zemstvo's franking privileges had implied that zemstvos were indeed part of the state apparatus. See *SPRDZ*, 1: 126, and 3: 135.

sized that given their knowledge of local affairs, not to mention their experience in finding loopholes in tax legislation, zemstvo members participating in these discussions might indeed conceive a plan to overhaul the tax system and provide the state with new sources of tax revenues.[105] Thus, neither Valuev nor opponents such as Reutern managed to exert the control over zemstvo affairs that they desired. The division in ministerial circles over state policy toward the zemstvo continued into the 1870s while the frequency of zemstvo–government conflicts diminished. In short, Alexander II's diffusion of ministerial authority, an arrangement that appeared almost experimental in nature in the late 1850s and signified his need to effect change while retaining political control, proved remarkably durable in subsequent decades. Unfortunately, it was not conducive to the establishment of a coherent government policy on local self-government.

Let us conclude with several generalizations about ministerial conflict and the development of local self-government in order to provide a framework for our analysis of the counterreform politics of the 1880s. While the zemstvo-bureaucratic conflicts of the late 1860s pointed up the untenable position of public self-government in tsarist Russia and the growing gulf between state and society, the zemstvos and peace arbitrators were a source of much conflict *within* ministerial circles. This is not surprising because the arbitrators and zemstvos, more than elected peasant officials, were key institutions to rural administrative development and ministerial policy enforcement, and because both institutions drew mainly on the gentry, the traditional rural support of the state. Still, this source of ministerial conflict must be understood in order to appreciate the administrative crisis that faced postreform officials. It helps explain why peasant and zemstvo self-government operated under adverse conditions and why the government was slow to rectify shortcomings of peasant and zemstvo self-government.

From the standpoint of local self-government, the reforms, for all of the emphasis on administrative decentralization and local initiative, failed to solve some perennial problems concerning personnel and authority. If anything, the legislation in this area in the 1860s and 1870s underscored the limits of autocratic power and tsarism's few options in governing the countryside in the century following the Provincial Reform of 1775. To maintain control over the emancipated peasants without greatly expanding its own rural bureaucracy, the state introduced peasant self-government in 1861 and placed it under public supervisory officials, the peace arbitrators. In essence, this reform and the zemstvo legislation introduced public self-government, in contrast to rural state and corporate bodies. The irony here was that the inadequacies of serfdom and the undergoverned nature of the prereform provinces prompted the reforms of the 1860s; yet the new peace arbitrators and later permanent members of the district bureaus – the key supervisory

[105]Gantvoort, pp. 95–6, 121–3.

element in the new self-government – and the zemstvo leadership came from the same limited pool of rural gentry as their corporate-elected predecessors and counterparts. Thus, whatever appeal the new ideas of decentralization and public self-government had, they alone could do little to correct the personnel shortages that had long hampered rural administration, or coordinate the many distinct rural institutions responsible for implementing the reforms.

By the same token, the issues of jurisdiction, initiative, and control became bones of contention to many ministries, not simply the Ministry of Internal Affairs, following the introduction of local self-government in the early 1860s. True, no official sought to use law and systematic administration as much as Valuev in order to direct the local population in rural development while simultaneously shoring up the traditional political order.[106] He fully understood that, in practical administrative terms, this was the great challenge posed by the reforms. Yet Valuev's plans were of vital interest to his ministerial peers because they had ramifications for the ministerial power balance in the capital and the provinces that helped maintain the personal power of the autocrat; over time, this ministerial conservatism would prove a formidable barrier to institutional reform. By the early 1870s, ministerial conflict over local self-government had the effect of dampening local enthusiasm for the new self-governing institutions while simultaneously encouraging local bureaucratic attacks on them.

More specifically, the ministerial divisions in the capital and in the provinces left tangible marks on local self-government. Granted, up to the mid-1870s the ministers of internal affairs were largely foiled in their numerous attempts to circumvent the principles of the Great Reforms and take control of self-government, notwithstanding the reactionary political climate in the capital following the Karakozov affair. But in their desire to revitalize local administration without sowing the seeds of gentry/zemstvo constitutionalism or providing the Ministry of Internal Affairs with total control over local development, the ministers put the zemstvos (and local self-government) in a legal no man's land. The Ministry of Internal Affairs in turn wanted neither elected officials who took their new role as public servants too seriously nor those who used public institutions for their material benefit, thus removing much incentive for those who served as zemstvo officials or as peace arbitrators. In these conditions, the legislation on the zemstvos provided no clear direction to these institutions, the local bureaucracy, or the various ministries for that matter. Hence, to paraphrase Korf, zemstvo and peasant institutions were left with competence and no power, and they suffered the administrative consequences throughout the 1870s. With the Balkans crisis of 1875 and the outbreak of the Russo-Turkish War in 1877, official concerns

---

[106]In this respect, Valuev sought to go beyond the old well-ordered police state and establish government by *Reglamentstaat*, that is, a more active government that through "a unified and efficient system of laws and administration . . . could weld a diverse and fragmented Russian society into a single national and social community." Quoted from Macey, p. 13.

over local self-government receded to the background. Within four years, however, the debate over local self-government reform again came to the forefront with the administrative and fiscal disorder in the countryside that, in the context of the crisis of the autocracy, led the government to reevaluate the record of local self-government and propose major changes in its organization.

CHAPTER 3

The breakdown of tsarist administrative order, 1875–81

Of the many documents depicting the corrupt, ramshackle state of peasant self-government during the period 1875 to 1881, few were more critical in their description than the memorandum of peasant Mikhail Aleksandrov. "What kind of *volost'* elder can we have," he complained, "when the office is attained by means of vodka?"[1] The memorandum, submitted to the minister of internal affairs in 1881, attacked the drunkenness, bribery, and various forms of intimidation that occurred during peasant elections, village meetings to repartition communal land, and *volost'* court deliberations. It blamed peasant officials for the empty grain warehouses during recent food shortages. To protect peasants from their elected officials (a request made in other peasant memorandums of the period),[2] Aleksandrov pleaded for government control over peasant self-government. "It would be most advantageous to the government and the peasants," he emphasized, "to abolish the system of elected peasant self-government and to allow each district bureau [for peasant affairs] to appoint *volost'* and village officials and scribes from among the peasants."[3]

Aleksandrov's memorandum provides not only rare evidence of peasant literacy, but also a peasant's viewpoint of a problem that aroused widespread concern in the government at the end of the 1870s. The administrative and fiscal anarchy of local self-government, the extent of which was revealed by the senatorial inspections of 1880–1 (and other official reports of the late 1870s), was the impetus for the reforms of local government elaborated in

[1] Tsentral'nyi gosudarstvennyi istoricheskii arkhiv SSSR [hereafter TsGIA], *fond* Osobaia komissiia dlia sostavleniia proektov mestnogo upravleniia (Kakhanovskaia komissiia) [hereafter *f*. Kakhanovskaia komissiia], 1881–1885, *opis'* 1, *delo* 59, *l*. 22.

[2] For instance, Grigorii Dorovskii, a peasant in Voronezh Province, argued that "more frequent visits by the authorities to the *volosti*, the courts, and the assemblies are necessary; their presence on the scene would restrain the scribe and *volost'* officials from arbitrariness." Ibid., *l*. 25. For similar peasant comments see ibid., *ll*. 190–2 *ob.*, 428–9.

[3] Ibid., *l*. 25.

the 1880s. Although historians have alluded to the inefficiency of local administration in the late 1870s and acknowledged that "the reorganization of local government was among the pressing issues of the day,"[4] few of them have analyzed these shortcomings in detail. Instead, they have concentrated on revolutionary terror, peasant disturbances, and other palpable signs of the autocratic crisis of 1878–82, and the government's reaction to it, to show how the government was isolated from educated society and plagued by ministerial division and confusion (as Valuev put it in 1879, "there are [only] fragments of a government. There is no whole. It is an idea, an abstraction.").[5] In these conditions, the tsar resorted to the "dictatorship" of Mikhail Tarielovich Loris-Melikov, who sought to end the autocratic crisis in 1880–1 by combining police repression of revolutionaries with promises of reform in local administration and other areas. According to these historians, Loris-Melikov's senatorial inspections (1880) and reforms were primarily political gestures intended to curry public support for the government. However, the crisis of autocracy ended only in 1882, a year after Alexander II's assassination and Loris-Melikov's downfall, when Alexander III appointed Dmitrii Tolstoi as minister of internal affairs. His appointment ostensibly marked a return to the regime of Nicholas I, with its emphasis on personal autocracy and arbitrary government (*proizvol*) over rule of law and administrative reform and, according to these historians, it led to the "new course" of land captain and zemstvo counterreforms that aimed at gentry support for the government.[6]

But revolutionary terror, however potent, was only one dimension of the autocratic crisis of the late 1870s. At the same time that terrorism and strikes escalated, a crisis of authority in the countryside, marked by peasant confusion over the numerous local officials introduced by the reforms (*mnogovlastie*) and the general breakdown of rural administrative and fiscal order (*bezvlastie*), eroded rural support for the government and magnified the ministerial confusion in the capital. As early as the mid-1870s, numerous governors, zemstvo officials, and ministers warned that the practical shortcomings of local administration, particularly peasant and zemstvo self-government, posed a growing threat to the regime. Yet it took the administrative and fiscal breakdown of local self-government in the late 1870s to convince top officials that these shortcomings jeopardized the autocracy itself. War Minister Miliutin was not alone in maintaining that more complex

[4]Michael T. Florinsky, *Russia: A History and an Interpretation* (2 vols.; New York, 1947), 2:1092.
[5]See the entry for 1 May 1879 in P.A. Valuev, *Dnevnik 1877–1884 gg.*, ed. V. Ia. Iakovlev-Bogucharskii and P. E. Shchegolev (Petrograd, 1919), p. 36.
[6]For this interpretation, see Kornilov, *Krest'ianskaia reforma*, pp. 236–8; Gessen, *Voprosy mestnogo upravleniia*; Veselovskii, *Istoriia zemstva za sorok let*, 3: 231ff., 318–19; Zaionchkovskii, *Krizis samoderzhaviia*; Solov'ev, pp. 27ff., 89; Itenberg, "Krizis samoderzhavnoi vlasti," pp. 90–120; and, among recent Western accounts, Taranovski, "Politics of Counter-Reform," pp. 371–2; and Hans Rogger, *Russia in the Age of Modernisation and Revolution 1881–1917* (London, 1983), p. 10. On the incidents and role of peasant disturbances and arsons in the "crisis of autocracy," see A. M. Anfimov, "Krest'ianskoe dvizhenie," in *Rossiia v revoliutsionnoi situatsii*, pp. 168–89.

work in reorganizing local administration lay ahead, as illustrated by his observation (1879) that "our entire state structure requires radical reform from top to bottom. The system of rural self-government, the zemstvo, local district and provincial administration, as well as central higher state institutions have all outlived their time and should be given new forms in accordance with the Great Reforms in the 1860s."[7]

In this context, the senatorial inspections initiated in August 1880 are properly seen not as an isolated political gesture on Loris-Melikov's part but as proof of the government's decision to overhaul all of local administration. Because the inspections were ordered by Loris-Melikov, an official famous for his overtures to the public for political support as "dictator" in 1880, historians have played down their importance.[8] Certainly, the inspectors were politically expedient in weaning public support away from the revolutionaries (a goal Loris-Melikov had accomplished as director of the Supreme Executive Commission prior to his appointment as minister of internal affairs in August 1880) and in reminding Alexander II of his political indispensability. And the substance of his 27 August 1880 instructions shows that Loris-Melikov had ambitious designs in dispatching the senatorial inspectors, namely to reorganize local government and the central ministerial hierarchy and in the process to consolidate his unofficial position as "prime minister" within the government.[9] Like his predecessors, Loris-Melikov understood

---

[7]Passage for 20 April 1879 in *Dnevnik D. A. Miliutina*, 3: 139. Miliutin drew up a rough plan for comprehensive administrative reform in November 1879; see ORGBL, *f.* D. A. Miliutin, 1879, *papka* 44, *delo* 12, *ll.* 1–8 *ob.* Other high officials criticizing local administration and self-governing institutions included Nikitenko (see the entry for 3 November 1874 in Nikitenko, *Dnevnik*, 3: 323), Valuev, Timashev, and Loris-Melikov. R. A. Fadeev, a Slavophile and general who served in the Caucasus with Loris-Melikov, and A. V. Golovnin likewise advocated administrative reforms in memoranda to Alexander II in 1879. Fadeev warned that police measures alone were insufficient to curb the terrorist threat and proposed to make zemstvo self-government efficient by eliminating government restrictions on its activity and by streamlining the bureaucracy. Such a reform, besides reducing the amount of red tape, would make funds and educated personnel available for zemstvo service and would distract the public from greater political demands. See Tsentral'nyi gosudarstvennyi arkhiv Oktiabr'skoi revoliutsii, vysshikh organov gosudarstvennoi vlasti i gosudarstvennogo upravleniia SSSR [hereafter TsGAOR], *fond* Aleksandr III, 1879, *opis'* 1, *delo* 512, *ll.* 4 *ob.*-5, 7 *ob.*-16; on the gentry's role, see Becker, pp. 57, 93.

Golovnin also favored autonomous zemstvos and worried that governors would abuse their recently acquired powers over the zemstvos. The argument did not impress Alexander II, who noted on the memorandum that he did not share Golovnin's fears. TsGIA, *fond* A. V. Golovnin, [1880?], *opis'* 1, *delo* 16, *ll.* 14–14 *ob.*

[8]There is still no published analysis of the administrative and economic problems revealed by the senatorial inspectors. Soviet historian Bol'shov merely outlines the territorial and subject areas of the inspections without really discussing the senators' findings. See V. V. Bol'shov, "Materialy senatorskikh revizii 1880–1881 gg. kak istochnik po istorii mestnogo upravleniia Rossii," *Vestnik Moskovskogo universiteta,* ser. 9, *Istoriia*, no. 4 (1976): 38–54. Other accounts provide either brief descriptions of the inspection procedures or dismiss the inspections as a political ruse by Loris-Melikov, the newly appointed minister of internal affairs. See I. A. Blinov, *Istoriia pravitel'stvuiushchego senata za dvesti let 1711–1911 gg.* (5 vols.; St. Petersburg, 1911), 4: 182; Zaionchkovskii, *Krizis samoderzhaviia*, pp. 238–43; Itenberg, "Krizis samoderzhavnoi vlasti," p. 104; M. I. Kheifets, *Vtoraia revoliutsionnaia situatsiia v Rossii (Konets 70-kh-nachalo 80-kh godov XIX veka). Krizis pravitel'stvennoi politiki* (Moscow, 1963), pp. 102, 105–6, 191; N. M. Druzhinin, *Russkaia derevnia na perelome 1861–1880 gg.* (Moscow, 1978), pp. 252–5; and Orlovsky, *Limits of Reform*, pp. 102, 180–5.

[9]Orlovsky, pp. 180–91.

that extensive reform of local self-government required a new ministerial power balance in St. Petersburg. Nevertheless, following measures taken by the government concerning local administration from 1877 to 1879 (see the next section), the comprehensive nature of the inspections – which E. S. Paina termed the most thorough of the nineteenth century[10]– shows that administrative and fiscal considerations of state were uppermost priorities in Loris-Melikov's mind.[11] In their reports, the senators made only brief mention of revolutionary terrorist activity and public dissatisfaction in the provinces, while dwelling at length on the administrative and fiscal breakdown of local self-government.

The evidence of administrative and fiscal mismanagement in local self-government that prompted Loris-Melikov to dispatch the senators was (1) the sharp rise in the number of zemstvo petitions sent to the ministry of internal affairs in the late 1870s calling for the revision and, in some cases, the abrogation of the 27 June 1874 statute; (2) the sudden rise in tax arrears of extraordinary amounts, which undermined the state budget and paralyzed the work of local self-government; (3) new frictions in zemstvo–state relations after the outbreak of the Russo-Turkish War in 1877, which intensified during the period of revolutionary terrorism and diverted many local zemstvos from their administrative work; and (4) the food supply crisis of 1880–1, particularly in the Volga provinces. These four developments necessitated the senatorial inspections in 1880–1 that brought to a climax the first phase (1877–81) of state activity on local self-government reform; and in turn the inspections and other reports from the provinces led to Loris-Melikov's reform plan and the ministerial conflict of 1881, the resolution of which verified again the connection between court politics and local self-government reform.

Autocracy and the crisis of local self-government

Proposals to reform the 27 June 1874 statute. If top officials harbored any illusions about the effectiveness of the 27 June 1874 statute, they were soon dispelled. Beginning in 1875, provincial governors, zemstvos, and district

---

[10]E. S. Paina, "Senatorskie revizii i ikh arkhivnye materialy (XIX-nachalo XX v.)," *Nekotorye voprosy izucheniia istoricheskikh dokumentov XIX- nachala XX v. Sbornik statei*, ed. I. N. Firsov (Leningrad, 1967), pp. 165–6.

[11]"Senatorskie revizii 1880 goda," *Russkii arkhiv*, vol. 50 (1912), pp. 417–29.

The text of Loris-Melikov's 11 August 1880 report to Alexander II, which proposed the senatorial inspections, is found in TsGAOR, *fond* M. T. Loris-Melikov, 1880, *opis'* 1, *delo* 87, *ll*. 1–5 *ob*. Loris-Melikov's efforts to gain Tsarevich Alexander Alexandrovich's support for the inspections are revealed in his letter of 3 September 1880 to the heir and the latter's reply on 11 September 1880 in "Perepiska Aleksandra III s M. T. Loris-Melikovym (1880–1881 gg.)," *Krasnyi arkhiv* 1, no. 8 (1925): 116–17. In February 1881, Loris-Melikov reiterated that the primary objective of the inspections in progress was to investigate current administrative, fiscal, and economic conditions in the provinces, to determine local needs, and to furnish material and recommendations for the reform work which the central government would soon undertake. Cf. "Konstitutsiia gafa Loris-Melikova," *Byloe*, no. 4–5 (1918), p. 168.

officials flooded the Ministry of Internal Affairs with complaints about the district bureaus' inefficiency in supervising peasant and police officials, especially in connection with the massive buildup of tax arrears in the late 1870s. So loud was the outcry that by 1879–80 zemstvos and other local administration officials were demanding the replacement of the district bureaus with new institutions that could provide effective personal supervision over peasant self-government and the village economy. In 1879–81, twenty zemstvos adopted resolutions to introduce zemstvo control through all-estate *volost'* assemblies, while five other assemblies debated measures to create zemstvo justices (*zemskie sud'i*) with administrative and judicial authority over peasant officials and petty peasant litigation.[12] A leading advocate of the latter approach was A. D. Pazukhin, the gentry marshal of Alatyr' district, a former justice of the peace (1872–8), and the head of the Simbirsk Provincial Commission. He became a recognized authority of local administration in the mid-1880s and played a major role in developing the counterreforms that were ultimately adopted in 1889–90. Yet, in 1881, his plan for elected zemstvo justices was but one of several such proposals that, along with fifty-nine zemstvo petitions from 1875 to 1882, proposed changes of one form or another in the 27 June 1874 statute.[13]

The petitions covered a wide range of shortcomings and gaps in the 1874 statute, the most important of which concerned article five. From 1875 to 1881, seventeen zemstvos petitioned to change this article on the procedure for electing permanent members of the district bureaus for peasant affairs, the official responsible for supervising peasant administration. With the ink on the 1874 statute barely dry, the provincial zemstvo assemblies of Vladimir, Khar'kov, and Riazan' provinces recommended in 1875 that permanent members be elected by district rather than provincial zemstvo assemblies, because the latter were generally unacquainted with the various district nominees for the post, and invariably made poor choices. Other provisions concerning the permanent members (who in theory were subordinate to the minister of internal affairs and the governor but in practice were supervised by neither) also came under zemstvo attack.[14] In 1876, the provincial assemblies of Riazan' and Tambov proposed that zemstvos have the right to elect two rather than one permanent member in cases warranted by local needs. They argued that in some areas, particularly the black earth provinces of Tambov and Riazan', the property arbitration and peasant-supervision responsibilities of the permanent member exceeded the capabilities of one man.

[12] TsGIA, *f.* Kakhanovskaia komissiia, *op.* 1, *d.* 114, *ll.* 52–52 *ob.*, 53 *ob.*–54. For details, see ibid., *d.* 103, *ll.* 1–3, 6–8 *ob.*, 14–14 *ob.*; *Materialy po preobrazovaniiu mestnogo upravleniia v guberniiakh dostavleny gubernatorami, zemstvom i prisutstviiami po krest'ianskim delam* (3 vols.; St. Petersburg, 1883–4), 1: 57–60; Gessen, *Voprosy mestnogo upravleniia*, pp. 194–6; V. Iu. Skalon, *Zemskie vzgliady na reformu mestnogo upravleniia. Obzor otzyvov i proektov* (Moscow, 1884), pp. 42, 50–3, 93–4.

[13] TsGAOR, *fond* T. I. Filippov, 1882 or later, *opis'* 1, *delo* 543, *ll.* 21–41.

[14] Ibid., *ll.* 22–22 *ob.*; Korelin, *Dvorianstvo v poreformennoi Rossii*, p. 192.

Unlike most zemstvo petitions submitted to the state in the late 1870s, those complaining about the district bureaus led to concrete legislation sponsored by Minister of Internal Affairs Timashev and his successor Lev Savich Makov (appointed 27 November 1878). The petitions of the Riazan' and Tambov provincial zemstvos were especially instrumental in breaking the ground for reform. On 1 February 1877, the State Council, on Timashev's recommendation, modified the 1874 statute to allow provincial assemblies to elect an additional member to the district bureau with the consent of the minister of internal affairs in order to provide adequate supervision of peasant affairs. The zemstvo also received the right to choose alternates for the office of permanent member in the event of his absence or illness. Finally, the State Council recognized that the 27 June 1874 statute suffered from gaps and shortcomings that would entail substantial legislative changes.[15] In short, already in 1877 the government acknowledged that the system of peasant administration as modified in 1874 required reform in order to furnish the necessary supervision over peasant self-government, and it began the preliminary work of collecting data on local government that would be used in reform discussions over the next decade.

On 14 June 1878, the Committee of Ministers made additional revisions in the 1874 statute and instructed the Ministry of Internal Affairs to make a systematic review of the legislation. It authorized permanent members to assume responsibility for the records of the district bureau, which were utterly disorganized (or even lost) in many districts, and to supervise peasant administration by conducting mandatory inspections of the villages and *volosti* at regular intervals. The permanent member would have the power to discipline peasant officials, a right that peace arbitrators previously possessed. Finally, the decree stipulated, the district bureau was to discuss as a collegial body only the most important business of peasant administration and to ensure the timely and proper payment of state and zemstvo taxes, heretofore an exclusive responsibility of the district police chief.[16] Thus, by mid-1878 the government and many zemstvos already viewed one-man supervision (*edinonachalie*) of the permanent member over peasant self-governing institutions as a means of organizing peasant self-government. As it turned out, this emphasis on one-man supervision over the peasant village was a major thread connecting all official work on peasant self-government reform over the next twelve years.

Escalation in tax arrears. Although the zemstvos and other local authorities pinpointed numerous shortcomings of the district bureaus from 1875 to 1878, it is unlikely that the government would have overhauled the 1874 legislation had it not been for the extraordinary increase in tax and redemption

---

[15] TsGAOR, *f.* Filippov, *op.* 1, *d.* 543, *ll.* 23 *ob.*-24.
[16] M. M. Kataev, *Mestnye krest'ianskie uchrezhdeniia 1861, 1874, i 1889 gg. (Istoricheskii ocherk ikh obrazovaniia i norm deiatel'nosti)* (3 pts.; St. Petersburg, 1911), pt. 2, pt. 113.

arrears in the late 1870s – arrears that provided the most tangible evidence of the absence of administrative authority in the village. Attributable largely to inadequate district bureau supervision of peasant administration, these arrears served as a barometer of rural administrative and economic disorder. They focused government attention on the absence of law and authority in the village and *volost'*, the fiscal insolvency and irresponsibility of various zemstvos, the interrelationship between mismanaged peasant administration and ruined village economies, and the ramifications of all the above for the state economy. Whereas at times the government, for political reasons, chose to ignore the petitions from certain zemstvo and gentry assemblies in the late 1870s, the growing arrears directly threatened those ministries with local administrative power (Internal Affairs, Finance, Education, and Justice), and demanded government action. Indeed, among the outcomes of the crisis of 1878–82 were new state policies to reduce redemption payments (1881), facilitate peasant resettlement, and establish a peasant land bank (1882) to offer cheap credit to peasants who sought to add to their landholdings.[17]

Contrary to the early 1870s, when relatively few, scattered *volosti* and districts had arrears exceeding their annual tax rates (leading the government to organize commissions in Smolensk in 1872 and Novgorod in 1874 to investigate the causes),[18] by 1878–80 exorbitant arrears were fast becoming a nationwide phenomenon. In nine provinces throughout the empire (Don Region, Moscow, Novgorod, Orenburg, Pskov, Samara, Smolensk, Ufa, Chernigov) the arrears for 1880 surpassed the annual rate of all taxes. In certain districts, they assumed astronomical proportions, for instance, 598 percent in Krasninsk (Smolensk province), 544 percent in Smolensk, 540 percent in Belebeevsk (Ufa), 611 percent in Surazhsk (Chernigov), and 232 percent in Mozhaisk (Moscow).[19] The state controller's report for 1880 put the arrears crisis in perspective, noting that

in Smolensk province the arrears have increased to 4,160,901 rub. [versus an annual tax rate of 1,874,234 rub.]; arrears exceeded the annual tax rate in the Don region and in the provinces of Moscow, Pskov, Olonets, Orenburg, Pskov, Samara, Ufa, and Chernigov; in fifteen provinces the amount of arrears is more than 10% the annual tax rate, namely in St. Petersburg (91%), Saratov (79%), Riazan' (57.5%), and Orel (50.5%).[20]

In fact, in thirty of forty-nine provinces in European Russia the arrears in state taxes during 1878 to 1880 were substantially higher than the arrears

[17]For details, see Zaionshkovskii, *Krizis samoderzhaviia*, pp. 249–54; and Macey, pp. 19–23.
[18]Chernukha, *Krest'ianskii vopros*, pp. 107, 111.
[19]See *Krest'ianskoe dvizhenie v Rossii v 1870–1880 gg. Sbornik dokumentov*, ed. P. A. Zaionchkovskii (Moscow, 1966), pp. 30–1; and A. M. Anfimov and A. M. Solov'eva, "Obostrenie nuzhdy i bedstvii ugnetennykh klassov," in *Rossiia v revoliutsionnoi situatsii*, p. 145.
[20]*Obiasnitel'naia zapiska k otchetu Gosudarstvennogo kontrolia po ispolneniiu gosudarstvennoi rospisi za smetnyi period 1880 goda* (St. Petersburg, 1881), pp. 64–5; quoted from Druzhinin, *Russkaia derevnia*, p. 252.

rate for even the mid-1870s.[21] Although increasing arrears rates alone did not signify a decline in peasant living standards, they forced local authorities in the late 1870s to juggle figures in order to cover up tax losses from the village level up – no small task in view of the fact that local police and peasant tax officials in 1881 collected only 15.9 percent of the taxes they were assigned to collect as opposed to 23.2 percent in 1878.[22]

Besides jeopardizing the state budget at a time when the Russo-Turkish War left a deficit of a half billion rubles and the government was more dependent than ever on rural revenues, the huge arrears in state taxes often had a calamitous impact on zemstvo services. The problem arose because the law required local police and peasant officials, over whom the zemstvo had no legal control, to collect zemstvo taxes. Subject to discipline by state authorities and mindful of accumulating arrears in redemption payments and state taxes, police and peasant tax collectors understandably invoked a law (passed in 1867) that allowed them to collect state and zemstvo taxes together[23] and to use the latter to cover redemption and state tax arrears. Two Soviet historians have noted that peasant payments were used first to pay the redemption debt, with the surplus used for other taxes.[24] This practice of robbing Peter to pay Paul exacerbated the already strained relations between zemstvo and state authorities at the end of the 1870s, and produced cases such as that in Tambov Province, where in 1880 the arrears rate for state taxes (6.5 percent) was kept down by expropriating taxes that should have gone to the zemstvos, thus inflating zemstvo tax arrears (40 percent).[25] In some provinces the rapid increase in zemstvo arrears all but paralyzed zemstvo work. In Samara Province, according to senatorial inspector I. I. Shamshin, the deficit of 710,443 rubles or 80.2 percent of the annual zemstvo tax rate (up 25 percent in the three previous years) resulted in a temporary suspension of salaries for teachers, physicians, fel'dshers, and zemstvo coachmen in 1880–1.[26] Even worse, by 1884 zemstvo arrears for all zemstvos totalled 50 percent of the budgeted annual zemstvo tax, and zemstvos in

---

[21]Druzhinin, pp. 251–2.

[22]Anfimov and Solov'eva, "Obostrenie nuzhdy," p. 142.

Among other factors during the 1870s, the number of peasants making redemption payments to the state rose from 55 percent (1870) to 85 percent (1881). Chernukha, Krest'ianskii vopros, p. 84. Anfimov and Solov'eva exaggerate the significance of arrears as evidence of peasant distress and "oppression" in "Obostrenie nuzhdy," p. 137.

[23]According to this law, the district treasuries, if they received partial or undifferentiated payments of various local taxes, were allowed to earmark 12 percent of the total sum for local zemstvo taxes and divide the remainder into three equal portions – one for the payment of state taxes, another for the payment of food supply duties of state peasants, and the third for payment of peasant redemption arrears. See PSZ, vol. 42, no. 44297, 27 February 1867. Since zemstvo taxes in nearly all provinces exceeded half the amount for state taxes, the zemstvos suffered from this procedure of arbitrary allocations.

[24]Anfimov and Solov'eva, "Obostrenie nuzhdy," p. 146.

[25]Materialy po vysochaishe utverzhdennoi osoboi komissii dlia sostavleniia proektov mestnogo upravleniia (10 vols.; St. Petersburg, 1884) [hereafter cited as MVUOK], 3: Po senatorskim reviziiam, pt. 2: Zapiski senatora Mordvinova, document 7, p. 2.

[26]TsGIA, f. Kakhanovkaia komissiia, 1881–1885, op. 1, d. 109, l. 71 ob. The Samara district zemstvos

Perm, Novgorod, and Samara provinces, to name a few, were completely bankrupt.[27]

Confronted with evidence of an arrears crisis paralyzing all branches of local government, successive ministers of internal affairs (Timashev, Makov, Loris-Melikov) and ministers of finance (Reutern, 1862–78; Samuil Aleksandrovich Greig, 1878–80) demanded explanations from local governors concerning the causes of the arrears buildup. Although many governors justifiably pointed to a succession of bad harvests, cattle epidemics, village fires, the drafting of peasants into the wartime army (1877–8), and police involvement with military recruitment, others, including A. N. Zhedrinskii of Kursk Province and V. S. Perfil'ev of Moscow Province, specifically accused police and peasant officials in the years 1878–9 of misplacing and, in some cases, embezzling the taxes they collected.[28] They likewise contended that these officials did not take the vigilant measures to collect arrears from landlords that they did with peasants, a claim prompted by the fact that, next to the state (85 percent), the peasants had the best record of meeting payments on their zemstvo land tax bill (60 percent).[29] Various governors and zemstvo officials in Samara, Viatka, Kherson, and elsewhere agreed that such losses usually occurred because the district bureaus failed to provide adequate supervision over tax collectors as required by law.[30] Governor E. V. Lerkhe, whose province of Novgorod had one of the highest rates of state tax arrears in 1878 (150.5 percent), spoke for many of his colleagues when he emphasized that the district bureaus, given their composition and extensive jurisdiction, were incapable of providing the personal supervision over peasant officials necessary to prevent losses or theft of taxes. Meeting only once or twice monthly and saddled with many other administrative obligations, the district bureau members (district gentry marshal, district police chief, zemstvo-elected permanent member) had little control over rural tax collection, as illustrated in Tambov Province in 1880. In that year, there were 123 cases in Tambov Province in which peasant officials misplaced or stole communal funds. Yet the district bureaus, too shorthanded to inspect each *volost'* administration (as required by law), rubber-stamped the records compiled by the *volost'* scribe on the amount of taxes collected in the district. Such procedures provided limitless possibilities for graft by the scribe and tax collectors. For instance, in the village of Guliny, where tax losses were the highest in the district, several minor tax collectors annually assisted the public tax collector in levying duties, and local records disclosed that a few individuals monopolized these posts for years at a time. The reason, as the

finally paid the salaries to these zemstvo personnel but only after receiving loans from the provincial zemstvo and the government.

[27]Atkinson, "The Zemstvo and the Peasantry," p. 106.

[28]TsGIA, *fond* Departament obshchikh del Ministerstva vnutrennikh del (MVD), 1878, *opis'* 69, *delo* 144, *ll*. 4–4 *ob.*; and ibid., 1879, *d.* 117, *ll*. 3–4.

[29]Atkinson, "The Zemstvo and the Peasantry," p. 106.

[30]Cf. TsGIA, *f.* Departament obshchikh del MVD, 1878, *op.* 69, *d.* 136, *l.* 25; and on the zemstvos Skalon, *Zemskie vzgliady*, pp. 50–3.

senatorial inspections subsequently revealed, was that these tax collectors embezzled sizable amounts of the taxes they collected and accused the peasants of not paying. The illiterate peasants could offer no proof of their payments, and the Morshan District bureau took no action because it could not prove who was criminally responsible – the public tax collector or the peasant volunteers.[31]

Such examples of fiscal corruption in the villages and negligence on the part of district bureaus triggered seventeen petitions from 1875 to 1881 to increase the number of permanent members or establish new supervisory officials to enforce the proper collection of taxes by police and peasant officials.[32] Unfortunately, the government's effort to rectify the problem through the above-mentioned stopgap legislation in 1877–8, a period when the state already had its hands full with the Turks and terrorists, proved inadequate. In its 11 August 1879 petition, the Orel provincial zemstvo complained that the district bureaus, authorized by the 1878 legislation to curb the inflation of local tax arrears and protect the peasant economy from capricious tax collection procedures of the district police, were more powerless than ever to do either. As evidence, the Orel zemstvo pointed out that the local police, who had a reputation for embezzling tax revenues,[33] ignored the advice of the district bureaus from 1876 to 1878 and collected tax arrears at inopportune times, for instance, in the spring when peasants were compelled to use their food supply loans for payment. Even worse, the police confiscated so much peasant property for nonpayment of taxes that virtually no unencumbered land remained in the province. On the other hand, the Orel assembly argued, the district bureau, which included on its staff zemstvo members familiar with local economic conditions, could take more prudent measures for collecting taxes.[34]

Not surprisingly, the Orel petition, with its attack on local police at a moment when revolutionary terrorism reached unprecedented levels and its proposed expansion of zemstvo authority, evoked a sharp rebuke from Minister of Internal Affairs Makov. Determined to retain control over local tax collection, he opposed further revisions in the 1878 legislation and insisted that the Committee of Ministers reject the petition. The matter, along with the government's reform plan, might well have died here, except for the intervention of Alexander II. Disturbed by the growing insolvency in his realm, the tsar ordered the petition forwarded to the Main Committee for Rural Welfare for consideration. His intervention in November 1879 was

---

[31]*MVUOK, Zapiski senatora Mordvinova*, document 8, pp. 21, 24; and ibid., document 5, p. 23. For Lerkhe's view, see TsGIA, *f*. Departament obschchikh del, *op*. 69, *d*. 136, *ll*. 6–7.

[32]The petitions came from Governor Lerkhe of Novgorod and sixteen provincial assemblies. See N. A. Karyshev, *Zemskie khodataistva 1865–1884 gg.* (Moscow, 1900), p. 106.

[33]Orlovsky points out that from 1863 to 1865 the Ministry of Finance proposed several times to conduct inspections of Orel Province, presumably to expose local police corruption, but Valuev blocked these attempts. Orlovsky, *Limits of Reform*, p. 255.

[34]TsGAOR, *f*. Filippov, *op*. 1, *d*. 543, *l*. 28 *ob*. On local police defiance of provincial administrative boards in general, see Robbins, "Viceroys," chap. 5.

not only an unusual display of imperial resolution at a time when, according to several top officials, he was disillusioned with state politics and rarely involved himself in them.[35] Even more, his decision guaranteed that wholesale changes in the system of peasant self-government were forthcoming. In this spirit, the Main Committee decided on 20 March 1880 that the 1874 statute required extensive revisions in light of the changes suggested by the governors and zemstvos in order to reduce arrears and collect taxes. It recommended that the minister of internal affairs solicit the views of the zemstvos and local bureaus for peasant affairs concerning reforms in the legislation, and to turn them over to the Main Committee for discussion.[36] Thus, by the spring of 1880 the government began the work of overhauling the 1874 statute and reevaluating the roles of local peasant, zemstvo, and police officials, a process that continued almost constantly until 1889, despite the accession of a new autocrat in 1881 and numerous ministerial changes.

New strains in government–zemstvo relations. In contrast to the collection of zemstvo taxes, in which the zemstvos were often the victims of local police indolence or inefficiency, the new strains in government–zemstvo relations frequently arose from the deliberate efforts of certain zemstvos (and their gentry leaders) to expand their political roles during a period of government weakness and confusion. Hence, it is easy to understand why such zemstvo petitions for "constitutional" reform were the most publicized aspect of the crisis of local self-government in the late 1870s and the focal point in studies of prerevolutionary "liberal" historians, even though, in comparison with other western states, the pressure for public participation in the Russian government did not reach massive, or even critical, dimensions prior to the twentieth century. Contrary to the views of most "liberal" historians, the government had reason to criticize these assemblies for using imperial appeals for support in its campaigns against the Turks (1877–8) and revolutionaries (1878–81) as a pretext for advocating national zemstvo congresses and certain civil liberties that Alexander II had consistently opposed. On 12 April 1877, Russia declared war on Turkey and the government called for public and zemstvo support during the period of hostilities. Concurrently, it imposed new obligations on the zemstvo that have been mentioned above. The zemstvos responded enthusiastically to the appeal, although their zeal did not always stay within the framework of the law, a fact that irritated high officials. The Usman district zemstvo assembly in Tambov Province, for instance, voted on 1 May 1877 to donate 8,000 rubles to his majesty for the war. But it proposed to cover the donation by imposing a surtax on all taxable property in the district, including state forests – a sensitive issue in this period of burgeoning arrears. This act infuriated Minister of State Properties

---

[35]See A. A. Polovtsov's diary entry for 2 August 1879 in TsGAOR, *f.* A. A. Polovtsov, 1879–1880, *op.* 1, *d.* 15, *ll.* 69–70; and Valuev's passage for 3 June 1879 in his *Dnevnik 1877–1884 gg.*, p. 38.
[36]TsGAOR, *f.* Filippov, *op.* 1, *d.* 543, *ll.* 28–31 *ob.*

Valuev who, in an act reminiscent of his stand in 1866 as minister of internal affairs, declared to the Committee of Ministers that such zemstvo expenses were unnecessary and outside the sphere of local economic affairs under its jurisdiction. Actually, the idea of wartime zemstvo donations did not disturb the committee as much as the prospect that state lands would be taxed to provide funds for a zemstvo donation. In accordance with the recommendation of the governor of Tambov and Valuev, the Committee of Ministers rejected the petition on 7 July 1877.[37]

Even more serious misunderstandings between the government and zemstvo developed over the zemstvo response to the emperor's proclamation of 20 August 1878 in the *Government Herald*. The imperial notice solicited public cooperation in the struggle against the revolutionaries, and three months later Alexander II personally made the same appeal to a group of public representatives in Moscow. Once again, however, several provincial zemstvo assemblies seized the occasion to declare their views on what was wrong in Russia. The most pointed attack came from the Chernigov provincial assembly in December 1878. Arguing that repressive measures alone would not quash terrorist activity and that the restoration of public respect for the law provided the only solution, it proposed that zemstvo institutions be given more authority in the area of public education, contrary to recent statements made on this subject by Count Tolstoi, minister of education. The address explained that the classical studies curriculum adopted by Tolstoi had no connection with current needs and as a result students dropped out in droves.[38]

The Chernigov zemstvo address, drafted by I. I. Petrunkevich, a prominent *zemets* and justice of the peace of the period, focused its sharpest criticism on the government's censorship of zemstvo publications, long a sore point with politically active zemstvos:

The zemstvo itself not only lacks any possibility of having a periodical for the free exchange of ideas on its most immediate needs; it is even denied the freedom to express opinions within the assembly and, in addition, to declare its needs to the government, despite the fact that feelings and motives such as the desire for the development and consolidation of the country's welfare may guide the zemstvo.[39]

The address closed with a warning that the price of government repression would be the loss of public support, and that only by giving the Russian people certain civil rights – namely, the freedom of speech, press, and petition – could respect for the law be reestablished. Thus, the Chernigov assembly implied by its address that it would refuse to support the autocracy in its struggle against the revolutionaries unless its demands were fulfilled immediately, and, to give substance to this warning, Petrunkevich made

[37]TsGIA, *f.* Komitet ministrov, 1877, *op.* 1, *d.* 3908, art. 298, *ll.* 31–33 *ob.*; and ibid., *d.* 3909, *ll.* 25–6.

[38]TsGAOR, *f.* Bakuniny, 1878, *op.* 1, *d.* 373, *ll.* 3–4.

[39]Ibid., *l.* 4 *ob.*

contact with other zemstvo assemblies to work out a coordinated zemstvo response on this issue.[40]

Other provincial zemstvo assemblies echoed these complaints and added a few of their own. In underscoring the political crisis of support that alarmed imperial officials, these addresses pinpointed some concrete problems that bureaucratic interference (or, conversely, official indifference) created for zemstvo activity. The Tver' provincial assembly, for instance, criticized the government for not allowing zemstvo institutions and justices of the peace to develop, and for limiting their spheres of jurisdiction. It chided the Ministry of Internal Affairs for refusing to reply to the most urgent zemstvo petitions. However, the Tver' demand that Alexander II give the Russians what he gave the Bulgarians in 1878, namely a constitution and civil liberties, especially vexed top officials.[41] Similar demands came from the provincial assemblies of Khar'kov, Poltava, and Chernigov in December 1878 and Moscow in 1879.[42] In the same year, the Chernigov provincial assembly, in discussing the tsar's appeal to the public a year earlier, launched a personal attack against its chairman, N. P. Nepliuev, over his powers as assembly chairman. Petrunkevich claimed that educated society, as an unorganized, inert body, could not respond to Alexander's appeal, but that the provincial zemstvo should send its own address to the government proffering its advice. Nepliuev, recognizing his responsibility as a government representative in accordance with the 13 June 1867 law, ruled that the zemstvo could not submit such an address without the government's invitation. Yet Nepliuev failed to silence the delegates led by Petrunkevich on this issue. Baited by Petrunkevich, he eventually threatened to strip the zemstvo leader of his voting rights, an act that prompted Petrunkevich and twenty-one other delegates to walk out of the session and to sign a declaration protesting Nepliuev's coercive tactics.[43]

The walkout of the Chernigov delegates typified the breakdown in zemstvo–government relations that occurred in many provinces at the end of the 1870s. Although certain zemstvo assemblies courted a confrontation with government officials, the government helped create a climate of hostility by

[40]Ibid., *ll.* 5–5 *ob.* On Petrunkevich and his efforts to organize inter-zemstvo congresses to pressure the government into constitutional reform, see I. I. Petrunkevich, "Iz zapisok obshchestvennogo deiatelia: Vospominaniia," *Arkhiv russkoi revoliutsii,* vol. 21 (Berlin, 1934); and Charles E. Timberlake, "The Birth of Zemstvo Liberalism in Russia: Ivan Il'ich Petrunkevich in Chernigov" (Unpublished Ph.D. dissertation, University of Washington, 1968). Petrunkevich's famous brochure, "Blizhaishie zadachi zemstva," which demanded civil liberties and a constituent assembly, is published in *1864–1914: Iubileinyi sbornik,* pp. 429–36. On zemstvo political efforts to establish inter-zemstvo congresses in 1878–9, see F. A. Petrov, "Nelegal'nye obshchezemskie soveshchaniia i sezdy kontsa 70-kh-nachala 80-kh godov XIX veka," *Voprosy istorii,* no. 9 (1974): 33–44.

[41]TsGAOR, *f.* Bakuniny, 1878 or later, *op.* 1, *d.* 375, *ll.* 2–2 *ob.*

[42]S. G. Svatikov, *Obshchestvennoe dvizhenie,* p. 87; A. A. Kornilov, "K istorii konstitutsionnogo dvizheniia kontsa 70-kh nachala 80-kh godov," *Russkaia mysl',* bk. 7 (1913), p. 39; and especially Veselovskii, *Istoriia zemstva,* 3: 230–9, who claims that the zemstvos showed new enthusiasm for their work in the late 1870s, although zemstvo members were frequently preoccupied with factional conflicts within their assemblies.

[43]V. M. Khizhniakov, *Vospominaniia zemskogo deiatelia* (Petrograd, 1916), pp. 151–3, 156.

the Committee of Ministers' Statute of 14 January 1877. It provided that, in the event of war, certain measures would be enforced in the provinces under martial law with respect to zemstvo and municipal institutions. First, zemstvo assembly and municipal duma sessions devoted to military exigencies would be considered legal no matter how many delegates showed up. This provision clearly revealed the government's willingness to sacrifice legality for administrative expediency – an issue that, as shown in Chapters 4 to 6, divided ministerial opinion on the methods of local self-government reform in the 1880s. Second, the zemstvo would have the right to transfer corvée duties related to military needs to monetary zemstvo taxes. Third, and most important, if the governor felt that the zemstvo or municipal duma had not discharged its legal obligation, he had the right to fulfill these needs and to require the zemstvo or municipal duma to pay for them.[44] By adopting Timashev's proposal, the committee aimed to ensure the expeditious fulfillment of military needs by increasing the governor's control over the zemstvos. It authorized governors to borrow up to 5,000 rubles from the State Treasury in the event of insufficient zemstvo or municipal resources, with the loan subject to repayment in the next collection of zemstvo or municipal taxes.[45]

The 14 January 1877 statute thus provided vivid proof that zemstvo concerns and needs were secondary to the state's military exigencies. Although the provision for gubernatorial action at the expense of the zemstvos was never enacted, the legislation itself signified official suspicion toward zemstvo institutions in fulfilling their responsibilities. Whereas Governor I. N. Durnovo claimed that the zemstvos in Moscow Province performed satisfactorily and enjoyed public confidence in 1877, Governor P. A. Bil'basov of Samara and Governor Lerkhe of Novgorod complained that many zemstvo delegates in their provinces pursued selfish, personal goals and that in general the zemstvos did a lot on paper but little in practice.[46] In their reports for the period, the governors usually pinpointed administrative shortcomings of the zemstvos along with criticizing them for raising political reform issues. A further limitation of self-government came on 4 April 1878 with the establishment of temporary governors-general in St. Petersburg, Khar'kov, and Odessa provinces to assist the government's campaign to suppress the terrorists. The governors-general received the right to close temporarily self-governing institutions that, by their declarations on behalf of constitutions or by their contact with revolutionaries, showed their opposition to the regime.[47] The vague guidelines allowed the governors-general to interfere at will in zemstvo affairs, a fact that provoked many complaints in the zemstvo resolutions of 1879.

---

[44] TsGIA, f. Komitet ministrov, 1877, op. 1, d. 3894, ll. 16–21 ob.

[45] Ibid., ll. 17, 20, 22–4; and PSZ, second series, vol. 52, no. 56837, 14 January 1877.

[46] See TsGIA, f. Departament obshchikh del MVD, 1878, op. 69, d. 96, ll. 17–18; ibid., d. 136, ll. 21–22 ob.; and ibid., d. 381, ll. 11 ob.-12.

[47] Ibid., f. P. A. Valuev, 1879, op. 1, d. 396, l. 2.

Ultimately, the government's measures to police the zemstvos and contain the spread of revolutionary propaganda backfired, not only because the legislation elicited more public criticism, but also because state ministers themselves broke ranks over these policies. On 14 August 1879, the Committee of Ministers approved Makov's recommendation to permit the governor to remove any zemstvo official who served by election or on the zemstvo payroll on the grounds of political or moral unreliability. Not surprisingly, Makov's proposal, which would have legalized the arbitrary interference of his ministry in all local self-government, provoked a bitter ministerial confrontation in the Committee of Ministers with Dmitrii Nikolaevich Nabokov, the newly appointed minister of justice (1878). In words recalling Dmitrii Miliutin a decade earlier, he contended that governors already possessed enough control over the zemstvos and that their capricious actions according to Makov's proposal would undermine public respect for administrative law. A jurist by education and a career official in the Ministry of Justice, Nabokov realized that the plan would eliminate the autonomy of his justices of the peace who, as zemstvo-elected and zemstvo-financed officials, could be removed at the whim of the local governors. Also, the project jeopardized his own plans to reestablish an autonomous judiciary and the prestige of his ministry, both in decline due to Count Pahlen's support for the methods of Shuvalov and Timashev in suppressing the revolutionaries. Prince S. N. Urusov likewise opposed the measure as unnecessary, claiming that all persons suspected of violating their office or sympathizing with revolutionaries could simply be placed under police surveillance. Nonetheless, Makov's concluding argument on the political unreliability of zemstvo personnel who had frequent contact with the peasantry and could easily propagate antigovernment ideas persuaded the majority of ministers to adopt his view in its 19 August 1879 statute.[48] A supplementary decree issued on 26 September clarified that the governor's authority covered the justices of the peace.[49] Thus, the decision of the Committee of Ministers for the moment signaled the defeat of Nabokov's position on the separation of the administrative and judicial branches of government and the need for a restrained policy in dealing with the revolutionaries.

Above all, this legislation illustrated how severely the government reacted to political pressure from the zemstvos. It left little doubt that the government in 1879 regarded the zemstvos as state institutions expected to function in accordance with its directives, especially during such critical periods. Yet many zemstvo leaders had a different concept of their role as public officials

---

[48]Ibid., *f.* Komitet ministrov, 1879, *op.* 1, *d.* 4044, *ll.* 72–93; *PSZ*, 2d ser., vol. 54, no. 59947, 19 August 1879; and TsGIA, *f.* Golovnin, *op.* 1, *d.* 16, *ll.* 63–63 *ob.* The most thorough account of the work of the Special Conference established under Valuev to combat terrorism is found in Zaionchkovskii, *Krizis samoderzhaviia*, pp. 98–112. Zaionchkovskii shows that the proposal for increasing gubernatorial control over zemstvo-elected officials originated in the Special Conference sessions in the spring of 1879.

[49]*PSZ*, 2d ser., vol. 54, no. 60043, 26 September 1879.

and attacked the restraints placed on zemstvo activity by this legislation. In the spring of 1880, Loris-Melikov convinced the emperor to revoke it in order to garner zemstvo support for his policies and to signify the restoration of the government's confidence in the zemstvo. The legislation of 1877 and 1879 was not the only barrier to zemstvo activity in the late 1870s, however. During the years 1875 to 1879 the zemstvos experienced much frustration in submitting petitions to the minister of internal affairs. N. A. Karyshev, who tabulated zemstvo petitions for the period 1865–84, noted that the government rejected a higher percentage of zemstvo petitions from 1875 to 1879 (59.1 percent or 323 out of 599 petitions) than during any other five-year period up to 1884; more revealing, it rejected 77.2 percent of zemstvo petitions concerning the organization of local government, a figure surpassed only by that (86.1 percent) for military duties.[50]

Thus, under the impact of the Russo-Turkish War and the government's campaign against the revolutionary terrorists, new antagonism developed in zemstvo-government relations that had to be eliminated if the zemstvos were to function effectively. As in the late 1860s, jurisdictional conflict with the government invariably absorbed the greater part of the attention of the zemstvos, to the detriment of the public welfare and economy under their management, although this should not obscure the fact that there were examples of zemstvo–state cooperation in the late 1870s. Still, the government–zemstvo conflicts revealed that, in its preoccupation with combating terrorist activity, the government spared no resources in dealing with the revolutionaries, even if this meant undermining an independent judiciary, zemstvo status and effectiveness, and discouraging zemstvo representatives from further service in the provinces.

The food supply crisis in the Volga provinces, 1880–1. In their addresses to the government at the turn of the decade, zemstvo leaders repeatedly protested the isolated and impotent status of the zemstvo in local administration and insisted that rural administration would improve only if the state heeded their practical advice on local economic needs. The food supply shortages in the Volga provinces in 1880–1, which already have been cited as an immediate reason for the senatorial inspections, were clear proof, according to these zemstvo officials, of the mismanagement of peasant self-government and the hostility between peasant, police, and zemstvo officials.[51] The most widespread of the "famines" to strike the empire prior to the great famine of 1891–2, it occurred in nearly all of the eastern and southeastern provinces in European Russia.[52] The food supply crisis began in Saratov and Samara

---

[50]Karyshev, pp. 2–4

[51][V. Iu. Skalon], *Mneniia zemskikh sobranii o sovremennom polozhenii Rossii* (Berlin, 1883), pp. 11–13.

[52]Besides Samara and Saratov provinces, the "famine" of 1880 and 1881 struck Astrakhan, Orenburg, Kazan', Pskov, Kherson, Vologda, Viatka, and, to a lesser extent, Khar'kov provinces. Cf. V. Iu. Skalon, *Zemskie voprosy. Ocherki i obozreniia* (Moscow, 1882); Anfimov and Solov'eva, "Obostrenie nuzhdy," pp. 135, 140–2; and D. Daragan, *Mysli sel'skogo khoziaina po raznym zemskim voprosam. Sbornik*

provinces in the winter of 1879–80 and peaked in the fall of 1880, precisely when Senator I. I. Shamshin began his inspection of the two provinces. He had an excellent opportunity to observe the starvation of peasants and their livestock, the outbreak of typhus, the emigration of peasants to areas (Tambov, Voronezh, Penza provinces) in search of food relief,[53] and the shortcomings of zemstvo and local peasant officials in calculating and distributing food supply loans. His reports to Count Loris-Melikov and the replies of the minister of internal affairs revealed that, as with tax arrears, the food supply crisis of 1880–1 was the result not only of a succession of poor harvests in the 1870s, which depleted grain reserves and minimized the collection of food supply duties from peasants at harvest time, but also of incompetent management of food supplies by zemstvo and peasant officials and their fraudulent use of state loans for food relief.

On 20 September 1880, Loris-Melikov reported to the tsar that the food supply situation in the Volga provinces presented no cause for grave concern.[54] However, his actions during August and September and subsequent comments in the 20 September report belied his reassurances. On 30 July 1880, he provided the Samara provincial zemstvo with a loan of 918,000 rubles from the Imperial Food Supply Fund in fulfillment of its request. On 27 August 1880, A. D. Sverbeev, governor of Samara Province, requested an additional 500,000 ruble loan on behalf of the provincial zemstvo because of the bad harvest of 1880. Loris-Melikov furnished this loan on 17 September.[55] In Saratov, the provincial zemstvo in December 1879 applied for and received a government loan of 454,000 rubles and six months later the district assemblies in Saratov Province claimed that they would need approximately 4.3 million rubles more in state loans to feed the local population and provide seed to sow crops in the spring of 1881.[56] As Loris-Melikov admitted in his 20 September report, the situation was alarming because arrears in these provinces had risen sharply in the first half of 1880, and immediate government loans to buy bread and seed alone would not be sufficient to arrest the problem. Loris-Melikov, by that time minister of internal affairs (as we shall shortly see), recommended that the government create public works jobs such as the construction of railroads, highways, and

statei po raznym zemskim voprosam, pomeshchennym v "Vestnike Pskovskogo Gubernskogo Zemstva" (St. Petersburg, 1884), pp. 107–15. For Viatka Province in particular, see V. V. Ivanovskii, *Opyt issledovaniia deiatel'nosti organov zemskogo samoupravleniia* (Kazan', 1881), pp. 192–3. On the impact of the poor harvest of 1880–1 on grain prices throughout the empire and Loris-Melikov's methods for dealing with grain speculators in St. Petersburg, see *Dnevnik E. A. Perettsa, gosudarstvennogo sekretaria (1880–1883)* (Moscow-Leningrad, 1927), p. 9; and Valuev, *Dnevnik 1877–1884 gg.*, pp. 122, 128.

[53] Anfimov and Solov'eva, "Obostrenie nuzhdy," pp. 141–2.

[54] "Graf Loris-Melikov i imperator Aleksandr II o polozhenii Rossii v sentiabre 1880 g.," *Byloe*, no. 4 (26) (1917): 35.

[55] TsGIA, *f.* Reviziia senatora I. I. Shamshina Saratovskoi i Samarskoi gubernii [hereafter cited as *f.* Reviziia senatora Shamshina], 1880–1881, *op.* 1, *d.* 6, *ll.* 8 ob.-14.

[56] Ibid., *f.* Kakhanovskaia komissiia, *op.* 1, *d.* 109, *ll.* 39–41. On the food supply shortages in Saratov Province, see ibid., *f.* Reviziia senatora Shamshina, *op.* 1, *d.* 14, vol. 1.

canals in the stricken provinces to provide the peasants with additional money to purchase grain and to forestall possible peasant unrest. The tsar gave his support to Loris-Melikov's proposals.[57]

As a result of increasing zemstvo requests for loans, Loris-Melikov instructed the governors of Samara and Saratov, along with Senator Shamshin, to pay particular attention to the management of public food supply resources by zemstvo and peasant officials. On 28 September 1880, he pointed out to Governor Sverbeev:

I consider it necessary to direct Your Excellency's special attention to the fact that food supply loans are used exclusively for the purpose for which they are intended, since unfortunately the Ministry of Internal Affairs has received information from several places concerning the possibility of diverting a certain part of these resources for monetary payments by the needy population to cover debts on various matters. Thus, food supply loans frequently do not attain their objective.[58]

The governors and Shamshin soon unveiled cases in which zemstvo and peasant officials had violated articles 186–214 of the Food Supply Statute and distributed loans for purposes other than providing food relief. In some villages, Shamshin informed Sverbeev, peasant officials had given out loans to wealthier peasants, and peasant communities, in theory bound by mutual guarantee to repay the loans, were unable to cover them. He also criticized the methods used by some district and provincial zemstvo boards in determining the needs of local peasants and the procedures for distributing bread. The absence of uniformity or coordinated inter-zemstvo measures, Shamshin emphasized, aggravated the food supply problems.[59]

By early November 1880, the food shortages in the two provinces reached a critical point. On 7 November 1880, Loris-Melikov reluctantly authorized an additional loan of one million rubles to the Samara provincial assembly. At the same time, he criticized the Samara District zemstvos for making an inflated request for 5,031,722 rubles, which, in his opinion, was not based on precise calculations. He ended his letter to Governor Sverbeev by admonishing the zemstvos to check the lists of the needy more carefully, and added that the resources in the Imperial Food Supply Fund were limited, particularly given the requests from other provinces.[60]

Shamshin's preliminary investigation revealed scores of instances in which the zemstvos in Saratov and Samara provinces had failed to check the lists of needy and to inspect the local areas suffering from bad harvests. On the basis of information provided by Shamshin, Loris-Melikov cited the cases of Novouzensk, Nikolaev, Buguruslan, and Bugul'min districts, where the

---

[57]"Graf Loris-Melikov i imperator Aleksandr II," p. 35.
[58]Quoted from Loris-Melikov's letter of 28 September 1880 to A. D. Sverbeev, governor of Samara, in TsGIA, f. Reviziia senatora Shamshina, op. 1, d. 6, ll. 17 ob.-18.
[59]Ibid., ll. 100–100 ob.
[60]Ibid., ll. 87 ob., 92 ob.

district zemstvos distributed loans according to lists compiled in 1879. The zemstvo boards in these districts failed to verify these lists and submitted inflated loan requests.[61] In Kamyshin District in Saratov Province, the board simply ratified the exaggerated loan requests of the *volost'* administrations.[62] Finally, Shamshin argued that in distributing state loans to the peasants, zemstvo and peasant officials failed to impress on them the terms of repayment. Hence, the peasants frequently viewed these loans as an imperial gift and the government stood little chance of recovering the funds.[63] In fact, by the time the food supply crisis abated in 1882, the government had loaned the zemstvos well over three million rubles for famine relief.[64]

In essence, top officials were led to believe that local zemstvo and peasant officials were greatly responsible for the food supply crisis because of their failure to estimate and verify the food relief needs of the population and their abuses in distributing government loans. These problems were emphasized by the senatorial inspector in Voronezh and Tambov provinces as well. Peasant officials who made fraudulent claims in presenting lists of the needy to the zemstvo and district bureau and who stole food supplies from the warehouses (in some cases to meet tax obligations that they regarded as their first priority) escaped punishment because the 1864 Zemstvo Statute gave the zemstvos no authority to require peasant officials to correct their lists. Moreover the zemstvos lacked the personnel and even the desire to supervise the peasant officials responsible for guarding the food warehouses and for collecting the food supply tax. As numerous governors pointed out, the more active zemstvos concentrated on public education and public health rather than on such traditional obligations as providing food relief.[65] Neither the zemstvos nor the district bureaus provided the necessary on-the-spot supervision over the peasant officials on whom they depended to develop the rural economy, and, under existing legislation, the government had few options for halting the mismanagement of local food supply funds short of terminating all loans and starving its population. The food supply crisis of

---

[61]Ibid., *ll.* 65, 79 *ob.*

In his 8 January 1881 reply to Loris-Melikov, Sverbeev presented figures to show that the Samara district zemstvo had submitted an inflated loan request for 1881. For example, it based its estimates on the assumption that 48,106 *pudy* of bread would be required each month for a seven-month period to feed the local population (a *pud* was equivalent to 36.113 English pounds). However, Sverbeev noted, in December 1880 the district board gave out only 34,256 *pudy*, and all the needy were satisfied. Such discrepancies in the estimates for the seven-month period, according to Sveerbeev, produced a loan request for money to purchase almost 100,000 more *pudy* of bread than necessary. Even taking into account the fact that peasants required more assistance in February and March than in December, owing to the depletion of food reserves, Sverbeev argued that the zemstvo could trim the cost of 27,700 *pudy* from the loan estimate. Ibid., *ll.* 173 *ob.*-174.

[62]Ibid., *f.* Kakhanovskaia komissiia, *op.* 1, *d.* 109, *l.* 41 *ob.*

[63]Ibid., *f.* Reviziia senatora Shamshina, *op.* 1, *d.* 6, *ll.* 102 *ob.*−103; and *MVUOK*, vol. 3, pt. 2: *Zapiski senatora Mordvinova*, document 12, pp. 16−20.

[64]Anfimov and Solov'eva, "Obostrenie nuzhdy," p. 147. All told, by 1883 the zemstvos owed 11,700,000 rubles to the state in outstanding federal food supply loans, the burden for which, according to the authors, would be imposed on the peasantry in the form of taxes.

[65]TsGIA, *f.* Departament obshchikh del MVD, *op.* 69, *d.* 136, *ll.* 21−22 *ob.*

1880–1 made tragically clear the lack of state and zemstvo control over peasant officials, and subsequently this problem became a focal point in all discussions over local self-government reform.

In sum, the shortcomings of the 27 June 1874 statute – as documented by zemstvo petitions, massive tax arrears, the new government–zemstvo tensions, and the food supply shortages of 1880–1 – all pointed up the disintegration of local authority in rural Russia. These factors, at the heart of the autocratic crisis from 1878 to 1881, induced Loris-Melikov to send the senators to investigate local conditions. True, peasant and zemstvo self-government were never models of legality and efficiency, and many of the conditions just noted antedated the administrative and fiscal crisis of 1878–81; zemstvo tax arrears first appeared in the late 1860s and Samara Province had suffered a more serious famine in 1873. But these problems had not occurred at the same time and with the same intensity, nor, for that matter, in a period of such political crisis, which focused government attention on its rural institutions. The insolvency of the zemstvo and the failure of local zemstvo and peasant officials to collect taxes and to distribute food loans properly were all the more critical given the huge state budgetary deficit (exceeding one billion rubles), the conflict and confusion in ministerial circles (evident by the state's reliance on extraordinary commissions and legislation), and the reports from the provinces of peasant indifference, and sometimes hostility, to local authorities. Convinced that the main terrorist threat had waned, Loris-Melikov decided in the summer of 1880 to begin rebuilding the local administrative foundations of the empire. The senatorial inspections initiated in September 1880 constituted the first step in this process.

Agenda for reform: the senatorial inspections and their implications

On 14 August 1880, Alexander II, on the advice of Loris-Melikov, appointed four senators to inspect ten provinces in Russia. Senator A. A. Polovtsov was appointed to inspect Kiev and Chernigov provinces, and Senator M. E. Kovalevskii was assigned to investigate Kostroma, Kazan', Ufa, and Orenburg provinces. The tsar ordered Shamshin to inspect Saratov and Samara provinces and Senator S. A. Mordvinov to review Tambov and Voronezh. Besides representing a cross section of four regions in the empire, these provinces were among those that had the highest rates of tax arrears and peasant land shortages, both of which were crucial concerns of the ministers of finance and of internal affairs. All of the senators except Polovtsov had served on the Supreme Executive Commission under Loris-Melikov from March through July 1880 and had impressed him with their studies of the administrative exile system, the Third Section, and the judicial institutions;[66]

---

[66]See the passages for 29 September and 15 December 1880 in *Dnevnik Perettsa*, pp. 4, 15; and for 14 August 1880 in TsGAOR, *f.* A. A. Polovtsov, 1879–1880, *op.* 1, *d.* 15, *ll.* 255–6. See also Bol'shov, pp. 40–1.

and on top of that, Kovalevskii and Shamshin were personal friends of Loris-Melikov. The appointment of the four senators made a favorable impression on the emperor, heir, and virtually all top officials except Valuev, who claimed that such inspections would denigrate the legislative accomplishments of the reign.[67] Valuev apparently had good reason to oppose Kovalevskii's inspection of Orenburg Province; as minister of state properties (1872–9), he and Orenburg Governor-General N. A. Kryzhanovskii had given out some state lands in Orenburg Province as estates to subordinates without consulting each other, as required by law. Kovalevskii's findings and the ensuing scandal prompted Valuev's resignation as chairman of the Committee of Ministers on 3 October 1881 and Kryshanovskii's dismissal as governor-general of Orenburg Province.[68]

The senatorial inspections warrant detailed treatment not only because they provided the material for the reform discussions of the 1880s, but also because the inspectors' recommendations on the ways to rectify the shortcomings in local administration initially constituted the agenda for debate. So thorough was the evidence presented by them and, in the case of peasant self-government and economy, so consistent with the reports of the governors and zemstvos during the previous five years, that no top official in 1881 disputed the need for local self-government reform. But the senators' allegation that the problems stemmed largely from bureaucratic interference in local self-governing institutions, a view that in the cases of Mordvinov and Kovalevskii seemed designed to suit the decentralist predilections of Loris-Melikov and his successor, N. P. Ignat'ev (1881–2), touched off a fervid debate among these officials over the next decade. The senators' explicit recommendations for zemstvo autonomy and legal limitations on the governors, along with more rigid supervision over the peasantry, were not always consistent with the data they collected, a point that the opponents of decentralization would make frequently. Consequently, the findings of the senatorial inspectors were a weapon used by both sides in the ministerial conflict over local self-government reform in the 1880s.

In their work, the senators followed usual procedures and reviewed the files of local institutions. In addition, they went to great lengths to receive complaints against local officials and collect testimony from zemstvo, state, and peasant officials, and attached much importance to this evidence, thereby dispelling any notion that this was a "paper" inspection. The findings of Senators Mordvinov and Shamshin are more pertinent to our study because they inspected provinces in the heartland of European Russia where the zemstvos and district bureaus for peasant affairs were introduced. In contrast, peace arbitrators still handled peasant supervision in Kiev Province, and the areas under Kovalevskii's purview were considerably different from Great

---

[67]See the entries for 17 October in *Dnevnik Perettsa*, p. 7; and for 13 October 1881 in *Dnevnik Miliutina*, 4: 111.
[68]For details on this scandal, see ibid., pp. 97, 102–3.

Russian provinces owing to their ethnic composition; still, many of the findings of Polovtsov and Kovalevskii (whose final report apparently did not include Kostroma Province) complement the material presented by Mordvinov and Shamshin. Finally, Polovtsov finished his inspection report only in 1883, a year after top officials in the Special Conference of the Kakhanov Commission (1881–5) in the capital began their discussion over plans for local administration reform based on the reports of Shamshin, Mordvinov, and Kovalevskii.

The district bureau for peasant affairs. In his general conclusions about peasant self-government in Tambov Province, Senator Mordvinov criticized the ineffectiveness of the district bureau for peasant affairs in supervising peasant self-government in the following terms:

One might say that from the resignation of the first peace arbitrators in 1863 until the present the peasants have lacked any administration. The peasant has not encountered any rational authority to inform him of his civil obligations, and has not found any protection against the oppression of the strong – either his neighbor or the authorities in their various forms. . . . He may finally lose faith in justice and the government, and become incapable of any self-government.[69]

The senator added that indifference, incompetence, and ignorance of local economic conditions characterized the activity of district bureaus for peasant affairs, and charged that these officials were mainly responsible for the decline of the peasant economy in the 1870s as well as the virtual disappearance of peasant self-government. And Mordvinov and his inspector colleagues warned that, in the absence of any supervision over the peasantry, the abuses of peasant officials and continued social stratification in the village might eventually turn the peasantry as a whole against all authorities.

In their reports, the inspectors reminded the ministers that, under the 27 June 1874 statute, the district bureaus were required to supervise peasant administration by (1) overseeing the collection of taxes by the district police chief and village and *volost'* officials; (2) conducting regular inspections of the *volost'* administration; and (3) reviewing peasant complaints against peasant officials and *volost'* court decisions. In particular, Mordvinov and Kovalevskii assailed the district bureaus and the permanent members for neglecting to carry out these functions. On the subject of tax and arrears collections, the inspectors added little new to the picture of arbitrary and corrupt peasant and police officials and district bureau indolence presented in the reports of governors and zemstvos (detailed earlier in this chapter); rather, they merely provided a more comprehensive analysis of bureau negligence. Mordvinov maintained that the unsupervised *volost'* scribe, often the only literate person in the *volost'*, was in a good position to siphon off tax revenues and accuse the conscientious tax collector of embezzlement in hopes

---

[69]Quoted from *MVUOK*, vol. 3, pt. 2: *Zapiski senatora Mordvinova*, document 1, p. 9.

of extracting a bribe from him.[70] In the few instances in which the district bureaus did intervene, the inspectors pointed out, they infringed arbitrarily on the rights of peasant officials.

Whereas the inspectors indiscriminately blamed the district bureaus for the abuses and arrears in tax collection, they were more judicious in calling the district bureaus to task for not conducting inspections of *volost'* administrations. In 1880 no district bureaus in Tambov Province inspected the *volosti* under their jurisdiction. Members of the district bureaus queried by Senator Mordvinov replied that they carried out inspections only in cases involving the loss of a significant amount of *volost'* funds. When they did occur, bureau inspections (or those of the peace arbitrators in Kiev, according to Polovtsov)[71] were notoriously superficial and rarely did district bureau members acquaint the *volost'* and village officials with their obligations.[72] In Voronezh Province, the authority of the permanent member who inspected the *volost'* administration was undermined by the fact that the district police chief, rather than the permanent members, imposed disciplinary punishments on the *volost'* elders. Finally, the large number of *volosti* (226) in Voronezh Province alone precluded effective bureau supervision, especially in such large districts as Ostrogozh, which encompassed twenty-nine *volosti* (each averaging roughly 2,000 male souls). Mordvinov emphasized the consequences of insufficient supervision:

The lack of supervision over peasant self-government increases the abuses on the part of *volost'* and village officials to such a degree that even the peasants are afraid to complain against these authorities and to expose their abuses. Complaints against officials in districts in which the *volost'* administrations are rarely or superficially inspected are notably fewer in number than in districts in which the administrations are actually inspected, and not simply surveyed or visited. For example, in the Zadonsk district where the permanent member annually conducts inspections, there are as many as 400 complaints filed each year. In other districts in which inspections are rare or superficial, only 40 to 85 complaints against officials are filed each year.[73]

The few bureaus that were willing to act on peasant complaints against drunken officials, forgeries, arbitrariness, losses of funds, and the like found their hands full with prosecuting peasant officials. Mordvinov confessed that other peasant official offenses such as extortion were commonplace but went unpunished because the guilty parties covered up their crimes and district bureau procedures made it difficult to bring them to justice.[74] In Kozlov

---

[70]Ibid., document 5, pp. 21, 24. Kovalevskii's criticism of the district bureaus' failure to prevent embezzlement of communal funds (*mirskie sbory*) in Ufa and Kazan' is found in ibid., vol. 2, pt. 1: *Zapiski senatora Kovalevskogo*, document 2, pp. 24–5.

[71]Gosudarstvennaia publichnaia biblioteka imeni M. E. Saltykova-Shchedrina, otdel rukopisei [hereafter cited as OR-GPBSS], f. A. A. Polovtsov, 1880s, d. 651, ll. 25 *ob.*-26. Polovtsov pointed out that some peace arbitrators did not even live within the area under their jurisdiction.

[72]*MVUOK*, vol. 3, pt. 2: *Zapiski Mordvinova*, document 5, p. 4.

[73]Quoted from ibid., document 3, p. 5.

[74]Ibid., document 5, p. 11.

District alone (Tambov Province), the district bureau in 1880 imposed administrative punishment on 118 peasant officials, including 71 village elders, in many cases because they lost important records. The Kirsanov District bureau initiated legal proceedings against 60 peasant officials who, among other offenses, allegedly stole grain from the public food supply warehouses and illegally distributed it.[75] But in most areas the district bureaus confined their supervision over peasant administration to the formal review of complaints against peasant officials and *volost'* courts in the district capitals, far from the scene of the offense. Such reviews in some cases led to disciplinary punishment of guilty peasant officials but did little to prevent the recurrence of such acts or provide on-the-spot guidance needed for village and *volost'* administration. In rare cases, the bureaus intervened in the *volost'* administration, for example, to transfer an unscrupulous *volost'* scribe from one *volost'* to another within the district, as if the change in environment would reform the scribe of his bad habits. Such acts attested to the scarcity of literate people available to serve as scribes, as well as the powerlessness of the district bureau to exert genuine control over peasant officials. At the same time, they convinced the latter that the district bureaus acted arbitrarily.[76] In Chernigov Province, Polovtsov observed, the lack of district bureau supervision was the primary reason for the deteriorating system of peasant self-government.[77]

The inability of district bureaus and permanent members to supervise peasant self-government largely stemmed from the composition of the district bureaus and their extensive jurisdiction. The bureaus consisted of three members – the chairman (district gentry marshal), the district police chief, and the permanent member – the first two of whom had their own service obligations unrelated to the bureau's activity. Thus, they considered their work in the district bureau a formality, a secondary matter. This was no small problem because bureau meetings were canceled if all members did not show up. In Voronezh Province, for instance, the Bobrov District bureau canceled about a third of its meetings in 1879, while its counterpart in Bogucharsk District failed to meet for eight of twelve scheduled sessions.[78] In addition, the permanent members, along with participating in bureau meetings and checking the records of the bureaus, were required to inspect the *volost'* administration and mediate land-related disputes between peasants and landlords. The size of some districts made it impossible for the permanent

[75] Ibid.; for Voronezh Province see ibid., no. 3, p. 4.

[76] Ibid., no. 5, p. 31.

[77] OR-GPBSS, *f.* Polovtsov, 1880s, *d.* 1333, *ll.* 55–55 *ob.*

[78] MVUOK, vol. 3, pt. 2: *Zapiski Mordvinova*, no. 3, pt. 1. see also TsGIA, *f.* Kakhanovskaia komissiia, *op.* 1, *d.* 11, *l.* 361 *ob.*; MVUOK, vol. 3, pt. 1: *Zapiski Kovalevskogo*, no. 1, p. 5; and Kataev, *Mestnye krest'ianskie uchrezhdeniia*, pt. 2, pp. 106–9. On the disorder in the records of the district bureaus and peasant complaints to the senators about the slowness of bureaus in processing protests and inquiries see MVUOK, vol. 3, pt. 2: *Zapiski Mordvinova*, no. 3, p. 3. On absenteeism at various Provincial Bureau meetings in the 1880s and 1890s (for similar reasons) see Robbins, "Viceroys," chap. 5.

members to fulfill all these tasks; on top of that, most permanent members were apathetic in their work, probably owing in part to the absence of disciplinary authority over them.[79]

In general, then, the senators complained that the institutions established by the 27 June 1874 statute were completely ineffective for providing vigilant guidance of peasant self-government. As for solutions to the problems, they cited the two methods recommended by zemstvo and district bureau officials, namely all-estate self-government in the village (with the village administered by a zemstvo-elected official), and a zemstvo-elected official to supervise exclusively peasant administration. Although there was much debate between the two groups over the merits and drawbacks of each proposal, both groups unimaginatively emphasized that one-man supervision similar to that provided by the original peace arbitrators was preferable to the bureaus. Both approaches met the desires of the landed gentry who dominated the zemstvos in the black earth and Volga provinces and, presumably, stood to be elected to the new positions.[80] Senator Kovalevskii presented the case for *edinonachalie* by succinctly concluding: "In general I shall permit myself to think that a collegial institution in no way can be suitable for such a vital matter requiring personal decision-making as the supervision over peasant self-government, which could be turned over with incomparably greater benefits to officials having more immediate ties with the peasantry."[81] Thus, the senatorial inspections amply corroborated the attacks made in the zemstvo petitions and gubernatorial reports of the late 1870s against the 27 June 1874 statute, and validated their appeal to replace collegial supervision with a more immediate, paternalistic supervisor at the subdistrict level. Otherwise, Mordvinov predicted, the continued breakdown of peasant self-government and family partitions of communal land would leave the *narod* destitute and add to "the smoldering spirit of the time" in the village.[82] The creation of one-man supervision in the countryside, the embryo of the Land Captain Statute of 1889, was an idea that had widespread support in the late 1870s and above all represented a response to the administrative shortcomings of the district bureaus.

Peasant self-governing institutions: assemblies, officials, and courts. In evaluating the impact of the 27 June 1874 statute on the peasantry, Mordvinov portrayed peasant self-government in familiar, somber colors:

Peasant self-government, established as the cornerstone of welfare in the villages according to the spirit of the 19 February 1861 legislation, has virtually ceased to exist. The village and *volost'* assemblies, which have the right to elect officials and decide economic matters, have lost all credit in the eyes of the people. Decent peasants do not show up at the assembly, or are brought there against their will.

[79]TsGIA, *f.* Kakhanovskaia komissiia, *op.* 1, *d.* 11, *ll.* 361–361 *ob.*
[80]*MVUOK*, vol. 3, pt. 2: *Zapiski Mordvinova*, no. 1, p. 21.
[81]Quoted from ibid., vol. 3, pt. 1: *Zapiski Kovalevskogo*, no. 1, p. 5.
[82]Ibid., vol. 3, pt. 2: *Zapiski Mordvinova*, no. 5, p. 9.

Not one matter is decided objectively, since there are no assemblies where persuasion with vodka by the interested parties does not occur. Very frequently, especially in Tambov province, the village assembly decisions are drawn up in advance by the scribe and, on his instructions, are signed by the illiterate delegates who do not attend the assembly. The village and *volost'* elders, who almost without exception are illiterate, play a secondary role. The peasants are indifferent toward elections, believing that even if a good person were to be elected, he would be corrupted by the office. Other peasants try to elect weak people, fearing arbitrariness and ambition. The same practices that occur in the assemblies prevail as well in the *volost'* court – the scribe under the pretext of reading the law, prompts the decision. As for the scribe, the peasants have remarked: "Before we were subordinate to the landlord; now it's the scribe." The abuses of and disorder in the village and *volost'* administration are proved by the number of complaints submitted to me. There are 100 written complaints and at least as many oral ones.[83]

Although Mordvinov's statement had the ring of a truism by 1881, with each year the peasant institutions described by the senators less resembled the model of peasant self-government outlined in the 19 February statute. Contrary to the provisions of the reform legislation, the *volost'* assemblies failed to do anything but elect *volost'* officials, and anarchy prevailed in village and *volost'* assemblies to such an extent that elderly and sober peasants declined to attend on the grounds that drunken peasants refused to let them speak. Peasants in the inspected provinces complained that the strong peasants and *miroedy* (village peasants who lived off the labor of their neighbors) controlled the assemblies and manipulated the village and *volost'* elders. Coercion and the stronger voice rather than a majority vote decided business. However, the main cause for chaos in peasant self-government, according to the senators (and the Pskov and Orel zemstvos, among others), was vodka. In almost every assembly the delegates with proposals to pass bribed their colleagues with vodka or promises of it. This and other peasant customs, so "alien" to the senators from St. Petersburg, provided a convenient and visible target for criticism, and hence their reports must be treated with some skepticism. Nevertheless, this picture of inebriated peasants voting for the desires of their benefactors at the assembly could only dismay officials who, two decades earlier, foresaw the imminent creation of genuine public self-government at the village level.[84]

The *volost'* and village elders elected by their respective assemblies came under special attack from the senators. Because most peasants shunned elected office, the *miroedy* often arranged for the election of weak officials, for instance, peasants in arrears to the commune. As a rule, persons desiring to serve as village elder were ruled out by the assembly on the grounds that they would pursue purely personal aims. Consequently, elected peasant officials rarely pretended to serve the needs of all the villagers they represented. And

[83]Quoted from ibid., no. 1, p. 11.
[84]Cf. TsGIA, *f.* Kakhanovskaia komissiia, *op.* 1, *d.* 11, *l.* 27 *ob.*; *MVUOK*, vol. 3, pt. 1: *Zapiski Kovalevskogo*, no. 2, pp. 82–3; and Skalon, *Zemskie vzgliady*, pp. 34–5.

although many village and *volost'* officials were reelected to office, the senatorial inspectors revealed that experience in office was no boon to efficient administration. They cited examples of *volost'* elders who embezzled property during many years of service or village elders who arranged for land repartitions in the interests of their *miroed* patrons.[85] True, in some cases village elders were more vigilant in punishing peasants who harmed the village than those who damaged state or gentry property; but this hardly gave comfort to state officials. It is little wonder that most peasants viewed self-government as a curse and, as they emphasized to Mordvinov, an important cause of their poverty.[86] They despised the *volost'* elders as junior police officials whose sole concern was collecting taxes and implementing orders of the district police chief, his precinct captains, and justices of the peace. In a few instances (for example, in several *volosti* in Kazan' Province in 1878 and Perm Province in 1879) peasants went as far as to remove by force their village and *volost'* elders from office.[87]

Without a doubt, an underlying cause for many of the other difficulties in peasant self-government was peasant illiteracy. Since the peasants were uneducated, they had no concept of written law, regular bureaucratic procedures, or division of responsibility, and most of them had no experience in administration outside of obeying their former landlords. Many *volost'* and village elders were illiterate and thus depended heavily on the *volost'* scribe. A survey of the literacy rates of peasant officials completed by the Ministry of Internal Affairs in January 1880 shows how uneducated peasant officials were and that, in such cases, a little literacy could be a dangerous thing. In the thirty-four provinces in which zemstvo institutions were introduced, there were 4,650 literate *volost'* elders and 3,227 illiterate *volost'* elders, and 15,951 literate village elders as opposed to 68,968 illiterate village elders. Widespread illiteracy of peasant officials was particularly noticeable in those provinces listed in the survey that the senators inspected. Of the eight provinces inspected by the senators (Kiev and Orenburg were not included on the list), the number of literate *volost'* elders exceeded the number of their illiterate counterparts only in Chernigov Province (146 literate, 28 illiterate). In Samara Province, exactly half the *volost'* elders were literate. In the other inspected provinces, the number of illiterate *volost'* elders exceeded the figure for literate elders, particularly in Tambov (157 literate, 174 illiterate), Kazan' (71 literate, 111 illiterate), and Ufa provinces (60 literate, 111 illiterate). The percentage of illiterate village elders was far higher. The data from the

[85] *MVUOK*, vol. 3, pt. 2: *Zapiski Mordvinova*, document 7, p. 3; and TsGIA, *f.* Kakhanovskaia komissiia, *op.* 1, *d.* 11, *l.* 28 *ob.*

[86] TsGIA, *f.* Kakhanovskaias komissiia, *d.* 11, *ll.* 31-31 *ob.*, 362–3; see also Mandel, chap. 2.

[87] Anfimov, "Krest'ianskoe dvizhenie," pp. 180–1; TsGIA, *f.* Kakhanovskaia komissiia, *op.* 1, *d.* 11, *l.* 362 *ob.*; *MVUOK*, vol. 3, pt. 1: *Zapiski Kovalevskogo*, no. 2, p. 81. The zemstvos and many district bureaus were likewise frustrated by the tendency of *volost'* elders to neglect their main responsibility for supervising village officials and assemblies and to concentrate on the collection of taxes, as noted in *Materialy po preobrazovaniiu*, 1: 85–8.

survey shows that overall 18.8 percent were literate, and the percentages in some provinces were much smaller – 3.9 percent in Kazan', 4.0 percent in Ufa, 5.0 percent in Voronezh, 6.2 percent in Chernigov, 7.5 percent in Tambov, and 8.6 percent in Saratov. Thus, an illiterate village elder was a foregone conclusion. Of all the provinces listed, only in Moscow and Iaroslavl' did the literate elders outnumber their illiterate counterparts (1,813 literate, 1,761 illiterate in Moscow, and 1,319 literate, 493 illiterate in Iaroslavl').[88]

The statistics on the literacy of peasant officials indeed emphasize that literate peasant officials not only were a rare phenomenon in 1880, but that the education of the peasantry, a goal of the reformers of the 1860s and one of the prerequisites for genuine public self-government in the village, had made little headway in the two previous decades. Widespread peasant literacy was not much closer in 1880 than in 1861, and without a literate peasant population, the peasants stood little chance of exerting legal control over their elected officials and developing a responsible administration. Rather, they were compelled to defer to other authorities and to rely on the *volost'* scribe, who usually succumbed to the temptation to exploit the peasants for his own personal profit.

The *volost'* scribe conducted all business in the *volost'* administration and directed the *volost'* elder because the latter was illiterate and unfamiliar with the law. Unfortunately, the scribe often used his knowledge to run the *volost'* administration in the interests of a small clique of *miroedy* who elected him and provided occasional bribes. The case of a certain Sobolev, a scribe in Spasski District (Voronezh Province), was by no means unusual. The peasants who submitted the complaint requested to remain anonymous out of fear of Sobolev, who allegedly enjoyed the support of fifteen *miroedy* who dominated the *volost'* assembly and prevented the majority of the assembly from acting in accordance with their convictions. Mordvinov's investigation corroborated the accusations made by the peasants, and the peasants interviewed by Mordvinov complained that Sobolev constantly made arbitrary decisions and arranged for the flogging of peasants who disagreed with him.[89] Yet, as N. M. Astyrev, one of Sobolev's counterparts in Voronezh Province, pointed out, sinister motives did not always account for such actions on the part of the scribe. Most peasant officials were so lethargic or servile toward local police and tax collectors that the scribe, in discharging the functions of six separate

---

[88]The survey is found in TsGIA, *f.* Kakhanovskaia komissiia, *op.* 1, *d.* 83, *ll.* 21 *ob.*-29 *ob.* The statistics in this report suggest, contrary to Raeff's assertion, that the peasant emancipation did not give peasants immediate access to elite literary culture, or limited participation in civic life. Raeff, *Understanding Imperial Russia*, p. 79.

[89]TsGIA, *f.* Kakhanovskaia komissiia, *op.* 1, *d.* 11, *ll.* 28-28 *ob.* Kovalevskii asserted that the process whereby district bureaus appointed the *volost'* scribes, often without taking into account the wishes of the *volost'* administration, was the cause of the problem. Under these conditions, the scribe was not dependent on the *volost'* administration and *volost'* elder, and instead issued orders to the elder on the pretext of representing the district bureau. See *MVUOK*, vol. 3, pt. 1: *Zapiski Kovalevskogo*, no. 2, pp. 85–6.

ministries at the *volost'* level, had to circumvent the law and local custom to get anything done;[90] and judging by Astyrev's comment (1881) on the official demands made on him by various ministries, such bribes were an inadequate, albeit dishonorable, compensation:

And what a mass of hodge-podge departments and officials turn to the *volost'* administration with the demand to carry out their instructions immediately! The district bureau for peasant affairs, the district and provincial zemstvo boards, the war bureau, school council, gentry trusteeship, police administration, fiscal chamber, provincial administration, administration of state properties, treasury, district assembly of the justices of the peace [*mirovoi sezd*], and the justices of the peace, district police chief [*ispravnik*], permanent member, district police officer [*stanovoi*], judicial investigator, bailiff, provincial statistical committee, zemstvo insurance agent, and so on and so on – all of them, and they all write: "furnish immediately," "to be enforced without delay," "carry out forth-rightly," "see to it personally" – to look for, compile, evaluate, send for, describe, investigate, watch over, etc. endlessly.[91]

In short, arbitrariness, apathy, corruption, peasant confusion over many officials (*mnogovlastie*), and police domination more than ever victimized peasant administration. The twin evils of *volost'* administration – vodka and illiteracy – were likewise the scourge of the *volost'* court, as noted in Chapter 2. *Volost'* elders and scribes exploited their role of providing legal instructions for the peasant judges in order to pressure them into rendering the decision they desired. *Volost'* judges often resolved cases slowly or postponed hearings because the defendant failed to show up, without bothering to fine the guilty peasant for his absence. In other cases, notably in Arapovskaia *volost'* in Tambov District and Kazachinskaia *volost'* in Shatskii District, even the peasant judges failed to appear since they already had signed a copy of the decision written out in advance on a separate piece of paper by the scribe, who later entered the decision in the *volost'* book.[92] As for the emphasis on local peasant custom as the primary determinant in *volost'* court decisions, the experience of *volost'* courts in the inspected provinces revealed that in many *volosti* the peasants rarely agreed on customs. All in all, argued Polovtsov, the *volost'* court, which rendered final decisions on cases under its jurisdiction, had ceased to function in the manner prescribed by the 1861 reform:

The *volost'* court serves not so much as the upholder of peasant customs as much as an institution for the arbitrariness of *volost'* scribes and elders, under whose influence it is always found. This arbitrariness is revealed sometimes by the immediate execution of decisions involving corporal punishment, without waiting out the period for the appeal of these decisions, and most often by the complete failure of the *volost'* elder to enforce the court's decisions, thereby depriving it of any real effect. As a

---

[90]N. M. Astyrev, *V volostnykh pisariakh: Ocherki krest'ianskogo samoupravleniia* (Moscow, 1886), pp. 150–1.

[91]Quoted in ibid., p. 32.

[92]*MVUOK*, vol. 3, pt. 2: *Zapiski Mordvinova*, no. 7, p. 15.

result of these factors, the peasants avoid their *volost'* court and sometimes submit to the decisions of special judges elected in the village communities.[93]

In essence, from the village assemblies to the *volost'* courts, the senatorial inspectors assailed peasant self-government as riddled with corruption and anarchy. Considering their one-sided view of peasant administration, one might indeed question whether the inspectors, for all their thoroughness, depicted actual conditions in the villages; their reports at times exaggerated the degree of social stratification and economic distress in the villages, just as they failed to appreciate the role of customary law in the village. Still, we should remember that their findings on peasant self-government sub-stantiated the reports of other officials and the handful of peasants who submitted memorandums to the ministries and Kakhanov Commission. Most important, the senatorial reports, unlike the Valuev Commission (1872), conclusively argued that the problems of tax collection, land redistribution, village stratification, peasant apathy, and lawlessness were inextricably rooted in elected peasant administration, and that the absence of real authority in the village posed a danger to the various ministries and autocracy as a whole.[94]

Zemstvo institutions: their activity and composition. If the absence of supervision over peasant self-government was the main problem in that area, according to the senatorial inspectors, the opposite was the case with zemstvo insti-tutions. The inspectors by and large blamed the arbitrary interference of state officials in zemstvo affairs and their lack of cooperation in fiscal matters as the main cause for zemstvo inefficiency. For these reasons, they concluded that the zemstvos functioned most effectively in areas in which they had to rely least on police and peasant officials – namely public health and, to a lesser extent, public education. In those areas, the zemstvos had their own physicians, *fel'dshers*, hospitals, schools, trustees, and inspectors (until Tolstoi deprived them of school inspectors in 1874). Even after the 1874 statute, the zemstvo retained two members on the school councils, along with the

---

[93]Quoted in *Istoriia pravitel'stvuiushchego senata*, 4: 210.

Although many zemstvos and district bureaus attacked the inadequacies of the *volost'* court, most of them (perhaps in consideration of gentry interests or mindful of the problems connected with the justices of the peace, as discussed in Chapter 3) recommended keeping the peasant court of custom as a means of providing simple and accessible justice for the peasantry. Some zemstvos advocated a low-level court for all social estates. See *Materialy po preobrazovaniiu*, 1: 100–29.

[94]Soviet historians admit that actual peasant disturbances in the late 1870s and 1880s were relatively few in number and that peasant rumors of a forthcoming "black partition" (*chernyi peredel'*) posed a wider threat to tsarism. They contend that of the 245 peasant disturbances in the empire from 1878 to 1882, 179 were related to land disputes, 39 stemmed from tax/*obrok* payments, 21 were directed against local administrative and judicial authorities, and 6 against local kulaks. In 47 cases, troops were needed to put down the disturbances. In fact, as the foregoing analysis of the inspection materials shows, such a categorization of causes for peasant disturbances is arbitrary and artificial; many of the land-related disputes reflected peasant dissatisfaction with the activities of the district bureaus and village and *volost'* elders, who were regarded as bureaucratic agents opposed to peasant interests. Moreover, it should be remembered that peasants (well known for having monarchistic tendencies and being suspicious of revolutionaries) generally turned to upheaval as a last resort. For the data, see Anfimov, "Krest'ianskoe dvizhenie," pp. 171–3.

gentry marshal who presided over them. In short, provided that they could collect the taxes to finance their work, the zemstvos had the personnel to introduce improvements in public health and public education. The sharp rise in the number of hospitals and schools in the provinces inspected by the senators attests to impressive zemstvo work in these areas. For example, the number of hospitals in Kazan' Province rose from eleven to twenty-three from 1865 to 1880 and the number of physicians in Tambov Province increased threefold during the same period.[95]

Unfortunately, even in these areas there were troubling signs in the implementation of zemstvo initiatives. Although many zemstvos lavished significant amounts of money on public health because they were subject to fewer central controls in this respect, zemstvos in some provinces (for instance, Kazan') came under criticism from their physician employees, who resented zemstvo interference in their work.[96] The inspectors added that the *feld'shers* and smallpox vaccinators hired by the zemstvos to provide the bulk of rural medical services were incompetent and lazy on the whole. The vaccinators were barely literate and unable to distinguish the right vaccines from the wrong ones and healthy children from sick ones.[97] As for public education, the senator inspectors depicted zemstvo activity in a positive, yet rather partial light. Mordvinov observed that the number of public schools and teachers had doubled and the number of pupils had tripled in Tambov Province, owing to zemstvo activity there;[98] in fact, Mordvinov asserted, the policy of former Minister of Education Tolstoi (who resigned under fire in April 1880) prevented even greater gains, because it restricted zemstvo activity to the financial upkeep of schools and, as a result of the 1874 Statute on Elementary Education, stifled zemstvo initiative by depriving the public of the right to inspect schools that they built and maintained. Resurrecting the perennial zemstvo complaint about having competence but no authority, Shamshin warned that zemstvos might reduce their appropriations for public education in retaliation against Tolstoi's inflexible policy.[99] What the two inspectors failed to mention was that many zemstvos had already played politics with public education. Moreover, although there was a marked increase in the number of schools between 1860 and 1880, the zemstvo (as

[95]*MVUOK*, vol. 3, pt. 1: *Zapiski Kovalevskogo*, no. 1, p. 10; and ibid., vol. 3, pt. 2: *Zapiski Mordvinova*, document 12, pp. 26–8. For Mordvinov's laudatory comments on zemstvo activity to improve public health facilities in Voronezh Province, see TsGIA, *f*. Kakhanovskaia komissiia, *op*. 1, *d*. 11, *ll*. 341 *ob*.-342.

[96]Nancy M. Frieden, *Russian Physicians in an Era of Reform and Revolution, 1856–1905* (Princeton, 1981), pp. 88–90.

[97]*MVUOK*, vol. 3, pt. 2: *Zapiski Mordvinova*, no. 12, p. 28; and TsGIA, *f*. Kakhanovskaia komissiia, *op*. 1, *d*. 109, *ll*. 28 *ob*.-29, 50–56 *ob*., 69–69 *ob*. For an analysis of zemstvo activity in providing public health care, see Frieden, *Russian Physicians*, pp. 77–104; and Samuel C. Ramer, "The Zemstvo and Public Health," *The Zemstvo in Russia*, pp. 279–314.

[98]*MVUOK*, vol. 3, pt. 2: *Zapiski Mordvinova*, no. 12, p. 48.

[99]TsGIA, *f*. Kakhanovskaia komissiia, *op*. 1, *d*. 109, *ll*. 58–60.

opposed to state and peasant) contribution to this process before 1890 was minimal in most provinces.[100]

But the most significant obstacle to zemstvo work was perhaps the lack of cooperation from police officials in collecting zemstvo revenues (as noted earlier in the growth of arrears in district and provincial zemstvo taxes). In Tambov Province, for example, zemstvo tax- and insurance-related arrears for 1881 totaled 1,311,142 rubles, with the highest percentage of zemstvo tax arrears found in the districts of Morshan (61 percent of the annual rate), Temnikov (58 percent of the annual rate), and Borisogleb (57 percent), of the annual rate); zemstvo arrears in Saratov and Samara provinces equaled 545,849 rubles (59.3 percent of the annual rate) and 710,443 rubles (80.2 percent), respectively.[101] Even worse, the senators revealed, the police had taken no steps since the mid-1870s to collect zemstvo taxes more effectively or more equitably. The Tambov District board cited a familiar litany of reasons for the increase in zemstvo arrears:

1. The bad economic condition of the peasantry;
2. The fact that the arrears of the zemstvo tax are collected by the police along with state taxes. The police officials are held strictly accountable if they fail to collect state taxes. *Volost'* and village elders are put under arrest by the district police chiefs, and hence their primary attention is devoted to the collection of state taxes without arrears, whereas the police are not at all interested in the successful collection of zemstvo tax arrears. Even though the law, in order to avoid irregularities, indicates the procedure for levying the zemstvo tax, in practice in the majority of cases all the collected state and zemstvo taxes initially are turned over to the district treasury. After covering all the arrears for the state tax, [the tax officials] count the surplus as the zemstvo tax, with the leftovers from the zemstvo tax serving as the insurance premiums.[102]

To alleviate their fiscal difficulties and reliance on police officials outside their control, many zemstvo leaders advocated that tax collectors be elected by the district assemblies – an arrangement that the ministers of internal affairs had long opposed for political reasons. Mordvinov added that the zemstvo should be given control over the sale of peasant property to pay zemstvo tax arrears on the grounds that such sales (and confiscation of food supply loans to the peasants) by local police officials ruined the peasant economy.[103]

[100]On this issue, see Ben Eklof, *Russian Peasant Schools: Officialdom, Village Culture, and Popular Pedagogy, 1861–1914* (Berkeley, 1986), pp. 70–88. Eklof concentrates mainly on Moscow Province, but his conclusions are valid for other provinces, including Tambov.

[101]TsGIA, *f.* Kakhanovskaia komissiia, *op.* 1, *d.* 109, *ll.* 24–27; and *MVUOK*, vol. 3, pt. 2: *Zapiski Mordvinova*, no. 12, pp. 25–6.

[102]Quoted from *Zapiski Mordvinova*, no. 12, p. 53. Senator Polovtsov reported similar problems in Chernigov Province and recommended that the law allocate a certain percentage of all taxes collected for zemstvo expenses. See OR-GPBSS, *f.* Polovtsov, *d.* 1333, *ll.* 43–4.

[103]TsGIA, *f.* Kakhanovskaia komissiia, *op.* 1, *d.* 11, *l.* 354. In 1881–2, zemstvos in Ufa, Kaluga, and Novgorod provinces made the same recommendations. Skalon, *Zemskie vzgliady*, pp. 55–9. On the inadequacies of the police (*stanovye*) see Yaney, *Urge to Mobilize*, pp. 59–62.

Yet nowhere was the gap between broad zemstvo responsibilities and its limited resources greater than in the zemstvo fire insurance programs, as noted by the Tambov District board. The immediate problem was the local police who, as in the case of zemstvo taxes, displayed little initiative in collecting insurance premiums and arrears from the village population, or used the funds collected to pay state tax arrears. By 1880, the zemstvos in Saratov Province, as one example, faced a critical situation. In that year, the amount of insurance claims paid out exceeded the amount in premiums by 63,749 rubles, with a government loan covering the difference; to provide insurance in 1880, the district zemstvos took additional loans from the government. In Samara Province the situation was even worse. The compensation for claims had exceeded the amount collected in premiums since 1877 (the figures for 1877 alone were 33 percent for mandatory insurance and 63 percent for voluntary insurance). At first, the Samara provincial board dipped into its *food supply fund* to cover the claims. When this source dried up, it resorted to state loans, which, together with the food supply funds spent for insurance compensation, amounted to a debt of 200,000 rubles.[104] In Tambov Province, the insurance arrears rate rose from 192,227 rubles in 1876 to an alarming sum of 467,621 rubles in 1880.[105]

The unwillingness of peasant and police officials to enforce the fire safety regulations established by the provincial zemstvo assemblies compounded the problem. Mordvinov pointed out that the village fire marshals existed only on paper and that the failure of peasant authorities and *volost'* courts to enforce the fire safety regulations was the main reason for the increasing number of fires (13.8 percent of which, according to one historian, were cases of arson directed against local landlords and *miroedy* in 1878–82).[106] In 1880, 916 fires occurred in Voronezh Province, many of which stemmed from the failure of peasant officials to enforce fire safety regulations.[107] Shamshin cited the case of Stavropol' District (Samara Province) as proof of such negligence by *volost'* officials. A district board check of the list of insured buildings compiled by the *volost'* administration disclosed approximately 2,000 buildings on the list that did not exist and another 4,000 buildings subject to insurance regulations that were not listed.[108] This situation was hardly surprising given the burdens of tax collection, law enforcement, food supply maintenance, and repartitioning that fell on peasant officials. They had no time to enforce fire insurance regulations, the details of which were beyond the comprehension of most of them anyway.

The provincial zemstvos themselves created additional difficulties by their

---

[104]TsGIA, *f.* Kakhanovskaia komissiia, *op.* 1, *d.* 109, *ll.* 48–48 *ob.*
[105]*MVUOK*, vol. 3, pt. 2: *Zapiski Mordvinova*, no. 12, p. 89.
[106]Anfimov, "Krest'ianskoe dvizhenie," p. 186. However accurate this figure, it is noteworthy that tsarist officials saw the fires as clear proof of the increasing lawlessness and authority crisis in peasant villages in the late 1870s.
[107]TsGIA, *f.* Kakhanovskaia komissiia, *op.* 1, *d.* 11, *l.* 346 *ob.*
[108]Ibid., *d.* 109, *l.* 48 *ob.*

slow handling of insurance claims, and added to widespread peasant belief that the introduction of the zemstvos brought only more taxes for the peasantry (an opinion substantiated by the fact that on the average peasant lands in the late 1870s were taxed by the zemstvos at one and a half times the rate of nonpeasant property). [109] Although the zemstvos had their own agents, regulations for building villages, and a classification system for insured buildings to expedite their claims service in the mid-1870s, none of these measures accelerated the process significantly. For instance, on 16 November 1880 the Vasil'evskaia *volost'* filed a claim with the Voronezh provincial zemstvo board for compensation to cover fire damages. Twice the *volost'* elder traveled to the local district board to receive the 2,397 rubles to pay the peasants whose property was damaged, and twice he returned home empty-handed. On 11 December 1880, the provincial assembly, recognizing that further delay in paying the compensation would entail extreme hardship for the peasants, adopted new regulations whereby the district treasury would pay insurance compensation to district boards on the special instructions of the provincial board. In cases in which compensation exceeded 3,000 rubles, payment would be made through a member of the district board within two weeks after receiving the instructions of the provincial board. But the settlement came too late to tide the peasants over the severe winter months or to temper the peasants' dissatisfaction with zemstvo insurance. [110]

In short, problems ranging from the incompetence of some zemstvo employees to the inefficiency of police and peasant officials in enforcing zemstvo regulations hampered zemstvo work in the areas of tax collection and fire insurance, not to mention the public food supply, as noted earlier. The senatorial inspectors attributed all these difficulties to the government's laxity in disciplining officials who did not work with the zemstvos. Yet the underlying cause of these problems was the recurrent shortage of state officials to handle enforcement-related functions in a countryside undergoing the initial phases of legal and industrial development, and the government's refusal to grant the zemstvos (or other nonministerial agencies) such authority. Zemstvos had no legal control over the officials who were available, whereas the latter complained that they already were overburdened in fulfilling directives of state ministries. Thus, the preconditions for efficient administration, as far as the zemstvos were concerned, were clarification of their status as either public or state institutions, and the creation of government or public executive agents to implement zemstvo decisions at the subdistrict level. Both points were frequently raised in zemstvo petitions of the period.

Still, the inspectors did not pin all the blame for zemstvo ineffectiveness on the government. The growing proportion of self-seeking, less-educated landlords elected as zemstvo delegates, and the high rate of absenteeism,

---

[109]Atkinson, "The Zemstvo and the Peasantry," pp. 112, 101–3.
[110]TsGIA, *f.* Kakhanovskaia komissiia, *d.* 109, *l.* 48 *ob.*

especially among peasant representatives, signaled the growing indifference of the provincial population toward zemstvo service. Most of the inspectors attacked the prominent gentry landlords for abandoning the responsibilities of zemstvo leadership that the government conferred on them. In fairness to these landlords, the senators acknowledged that state interference in zemstvo affairs had played no small role in dissuading the prominent gentry from zemstvo activity.

More to the point, the rising tide of absenteeism in the zemstvo assemblies convinced the senatorial inspectors that changes were necessary in zemstvo election and representation procedures. Shamshin indicated that in the district assembly sessions in Saratov Province for 1879 and 1880, no more than 57 percent of the delegates on the average attended any one session. In contrast, in Petrov District, an average of only 33 percent of the delegates were present. In Samara Province, the figures were better, with 73 percent the high average in Novouzensk District and 38 percent the low average in Buguruslan. Although no zemstvo assembly sessions in either province were canceled owing to a shortage of delegates, the sessions in Aktarsk, Balashov, Kuznets, and Saratov districts were delayed several days until a quorum of delegates appeared.[111] At the provincial assembly level (where gentry landlords had overwhelming majorities in representation), the problem was even worse, as illustrated by the history of the Voronezh provincial assembly from 1865 to 1880. Of the twenty sessions called during those years, in only three cases did the assembly meet on time. Usually the openings were delayed by two to four days, and in 1878 the provincial assembly opened ten days late. And as the writings of zemstvo publicist V. Iu. Skalon show, such absenteeism was commonplace in many other provincial assemblies (Khar'kov, Ekaterinoslav, Simbirsk, Riazan', Novgorod, Saratov) in 1881.[112]

Understandably, the absentee rate was highest among the peasants. Zemstvo service remained unattractive to them owing to the expense of traveling annually to the zemstvo assembly and living for one to three weeks in the district capital. Like all zemstvo delegates, the peasants received no compensation for their participation and lost valuable work time. In addition, peasant officials who were elected delegates intimidated other peasant delegates, who consequently were afraid to express their opinions in the assemblies. Mordvinov insisted that as a rule the peasants lacked the educational background to understand zemstvo affairs, and suggested a change in the procedure for electing peasant delegates, whereby the *volost'* assembly, under the chairmanship of the local justice of the peace, would elect its own delegates to the district assembly. This would enable the peasants to elect candidates they knew and trusted instead of simply deferring to the gentry.[113]

---

[111]Ibid., *ll.* 18 *ob.*-19.

[112]Ibid., *d.* 11, *l.* 352; and [Skalon], *Mneniia zemskikh sobranii*, p. 2.

[113]According to Atkinson, although peasant population in the zemstvo provinces increased by 34 percent between 1863 and 1885, the peasants continued to have less than 40 percent of the delegates in the district assembly. More revealing is the fact that in 1885 the peasant curia chose only 85 percent of

He even drafted a plan to reapportion representation in district assemblies according to the relative amounts of zemstvo taxes paid by each electoral group; hence, according to his plan, the number of delegates from the village communities in the district assemblies of Tambov Province would increase fom 267 to 360, whereas the figure for private landlords would decline from 284 to 229. Yet Mordvinov's contention that the elimination of the arbitrary quotas established by the 1864 Zemstvo Statute would rekindle peasant interest in zemstvo affairs was illogical and naive.[114] Only when peasants possessed sufficient education and the financial independence to participate meaningfully in zemstvo affairs and to recognize the potential benefits and not merely the tax burden of zemstvo representation, would they become enthusiastic about zemstvo work.

Thus, the public enthusiasm that greeted the establishment of zemstvo institutions in European Russia had long since waned by the late 1870s. The peasants rejected zemstvo service because of its cost and because zemstvo assemblies during the 1860s and 1870s devoted themselves primarily to the landowners' interests, as illustrated by their taxation and food supply policies. The peasants benefited primarily from public health and public education, and not surprisingly, in those few provinces in which peasants held the majority of seats in the district assemblies in the late 1870s, the zemstvos appropriated larger shares of their budgets to public education. Such was the case in Viatka, Olonets, Vologda, Orenburg, Kursk, and Tavrik provinces. By contrast, in those provinces (for example, Bessarabia, Tambov, Smolensk, Saratov) in which landlords predominated in the district assemblies, substantially less was budgeted for public education. The exception was Chernigov province, in which peasants accounted for only 42 percent of the district representatives; yet 17.1 percent of the budget went for public education.[115]

The townsmen in turn were disillusioned with zemstvo self-government because, as shown in Chapter 2, it likewise meant high taxes and few benefits. The senatorial reports revealed that in most provinces urban representatives constituted less than 10 percent of the delegates in the district assemblies. Finally, many prominent landowners were disenchanted with zemstvo service as early as the late 1860s, when their initiative and enthusiasm were thwarted by the governors and Minister of Internal Affairs Timashev. So, by the late 1870s, the zemstvos were run more and more by petty landowners, whose unfavorable influence on zemstvo activities provoked the inspectors' criticism of zemstvo representation. Indeed, Mordvinov and Shamshin recommended a reduction in the property requirement for educated people in order to weed

---

its representatives from peasant ranks, with 12 percent coming from the gentry (as opposed to earlier figures of 90 percent and 8 percent, respectively). In essence, the peasants were already leaving the zemstvo to the gentry. Atkinson, "The Zemstvo and the Peasantry," p. 86.

[114] *MVUOK*, vol. 3, pt. 2: *Zapiski Mordvinova*, no. 12, pp. 59–60; and TsGIA, *f.* Kakhanovskaia komissiia, *op.* 1, *d.* 11, *l.* 351 *ob.*

[115] M. Slobozhanin, *Iz istorii i opyta zemskikh uchrezhdenii* (St. Petersburg, 1913), pp. 313–15.

out delegates seeking to further personal interests rather than the public welfare. Besides illuminating the shortcomings in zemstvo activity between 1865 and 1880, the senatorial reports also emphasized that successful zemstvo work depended on reducing interministerial conflict in the provinces, resolving the status of the zemstvos vis à vis the state administration, and creating conditions that would allow true public servants, rather than petty gentry careerists, to play the leading role in the zemstvos.

The justices of the peace. Compared with the zemstvos and particularly peasant institutions, which were sharply criticized by the senatorial inspectors, the justices of the peace fared well. For example, Polovtsov concluded that the justices of the peace in Chernigov Province performed satisfactorily, with each regular section justice (*uchastkovyi sud'ia*) reviewing approximately 800 cases a year without noticeable delay; and Mordvinov contended that the majority of justices in his provinces were effective (even though he recommended that the Senate initiate prosecution against six of them).[116] Yet, on closer inspection, their reports provided a grass roots view of the basic shortcomings of the justices of the peace – specifically, the shortage of good candidates for the position, the dependence of elected justices on the zemstvos, and peasant confusion over the sophisticated cassation procedures that justices attempted to follow in hearing minor civil and criminal cases – that came under attack from the justices themselves in the 1870s and 1880s.[117] The senators' criticism of the zemstvo's role in the justices' election and activity and the peasant disenchantment with their legal procedures deserve special attention, given the role that the justices were supposed to play in educating the peasants in the law and in providing them with expedient and simple justice. As the reports showed, however, the complicated procedures adopted by the justices increased the role of secretaries and petty lawyers in rural judicial affairs, thus contradicting the aim of the 1864 Judicial Statutes. The peasants repeatedly complained to Polovtsov that the justices of the peace had nothing in common with justice.[118]

In their investigation of the justices of the peace, Senators Polovtsov, Mordvinov, and Shamshin contended that there was a shortage of qualified personnel for the office and they gave credence to the public perception of the declining caliber of justices in the late 1870s. Their data reveal that nearly all section and honorary justices of the peace were landed gentry and bureaucrats with the equivalent of a secondary education or above. For example, of the 55 regular justices of the peace in Tambov, twenty possessed a higher education, eleven a secondary education, and fifteen a specialized military education. Only nine (16.4 percent) had just an elementary edu-

---

[116]*MVUOK*, vol. 3, pt. 2: *Zapiski Mordvinova*, document 20, p. 23.
[117]The criticisms made by the justices in their memoirs and articles are discussed at length in Thomas S. Pearson, "Russian Law and Rural Justice: Activity and Problems of the Russian Justices of the Peace, 1865–1889," *Jahrbücher für Geschichte Osteuropas*, no. 1 (1984): 52–71.
[118]OR-GPBSS, *f.* Polovtsov, *d.* 1333, *ll.* 14–15a; ibid., 1882, *d.* 1506, *ll.* 80 *ob.*-81.

cation or had received tutoring at home, and thus did not fulfill the education requirement for the office. Polovtsov similarly found that only 8 of 52 section justices, or less than 15 percent, had less than a secondary education in Chernigov Province.[119] Nonetheless, the senators agreed, the justices lacked the legal background to comprehend complicated cassation procedures and the familiarity with peasant customary law to render quick decisions on peasant cases. Under these circumstances, the office of justice of the peace appealed mainly to those petty gentry who sought to use it as a springboard to a career in state service.

Even worse, with little in salary and benefits to recruit and retain competent justices, the district zemstvo assemblies in most cases permitted the prospective justice of the peace to select the location of his court (*kamera*). Invariably, he chose to hear cases on his landed estate rather than travel to the district capital or the largest city in the region. The peasants justly complained to the inspectors that in view of the turnover in the justices of the peace, they never knew where to go to submit their cases. Nor could they afford to travel great distances to serve as witnesses or to lodge a complaint. And with every relocation of the court within the section it was necessary to transfer all the records, and inevitably documents were lost. Thus, district zemstvos faced the dilemma of either adhering to the public interest and establishing a fixed location of the court, or acceding to the demands of the elected justices in hopes of attracting volunteers for the post. Unlike Polovtsov, who offered no solutions to the problem, Mordvinov proposed that the government authorize zemstvos to define permanently the number of judicial sections, their boundaries, and the location of the courts in accordance with the needs of the population.[120]

While commending the overall work of the justices of the peace in Chernigov Province, Polovtsov pointed out additional shortcomings: their slowness in handling some cases, especially in the Chernigov region, where hearings were postponed for six or seven months; and the lack of supervision by the district assembly of the justices of the peace over the activities of the local justices. These district assemblies repeatedly failed to prosecute justices suspected of negligence in their work, a fact that Polovtsov found difficult to justify since justices in Chernigov Province were not overloaded with litigation (each handling an average of 802 cases in 1881).[121] Not surprisingly, however, the justices of the peace who made up a district assembly usually resisted supervising each other's work too closely, and neither the zemstvos nor the Ministry of Justice pressed the issue.

Still, it was the buildup of cases backlogged in the *mirovoi* courts at the end of the 1870s that most concerned the senatorial inspectors, the Ministry of Justice, certain zemstvos, and reform-minded publicists of

[119]Cf. *MVUOK*, vol. 3, pt. 2: *Zapiski Mordvinova*, no. 20, p. 10; and OR-GPBSS, *f.* Polovtsov, *d.* 1506, *ll.* 61–61 *ob.*

[120]*MVUOK*, vol. 3, pt. 2: *Zapiski Mordvinova*, p. 8.

[121]OR-GPBSS, *f.* Polovtsov, *d.* 1506, *ll.* 69–74 *ob.*, 19 *ob.*-22 *ob.*

the day. The inspections and a statistical survey conducted by the Ministry of Justice revealed that of the thirty-four provinces surveyed for the period, nearly half (sixteen) had 1,000 more cases unresolved by justices at the end of 1882 than at the end of 1879. In some provinces a huge backlog of undecided cases lay in the *mirovoi* courts in 1882 – 13,090 cases in Bessarabia, 25,456 in Viatka, 6,004 in Novgorod, 7,351 in Saratov, 14,257 in Ufa, and 11,543 in Chernigov. Even more telling, in fourteen of the provinces each section justice received an average of fewer than 1,000 cases each year (in Kaluga, Tambov, Kursk, and Novgorod provinces the figure was less than 700 per year). In nine other provinces the increase for the same three-year period was between 500 and 1,000 cases, whereas only Olonets, Orel, Iaroslavl', and Smolensk provinces saw a reduction in the number of undecided cases. Worst of all, the steady increase of undecided litigation throughout the thirty-four provinces from 185,187 or 13.1 percent of the cases initiated in 1876 to 261,278 or 18.5 percent of all cases initiated in 1881, served as a more troubling sign that the wheels of *mirovoi* justice were slowing down.[122]

What accounted for this backlog of undecided petty litigation? Like the zemstvo leaders and justices who analyzed the phenomenon, the senators blamed it on the justices' confusion over their purpose and the procedures followed in rendering decisions, which was due to the instructions issued by the Senate Cassation Departments from 1867 on. Originally established as courts of reconciliation to render expedient justice at their own discretion, the justices increasingly fell under the purview of the Senate and the Ministry of Justice, and decided cases on the basis of the Judicial Statutes, the *Svod Zakonov*, legal precedents, and other criteria followed by the regular courts. To be sure, the justices' conflict with local police and peasant officials in getting subpoenas served and sentences enforced, not to mention zemstvo manipulation of the elected justices, contributed to the delays in deciding cases. But the formalism in *mirovoi* decision making clearly prevented the justices from keeping pace with the mass of undecided petty litigation, a fact that discredited the justices in the eyes of the provincial public and threatened the political order. Even the introduction by the zemstvos of a judicial duty (1877) on all cases submitted to the justices to reduce the influx of petty litigation and to subsidize the justices failed to stem the tide of cases (many of which were appealed to higher courts), and it proved only to be another unpopular tax.

The findings of the inspectors on the justices, along with other official reports, help explain why the reform of the *mirovoi* system became a lively topic of official and public debate in the 1880s quite apart from the autocracy's attack on other judicial institutions, most notably public jury trials, and the political designs of the minister of internal affairs to control all local

[122]TsGIA, *f.* Kakhanovskaia komissiia, *d.* 114, *ll.* 69 *ob.*-71 *ob.*

institutions. By the early 1880s, the government had two alternatives for reducing the quantity of unresolved petty litigation and reestablishing expedient and accessible justice for the rural population – prerequisites for building respect for autocracy in the countryside. It could either increase the number of justices of the peace in the section, which would entail additional expenses for the financially troubled zemstvos; or it could remove petty civil and criminal cases from the jurisdiction of the justices and turn them over exclusively to the *volost'* court or to a section chief, who would supervise peasant self-government and administer justice. As the following chapter shows, the most intense discussions in the Kakhanov Commission revolved around this issue.

Recommendations of the senatorial inspectors. In their investigations of local self-government in 1880–1, the senatorial inspectors provided an analysis of its shortcomings that was unprecedented in scope and depth. Their work revealed that, at the turn of the decade, local self-governing institutions suffered from serious administrative and fiscal problems that undermined the confidence of all social estates in them, and (for different reasons) required immediate solutions. Zemstvo publicist V. Iu. Skalon echoed the senators' conclusions in admitting in 1881–2 that

Never, it seems, has interest in the activity of [our] organs of public administration decreased to such an extent as now; never has [public] dissatisfaction with this activity reached such dimensions as in recent months. Russian society has seemingly lost faith in these institutions which alone serve as its representatives and alone are found under its direct influence. The abnormality in the state of the institutions is recognized by all; proposals for their reform are heard from all sides.[123]

But in proposing solutions to these problems, as Loris-Melikov had instructed them to do, the inspectors never questioned the usefulness of the reforms of 1861 and 1864 or the concepts of decentralization and public self-government, the efficacy of which, in their view, was fettered by ministerial conflicts (usually between local representatives of the Ministries of Internal Affairs, Justice, and Finance), arbitrary government interference, and vague legislation. Such a view was not surprising. During the previous two decades the four senators had worked in one capacity or another (for instance, as peace arbitrators, jurists, and senators) in implementing these reforms;[124] and Loris-Melikov himself had called for further decentralization prior to the beginning of these inspections. Perhaps most important, overwhelming numbers of zemstvo and gentry leaders supported these ideas. The senators thus reasoned that further decentralization and zemstvo (gentry) supervision over village self-government not only was consistent with their own views, but also

---

[123]Quoted in [Skalon], *Mneniia*, p. 1.
[124]For a social profile of the Senate in 1879, see I. V. Orzhekhovskii, *Iz istorii vnutrennei politiki samoderzhaviia v 60-70-kh godakh XIX veka* (Gor'kii, 1974), pp. 51-4.

was the most practical solution. It logically followed from their own paternalistic and rather patronizing view of the peasantry.

Unlike Polovtsov, who made a few technical suggestions for improving local self-government, Senators Kovalevskii, Shamshin, and Mordvinov presented concrete plans for reform.[125] Kovalevskii recommended establishing a *volost'* encompassing all social estates under zemstvo jurisdiction. He argued that the village community and *obshchina* currently managed all the economic and administrative affairs of the peasantry. These institutions should receive legal protection from government and zemstvo domination. Thus, the peasants at the village level were capable of governing themselves without outside supervision, an assertion based more on political conviction than the evidence collected. This argument distinguished Kovalevskii from all the other inspectors. As for the zemstvo, he proposed that its jurisdiction be expanded. Since he did not dwell on zemstvo institutions in his report, he did not offer more specific changes.[126]

Shamshin presented what amounted to a detailed and comprehensive plan to reform local peasant and zemstvo self-government. He argued much in the manner of zemstvo leaders that the current system suffered from administrative and political shortcomings: in the former case, the main problem was the lack of an executive agent for the zemstvo at the subdistrict level to implement its decisions; in the latter case, the political isolation of the zemstvo outside the state administration made cooperation with the local bureaucracy in daily work unlikely:

The need of the zemstvo to rely on the assistance of the police and the *volost'* administration at every step stems not only from the small number of zemstvo executive agents, but also from the general position of the zemstvo in our state system. The zemstvo is not established alongside the administration as much as it is placed in opposition to it. The law, *and even more actual practice*, are not as conducive to joint activity between the zemstvo and administration as the possibility for the former to exceed its authority or to be apathetic, and for the latter to frustrate or put pressure on the zemstvo. . . . The attempts at joint work rarely lead to the desired objective, because neither side is accustomed to viewing the other as a partner in general matters.[127]

Yet the senator rejected the idea of an all-estate *volost'* because, in his view, the prominent landlords would dominate the *volost'* assembly as they did the district assembly, while the peasants would shoulder the major share of taxes. Instead, he proposed the creation of a section chief elected by the district assembly to supervise peasant self-government on the grounds that

---

[125]For Polovtsov, see OR-GPBSS, *f.* Polovtsov, *d.* 1333, *ll.* 44–5.

[126]*MVUOK*, vol. 3, pt. 1: *Zapiski Kovalevskogo*, no. 1, pp. 4–7; Bol'shov, p. 49.

[127]Quoted from TsGIA, *f.* Kakhanovskaia komissiia, *op.* 1, *d.* 109, *l.* 73. Italics added. For a nearly identical statement, see the address of the Samara provincial zemstvo assembly commission (1881) in Skalon, *Zemskie vzgliady*, p. 32.

a section administrator, in enforcing instructions concerning zemstvo affairs and handling those matters which require on-the-spot supervision or enforcement, can be organized not only for zemstvo functions, but also for all administrative and some judicial activity. The combination of administrative and judicial functions in one administrator at the lower level will serve as the basis for merging the zemstvo and government. The combined activity on the one hand by the section officials, and on the other by the board members, will transform the zemstvo into a vital institution completely corresponding to its important purpose.[128]

In effect, Shamshin proposed to create an executive official at the subdistrict level who would implement all zemstvo and government orders, and thereby bridge the gap between public and state institutions. In doing so, he introduced another important concept of the Land Captain Reform – the combination of administrative and judicial powers in one official – into the government debate over local administrative reform.

At first glance, Shamshin's recommendations for a paternalistic section chief (and the concept of *edinonachalie*) appear to be nothing more than support for the zemstvo and gentry desire to play a greater role in local affairs.[129] Yet, as an administrative approach, *edinonachalie* offered numerous advantages over the existing district bureaus, especially in the state's perennial quest to strike a balance between local initiative and bureaucratic control in the provinces. As Hough shows in his study of local party officials in the Soviet period, *edinonachalie* does not mean unlimited personal authority. Rather, it is an approach to reduce bureaucratic formalism by granting the local manager wide authority to handle routine administrative matters while also requiring him to obey his superiors and holding him accountable for his actions.[130] To be sure, Soviet authorities have had greater means to police and discipline local officials than their tsarist predecessors; the point to emphasize, however, is that even in the early 1880s state and zemstvo officials advocating the introduction of section chiefs saw the need for some administrative control over them. At the same time, they agreed that on-the-spot supervision of peasant officials and broad powers for the section chiefs were the most expedient and effective way to curb anarchy in peasant administration. After all, the collegial decision-making process of the various bureaus existed largely in the law codes, not in actual local administration – one of many instances in which the principles of the Great Reforms had failed to take root in the countryside.[131]

To incorporate zemstvo institutions into the state apparatus, Shamshin

---

[128]Quoted from TsGIA, *f.* Kakhanovskaia komissiia, *d.* 109, *l.* 80 *ob.*

[129]Mandel, chap. 2.

[130]Hough, pp. 81–5. Hough claims that *edinonachalie* was introduced as a Soviet administrative approach in 1918, whereas Armstrong dates its beginning in 1920. Armstrong, *European Administrative Elite*, p. 265.

[131]Referring to statistics collected by the senatorial inspectors in the 1880s and the Ministry of Internal Affairs in the early 1900s, Robbins estimates that the Provincial Bureau (that assisted the governor) made only 2–5 percent of all its rulings based on genuine collegial examination and discussion. Robbins, "Viceroys," chap. 5.

proposed the creation of a district and provincial college consisting of elected zemstvo officials and personnel from the appropriate state ministries in matters under their jurisdiction. The colleges would reduce interministerial jurisdictional disputes and coordinate zemstvo and government activity in the district. The senator emphasized that, by establishing such colleges, the zemstvo would have power to issue mandatory regulations along with the executive authority to enforce them, because the colleges as state institutions would issue orders that the police would obey. Although Shamshin's innovation drew the support of Polovtsov (because it would reduce the number of state institutions at the provincial level), this point and several others in Shamshin's recommendation were opposed by Mordvinov. Specifically, the latter, in his plan, insisted that no changes be made in the organization of the zemstvos and that the section chiefs *not* have both administrative and judicial powers. Rather, he proposed that the section chief be elected by the zemstvo solely on the basis of educational qualifications and that he wield the same supervisory authority over the *volost'* administration as did the former peace arbitrators. Mordvinov's main suggestion to improve peasant administration entailed subdividing the current *volosti*, because his inspection of Voronezh and Tambov provinces revealed that most *volosti* were too large to be manageable. In some districts, such subdivisions already existed even though they were not sanctioned by law.[132]

In September 1881, Shamshin completed his inspection and submitted his report to Count Nikolai Pavlovich Ignat'ev, Loris-Melikov's successor as minister of internal affairs. In reviewing the report, the new emperor Alexander III lamented that the inspections revealed "a dreadful picture, although one not new," and that it deserved the attention of all ministers.[133] Mordvinov completed his report a month later and Kovalevskii finished the following spring. On the whole, the reports provided a distressing account of the Great Reforms in action, and accordingly the senators' perceptions of various local self-governing institutions hereafter provided the frame of reference for official reform discussions in this area in the 1880s. As Shamshin pointed out to State Secretary E. A. Peretts, chaos, laziness, apathy, and corruption characterized the provincial and district administration, and the reforms of the past reign, notwithstanding their benefits, required substantial changes. Peretts, who was impressed with Shamshin's analysis and conclusions, remarked that "the basic idea in all the [senatorial] memorandums is that we [our local government] suffer above all from inertia and a lack of skill, which can have very bad repercussions."[134] Yet substantive and expeditious reform of local self-government required interministerial cooperation and impe-

---

[132]For Polovtsov, see OR-GPBSS, *f.* Polovtsov, *op.* 1, *d.* 20, *ll.* 6 *ob.*-7; for Mordvinov, see TsGIA, *f.* Kakhanovskaia komissiia, *d.* 11, *ll.* 31-31 *ob.*, 363 *ob.*-364.

[133]Quoted from Polovtsov's diary entry for 21 September 1881 in TsGAOR, *f.* Polovtsov, *op.* 1, *d.* 20, *l.* 10.

[134]See the passages for 20 April and 13 October 1881 in *Dnevnik Perettsa*, pp. 62, 102.

rial support and, as analyzed below, dramatic and tragic events in 1881 would block Loris-Melikov's efforts to decentralize local self-government further.

Moment of opportunity: Loris-Melikov's "dictatorship" and local self-government reform

In recent years, Soviet and Western historians have written extensively about Loris-Melikov's "dictatorship of the heart" and his plans to establish his control over all ministries in the empire. Hence, we need not dwell at length on Loris-Melikov's background, his activity as head of the Supreme Executive Commission, or his political reform project of 1881 (and its defeat) — topics that are central to the recent studies of Zaionchkovskii, Solov'ev, Itenberg, and Orlovsky, among others. Rather, in the light of the official work on local self-government reform from 1877 to 1881 noted in the preceding section, it is important here to trace Loris-Melikov's impact on the traditional ministerial power balance at court and in the provinces, and his political evolution from a dictator in early 1880, who used his extraordinary power to coordinate state activity and quash revolutionaries, to the most powerful minister in Russia a year later. Such actions led some contemporaries and certain historians (especially Soviet scholars) to attribute all of his policies to personal ambition and to question the sincerity of his political convictions.[135] Yet for all of his egotism, Loris-Melikov sought as minister of internal affairs to go beyond Bonapartist gestures to win public support of the government. Indeed, the variety of practical reforms that he sponsored (in peasant redemption, various taxes, public education, local government), not to mention the extensive preparations that went into such measures, revealed Loris-Melikov's belief in the positive value of reform and of Russia's gradual evolution toward greater public participation in the administrative process. In this respect, his celebrated reform proposals of 28 January 1881 provided a framework for public involvement in the reform of local government and ushered in a new stage in government work on local self-government reform (that overlapped with the Kakhanov Commission's work in 1881–5). Officials and leading public figures (A. F. Koni, D. A. Miliutin, A. I. Koshelev, Professor A. D. Gradovskii) who adhered to Loris-Melikov's political views recognized this change in his priorities as minister of internal affairs and his aim to introduce reforms for years to come, although they were less cognizant of his ambition to act as a "prime minister."[136]

Historians generally concur that no official from 1855 to 1905 wielded as much power within the government as Loris-Melikov did in the year following his appointment on 8 February 1880 as dictator of the Supreme

[135]For a discussion of Loris-Melikov's "Bonapartist" policies, see Kheifets, *Vtoraia revoliutsionnaia situatsiia*, pp. 102, 191; and Itenberg, "Krizis samoderzhavnoi vlasti," p. 100.
[136]See A. F. Koni, "Graf M. T. Loris-Melikov," *Sobranie sochinenii*, 5: 194–6; and A. I. Koshelev, *Zapiski Aleksandra Ivanovicha Kosheleva (1812–1883 gody)* (Berlin, 1884), pp. 262–3.

Executive Commission – a year in which the traditional ministerial equilibrium was disrupted for two reasons.[137] Most important, Alexander II withdrew from active participation in state affairs. Hounded by would-be assassins (exemplified by S. N. Khal'turin's attempt to blow up the Winter Palace on 5 February 1880, which led to the establishment of the Supreme Executive Commission), distressed by his ministers' failure to agree on methods to eradicate the terrorists, and depressed by reports from the provinces documenting the shortcomings of the institutions created by his early reforms and the erosion of public support for autocracy, the tsar retreated to his estates at Tsarskoe Selo and Gatchina. Accordingly, Loris-Melikov had full latitude in devising administrative reform and in recommending changes in ministerial personnel in 1880–1 to make the government function efficiently and to preserve his leading role in the government during this crisis period.

By the same token, Alexander II's appointment of Loris-Melikov, an arrivé, as director of the Supreme Executive Commission, served notice to the ministers that the tsar would not tolerate the usual infighting and inertia during this emergency period. The son of an Armenian merchant in Tiflis, Loris-Melikov had distinguished himself by military service in the Caucasus during the Russo-Turkish War and by his success in eliminating the plague epidemic in the lower Volga while saving the government a considerable amount of money earmarked for this purpose. But his repression of terrorists and cultivation of public support for the government (a favorite tactic he employed as temporary governor-general in Khar'kov in 1879) was no doubt the main factor in his appointment. The sovereign gave Loris-Melikov virtually dictatorial powers to eradicate the revolutionary threat, and the latter appeared to be so successful in this respect that he proposed the closure of the commission five months later.[138]

Armed with extraordinary powers and confident of Alexander's complete backing, Loris-Melikov had every opportunity to accomplish his task and to lay the groundwork for his reform proposals. Yet it is a testament to his intelligence and political acumen that from the outset he secured the support of nearly all top officials of diverse views for his policies, when a tactical mistake or imperiousness on his part might well have eroded tsarist confidence in him. Naturally, the urgent circumstances surrounding Loris-Melikov's appointment made other high officials reluctant to complain to the tsar about his incursions on their jurisdictions. Nonetheless, the dictator sought to avoid such misunderstandings and personally solicited the support of the

---

[137] Orlovsky, *Limits of Reform*, p. 103.

[138] For background on Loris-Melikov's policies in Khar'kov and a detailed survey of his activities as director of the Supreme Executive Commission and as Minister of Internal Affairs, see ibid., pp. 170–80; and Zaionchkovskii, *Krizis samoderzhaviia*, pp. 116–378. Loris-Melikov's background in school and the army is described in N. A. Belogolovyi, *Vospominaniia i drugie stat'i* (4th ed.; St. Petersburg, 1901), pp. 156–93; on his work in the plague-stricken provinces, see A. F. Koni, *Sobranie sochinenii*, 5: 194–6; and *Dnevnik Miliutina*, 3: 113.

heir (who had convinced his father to establish the Supreme Executive Commission)[139] and other influential officials. For example, he advised the heir about the nature of his reform proposals before submitting them to the tsar, as illustrated by the series of letters he sent to Alexander Alexandrovich in 1880; and in September 1880 he sought the support of Konstantin Petrovich Pobedonostsev, the tsarevich's tutor and the ober prokuror of the Holy Synod appointed in April 1880, by assuring both the heir and Pobedonostsev that he would push for Podedonostsev's inclusion in the Committee of Ministers.[140] Loris-Melikov remained on good terms with both until July 1880, when he attended Alexander II's secret morganatic marriage to Princess E. M. Iur'evskaia, a match that the heir and Pobedonostsev bitterly opposed.[141]

The variety of methods that Loris-Melikov employed to maintain imperial favor and gain ministerial support – keys to substantial reform of local administration and public self-government – revealed that the parvenu Loris-Melikov learned quickly in the realm of court intrigue. For instance, he did not hesitate to flatter Alexander in his reports, referring to him as the tsar-emancipator and lauding his reforms of the 1860s as monumental achievements. Although this was the very legislation that required overhauling, as Loirs-Melikov made clear in the same reports, Alexander did not comment on the dictator's contradictory evaluations. But judging from these memoranda to the tsar, Loris-Melikov's favorite ploy was to remind the emperor of his progress in suppressing the revolutionaries and to warn that unless all his projects were implemented the terrorists would no doubt reappear in greater numbers. Not only did the crisis situation bring him to power; in addition, the government functioned with rare efficiency and cohesion during such periods, provided a powerful figure such as Loris-Melikov directed its activity.

Yet nothing demonstrated Loris-Melikov's authority more clearly than his ability to pressure other ministers into supporting his projects and, when necessary, securing the removal of those who did not cooperate. For example, on 11 April 1880 he urged Alexander II to dismiss Tolstoi as minister of education, because his harsh and inflexible policies and classical curriculum had alienated students, teachers, and parents. Two weeks later, Andrei Aleksandrovich Saburov, an official of little distinction, replaced Tolstoi in a move that evoked widespread public jubilation, but more important, gave Loris-Melikov the control over public education necessary to maintain domestic order (as shown by the enactment on 18 February 1881 of his proposal

---

[139]According to Itenberg, the heir got the idea of a dictatorship from Katkov; see Itenberg, "Krizis samoderzhavnoi vlasti," p. 99.

[140]See "Perepiska Aleksandra s M. T. Loris-Melikovym," pp. 101–31; Zaionchkovskii, *Krizis samoderzhaviia*, p. 232; and Koni, *Sobranie sochinenii*, 5: 190.

[141]See Polovtsov's diary passage for 18 December 1880 cited in Zaionchkovskii, *Krizis samoderzhaviia*, p. 234; also *Dnevnik Miliutina*, 4: 78; *Dnevnik Perettsa*, p. 5; and E. M. Feoktistov, *Vospominaniia E. M. Feoktistova. Za kulisami politiki i literatury*, ed. Iu. G. Oksman (Leningrad, 1929), pp. 196–7.

to legalize student meetings and to subordinate the inspectors of the Ministry of Education to the university rector).[142] Similarly, when Valuev and Makov intrigued against Loris-Melikov on the grounds that he had exceeded his powers, the dictator recommended the closing of the Supreme Executive Commission and the abolition of the Third Section. His intrigue against Valuev and Makov paid off when the emperor named Loris-Melikov to succeed Makov as minister of internal affairs in early August, and agreed with Loris-Melikov that new measures to reorganize state and public institutions were necessary to guarantee public support for the government.[143]

Consequently, by the time Loris-Melikov called for the senatorial inspections, he had control of all the key ministries in local government except finance, where his final and most startling coup came in October 1880. As we have seen, finance ministers had opposed Loris-Melikov's predecessors on rural administration and local government reform; the conflict between Finance Minister Greig (Reuter's successor in 1878) and Loris-Melikov occurred over the latter's proposal to abolish the odious salt tax for peasants in light of provincial food shortages. When Greig refused to give in, Loris-Melikov went so far as to denounce him to the emperor, to submit a memorandum calling for his dismissal, and to boast about the results. Loris-Melikov's willingness to use underhanded tactics against a fellow minister so violated the unwritten rules of ministerial behavior that State Secretary E. A. Peretts expressed shock.[144] But in another demonstration of imperial confidence, Alexander II appointed Loris-Melikov's choice, Aleksei Ageevich Abaza, as the new minister of finance. No sooner did Abaza take office than he received a list of guidelines from the tsar concerning the activity of the finance minister. Unsigned and dated only October 1880, the instructions probably were drafted by Loris-Melikov because they conformed to his ideas on economic policy, particularly in regard to alleviating the fiscal burdens of the peasants.[145] Thus, by holding his own ministerial post and by having supporters in other key ministries (among them Justice Minister Nabokov, a professional jurist appointed in 1878 and an advocate of independent courts, and War Minister Miliutin), Loris-Melikov seemed virtually assured of implementing his reform program as long as he held Alexander's trust. There is little evidence that his majesty's confidence in Loris-Melikov ever diminished or that Alexander II planned to return to his previous system of ministerial government in the foreseeable future. At last Loris-Melikov had in his hands the ministerial unity and auto-

[142]See "Konstitutiia grafa Loris-Melikova," pp. 157–8, 160; *Dnevnik Miliutina*, 3: 280; and G. I. Shchetinina, *Universitety v Rossii i ustav 1884 goda* (Moscow, 1976), pp. 92–5, 97.
[143]See the 28 September 1880 entry in *Dnevnik Perettsa*, pp. 1–2; and Zaionchkovskii, *Krizis samoderzhaviia*, pp. 222–5.
[144]See the entry for 21 October 1880 in *Dnevnik Perettsa*, p. 7.
[145]Zaionchkovskii, *Krizis samoderzhaviia*, p. 252.

cratic support required to overhaul local self-government and establish his ministry as the linchpin in the process.

Local self-government was an area of special concern in Loris-Melikov's reform plans, as he pointed out in discussions in September 1880 with editors of the leading newspapers in St. Petersburg. His arguments reveal his conviction that the time was ripe for reforms not solely to galvanize public support for the regime, but, more important, to make the governing apparatus more efficient, which in turn would raise public confidence in the autocracy. He had first outlined his zemstvo reform program in May 1880 in a letter to Makov, then the minister of internal affairs, and emphasized the need to take measures that showed the government's concern for the estates of the realm and public institutions. In addition, he urged the revision of separate provisions of the 1864 Zemstvo Statute and advised Makov to send a list of questions concerning local government reforms that could be discussed in zemstvo assemblies which would then submit their comments to a government commission. Actually, it was Loris-Melikov who sent these lists to the zemstvos on 22 December in his circular to the governors.[146] As a regular minister, Loris-Melikov stressed the need for increased public participation and administrative decentralization in order to make government more systematic. His military and administrative experience in the Caucasus and in the provinces convinced him that the local public, especially the landed gentry, could manage their own affairs without being under the watchful eye of St. Petersburg.

With this in mind, Loris-Melikov drafted his proposal of 28 January 1881 to invite zemstvo representatives to participate in the discussions of reforms in local administration. Although contemporaries, publicists, and scholars subsequently called the project Loris-Melikov's "constitution," it bore little resemblance to one. In fact, prior to the confusion and near hysteria in state circles following the assassination of Alexander II, few officials viewed the project as anything close to a constitution; only in the aftermath of that event did the opponents of public self-government and officials seeking to ingratiate themselves with the new sovereign utter the frightening word "constitution" in order to induce Alexander III to reject Loris-Melikov's proposals and, in effect, restore the traditional ministerial power balance that characterized the earlier years of Alexander II's reign. Loris-Melikov's project was certainly more limited in scope than the projects resubmitted a year earlier by Valuev

---

[146]TsGAOR, *f.* Loris-Melikov, 1880, *op.* 1, *d.* 54, *ll.* 3 *ob.*-7 *ob.* The list of questions drawn up by Makov is found in ibid., *d.* 63, *ll.* 3–15 *ob.* The questions were essentially those raised by zemstvo assemblies in their petitions of the late 1870s and early 1880s. The 22 December 1880 circular to the governors is published in *Sbornik tsirkuliarov ministerstva vnutrennikh del za 1880–1884 gg.*, comp. D. V. Chichinadze (St. Petersburg, 1886), pp. 106–7, 133–9. For an account of Loris-Melikov's policy on local self-government reform that emphasizes his political considerations, see Orlovsky, *Limits of Reform*, pp. 176–7, 189–91.

and Grand Duke Konstantin Nikolaevich, both of which aimed to call to arms the conservative forces of the empire and to satisfy the desire of educated society to participate in the administration (by including public representatives in the State Council).[147] The Special Conference of ministers called in late January 1880 voted down both proposals following Tsarevich Alexander Alexandrovich's condemnation of Western-type constitutions. As for Loris-Melikov's proposal, it is especially revealing that once the initial shock and grief following Alexander II's assassination dissipated, Alexander III's government discussed projects for local administration reform in the Kakhanov Commission along the very guidelines specified by Loris-Melikov in his 28 January memorandum.

Determined to implement his project as a second step in local government reform, Loris-Melikov took pains in 1880 and early 1881 to convince the heir that he, too, opposed Western constitutions and parliaments, and that he desired only to give zemstvo representatives a consultative voice on proposals to reform local self-government. He assured Alexander II and his son that he opposed any political reforms along Western lines, European-type national assemblies, or the convocation of a Russian *zemskii sobor*.[148] Rather, his proposal in 1881 for a limited degree of public participation in the local self-government reform process was modeled on a plan drafted in 1879 by M. S. Kakhanov, a former governor of Pskov Province and the current deputy minister of internal affairs (and, along with S. S. Perfil'ev, one of Loris-Melikov's confidants within that ministry).[149] The memorandum began with a summary of Loris-Melikov's activity as the director of the Supreme Executive Commission and minister of internal affairs to eliminate terrorism, and then outlined his reform plan. Loris-Melikov wrote that the senatorial inspections were providing much material on conditions and local needs in the provinces, along with suggestions on possible reforms. However, such evidence, he maintained, would be insufficient without the practical counsel of local experts. He advocated the formation of two preparatory commissions (one dealing with administrative-economic affairs and the other with financial matters) modeled on the Editorial Commissions of 1859–60. These com-

---

[147]TsGIA, *f.* Golovnin, *op.* 1, *d.* 16, *ll.* 3–3 *ob.* For a similar interpretation, see Whelan, pp. 35, 37. For details on the proposals of Valuev and Grand Duke Konstantin and on the Special Conference's discussions of them, see Valuev, *Dnevnik 1877–1884 gg.*, pp. 38–40, 50–4; *Dnevnik Miliutina*, 3: 187; and Zaionchkovskii, *Krizis samoderzhaviia*, pp. 137–46. Besides Valuev and Grand Duke Konstantin, the participants in the conference were the heir, Prince Urusov, Makov, and Aleksandr Romanovich Drentel'n, the chief of the Third Section. According to Valuev, the heir's criticisms turned Makov and Prince Urusov from supporters to opponents of the reform.

[148]See the entries for 21 October and 10 November 1880 in *Dnevnik Perettsa*, pp. 8, 10, 11; "Konstitutsiia grafa Loris-Melikova," p. 159; Zaionchkovskii, *Krizis samoderzhaviia*, pp. 235–6, 260–1; and Orlovsky, *Limits of Reform*, pp. 185–6, who argues that Loris-Melikov's goal was "to redesign autocratic politics and alter the traditional ministerial power ethos without threatening Alexander. Thus the myth of autocracy had to be maintained long enough to institutionalize the elements necessary for renovations."

[149]See Polovtsov's diary entry for 4 February 1882, which reveals that Kakhanov drafted the plan following the assassination of Gendarmes' Chief Nikolai Vladimirovich Mezentsov by the Populists on 4 April 1879. TsGAOR, *f.* Polovtsov, *op.* 1, *d.* 20, *ll.* 47 *ob.*-48. On Perfil'ev and Kakhanov as Loris-Melikov's confidants, see Orlovsky, *Limits of Reform*, p. 185.

missions, in dealing with two vital areas of local self-government, would consist of central government representatives, the four senatorial inspectors, and of imperially invited local experts known for their scholarly work or practical experience in the areas of local administration. The tsar would appoint the chairman of each commission, which would draft projects for local administrative reform on the basis of the materials furnished by the senatorial inspections and the government chancelleries. The administrative-economic commission would concern itself with such practical needs as provincial administrative reform, updating the 19 February 1861 peasant statute, mandatory peasant redemption, revitalizing the zemstvo and municipal institutions, organizing public food supply, and designing measures to protect cattle breeding.[150]

A General Commission under an imperially appointed chairman and consisting of the members of the Preparatory Commissions along with elected representatives from the provincial zemstvos and several significant cities, would review the projects drafted by the Preparatory Commissions. Loris-Melikov emphasized that the participation of zemstvo delegates as members of the Preparatory Commissions would furnish the government with a grass-roots view of local needs and concrete suggestions for fulfilling them. Projects approved or corrected by the General Commission would then be submitted to the State Council, along with the opinions of the appropriate ministers. Loris-Melikov suggested that the emperor might order ten to fifteen public representatives to sit in the State Council with the right to vote. They would be imperially appointed on the basis of their practical knowledge, outstanding abilities, and presumably their loyalty to the government. Both the Preparatory Commissions and General Commission would consider only the business presented to them by the government, and the General Commission would meet at the sovereign's pleasure for no more than two months at a time.[151]

In essence, although his reform plan curried public support by giving educated society a way to participate in political life (Kakhanov's aim in 1879),[152] not to mention that it offered means to revitalize the ministerial bureaucracy, Loris-Melikov's main objective was much simpler – to gain the advice of representatives from local self-governing institutions on the material gathered by the senatorial inspectors. As such, the establishment of such commissions signified a second step in his plan to reactivate local self-government and a logical corollary to state initiatives taken in local self-government reform from 1877 on. In his memorandum he emphasized that his proposals to allow public participation in the Preparatory and General

---

[150]See the 28 January 1881 memorandum in Bermanskii, "Konstitutsionnye proekty," pp. 284–91. It is translated into English in Marc Raeff, ed., *Plans for Political Reform in Imperial Russia, 1730–1905* (Englewood Cliffs, N.J., 1966), pp. 132–40.

[151]Bermanskii, pp. 288–9.

[152]This is the contention of Orlovsky, *Limits of Reform*, p. 191; and Yaney, *Urge to Mobilize*, p. 69, who argues that the project proposed to increase the gentry's responsibility for local self-government.

Commissions had nothing in common with Western constitutional forms, and many of his fellow officials agreed. Peretts, a confidant of Grand Duke Konstantin Nikolaevich, maintained that Loris-Melikov's proposal fell far short of introducing the permanent public representation in the State Council that Grand Duke Konstantin and Valuev advocated in their projects. Valuev dismissed the proposal as "a monument of intellectual and moral mediocrity" filled with course flattery of the tsar.[153]

The proposal evoked little criticism in the Special Conference sessions held in February 1881 because prior to the Special Conference meetings, the participants of which included the heir, Grand Duke Konstantin, Loris-Melikov, Prince Urusov, Valuev, Nabokov, Abaza, and Count Aleksandr Vladimirovich Adlerberg (minister of the imperial household), the minister of internal affairs secured the tsarevich's approval of the proposal. Loris-Melikov apparently convinced the heir that the proposal lacked constitutional implications, because the latter raised no objections of this nature in the conference sessions.[154] In addition, the absence of Pobedonostsev, a notorious opponent of reform, was conspicuous. The other participants were by and large sympathetic to the stipulations of the project, although they made two important changes. They deleted the most controversial provision of the project, which called for the appointment of public representatives with voting rights to the State Council. Second, they noted that the details of the project concerning the General Commission required further elaboration. On 17 February 1881, Alexander II signed the conference journal and ordered that the project be implemented. He also authorized Loris-Melikov to draw up a project for the announcement of the reform.[155]

Although the assassination of Alexander II on 1 March 1881 disproved Loris-Melikov's claim that the police had handcuffed the revolutionary terrorists, it alone did not precipitate his downfall, nor rule out his approach to local self-government reform. Neither was Pobedonostsev's influence on the new tsar the primary factor, despite the fact that the synod chief raised the main challenge to Loris-Melikov's authority in the turbulent weeks following the assassination. In the immediate aftermath, Alexander III staunchly resisted Pobedonostsev's appeals to replace Loris-Melikov.[156]

---

[153]*Dnevnik Perettsa*, p. 21; and Valuev, *Dnevnik 1877–1884 gg.*, p. 142.

[154]Loris-Melikov had so convinced him of the harmlessness of the proposal that the tsarevich was shocked on 1 March 1881 when he heard his father refer to it as the first step toward a constitution. The shock was compounded by events later that day that brought Alexander III to power. In recalling the events surrounding Alexander II's assassination, Miliutin wrote on 4 July 1881 that the tsar's words made an indelible impression on his son. No doubt he felt that Loris-Melikov had deceived him, a feeling that grew in view of Loris-Melikov's behavior in the weeks following the assassination. See *Dnevnik Miliutina*, 4: 96–7.

[155]TsGAOR, *f.* Loris-Melikov, 1881, *op.* 1, *d.* 97, *ll.* 1–6.

[156]Feoktistov, p. 198.

Historians have offered a variety of reasons to explain Loris-Melikov's downfall. For instance, Hans Heilbronner attributes it not to Alexander II's assassination as much as Pobedonostsev's intriguing, especially in his 6 March 1881 letter to Alexander III. See Hans Heilbronner, "Alexander III and the Reform Plan of Loris-Melikov," *Journal of Modern History*, no. 4 (1961): 386. In contrast, Veselovskii

Rather, in the wake of Alexander II's death, Loris-Melikov, eager to protect his reform projects and his favored position within the ministerial system, committed a number of blunders that undermined Alexander III's confidence in him. The climate of shock, sorrow, and alarm that prevailed in ministerial circles following the assassination gave Loris-Melikov's political opponents an excellent opportunity to turn the tsar against Loris-Melikov's ministerial system and his reform proposal by distorting and exaggerating its political significance.

First, Loris-Melikov, overestimating Pobedonostsev's influence over the tsar and fearing that it would grow, tried to pressure Alexander III into adhering to his father's will. Immediately after the assassination, the emperor was willing to accept Loris-Melikov's project as the legacy of his father, and directed the minister of internal affairs to prepare the original announcement project for publication. But on 3 March he changed his mind (probably persuaded by Pobedonostsev's letter on that day urging the tsar to be firm in his will)[157] and he ordered Loris-Melikov to rewrite the announcement of the project in light of recent events.[158] The new tsar resented his minister's attempt to ram his project through in the confusion that prevailed immediately after 1 March. Consequently, he gave copies of the reform proposal and announcement project to Pobedonostsev and Sergei Grigor'evich Stroganov, the two leading opponents of such reforms, for criticism and invited them to attend the 8 March meeting of the Council of Ministers.[159] In effect, the Loris-Melikov system, as opposed to his approach to local administration reform, was already under attack, because the new tsar decided to intervene directly in state politics, at least in these first weeks, and to reopen the question of reform. His invitation to Pobedonostsev and Stroganov was reminiscent of the tactics used by his father in disposing of Valuev's reform project in 1863 and 1880, and showed that Loris-Melikov would receive no

argues that the assassination of Alexander II signified the turning point to reaction. See Veselovskii, *Istoriia zemstva*, 3: 264–5. Recent works, particularly by Soviet scholars, maintain that the government's position remained ambiguous, with the period of 8 March to 29 April 1881 representing the climax of the autocratic crisis. According to this interpretation, first developed by Iu. V. Got'e, the conflict between the "liberal" faction (led by Loris-Melikov) and the "reactionaries" (led by Pobedonostsev) paralyzed the government until the last week of April, when Pobedonostsev exerted the decisive influence over Alexander III. Thus, Loris-Melikov's policies had a chance for adoption until the spokesmen for traditional personal autocracy prevailed over the liberals (or those ministers who defended the principles of the Great Reforms). See Iu. V. Got'e, "Bor'ba pravitel'stvennykh gruppirok i manifest 29 aprelia 1881 g.," *Istoricheskie zapiski*, 2 (1938): pp. 287–99; Zaionchkovskii, *Krizis samoderzhaviia*, pp. 333–4; Tvardovskaia, *Ideologiia poreformennogo samoderzhaviia*, pp. 205–9; Itenberg, "Krizis samoderzhavnoi vlasti," pp. 110–17; Rogger, *Russia in the Age of Modernisation and Revolution*, pp. 6–7.

[157] *Pis'ma K. P. Pobedonostseva k Aleksandru III* (2 vols.; Moscow, 1925), 1: 315.

[158] "Konstitutsiia grafa Loris-Melikova," p. 137; and *Dnevnik Miliutina*, 4: 28.

[159] In his 3 March 1881 letter to E. F. Tiutcheva, Pobedonostsev vented his irritation with Loris-Melikov for being excluded from the Special Conference sessions on the reform project. During February 1881, the tsarevich had asked Loris-Melikov to send a copy of his project to Pobedonostsev. Loris-Melikov failed to do so, and finally, on 6 March, Alexander III personally had to deliver a copy to Pobedonostsev. See "Pervye nedeli tsarstvovaniia imperatora Aleksandra Tret'ego: Pis'ma K. P. Pobedonostseva iz Peterburga k E. F. Tiutchevoi, 1881," *Russkii arkhiv*, no. 5 (1907): p. 90.

special imperial favor among ministers. In short, the death of Alexander II paved the way for a return to the previous system of ministerial government with ministers competing for favored status with the tsar — an arrangement that had adverse ramifications for local government reform.

Second, Loris-Melikov defended his project poorly at the Council of Ministers meeting against the criticisms of Pobedonostsev, Stroganov, Makov, and others. The tsar shocked Loris-Melikov and the supporters of his project by announcing at the start of the meeting that the outcome of the project had not been decided. He then instructed Loris-Melikov to read his reform proposal and revised announcement project. Rather than rewrite the initial project, Loris-Melikov merely had crossed out the words "Sovereign Emperor" and replaced them with "Deceased Emperor." He also had added an appendix that stated Alexander III's determination to execute his father's will and implement the reform as a dignified farewell of Alexander II to his people.[160] Consequently, Loris-Melikov read a document filled with embarrassing references to the deceased emperor. The reading made a bad impression on nearly all the participants at the meeting, some of whom — for example, Makov — used the occasion to settle old scores with Loris-Melikov. Pobedonostsev was especially incensed at Loris-Melikov for shamelessly reiterating the arguments he used before 1 March — namely that tranquility reigned and treason had been crushed.[161] According to Miliutin, the reading opened the way for Pobedonostsev's impassioned attack on the "constitutional" aspects of Loris-Melikov's reform plan (specifically, institutionalized public consultation in the reform process), Alexander II's reforms in general, and on the entire basis of European civilization, which he discerned in all the reform projects.[162] It was largely Pobedonostsev's speech *and* Loris-Melikov's poor defense that influenced Alexander III to postpone further consideration of reform for the time being.

The outcome of the 8 March meeting unnerved Loris-Melikov, Miliutin, Abaza, and other supporters of the reform plan. A month later (12 April

---

[160]TsGAOR, *f*. Aleksandr III, 1881, *op*. 1, *d*. 528, *ll*. 1–9 *ob*. A printed version is found in "Konstitutsiia grafa Loris-Melikova," pp. 177–80.

[161]See Pobedonostsev's letter of 11 March 1881 to Tiutcheva in "Pervye nedeli tsarstvovaniia," p. 94.
    Space limitations preclude a detailed review of the Council of Ministers' meeting of 8 March 1881. A nearly verbatim account of the discussion, along with the tsar's sarcastic comments during Loris-Melikov's reading, is found in *Dnevnik Peretsa*, pp. 31–46. Other accounts by participants in the meeting are contained in Valuev, *Dnevnik 1877–1884 gg.*, pp. 151–7; and *Dnevnik Miliutina*, 4: 32–7. Loris-Melikov's version, which erroneously claimed that the tsar accepted the view of the majority of the participants and supported the reform proposal, is published in "Gosudarstvennoe zasedanie 8 marta 1881 goda," *Russkii arkhiv*, no. 7 (1906): pp. 445–8.

[162]Miliutin added that during Pobedonostsev's speech it was difficult for many of those present to conceal their irritation at several statements of the "reactionary fanatic." See *Dnevnik Miliutina*, 4: 35. Valuev simply termed the oration "impossible," as noted in Valuev, *Dnevnik 1877–1884 gg.*, p. 152. Nonetheless, contemporaries and historians have generally agreed that Pobedonostsev's speech was the turning point of the 8 March meeting and that it made an enormous impression on nearly all present, particularly the emperor. See *Dnevnik Peretsa*, p. 40; and Robert F. Byrnes, *Pobedonostsev: His Life and Thought* (Bloomington, Ind., 1968), pp. 155–6.

1881), Loris-Melikov submitted a report that sought to salvage his plan for local administrative reform by playing down its political significance. For instance, his report called for public participation in the reform process but did not specify what forms it should take; and he reemphasized the need to reform the 27 June 1874 statute and the 1864 zemstvo legislation. These proposals were the means by which Loris-Melikov hoped to reunify the government and reassert his control over state policies. Having held a preeminent position among top officials, and being shrewd enough to recognize it as necessary for his long-range reform plans, Loris-Melikov could not accept his demotion to a position of equality with other ministers. By 1 April 1881, however, Valuev perceived that "Michel I" was dethroned, and that there was no unity in the government. After 8 March, Pobedonostsev increasingly took over as the major figure in making appointments; for example, he was responsible for replacing Loris-Melikov's choice, Saburov, as minister of education with Baron Aleksandr Pavlovich Nikolai. Equally telling, given Loris-Melikov's evident loss of power, Miliutin hastily drafted his own proposals on local administration reform in April 1881. He pointed out that the peasant question was the first priority of state business and that the zemstvo had to assist the government in legislative work in order to enable the bureaucracy to ascertain local needs and coordinate its reforms with local conditions.[163]

The showdown between the Loris-Melikov and Pobedonostsev factions occurred at a meeting of ministers at Gatchina on 21 April. Recognizing that he no longer was the leading minister, Loris-Melikov agreed with Abaza's suggestion to form a cabinet of ministers to counter Pobedonostsev's growing influence and to restore the unity within government that had all but vanished in the weeks following Alexander II's death. According to Peretts, Finance Minister Abaza reminded the Gatchina conference participants of the dangers that the return of the traditional ministerial power ethos posed for future reform:

Count Loris-Melikov and certain other ministers correctly note that we suffer from an absence of unity in administration. Each of our ministries virtually considers itself a separate state. Very frequently one does not know what the other is undertaking; not only can one not always count on the help of his colleagues, but from some of them you meet opposition. The result of this is complete discord. The objective pursued by the government is not achieved. Such a state of government is impossible. Society does not have the necessary confidence in government; more to the point, one can say that society does not trust the government.[164]

---

[163]"Konspekt rechi D. A. Miliutina: Mysli, nabrosannye na sluchae novogo soveshchaniia," *Vsesoiuznaia biblioteka im. V. I. Lenina. Zapiski Otdela rukopisei*, vol. 2 (Moscow, 1939), pp. 26–39. For Valuev's comments on Loris-Melikov's status, see Valuev, *Dnevnik 1877–1884 gg.*, pp. 151, 160. The text of Loris-Melikov's 12 April 1881 report is found in "Konstitutsiia grafa Loris-Melikova," pp. 180–3.
[164]Quoted from *Dnevnik Perettsa*, p. 64.

There is little doubt that top officials saw the need for a cabinetlike institution at the turn of the decade to promote state coordination, and in fact the government never came closer during Alexander III's reign to establishing such a system. At the 21 April meeting, the tsar consented to the formation of a cabinet in accordance with the plan of Abaza, Miliutin, and Loris-Melikov. But Alexander was not serious in his commitment, and privately he fumed about the three ministers in his letters to Pobedonostsev. Seizing a golden opportunity to undermine Loris-Melikov and his supporters once and for all while strengthening his own position with the tsar, Pobedonostsev drafted a manifesto signed by Alexander III on 29 April 1881. It proclaimed the inviolability of autocracy and led to the resignations of Loris-Melikov and Abaza the next day, and Miliutin three weeks later.[165] Although the manifesto is usually remembered for bringing down Loris-Melikov and for signifying tsardom's victory over legal bureaucracy, its exaltation of central authority also signaled Alexander III's determination to extirpate anarchy (*bezvlastie*) in the countryside and reforge the bond between tsar and *narod*.[166]

Six days later, Pobedonostsev's choice for minister of internal affairs, Count N. P. Ignat'ev, succeeded Loris-Melikov. But Ignat'ev, a Slavophile, soldier, and diplomat who helped negotiate the San Stefano and Berlin Peace treaties at the end of the Russo-Turkish War, soon disillusioned his patron. In a circular sent to the provincial governors on 6 May, he stressed the need to restore order and the authority of the local institutions created by Alexander II. The memorandum ended with Ignat'ev's promise that the rights and autonomy granted to the zemstvo and municipal institutions would remain inviolable. In short, the circular signified a continuation of Loris-Melikov's policies toward local self-government, and was hailed accordingly in the editorials of *Zemstvo* and other "liberal" newspapers. More important, along with a second circular on 22 May, it underscored the government's commitment to eradicate the disorder in village administration, taxation, and economy.[167]

Like Loris-Melikov, Ignat'ev proposed to invite local experts to participate with government officials in discussing important issues such as methods to

---

[165]On the 21 April 1881 meeting at Gatchina, see *Dnevnik Miliutina*, 4: 56–7; and *Dnevnik Perettsa*, pp. 62–6. Alexander III attacked the tactics of Loris-Melikov, Abaza, and Miliutin in his letter of 21 April to Pobedonostsev. See *K. P. Pobedonostsev i ego korrespondenty*, vol. 1, pt. 1: *Pis'ma i zapiski* (Moscow-Petrograd, 1923), p. 49. In his letters of 23, 25, and 26 April, Pobedonostsev urged the tsar to declare his resolution to uphold autocracy. He claimed that only insane Russians wanted a constitution, clearly implying Loris-Melikov, Abaza, and Miliutin. According to Pobedonostsev, a tsarist manifesto would stifle the rumors disseminated by the liberal press in St. Petersburg that a constitution for Russia was imminent. *Pis'ma Pobedonostseva k Aleksandru III*, 1: 332. For the manifesto itself, see *PSZ*, 3d ser., vol. 1, no. 138, 29 April 1881.

In his resignation letter (29 April 1881), Loris-Melikov cited poor health as the reason for stepping down. Alexander III replied in a letter that the government had parted completely from Loris-Melikov's views. For the pertinent correspondence see "Perepiska Aleksandra III s Loris-Melikovym," pp. 127–8.

[166]Rogger makes this point in *Russia*, p. 3.

[167]Zaionchkovskii, *Krizis samoderzhaviia*, pp. 385–6; Itenberg, "Krizis samoderzhavnoi vlasti," p. 116.

reduce arrears in redemption payments. The first group of thirteen local experts arrived in St. Petersburg in the second half of May 1881. They were gentry marshals and zemstvo leaders distinguished by their opposition to reform. In September 1881, a second delegation of thirty-two local experts came to the capital to discuss the opening of taverns and the resettlement of peasants. Although these discussions produced no concrete results, the fact that local representatives were invited demonstrated a continuity between the Loris-Melikov and Ignat'ev administrations that, notwithstanding the adoption of the repressive police regulations of 14 August 1881, zemstvo and municipal leaders recognized.[168] In his diary entry for 17 November 1881, Peretts noted that Ignat'ev had just sent a circular to the governors that Loris-Melikov could have signed, and that Pobedonostsev was furious over it.[169]

Yet Ignat'ev followed quite a different approach in dealing with zemstvo petitions. He complained that the zemstvo assemblies had abused the offer made to them in the 22 December 1880 circular and had raised national political issues in their replies. The zemstvos frequently had exceeded their jurisdiction in past petitions, he contended, but government reprimands or punishments had led to the participation of even worse elements in the zemstvo assemblies. Consequently, following a petition from the Tver' provincial assembly in 1881 for a national assembly of popularly elected representatives, Ignat'ev ordered the governors to shelve rather than to veto such petitions. He claimed that this method would eliminate the raucous discussions in the zemstvo assemblies which followed gubernatorial vetoes.[170]

This episode notwithstanding, however, Ignat'ev generally adhered to Loris-Melikov's policy toward local self-governing institutions, as illustrated by his decision to institute the Kakhanov Commission and his arguments in favor of expanding the sphere of zemstvo activity in his circulars to the governors. Significantly, Alexander III (and Pobedonostsev) tolerated Ignat'ev as minister (despite his reputation as an intriguer with other ministers)[171] until he presented his ill-fated plan to create a *zemskii sobor* in April 1882. The proposal had no relation to his zemstvo policy or to the work of the Kakhanov Commission; and Alexander, following a meeting on 26 May with Pobedonostsev, Ignat'ev, Reutern (the new chairman of the Committee of Ministers), Mikhail Nikolaevich Ostrovskii (the new minister of state properties), and Ivan Davidovich Delianov (the new minister of education), decided that Ignat'ev had to go.[172] Four days later, Count D. A. Tolstoi, a bureaucrat with fundamentally different political views on the relationship

---

[168]Veselovskii, *Istoriia zemstva*, 3: 267–75.

[169]*Dnevnik Perettsa*, p. 107.

[170]Zaionchkovskii, *Krizis samoderzhaviia*, pp. 434–5, 490–3.

[171]For instance, see Feoktistov, p. 199.

[172]The most detailed published account of the 26 May 1882 meeting is Ostrovskii's version, found in ibid., pp. 204–11. See also *Pis'ma Pobedonostseva k Aleksandru III*, 1 : 385. On Ignat'ev's plan for a *zemskii sobor*, which is not directly pertinent to this study, see Zaionchkovskii, *Krizis samoderzhaviia*, pp. 450–67.

of autocracy and public institutions, replaced Ignat'ev as minister of internal affairs.

Ignat'ev's dismissal had profound implications for the course of local self-government reform. For the time being, it ended a process that had begun in 1877 under Timashev, in which the ministers of internal affairs (with the exception of Makov) were initiators in state circles of local government reform. Loris-Melikov and Ignat'ev were, in particular, champions of decentralized local administration and public self-government. Although Tolstoi's position on local self-government reform in 1882 was not immediately apparent, not even the most optimistic partisans of self-government saw him as a spearhead for their reform ideas in the manner of Loris-Melikov or even Ignat'ev. Their fears, as shown in the following chapters, proved well-founded, if not immediately realized.

This lengthy chapter began with a discussion of historians' views on the crisis of autocracy and the relationship between developments in the capital and countryside from 1875 to 1881. By way of conclusion, let us summarize the main arguments in this chapter and raise the issues in local self-government reform that preoccupied Alexander III's bureaucracy. The standard interpretation is that the crisis of autocracy began in 1878 with the revolutionary attacks on state officials, reached a climax with the assassination of Alexander II and the defeat of Loris-Melikov's reform plan, and ended with Tolstoi's appointment in 1882. In terms of revolutionary activity against the regime, this interpretation is quite valid. However, as this chapter has shown, the government faced a more pervasive crisis of authority in the countryside that intensified in the mid-1870s and grew throughout the 1880s and 1890s, a crisis measured not by peasant disturbances as much as by the mismanagement and unpopularity of peasant self-government, the excessive arrears in state and zemstvo taxes, the widespread food shortages and epidemics (and the failure of local zemstvo and peasant institutions to provide relief), and the conflict between local police and zemstvos. To be sure, the terms *bezvlastie* and *mnogovlastie* were conveniently ambiguous labels for officials and publicists to attack local self-government and advocate particularistic (ministerial, gentry) solutions. Nevertheless, these terms were fitting descriptions of the nature of local self-government, which to many peasants meant more taxes, more food shortages, and more opportunities for the wealthy peasants at the expense of the whole community. To many gentry, local self-government signified an opportunity to stave off impoverishment or, for those who took public service seriously, frustration in organizing public services due to official resistance, revenue shortages, and peasant suspicion of outsiders. Indeed, the attitude of many in the countryside regarding local self-government in the early 1880s was summed up in the words of K. F. Golovin, a well-informed spokesman for the gentry: "There are too many authorities and too little authority."[173] The autocratic crisis, at least as it pertained to local government, furnished telling proof that the Great Reforms had not succeeded in practice in bringing a new legal order to the countryside, decentralizing administration, or mobilizing public participation in self-government – the keys to state control over the provinces. On the contrary, the crisis in local government continued to grow, in contrast to the temporary demise of revolutionary terrorism in the 1880s, and state and public officials emphasized that it threatened to deprive tsarism of peasant and gentry support.

By the same token, the government's policy to reform local self-government did not originate with Loris-Melikov in 1880 or represent a political gesture to wean public support from the revolutionaries. Loris-Melikov's policies (especially the senatorial inspections and political reform plan of 1881) were a logical step, following the piecemeal legislation of 1877–9, to restore administrative order and fiscal responsibility in local self-government. The revolutionary terrorism and ministerial conflict that brought Loris-Melikov to power in 1880 were important in convincing the government to undertake a comprehensive reform of local self-government, as opposed to a series of deliberate, piecemeal reforms; but these events were more the catalyst than the cause of local self-government reform in the 1880s. The escalation of revolutionary terror likewise provided Loris-Melikov with a rare opportunity to establish himself as Alexander II's "first minister," remove traditional ministerial opponents who had thwarted local government reorganization, and bring the local educated population more vigorously into rural administration. In this respect, the assassination of Alexander II was critical because, under Alexander III, the traditional system of ministerial government was quickly reestablished. Following Loris-Melikov's fall, ministers pursued separate and often contradictory objectives, as evidenced in one case by the conflict between Tolstoi and Nikolai Khristoforovich Bunge, Abaza's successor as finance minister (1882–7), over the economic development of the countryside; meanwhile, Pobedonostsev attacked the idea of reform altogether. The situation again required the tsar to take an active role in state politics in order to coordinate state policy, and Alexander III, who had an intuitive distrust for bureaucracy and legal administration, began his reign ready to do his part.

Despite these changes in ministerial politics, the government's commitment to reform local administration outlasted Loris-Melikov, Ignat'ev, and the last vestiges of *Narodnaia volia* by nearly a decade. More than ever the government recognized the need to solve the administrative and fiscal problems of local self-government, to transmit its authority to the rural village, and to reassure peasants and gentry alike. These officials in St. Petersburg recognized that terrorist attacks against state officials were symptomatic of

[173]K. F. Golovin, *Nashe mestnoe upravlenie i mestnoe predstavitel'stvo* (St. Petersburg, 1884), p. 6.

a larger administrative crisis that enveloped the local self-governing institutions (and to a lesser extent the local state bureaucracy) hampered by insolvency, absence of supervision, and lack of executive authorities. By the late 1870s, local peasant and zemstvo institutions, short of extraordinary efforts by their officials, were virtually incapable of functioning efficiently, and almost all state ministers and public officials agreed on the urgency of reform. But as Chapters 4–7 show, they clashed over the methods to reform them.

CHAPTER 4

The debate revived: state, social change, and ideologies of local self-government reform, 1881–5

In its predominantly bureaucratic composition and in its method of activity, the Kakhanov Commission, established in 1881 to draft reform projects for local administration, differed little from previous legislative commissions in nineteenth-century Russia. Yet owing to recent court politics and the deepening administrative and economic crisis in the provinces, the debate in the Kakhanov Commission exhibited a fervor unusual for such bodies. The participants not only clashed over proposals to reorganize peasant and zemstvo self-government, but they used the occasion to debate issues vital to the fate of the old regime, such as the future roles of the peasantry and gentry in local administration; the feasibility of dissolving legal and political distinctions between peasants and nonpeasants and establishing a common comprehensive system of public self-government from the village level up; the type of executive agent needed at the *volost'* level to enforce government and zemstvo decisions; and, finally, the benefits and shortcomings of the reforms of the 1860s and their guiding concepts of public participation in local government and the separation of administrative and judicial authority. Even though commission members failed to come up with definitive answers on these matters (these issues dominated official and public discussions of reform until tsarism fell in 1917),[1] they nevertheless agreed that in the early 1880s Imperial Russia stood at a crossroads in terms of political development and social support.

[1]These same questions were discussed by the Special Conference on the needs of agriculture, established by Tsar Nicholas II in 1902 and headed by Finance Minister S. Iu. Witte; the commission to review peasant legislation in 1903–4, established under the Ministry of Internal Affairs and headed by V. I.Gurko; and the commissions that met in conjunction with the enactment of the Stolypin reforms. There is a vast historical literature on this period treating these issues at length. For two accounts illustrating the similarity of the topics discussed in the Kakhanov Commission and the later Witte conference and Gurko commission, see Yaney, *Urge to Mobilize*, pp. 201–11, 217–25; and M. S. Simonova, *Krizis agrarnoi politiki tsarizma nakanune pervoi Rossiiskoi revoliutsii* (Moscow, 1987), pp. 155–219, passim.

The activity of the Kakhanov Commission likewise provides an in-depth look at ministerial politics within one ministry, namely the Ministry of Internal Affairs. The participation of senators, governors, gentry, zemstvo leaders, and ministerial representatives at various stages of the commission's work on local government reform shows the conflicting aims of different interest groups and the relative importance of their views to the minister of internal affairs. Indeed, the disagreement within the commission between the faction advocating the systematic establishment of public self-government from the village to the provincial levels, and their opponents, who favored either gentry or state control, severely hampered the enactment of concrete reform proposals. This conflict, which mirrored the division at higher levels within the government, prompted Tolstoi to attempt a reorganization of local government that would give his ministry control over local affairs and over central policy making. Consequently, the Kakhanov Commission's dismissal in 1885 was evidence of important changes in ministerial politics under way in the mid-1880s. Minister of Internal Affairs Tolstoi sought once and for all to establish his leadership in ministerial circles much in the manner of his former adversary Loris-Melikov, although the ramifications of his policy for local self-government were far different.

As we shall see in this chapter, the activity of the Kakhanov Commission constituted an integral second stage in the origins of the land captain and zemstvo counterreforms, coming as it did on the heels of the senatorial inspections. During this period all factions in the commission agreed on the administrative need for local self-government reform. Yet each sought to design the reform to suit its own political interests. Although scholars have generally acknowledged the commission's achievement in providing a comprehensive survey of local administration that would benefit later commissions and historians, they contend that the Kakhanov Commission's role in the elaboration of the counterreforms was negligible, and that the counterreform process began with Pazukhin's collaboration with Tolstoi in 1885. Soviet historian B. S. Itenberg overstates the traditional view only slightly in dismissing the Kakhanov Commission as a "stillborn" institution and as a demagogic trick of Ignat'ev.[2] However, this interpretation exaggerates

---

[2]Itenberg, "Krizis samoderzhavnoi vlasti," pp. 123–4. Most recent accounts on the origins of the counterreforms virtually ignore the Kakhanov Commission's work and argue that Pazukhin was the architect (or coarchitect) of the counterreforms, although Taranovski, Whelan, and Yaney maintain that Tolstoi (notwithstanding Pazukhin's contribution) did not devise counter reforms simply as part of a "gentry reaction." Still, Taranovski hardly touches on the Kakhanov Commission's activity and attributes the counterreforms to the spirit of political reaction following Tolstoi's appointment in 1882; see "Politics of Counter-Reform," pp. 373–440. Yaney argues that Tolstoi saw no value in the commission's work (which he had filed in his ministry's archive), and maintains that his "vision" for the land captains came from Pazukhin and his writings in 1884–5. See his *Urge to Mobilize*, pp. 70–2. Whelan contends that Tolstoi's plans for rural administrative reform were "inchoate" prior to Pazukhin's work on the counterreform projects in 1885. Whelan, *Alexander III and the State Council*, pp. 174–5.

Few studies on late nineteenth-century Russia go beyond mentioning the commission's existence. There is the official summary of M. V. Islavin, *Obzor trudov Vysochaishei utverzhdennoi, pod predsedatel'stvom Stats-Sekretaria Kakhanova, Osoboi Komissii* (2 pts; St. Petersburg, 1908), which provided the architects

Pazukhin's influence over Tolstoi, misconstrues Tolstoi's purpose in introducing the land captain and zemstvo counterreforms, and ignores the Kakhanov Commission's contribution to the minister's own plans on local self-government reform. Not only did the commission hammer out diverse reform proposals and collect the material that would be used to draft the Land Captain and Zemstvo statutes of 1889 and 1890, but, in failing to approve a comprehensive and simultaneous reform plan of local government, it allowed Tolstoi to advocate piecemeal peasant and zemstvo administration reforms. He was able to claim with some accuracy that such proposals were consistent with the conclusions of the Kakhanov Commission. Moreover, Tolstoi drew heavily on the criticisms of the initial commission recommendations by the governors and the local experts in the full commission, for administrative and political purposes, in drafting his proposals for local self-government.

Beyond the Great Reforms: the case for public initiative

The establishment of the Kakhanov Commission. Despite the demise of Loris-Melikov's ministerial system, the central government pushed on with the business of local self-government reform. On 4 September 1881, Minister of Internal Affairs Ignat'ev proposed to Alexander III that a commission be established to draft local administration projects. He recommended Kakhanov as its chairman on the grounds that his prior experience as governor of Pskov Province, secretary to the Committee of Ministers, and deputy minister of internal affairs under Loris-Melikov qualified him for the post. Ignat'ev emphasized that the senatorial inspections had revealed the urgent need for reorganizing local government. The prereform administrative and judicial institutions that survived the reforms of the 1860s were outmoded, and such obsolete institutions as the rural police hampered the activity of local zemstvo and government institutions created by the Zemstvo and Judicial Reforms. He dismissed the idea of limiting reform to reestablishing peace arbitrators or creating similar supervisory officials, claiming that only a comprehensive reform of local government would coordinate the activities of various state and public institutions. The emperor approved the proposal and Kakhanov's nomination as commission chairman, and on 20 October ratified a tentative plan of the commission's activity and authorized the chairman to invite local experts to the commission for consultation.[3]

of the Stolypin agrarian reforms with the background information. But most historians, like memoirists Meshcherskii and Feoktistov, confine their remarks to a few brief criticisms of the commission's reform proposals. The most detailed accounts of the Kakhanov Commission debates are found in Gessen, pp. 134–92 (especially good concerning commission proposals to reform peasant self-government); and Zaionchkovskii, *Rossiiskoe samoderzhavie*, pp. 217–33, which summarizes the proposals of various factions in the commission but does not analyze their arguments in detail.

[3] Ignat'ev's proposals in his 4 September and 19 October 1881 reports are found in TsGIA, *fond* Departament obshchikh del MVD, 1881, *opis'* 241, *delo* 83, *ll.* 210–12 ob., 213 ob.–215; and ibid., *ll.* 275 b–276 ob., 277–80. Ignat'ev tactfully chose not to mention that Kakhanov had written much of Loris-

Far from relegating the commission to an obscure role in the reform process, Ignat'ev's plan gave it the entire responsibility of drafting projects, which, with the consent of the minister of internal affairs, would have been submitted directly to the State Council for legislative review. Thus, Ignat'ev's proposals demonstrated his commitment to carry through the local administration reform work begun by his predecessor Loris-Melikov.[4] He did not plan sham constitutional reforms to garner public support for the autocracy, but in his two reports presented concrete administrative reasons for reorganizing local government. Nor did his efforts on behalf of the commission cease in October 1881. In April 1882, he persuaded the Committee of Ministers to endorse the proposed agenda of the commission and the comprehensive reform plan elaborated by Kakhanov and several commission members that aimed at increased public participation in local administration. To prove that they had comprehensive reform in mind, the members listed twenty-nine areas requiring reform that included the village, *volost'*, municipal, district, and provincial administrations; the local police forces; the zemstvos; and all matters concerning the organization, jurisdiction, and supervision of these institutions.[5]

The Kakhanov Commission began its legislative work on a promising note with the endorsement of the Committee of Ministers and the support of Ignat'ev; and judging by his marginal comments on Ignat'ev's reports, Alexander III approved of the goals and the methods of the commission's work. In granting Chairman Kakhanov the privilege of direct access to the tsar at its 20 April 1882 meeting, the Committee of Ministers in fact gave him a right usually reserved in practice for ministers, and in theory made him less dependent on the minister of internal affairs in planning local administrative reforms. Besides underscoring the importance of the commission's work, as top officials recognized, this act could play into the hands of a strong-willed, politically resolute chairman. He could dictate the commission's proposals by muzzling his adversaries within the commission and by declaring that his views represented the wishes of the autocrat.

Melikov's ill-fated 28 January 1881 reform memorandum. Orlovsky, *Limits of Reform*, p. 174.

Many state officials, among them Polovtsov and Peretts, who saw the logic in Ignat'ev's proposal of the Kakhanov Commission, were nevertheless amazed at Alexander's confidence in Ignat'ev. They distrusted him as a vain and ambitious official who stopped short of nothing, including lies, to enhance his position with the tsar. See Polovtsov's remarks for 29 January 1882 in his diary in TsGAOR, *f.* Polovtsov, *op.* 1, *d.* 20, *ll.* 44–44 *ob.*; and the entries for 28 July and 17 November 1881 in *Dnevnik Perettsa*, pp. 86–7, 107.

[4]Golovin, *Moi vospominaniia*, 2: 53–4.

[5]TsGIA, *f.* Komitet ministrov, 1882, *op.* 1, *d.* 4234, *ll.* 165–6, 126–142 *ob.*

Yaney ridicules the Kakhanov Commission's comprehensive approach as another wayward capital-city scheme and contends that Ignat'ev's ideas of government "were not profound," and that the Minister "wanted a piece of paper that would eliminate the bad features of the bureaucracy and preserve all the good ones." Yaney, *Urge to Mobilize*, p. 69. Although the Kakhanov Commission's approach had its flaws and inconsistencies, as elaborated below, Ignat'ev and Alexander III were more determined to improve local administration than Yaney suggests – in fact, Ignat'ev finally agreed with Kakhanov that the commission, in order to coordinate local government, should have the authority to propose reforms for the local police (but not the gendarmes). TsGAOR, *f.* Polovtsov, *op.* 1, *d.* 20, *ll.* 42 *ob.*, 45–46 *ob.*

From the outset, however, several factors jeopardized the prospects for the enactment of the program of increased decentralization and zemstvo control drafted by the ten-member Special Conference (*Osoboe soveshchanie*) of the Kakhanov Commission. Most important, Kakhanov received little concrete support from Alexander III during the commission's activity. The emperor disliked him personally and regarded the chairman as one of Loris-Melikov's confidants. For example, when the position of minister of state properties became vacant in 1881 and Ignat'ev recommended Kakhanov as his successor, the tsar appointed the less experienced Ostrovskii instead.[6] The appointment of Kakhanov as commission chairman several months later was apparently a reaffirmation of imperial confidence in Ignat'ev. The absence of firm imperial support for the chairman undoubtedly had adverse consequences for the commission's work. Even commission member Polovtsov warned the emperor that the Kakhanov Commission would not fulfill its objective of comprehensive local government reform unless he supported Kakhanov, because the latter, while possessing experience, lacked the firm disposition to deflect criticism against the commission proposals.[7] The tsar's distrustful attitude toward Kakhanov prevented the chairman from exploiting his personal access to the tsar; and as if this alone were not a sufficient obstacle, the commission no longer had a patron in the minister of internal affairs following Ignat'ev's dismissal in 1882. As a new minister, Tolstoi was not about to risk his position defending decentralization and public self-rule, concepts that he had long regarded as antithetical to autocracy.

Furthermore, Kakhanov was not the strong chairman needed to ramrod proposals through a commission regardless of ministerial opposition. True, he possessed many of the qualities desirable in a chairman – brilliance, expertise, desire to achieve great results, patience, tolerance, and a willingness to listen to even the most absurd opinions. Yet, in his desire to be impartial, he allowed commission members to disrupt the plan for comprehensive administrative reform by their petty conflicts over jurisdictions. Since he could not speak for the tsar as chairman, he concluded that the airing of all views in the commission would produce the most practical reform. But his actions had fateful consequences for the Special Conference decentralists who under Kakhanov drafted the original reform proposals. He failed to defend the decentralist program and vacillated when confronted by stiff opposition.[8] In the antibureaucratic climate that prevailed at court for several years after Alexander II's assassination, Prince Meshcherskii, the editor of the conservative newspaper *Citizen*, scorned Kakhanov as the typical St. Petersburg bureaucrat – a "liberal" reformer completely out of touch with

---

[6]See Polovtsov's diary entry for 20 January 1884 in *Dnevnik gosudarstvennogo sekretaria A. A. Polovtsova v dvukh tomakh*, ed. P. A. Zaionchkovskii (2 vols.; Moscow, 1966), 1: 170.

[7]TsGAOR, *f.* Polovtsov, *op.* 1, *d.* 20, *l.* 45 *ob.*

[8]See the entry for 4 December 1882 in ibid., *l.* 102; and Meshcherskii's 14 November 1884 diary-letter to Alexander III in ibid., *f.* Alesksandr III, 1884–1885, *op.* 1, *d.* 111, *ll.* 9–9 *ob.* This diary-letter was written during the debates in the full commission, in October and November 1884.

reality.[9] Kakhanov's inability to maintain control over the debate in the full commission and his reluctance to defend the conference's proposals played no small role in their eventual rejection by the commission.[10] Thus, the government's repudiation of the Kakhanov Commission program in 1885 was by no means inevitable in 1882; rather, it resulted from the repeated defeats sustained by the decentralists in the commission debates for various reasons and from Tolstoi's change in policy on local administrative matters as minister of internal affairs between 1882 and 1885.

The case for decentralization: the special conference and its program of public self-government and zemstvo control. Although several of the local experts invited to the Kakhanov Commission advocated self-government of all classes and zemstvo control, the members of the Special Conference were the main contingent who proposed and defended these ideas from 1882 to 1885. Beginning their work in September 1882, the conference consisted of chairman Kakhanov and three of the four senatorial inspectors (Shamshin chose not to be a member); P. P. Semenov, a senator, statistician, vice-present of the Imperial Russian Geographical Society, and former secretary to chairman Rostovtsev in the Editing Commissions; F. L. Barykov, a senator and former director of the Land Section in the Ministry of Internal Affairs; I. E. Andreevskii, a professor of law at St. Petersburg University; N. A. Vaganov, a member of the Ministry of the Imperial Household and formerly a zemstvo leader in Pskov Province; I. N. Durnovo, the deputy minister of internal affairs; and G. P. Galagan, a member of the State Council and previously a member of the Editing Commissions. Not surprisingly, this group of bureaucrats and legal experts were committed to the ideas of decentralization and public self-government embodied by the Peasant and Zemstvo Reforms, which some of them had helped prepare. At the same time, all the conference members, with the exception of Kovalevskii and Vaganov, tended not to defend their ideas very forcefully when challenged by opponents.[11]

The goal of the Special Conference was to draft proposals that would provide for effective administration at all levels and in all areas of local government in accordance with the Great Reform principles of *zakonnost'*

[9]Ibid., *d.* 108, *l.* 79.

Curiously, years later Meshcherskii described Kakhanov as one of the most talented officials in Alexander II's reign, a good man loved and respected by all. Even so, Meshcherskii remarked that Kakhanov was compliant and easily succumbed to the liberal views of people like Loris-Melikov. V. P. Meshcherskii, *Moi vospominaniia* (3 vols.; St. Petersburg, 1897–1912), 3: 142. Katkov's role in leading the backlash against legal bureaucracy is detailed in Tvardovskaia, *Ideologiia poreformennogo samoderzhaviia*, especially pp. 200ff.

[10]*Zhurnal Vysochaishe uchrezhdennoi Osoboi Komissii dlia sostavleniia proektov mestnogo upravleniia* [hereafter cited as *Zhurnal Osoboi Komissii}* (19 nos.; St. Petersburg, 1884–5), no. 4, pp. 34–6, 44.

[11]Polovtsov made this observation in his diary entries for 8 October 1881, 13 April, and 4 December 1882 in TsGAOR, *f.* Polovtsov, *op.* 1, *d.* 20, *ll.* 14 *ob.,* 68, 101–3 *ob.*

Polovtsov participated in the Special Conference until he was appointed secretary to the chairman of the State Council on 1 January 1883. On his influence in State Council affairs in the 1880s, and his tendency to exaggerate his own significance, see Whelan, pp. 116–18.

and *glasnost'*. Although the conference made a number of innovative proposals with that in mind, perhaps none was more controversial or had greater implications than its plan to establish self-government of all social estates at the village and *volost'* levels. Although conference members did not advocate the abolition of social estate distinctions as such, and their plan allowed for gentry predominance in the all-estate (*vsesoslovnye*) assemblies, their goal was to have the new village and *volost'* institutions act as melting pots for a new rural society based on classes much as the Great Reformers had envisioned with the zemstvos at the district and provincial levels.[12] Thus, in managing economic and administrative matters at the grass-roots level, the new institutions would function as truly public (*bessoslovnye*) organizations serving (and even creating) common interests. However, such distinctions between the composition (*sostav*) and purposes of the proposed village and *volost'* assemblies, at least as they pertained to the gentry, escaped various gentry leaders and their journalistic champions Katkov and Prince Meshcherskii; they were, on the contrary, convinced that the Special Conference had the imminent destruction of the entire *soslovie* system in mind. Fearing increased losses in gentry landholdings, they pleaded with Alexander III for financial and political support for the gentry and, during the period of the conference deliberations, they reminded the government that the traditional estates organization, headed by the landed gentry, had constituted a bulwark of tsarist control over the villages for centuries.[13] Thus, the introduction of the conference's proposal, by abolishing a separate peasant administration, in effect portended a more democratic system of public self-government based on territorial rather than estate (or curial) representation. Indeed, the radical nature of this recommendation is emphasized by the fact that even after the 1905 Revolution, when social estate distinctions disappeared in practice for all intents and purposes, the crown refused to abolish separate village and *volost'* administrations for peasants.

Why did the conference propose a reform of this nature? In devising a plan for all-estate self-government in the village and *volost'*, the members

---

[12]TsGIA, *f.* Kakhanovskaia komissiia, 1882, *op.* 1, *d.* 64, *l.* 39 *ob.*

[13]Beginning with the memoranda that A. R. Shidlovskii, the gentry marshal of Khar'kov province, submitted to the Ministries of Internal Affairs and Finance in 1881–2, prominent landed gentry (magnates) campaigned for cheaper state credit, a gentry land bank, and entailment of hereditary lands in order to preserve gentry landholdings. From December 1883 to May 1885, thirteen provincial marshals and gentry assemblies and six provincial zemstvo assemblies joined in the call for a gentry land bank. These addresses, in the wake of Alexander II's assassination and in the midst of a rural economic crisis, played on the government's generosity and "fear," in contending that the gentry was the government's rural support and that, accordingly, separate social estates had to be preserved. Similar arguments were made by Meshcherskii and other progentry publicists although, as Hamburg shows, the gentry bank campaign was not well organized or widespread. Whereas provincial gentry marshals desired cheap credit to protect gentry landlords from the vicissitudes of the market, Meshcherskii and his counterparts, who kept close watch on the Kakhanov Commission's work, had ideological reasons (fear of liberalism) for advocating state patronage of the gentry. Such differences in the motives of provincial gentry leaders in the provinces and their spokesmen in the capital were one factor that limited the effect of gentry "class" pressure on the government. G. M. Hamburg, *Politics of the Russian Nobility 1881–1905* (New Brunswick, N.J., 1984), pp. 103–11.

were convinced that traditional estate divisions in the countryside were disappearing in practice, and that new institutions encompassing the new residents and economic arrangements in the villages and on landed estates were needed; in turn, this would build support for the government from the ground up. Although a separate administration for the peasantry, which comprised over 80 percent of the population in Russia, was necessary during the period of temporary obligations, the mandatory peasant redemption law of 29 December 1881 ended all temporary peasant obligations as of 1 January 1883. In practice, they had terminated much earlier in the European part of Russia. The conference members remarked that peasant officials no longer provided supervision over peasant assemblies and tax collectors, their primary responsibility according to the 19 February statute. Instead, they discharged police functions for the entire district administration – proof in itself that village administration involved much more than the land affairs of the peasant *obshchina*.[14]

The most tangible evidence of the erosion of a separate peasant administration, according to the conference members, was the influx of an ever-increasing number of nonpeasants into the village. They had no doubt that this trend would continue in the future, primarily because of the government's resettlement policy spelled out in the 30 June 1881 instruction to the governors. On the basis of this document, entire peasant villages were transferred to the Volga provinces and reclassified as nonpeasant communities.[15] Yet here the conference members overstated their case, because they cited very few examples in which nonpeasants made up a substantial proportion of the village community. The situation in Balakov village in Samara Province, in which there were 1,252 peasants and more than 10,000 nonpeasants, was truly exceptional.[16] The data of the senatorial inspectors, which ostensibly provided the material on which the conference made its recommendations, revealed that in nearly all villages nonpeasants constituted less than 5 percent of the community. Hence, the process of social estate interaction in the village was under way, but, contrary to the conference members' arguments, it hardly had reached a critical point.

More likely, the signs of diminishing gentry landholdings in the countryside and of gentry seeking professional careers in the towns convinced conference members that the traditional estates order, especially with regard to local self-government, would soon be obsolete. From 1861 to 1882, gentry landholdings in forty-five provinces decreased by 18 percent, with the heaviest losses suffered by gentry magnates (those holding more than 1,000 *desiatiny*) in the southern steppe and non–black earth provinces (for instance, Moscow, Kostroma, Iaroslavl', Smolensk); gentry magnates in the mid-Volga provinces (Saratov, Simbirsk, Penza) were also hard hit.[17] Although confer-

---

[14]TsGIA , *f*. Kakhanovskaia komissiia, *op*. 1, *d*. 64, *l*. 3.
[15]Zaionchkovskii, *Krizis samoderzhaviia*, p. 425.
[16]*MVUOK*, 1–2: 8; and TsGIA, *f*. Kakhanovskaia komissiia, *op*. 1, *d*. 64, *l*. 5.
[17]For the figures, see Korelin, "Dvorianstvo v poreformennoi Rossii (1861–1904 gg.)," *Istoricheskie*

ence members did not calculate precisely the losses of gentry land, they rightly observed the beginnings of this trend. Consequently, there was a note of urgency in their plan to allow gentry landlords to participate in the village and *volost'* administration in order to guide the peasants in matters of local government.[18] Yet it should be kept in mind that the conference did not make the proposal simply because it was in the interests of the gentry (whatever benefits the middle-landholding gentry might have derived from it).[19] Rather, with England's decentralized local administration and justices of the peace in mind, they saw it as the most expedient way to raise standards of peasant conduct and make village self-government more honest, if not more efficient. Such an optimistic view of peasant and gentry cooperation in an all-estate village administration was perhaps more the product of the wishful thinking of St. Petersburg bureaucrats than of sound conclusions based on the data at hand. After all, the landed gentry were not always known for their efficiency in self-government, as the senatorial inspectors had emphasized in their reports. They had used the zemstvo to their advantage and had put pressure on peasant delegates. Moreover, what benefits could gentry landowners receive from participating in the village assemblies? How could the peasantry hope to participate as equals given their relative deficiencies in education and administrative experience? The conference mem-

zapiski, vol. 87 (1971), p. 143; Becker, pp. 28–36; and Hamburg, *Politics*, pp. 90–7. Hamburg contends that between 1877 and 1905 gentry landholdings fell 46 percent in the non–black earth and southern steppe zones, and 34 percent in the black earth region (although the declines for Simbirsk, Saratov, and Penza provinces in the black earth zone were 46, 42, and 47 percent, respectively). On the whole, during 1877–1905 the landholdings of gentry magnates fell by 30.4 percent; for the middle gentry and petty gentry, the figures were 18.8 percent and 13.7 percent, respectively. Hamburg attributes the loss of gentry lands primarily to the Great Depression, which struck Europe (and Russia) from the mid–1870s to the mid–1890s, and argues that such differences in landholding losses, not to mention occupational status, educational and religious background, and regional affiliation make it difficult to speak of the landed gentry as a distinct "class" in postreform Russia. Becker disputes this argument in *Nobility*, pp. 10, 40–7.

[18]*MVUOK*, 1–2: 11–12; and TsGIA, *f.* Kakhanovskaia komissiia, *op.* 1, *d.* 64, *l.* 5 *ob.*

[19]Such a claim is made by Yaney and, to a lesser degree, Whelan. In evaluating the Special Conference's program, Yaney maintains that the conference members proposed reforms with the intention of reestablishing gentry tutelage over the peasants and the zemstvo. He is puzzled over the traditional characterization of the Special Conference's proposals as "liberal," as opposed to Alexander III's establishment of "reactionary" gentry land captains; the latter, according to Yaney, were government servitors rather than "delegates of local privilege." Yaney, *Systematization*, pp. 350–1; idem., *Urge to Mobilize*, p. 69; and Whelan, p. 174. Yaney correctly points out that the conference members regarded the gentry as paternalistic leaders in local administration, but so did their adversaries in the full commission. If perpetuating gentry control was the reason for reform, it made little sense for the conference members to advocate abolishing estate distinctions between peasants and nonpeasants in village and *volost'* administration. Conversely, most historians portray the conference members as liberals who aimed to weaken the gentry's position in the countryside; for example, Zaionchkovskii, *Rossiiskoe samoderzhavie*, pp. 225, 228–9; and Kornilov, *Krest'ianskaia reforma*, p. 236. Meshcherskii argued that, above all, the Special Conference desired to weaken the authority of the governors and the landed gentry. Meshcherskii, *Moi vospominaniia*, 3: 143–4. This contention also misconstrues the conference's objective. Here we will argue that although the conference's proposal had long-term political ramifications, its aim in 1882–3 was much more limited and pragmatic. Recognizing the gentry's experience as leaders in local self-government as well as the processes of social change under way in the countryside, the conference advocated gentry leadership over all-estate village and *volost'* administration as a transitional measure – one that benefited the gentry in the short run but allowed for their eventual demise.

bers in fact faced the dilemma of establishing an all-estate village administration, which would require significant adjustments in the attitudes of peasants and gentry, or of maintaining an obviously inefficient peasant administration. In the interests of administrative efficiency and in accordance with the social changes already under way, they opted for the former course.

The Special Conference plan called for the replacement of the peasant village administration with a village government of all social estates. It clarified the legislative distinction between the village community and the landed *obshchina* introduced in the statute of 19 February, and specified that the *obshchina* would remain an exclusively peasant institution.[20] The conference members justified the sweeping change by the need to furnish nonpeasant villages with an administration and the district zemstvo and government with local agents to enforce their decisions. Yet, curiously, no reforms were proposed in the types of village institutions and officials, the targets of so much criticism in the senatorial inspections. The elders, their assistants, the village assemblies and tax collectors would conduct their affairs autonomously, and peasant and nonpeasant residents owning property in the village (in either private or communal land tenure) would be eligible for office.[21]

The merging of peasants and nonpeasants into a common village administration underscored the conference members' belief that only fundamental reforms would create efficient self-government at the village level. Their proposal went far beyond previous reforms of local administration. In contrast to the division of zemstvo representation into three separate groups that provided for gentry predominance, the conference proposed that all village landowners at least twenty-five years of age participate as equals in one village assembly. Whereas the Zemstvo Reform of 1864 perpetuated the semblance of the traditional estate organization in the form of separate electoral assemblies for various categories of property owners, the conference's proposal did nothing of the kind. On the other hand, their recommendation to preserve the peasant *obshchina* and the mutual guarantee contradicted other aspects of their plan for an all-estate village administration. This is explained by their reluctance to cut all the bonds of government control over the peasantry. Rather, they wished to loosen these bonds gradually and to use the all-estate village administration as a means of educating peasants in their civic responsibilities and facilitating the bases for peasant resettlement. Some

[20]The dual nature of the *obshchina* (commune), as analyzed by Boris Mironov, helps explain why the Special Conference had difficulty distinguishing between the functions of the village community and the commune (while recognizing the state's dependence on both). Mironov notes that "the formal structure [of the commune] enabled the state to extend its policies and its ideology to the peasants, to impose fiscal, administrative, and policy functions on the commune, and hence to transform the commune into a state institution. The informal structure enabled the peasants to defend themselves against the state, performed essential functions in daily life, and preserved the commune as an institution of customary law." Boris Mironov, "The Russian Peasant Commune after the Reforms of the 1860s," *Slavic Review* 44, no. 3 (Fall 1985): 443, 448–9. The article was translated by Gregory Freeze.

[21]MVUOK, 1–2: 10; TsGIA, *f.* Kakhanovskaia komissiia, *op.* 1, *d.* 64, *l.* 3 *ob.*; and Gessen, p. 135.

freedom of peasant movement came, but only in 1903 when the government abolished the mutual guarantee in an effort to overcome an agricultural crisis.

The Special Conference's proposals for *volost'* administration reform were more consistent with the data found in the senatorial reports. The members suggested replacing the peasant *volost'* administration, notorious for its arbitrariness and inefficiency, with a *volostel'* (a *volost'* manager) elected by the district assembly from among local *volost'* residents at least twenty-five years of age and with a secondary education. Although the government had the right to approve or reject a *volostel'* elected by the zemstvo, this stipulation was a mere formality. If approved, he would receive the privileges of state service. The district zemstvo would provide the salary and expenses for the *volostel'* and his assistants, in the event the latter were necessary.[22]

The *volostel'* would serve as an executive agent for the district zemstvo and the government in the *volost'*. All other institutions and officials except the *volost'* court would be abolished.[23] Conference members Kovalevskii and Barykov, who took the most active part in elaborating the reform proposals, emphasized that the village administration provided all the local services for the peasants. Past experience had shown that the *volost'* assembly confined its activity to electing officials who took no interest in public affairs.[24] The *volostel'*, on the contrary, would implement the decisions of the district assembly and administration within the *volost'*, watch over all zemstvo property, and oversee the collection of zemstvo taxes by village officials. As a secondary responsibility, he would supervise all public institutions within this territory, and would suspend village assembly decisions that exceeded their jurisdiction. The members briefly discussed the possibility of granting the *volostel'* disciplinary authority over village officials, but postponed detailed consideration of this issue until they had discussed the rights and responsibilities of local officials in general.[25]

In essence, the conference decentralists saw zemstvo control over local administration at the district and subdistrict levels as the most practical and least expensive solution to the current anarchy in peasant and zemstvo self-government. Not surprisingly, their proposal was popular with many zemstvos, who had impressed upon the senatorial inspectors the need for such control. By virtue of his election, functions, and source of income, the *volostel'* was above all a zemstvo executive agent. The state service privileges did not convert him into a full-fledged subordinate of the Ministry of Internal Affairs, contrary to the claims of some historians.[26] Rather, these privileges were

---

[22]*MVUOK*, 1–2: 17–18.

[23]The only significant change in the *volost'* court would be its reclassification as a local court for all estates. The majority of conference members naively expressed confidence that nonpeasants residing in the village would adapt to the local customs of peasant justice and accept the decisions of the *volost'* court. Cf. TsGIA, *f*. Kakhanovskaia komissiia, *op*. 1, *d*. 64, *ll*. 14–14 *ob*.; and *MVUOK*, 1–2: 21–2.

[24]TsGIA, *f*. Kakhanovskaia komissiia, *op*. 1, *d*. 64, *ll*. 8–9; and *MVUOK*, 1–2: 14.

[25]Ibid., pp. 19–20.

[26]For example, see Gessen, p. 171. He viewed the *volostel'* as primarily the agent of the district admin-

recommended to attract the most competent and conscientious local residents to seek election. On the other hand, the conference members did not go so far as to create the all-estate *volost'* assembly that many zemstvos desired. They reasoned that such an organization would be premature as long as the intellectual level of the peasants remained low and village communities were not independent units of public activity.[27] The conference never provided a satisfactory explanation as to why peasants and nonpeasants could participate together in the village assembly, but not in the *volost'* assembly, and this omission was pointed out to their embarrassment during the debate in the full commission. Their failure to resolve this contradiction cost them the support of local zemstvo experts in the commission who favored an all-estate *volost'* and paved the way for the rejection of the conference's proposal.

The conference members' conviction that greater public initiative would rectify the problems of local self-government is likewise evident in their proposals to reorganize the district administration and to expand zemstvo jurisdiction. They adopted several guidelines for district administration reform. First, the zemstvos were to be integrated into the state administrative system, but unlike government institutions, they would continue to be filled by public election. Second, zemstvo jurisdiction was to be defined explicitly by law in order to prevent conflicts in local economic administration between zemstvos and other local institutions. The conference members dogmatically asserted that elected zemstvo representatives were better able to identify local needs and the resources to meet them than government officials. Given the zemstvo record in the areas of public food supply and public charity, among others, this contention not surprisingly raised eyebrows in the full commission; indeed, it was reminiscent of the type of statement found in zemstvo petitions. Likewise, the conference's talk of integrating the zemstvo into the hierarchy of local state institutions while preserving their identity as public self-governing institutions (with their subordinate *volosteli* as public officials) only confused the issue further, as did its claim that the district zemstvos would discharge as many functions related to the local economy as possible; the core of the problem, as shown in the past, was the conflicting views of zemstvo and government officials over the capabilities of the zemstvos.[28]

What the conference did propose was a Bureau of District Administration to coordinate government and zemstvo activity. It would replace six district bureaus that over the years had functioned ineffectively and would supervise district zemstvo activity. The size of the Russian empire, the shortage of roads and communications, and the diversity of local needs, according to

---

istration and not the zemstvo, because it would be subordinate to a Bureau of District Administration (discussed in this section) consisting of both government and zemstvo representatives. Gessen claimed that the *volostel'* was an impractical compromise between a zemstvo *volost'* and a *volost'* administration organized on purely bureaucratic lines. In his opinion, Russian political history repeatedly demonstrated the futility of applying the electoral principle to bureaucratic institutions.

[27] *MVUOK*, 1–2: 15.

[28] TsGIA, *f.* Kakhanovskaia komissiia, *op.* 1, *d.* 64, *ll.* 35, 66–66 *ob.*; and *MVUOK*, 1–2: 47–50.

the conference majority, ruled out rigid state control over the zemstvo. Instead, they preferred the formal supervision of local district bureaus and specific laws on zemstvo jurisdiction as a way of minimizing conflicts between the government and the zemstvos.[29]

The numerous functions of the bureau would encompass supervising the activity of *volost'*, village, and town officials; inspecting elementary public schools and charity institutions; checking and certifying reports of separate district institutions and drafting a budget for the entire district administration; reviewing complaints against the orders and activities of various institutions and officials within the district; and rendering collegial decisions on matters previously handled by the separate District Bureaus for Peasants Affairs, for Police Administration, and for Military Affairs, as well as by the Guardianship Committee, the District Committee on Public Health and Vaccinations, and the District School Council. The conference members naively assumed that collegial discussion and supervision by the bureau over matters under zemstvo jurisdiction would coordinate the activity of the government and zemstvo institutions.[30] However, they failed to explain why the Bureau of District Administration, with its collegial organization, would function any more efficiently than the current district bureaus, which made decisions in collegial fashion, but could not enforce them owing to the pressing administrative obligations of individual bureau members and an overburdened rural police force. More important, what guarantee was there that formal supervision of the Bureau of District Administration, designed not to restrict the autonomy of zemstvo and government institutions, could force the zemstvo and police to cooperate, especially since the zemstvos, according to the conference's proposals, still retained their separate but equal status with government institutions?

Since the bureau would deal largely with zemstvo affairs, the Special Conference insisted that its chairman be elected by the district assembly for a three-year term and approved by the government. Although they encouraged the election of the district gentry marshal as chairman, in recognition of his experience as chairman of the various district bureaus and of the district assembly, they opposed his *ex officio* appointment to the post.[31] Such a stipulation, they emphasized, might be misconstrued as nothing more than government support for the narrow estate interests of the gentry. Besides the chairman, the only other permanent members of the Bureau of District Administration would be the district police chief, the district representative of the Ministry of Finance (the two representing the most powerful ministries in the countryside), and the chairman of the district zemstvo board. The remaining members of the bureau would vary according to the type of business under consideration, and, as appropriate, represent the local interests

[29]Ibid., p. 81.
[30]Ibid., p. 61.
[31]TsGIA, *f*. Kakhanovskaia komissiia, *op*. 1, *d*. 64, *l*. 51 *ob*.; and *MVUOK*, 1–2: 63–4.

of their ministries. For example, in matters of public health the district physician would participate, and for education-related business the district inspector of public schools would sit on the bureau.[32] The conference members reasoned that the flexible organization of the Bureau of District Administration would curb the bureaucratic inefficiency and burdensome expenses of separate district bureaus. With a zemstvo-elected bureau chairman and *volosteli* to implement the decisions of the district zemstvo and bureau, the conference majority predicted confidently, the zemstvo would finally play the leading role in district administration that the architects of the 1864 statute had in mind for it.

Given the breadth of the conference's proposals for local administration reform, it is not surprising that their projects in some cases suffered from inconsistencies and gaps that required clarification and supplementation. Yet far more critical was the conference's failure to rectify contradictions in previous legislation that caused problems in the past, such as the relationship of the zemstvo to the government. Instead, their program perpetuated an unwieldy system of local government divided not only into public, corporate, and state sectors, but, in the latter case, compartmentalized along ministerial lines. Blaming past conflicts between the zemstvo and local bureaucracy on ambiguous zemstvo legislation (1864), the Special Conference assumed that an exact delineation in law of zemstvo jurisdiction would end disputes in organizing public health clinics, combatting epidemics, and the like. This belief in the efficacy of precise legislation can be explained in part by the senatorial careers of several conference members who, in the late 1870s and early 1880s, had reviewed many unfounded protests from governors against zemstvo resolutions. Thus, they ostensibly favored explicit laws on zemstvo jurisdiction to shield public self-government from bureaucratic incursions on its autonomy – a viewpoint boldly contrary to the reactionary political temper at Alexander III's court in 1882–3. And although the conference majority did not dwell on long-range political implications, the nature of their arguments, especially on the need for public self-government and precise legislation in that area, suggests that they saw zemstvo representation as a first step to eventual public participation in the national administration. In essence, Alexander II's reforms and the concepts of *glasnost'* and *zakonnost'* implicit in them received no more eloquent defense in Alexander III's reign than in the private sessions of the Special Conference.[33]

Yet when the time came to recommend changes in zemstvo jurisdiction, the conference members merely called for fewer legal limitations on zemstvo

---

[32]TsGIA, *f.* Kakhanovskaia komissiia, *op.* 1, *d.* 64, *l.* 51; and *MVUOK*, 1–2: 42, 62.

[33]Taranovski and Whelan emphasize that top officials in the State Council and various ministries later in the 1880s defended the concept of a *Rechtsstaat*; however, as we shall show in the following chapters, these officials generally used the ideology of *Rechtsstaat* as a means of attacking the centralist ideology of their opponents, quite unlike the conference majority, whose arguments still reflected the reform optimism and philosophy of the 1860s. On the ethos of *Rechtsstaat*, see Taranovski, "Politics of Counter-Reform," pp. 227–91; Whelan, pp. 90–2.

activity in public health and sanitation, public food supply and education, public charity, fire safety and construction regulations, and local transportation facilities. The members decided to listen to the advice of local experts to the full commission before making specific recommendations, a decision that would put them at a great disadvantage in the Kakhanov Commission debate. Kovalevskii and Andreevskii did convince the conference members to propose tighter restrictions on governors' supervision over the zemstvos by spelling out the cases in which they could veto zemstvo resolutions. This would help curtail arbitrary interference of governors in zemstvo affairs without jeopardizing their role as custodians of the law within their provinces.[34] In essence, the recommendation, if adopted, would have reduced the governor from provincial *nachal'nik* (chief), with its overtones of indisputable political control over local activity, to merely the highest guardian of the law within the province.

In keeping with the senatorial investigations, governors' reports, and private memoranda submitted to the Kakhanov Commission, the conference members expressed alarm over the growing representation in district assemblies of delegates more concerned with personal interests than with the local economic welfare.[35] Firmly committed to the property requirement as the basis for zemstvo representation, they acknowledged that some changes in the electoral system were in order. The postemancipation changes in land tenure had benefited the petty landlords who were represented indirectly by virtue of owning 5 percent of the property required for direct participation. Many of their representatives, according to the conference majority, were the selfish elements concerned only with making careers of zemstvo service. To deal with this problem, especially in the provinces around Moscow, the conference members proposed to reduce the property requirement for direct representation in the landlords' electoral assembly. They recommended an even lower property requirement for persons with at least a secondary education in order to allow segments of the urban intelligentsia to participate more regularly in zemstvo affairs. Prominent landlords with ten times the amount of property necessary for personal participation in the electoral assembly would become *ex officio* members of the district assembly.

Although conference members considered the gentry the most desirable participants in zemstvo administration, it is noteworthy that they were unwilling to introduce artificial regulations, for example, an estate affiliation requirement, to guarantee gentry predominance. Rather, with gentry land-

---

[34] TsGAOR, *f.* Polovtsov, *op.* 1, *d.* 20, *ll.* 37 *ob.*-38; and *MVUOK*, 1–2: 74, 76, 78.

The conference recommended parallel institutional changes at the provincial level. For example, a Bureau of Provincial Administration headed by the governor would supervise all provincial institutions, coordinate their activities, and rule on decisions of the Bureau of District Administration appealed by the district marshal. Second, the members maintained that the provincial zemstvos were useful institutions and should not be abolished. For instance, they coordinated famine and epidemic relief measures among separate districts. In addition, they were to be preserved because they served as useful forums for petitioning the central government on behalf of local needs. Ibid., 67–71.

[35] Most of the private memoranda are found in TsGIA, *f.* Kakhanovskaia komissiia, *op.* 1, *d.* 59–61.

holdings diminishing, they preferred to bring new educated elements into local administration, thus reaffirming their belief that the government's fate hinged on its ability to educate the population, enlist them in domestic administration, and diversify its base of social support. Along with the proposal to include the landed gentry in village administration as equal members without special privileges, the conference's recommendation left little doubt about their view on the relevance of the traditional estates order to zemstvo service. These officials expected the gentry to educate nongentry delegates in the ways of zemstvo administration so that the latter could manage local economic needs in the future. Not surprisingly, the gentry marshals were the foremost critics of proposals that would use them to ease the transition to equal representation for all. However, the gentry marshals, themselves divided on the ways to strengthen the gentry's position in the countryside, would soon discover that Tolstoi, a staunch critic of the conference's proposals, would also manipulate them to establish his own ministerial control over the zemstvo.

The proposed changes in zemstvo jurisdiction and composition were among the last outlined by the Special Conference, which finished its work in November 1883. Despite gaps and ambiguities in certain areas, the plan drafted by the Conference was the most comprehensive and coherent official program for decentralization and public self-government submitted prior to 1905. It called for an end to social estate distinctions at the village level, at least in terms of administration, and rejected government or gentry control of the village. In repudiating these traditional foundations of autocratic rule in Russia, it implied that the time had come to make the peasants equal partners in local self-government with other estates of the realm and to prepare the way for a more democratic system in local self-government in the near future. Acknowledging the stratification of both the rural peasantry and gentry, the conference proposed to introduce public self-government attuned to the needs of social classes rather than traditional estates of the realm. No wonder Pobedonostsev, a spokesman for autocracy, balked at proposals that he felt would diffuse all power and, through the democratic rule of peasants, produce complete anarchy. He complained to Tolstoi that

I have read many senseless, stupid, incoherent, and worthless projects in recent years – but never anything like this. It is literally the work of children playing at the game of making government legislation.

Here, there is even no ulterior motive – an ingenious mind would be required for that. Here all the cards are displayed, and they reveal some kind of idiotic game. The realization of such a project is inconceivable to me; may we never live to see such a thing. It would signify such an utter decline in the administrative mind of Russia, that my spirit is unwilling to contemplate it. The project is written, as luck would have it, to destroy all authority in Russia, to splinter it into myriads of unconnected grains of sand.[36]

[36]Quoted from Pobedonostsev's letter of 11/23 September 1883 in ORGBL, *fond* K. F. Pobedonostsev,

Pobedonostsev concluded the letter by asking Tolstoi to find out who drafted the project. He suspected Barykov and Andreevskii, whom he belittled as academic theoreticians ignorant of real conditions in Russia; and in fact they along with Kovalevskii were the primary authors.[37] Such sarcasm was not an unusual reaction of governors and other local officials to the recommendations of the Special Conference, as the conference members ruefully discovered during the next eighteen months.

The turning point: the provincial governors respond

During the next stage of the Kakhanov Commission's activity, from the fall of 1883 to midsummer 1884, the provincial governors evaluated the Special Conference's proposals for local government reform. Previous studies of the Kakhanov Commission have overlooked this pivotal phase in its work (probably because governors routinely criticized proposals on local administrative reform), and have argued that the local experts invited to the full commission in the fall of 1884 initiated the fateful attack on the Special Conference's proposals. In fact, it was the governors' opposition to the reform proposals that put the decentralists on the defensive and persuaded Tolstoi to undermine the Special Conference by inviting local officials opposed to all-estate self-government to sit on the full commission in October 1884. This represented an important breakthrough for the governors too, because Tolstoi, despite his centralist inclinations as minister, began his administration highly critical of his provincial chiefs and their administrative abilities.[38]

As shown in Table 4.1, the governors rejected many of the conference's recommendations, especially in the areas of village and *volost'* administration and zemstvo jurisdiction. Well over half of the governors responding to Tolstoi's circular of 22 July 1883 opposed the abolition of exclusively peasant village and *volost'* self-government. Instead, the majority of them preferred to restore the firm one-man supervision over the peasants that typified the activity of the original peace arbitrators. That the governors advocated such control is not surprising; after all, as Taranovski has pointed out, the provincial governors were the most outspo-

1883, *karton* 4392, *delo* 3, *ll*. 11–11 *ob*. It is published in *K. P. Pobedonostsev i ego korrespondenty*, 1, pt. 1, pp. 315–17.
[37]ORGBL, *f*. Pobedonostsev, *k*. 4392, *d*. 3, *l*. 13.
[38]In June 1883, Tolstoi allegedly complained to Polovtsov about the shortage of "good people" in the provinces, a favorite cliché of conservatives of the period. Feoktistov maintains that on more than one occasion Tolstoi derided the governors in words to the effect: "It is impossible to imagine how bad our governors are." See Feoktistov, p. 231; and Solov'ev, p. 61, who cites numerous statements of this type to prove the crisis of Russian tsarism. Tolstoi's hostility toward governors apparently dated from his years as minister of education, when he opposed all attempts of the minister of internal affairs to centralize provincial administration and take control of local schools. Yaney, *Urge to Mobilize*, p. 65. Tolstoi's change of opinion on the governors within the next two years, as we shall see, stemmed from his own political interests as minister of internal affairs in local administration reform, and from his perceptions of grass roots problems in local self-government, derived from the gubernatorial, police, and senatorial inspection reports.

Table 4.1. *Some of the governors' responses to Tolstoi's circular (22 July 1883)*
concerning proposals of the Special Conference of the Kakhanov Commission

	Governors in favor	Governors opposed
A. Project for organizing the village and *volost'* administration		
Proposition 2. While retaining the peasant *obshchina*, it is necessary to establish an all-estate village community for police purposes that would include all lands of separate landowners who are not already members of the village community.	2	27
Proposition 4. (a) The *volost'* should be established as an all-estate territorial unit.	10	20[a]
Proposition 4. (b) The all-estate *volost'* should be administered by a zemstvo-elected *volostel'*.	7	3[b]
Proposition 7. The peasant *volost'* court should be replaced by village courts with jurisdiction over all estates.	9	21[c]
B. Supervision over peasant self-government		
Proposition 8. Given the unsatisfactory state of supervision over peasant administration, the current district bureaus for peasant affairs should be replaced by peace arbitrators or similar officials with direct control over peasant administration.	25	4
C. Projects to reform district administration		
Proposition 17. It is necessary to establish a general district administration [Bureau for District Administration] . . . for the purpose of direct supervision over the entire district administration.	20	10
Proposition 19. The chairman of the bureau [for district administration] should be . . . a person elected by the district zemstvo and approved by the minister of internal affairs.	3	29[d]

ken defenders of bureaucratic control and the wording of some questions in Tolstoi's circular clearly hinted at the minister's own political views.[39] Undoubtedly some governors used the opportunity to ingratiate themselves with Tolstoi by anticipating his political views.[40] Nevertheless, the detail and diversity of many replies shows that the governors had prag-

---

[39]Taranovski, "Politics of Counter-Reform," pp. 318, 442.

[40]M. Akhun argues that governors often provided distorted accounts of local self-government for precisely this reason. Yet in replying to Tolstoi's 1883 circular, it should be noted, a significant number of governors (10) voiced support for an all-estate *volost'*, as shown in Table 4.1; and the length of many gubernatorial replies shows that the governors took their task seriously and provided as accurate an evaluation as possible. For Akhun's view see M. Akhun, "Istochniki dlia izucheniia istorii gosudarstvennykh uchrezhdenii tsarskoi Rossii (XIX-XX vv.)," *Arkhivnoe delo*, no. 1 (1939): p. 84.

Table 4.1. (*continued*)

	Governors in favor	Governors opposed
D. Projects to reform zemstvo jurisdiction		
Proposition 23. (a) It is necessary to change article 2 of the 1864 statute in order to define more precisely the areas of zemstvo jurisdiction.	19	10
Proposition 23. (b) The zemstvos, under the supervision of the inspector of public schools, should have control over the economic and pedagogical aspects of elementary education.	11	17
Proposition 25. The cases . . . in which zemstvo assembly resolutions are subject to government [Ministerial/Gubernatorial] approval should be reduced.	9	19

*a*Five of these governors favored the abolition of the peasant *volost'*; the other fifteen recommended preserving it.
*b*These governors favored a government-appointed *volostel'*.
*c*Four governors favored the abolition of the *volost'* court; seventeen favored retaining the peasant *volost'* court.
*d*Twenty-four of these governors preferred gubernatorial appointment of the chairman; five favored the ex-officio appointment of the district marshal.
Source: TsGIA, *f.* Kakhanovskaia komissiia, *op.* 1, *d.* 106, *ll.* 29 *ob.*-31, 36 *ob.*-50, 65–7, 68–9, 73 *ob.*-78, 88 *ob.*-90. The information is taken from "Svod mnenii i materialy gubernatorov po preobrazovaniiu mestnogo upravleniia."

matic reasons for criticizing the Special Conference's program and advocating government control over the peasantry. They argued that some of the proposals were unrealistic in light of the breakdown in local government described by the senatorial inspectors. Rather, the inspectors' depiction of peasant self-government provided every reason to conclude that the peasants were incapable of governing themselves, much less of working responsibly with nonpeasants on an equal basis in administering the village and *volost'*. And although allowance should be made for the governors' bias (some of them indiscriminately pinned all the blame for zemstvo–government conflicts on the zemstvo), there is much substance to their claim that the conference's proposals were illogical and impractical, given the absenteeism, material condition, and educational deficiencies of the peasants.

Although most governors simply answered the thirty-one questions in the circular dealing with the conference's project, some, such as I. M. Sudienko (Vladimir), A. N. Mosolov (Novgorod), A. A. Zubov (Saratov), and N. M. Baranov (Nizhnii Novgorod), presented detailed reform plans. They focused their attacks on the conference's proposals on village and *volost'* administration, and in this area their views made a deep impression on Tolstoi. Looking beyond the publicized shortcomings of peasant self-government, these governors, as illustrated by Baranov's comment, pinpointed some of the underlying causes:

If we look closely at the peasant administration and the *volost'* courts, it is impossible not to be convinced that a large share of the problems in peasant life are simply an ugly manifestation of the abnormal organization of peasant self-government. The exploitation by scribes, *miroedy* and solicitors, the ruinous family partitions, the general collapse of the economy, and finally, drunkenness itself and its prevalence in the assemblies and courts – these are only various symptoms of one and the same malady. This malady is the extensive right of peasant self-government, which gives peasants the right to govern themselves according to their customs instead of the law. But there are no firmly established customs.[41]

The governors had reason to express concern. The number of peasant disturbances in 1883–4, owing largely to land repartitioning in the village communities, more than doubled the total for 1879–81. Although the impact of this unrest should not be exaggerated (most of the "disturbances" listed by Soviet historians were acts of petty insubordination),[42] these incidents, set against a backdrop of growing lawlessness and insolvency in rural administration, provided the governors (and Tolstoi) with a convenient pretext for taking control of local self-government. Under these circumstances, only two governors considered it possible to introduce an all-estate village administration, whereas the overwhelming majority advocated the reestablishment of personal supervision over the peasants.[43] They maintained that the establishment of a common village government for peasants and nonpeasants would be premature, if not harmful. I. A. Zvegintsev, governor of Kursk province, complained that there was already too much disunity in the activity of local institutions, and that vigilant supervision over peasant institutions, not more autonomy for village residents, would improve local administration.[44] Governor Mosolov rejected an all-estate village administration for different reasons, claiming that its establishment would enable landlords to use their superior education and experience to manipulate the village assembly on their behalf. To reestablish peasant self-government, he

[41]Quoted from TsGIA, *fond* Kantseliariia Ministerstva vnutrennikh del, 1883, *opis'* 2, *delo* 12, *ll.* 413–413 ob.

[42]Cf. *Krest'ianskoe dvizhenie v 1881–1889 gg. Sbornik dokumentov*, ed. A. V. Nifontov and B. V. Zlatoustovskii (Moscow, 1960), p. 20; and A. M. Anfimov, *Ekonomicheskoe polozhenie i klassovaia bor'ba krestian Evropeiskoi Rossii 1881–1904 gg.* (Moscow, 1984), pp. 199–202. Nifontov and Zlatoustovskii claim that roughly 20 percent of the 659 "disturbances" in the 1880s were in response to the arbitrariness of local peasant and police officials, although such categorizations are quite artificial, as we have already noted. Anfimov acknowledged (p. 201) that the "disturbances" were more noteworthy as a sign of rural agrarian distress than as a reflection of political opposition to autocracy; indeed, a more telling point here is that only 115 of the 659 "disturbances" (or approximately 16 percent) in the 1880s were put down by troops, as opposed to 88 of the 399 incidents (approximately 22 percent) in the 1870s. Anfimov, pp. 195, 199.

[43]TsGIA, *f.* Kakhanovskaia komissiia, 1883, *op.* 1, *d.* 106, *ll.* 26–47 ob.

[44]Ibid., *f.* Kantseliariia MVD, *op.* 2, *d.* 12, *ll.* 360 ob.-361.

suggested increasing the salary and disciplinary powers of the *volost'* elder and introducing a government-appointed watchdog (*bliustitel'*) at the *volost'* level to oversee peasant officials.[45] From the standpoint of the minister of internal affairs, this proposal had an important advantage over the reintroduction of peace arbitrators because it would bring peasant administration under his direct control and would enable him to punish inefficient and corrupt peasant officials. When Simbirsk Governor N. P. Dolgovo-Saburov urged in March 1884 that such an official be given broad administrative and judicial functions in order to restore peasant respect for the law,[46] Tolstoi had in his hands, almost a year before Pazukhin's celebrated proposal, actual guidelines for imposing state control over the countryside and for asserting his leadership in state affairs.

Whereas nearly all governors attacked the conference's proposal for village administration reform as too radical, a significant number of these same governors claimed that its program for *volost'* administration under the zemstvo-elected *volostel'* was too limited. Ten of them contended that the peasant *volost'* officials were no longer peasant administration officials but merely enforcement agents for the government, police, judiciary, and zemstvo. However, the proposed *volostel'* was unacceptable because the representatives in an all-estate *volost'* assembly would be more competent to elect experienced and trustworthy officials familiar with local conditions than the district assembly. In addition, the *volostel'* elected by the district zemstvo might well have plans at variance with the desires of the *volost'* population. In fact, like the ten governors who advocated the preservation of the peasant *volost'*, these governors opposed the conference's plan for a *volostel'* because it would establish zemstvo control at the subdistrict level, thereby challenging their own authority over all officials in the village and *volost'*.[47] Past conflicts between the zemstvos and governors had soured the latter on new experiments in public self-government, especially since the senatorial reports revealed the peasants' antipathy for self-government.

In effect, the governors' criticisms amounted to a sweeping repudiation of the Special Conference's proposals for village and *volost'* administration

---

[45]Ibid., *ll.* 462–462 *ob.*

[46]Ibid., *op.* 2, *d.* 15, *ll.* 305 *ob.*-306.

Zubov, the governor of Saratov, made the most detailed case for retaining peasant administration. He did not deny that problems existed in peasant administration. To rectify them, he proposed to allow large peasant communities to subdivide, on the grounds that the root of all abuses in village administration was the huge size of many communities (for instance, those with 500 or more heads of household). Since articles 52–54 of the Emancipation Statute required two-thirds of all village heads of the household to participate in the assembly's decision to be legal, the problems of convoking and maintaining order in such assemblies were ever present. To ease the fiscal burden of village administration for the peasants, he recommended that all residents of the village, regardless of their estate affiliation, pay a share of community taxes because they enjoyed the services of the village government. To ensure that peasants implemented these changes, Zubov favored the creation of a *volost'* guardian or watchdog, an official akin to a peace arbitrator appointed by and subordinate to the district administration. He would handle all the duties of the former arbitrators except land settlements. See ibid., *d.* 13, *ll.* 540–3, 548, 561–561 *ob.*

[47]See ibid., *d.* 15, *ll.* 99, 148 *ob.*–149; and ibid., *d.* 14, *l.* 222.

and a plea for quick and firm government control over the peasantry. Just as the idea of state control over the peasants attracted Tolstoi's attention from 1884 on, so did the criticisms of the conference's zemstvo reform program by some governors. Even though the majority of governors approved the organization of a Bureau of District Administration under the conference's proposal, they clearly had no intention of allowing the zemstvo control over the district administration that was the objective of the proposal, and Tolstoi later used their resistance effectively in dismissing the commission. These governors, as illustrated by their insistence on government-appointed bureau chairmen, urged Tolstoi to systematize local government from top to bottom by bringing all local organs under his ministerial control. Governors in favor of appointed chairmen emphasized that a zemstvo-elected chairman for a government institution would violate a basic practice of Russian government – namely that all officials in local state institutions were appointed and paid by the central government.[48] In other words, in order to establish state control over all local institutions, which these governors viewed as the prerequisite to establishing order in local administration, all local officials would have to be appointed by the government.

This argument for centralization certainly appealed to Tolstoi, who did not conceal his preference for local officials under the control of the minister of internal affairs. On the report of S. P. Ushakov, governor of Tula Province, he scribbled that it would be better to appoint rather than elect the district chief (to supervise the entire district administration), and that the latter should have the comprehensive discretionary powers of a governor in his district.[49] And on other gubernatorial reports he acknowledged his agreement that the conference's proposals for the village and *volost'* administration were premature, and that the provinces needed "a *volost'* chief with combined administrative and judicial responsibilities."[50]

In short, practical experience and political opportunism accounted for the governors' opposition to the conference proposal. Yet more important than their motives in opposing such proposals was the impact of their arguments for centralization on the course of official debate and on Tolstoi himself. First, they established the notion that the conference's proposals were impractical and that the authors of these reform plans had no knowledge whatsoever of local conditions – an inaccurate claim, to be sure, but one that opponents of the conference proposals in the Kakhanov Commission frequently reiterated in order to discredit the decentralist position. Clearly, the governors and some of the local experts in the full commission criticized the proposals as impractical for political reasons, because the reforms, if enacted, would have curbed their own

---

[48]Ibid., *f.* Kakhanovskaia komissiia, *op.* 1, *d.* 106, *ll.* 68 *ob.*-69; and ibid., *f.* Kantseliariia MVD, *op.* 2, *d.* 12, *ll.* 457–457 *ob.*

[49]Ibid., *ll.* 227 *ob.*-228.

[50]See ibid., *l.* 173; and ibid., *d.* 15, *l.* 306 *ob.*; and Tolstoi's marginalia on the governors' reports in ibid., *d.* 13, *l.* 556 *ob.*; ibid., *d.* 14, *l.* 222 *ob.*; and ibid., *d.* 12, *l.* 396.

authority over zemstvo activity and would have given the zemstvo control of district administration. Given the authoritarian attitudes of some governors, they were no doubt right in warning that zemstvo control at the district level and below would lead to difficulties in the form of paralyzing conflicts between the state and zemstvo.

Second, and more important, the governors' criticisms of the conference program educated Tolstoi on local conditions and reinforced his belief that such reform proposals were incompatible with autocracy, thus prompting the minister to invite local experts notorious for their attacks against the local government reforms of the 1860s to lead the full commission's attack against decentralization. At the same time, the governors' demand for state-appointed local officials (as opposed to peace arbitrators), gubernatorial control over the zemstvos, and the supervision by an official with administrative and judicial authority provided Tolstoi with the rudiments of his centralization and counterreform policy. As we have already seen, some of these ideas had been suggested earlier by certain gentry and zemstvo leaders. But in the fall of 1884 Tolstoi, in evaluating the Kakhanov Commission's recommendations and devising his own proposals, attached more importance to the governors' views than to the arguments of gentry and zemstvo leaders or of rival ministerial officials. Whereas gentry/zemstvo leaders often acted according to "public" interests that frequently clashed with state aims and rival ministries had their own particularistic concerns, the governors, according to Tolstoi, were the only local officials to put the interests of autocracy above all others. As such, Tolstoi had come to regard them as his plenipotentiaries in the provinces and to believe that their knowledge of local conditions and political reliability made them eminently more qualified than St. Petersburg bureaucrats or zemstvo leaders to propose effective reforms.

In the wake of the governors' response to his 1883 circular, Tolstoi, even though he did not intervene directly in the Kakhanov Commission, took measures to prevent the adoption of the conference's recommendations, and, he hoped, to force the commission to propose reforms more congruent with his views. His main step in that direction was to invite several governors and a number of traditionally minded gentry marshals to participate in the full commission. Still, it must be emphasized that in the fall of 1884 he was willing to wait for the final recommendations of the commission and to judge them on their merits. Only six months earlier he had expressed this view to Judicial Minister Nabokov.[51] His break with that body would come in the following year when, in con-

---

[51] See Tolstoi's 10 February 1884 letter to Nabokov noted in ibid., *fond* Departament zakonov Gosudarstvennogo Soveta, *opis'* t. 11, *delo* 23a, *ll.* 598 *ob.*-599; the passage for 26 November 1883 in *Dnevnik sekretaria Polovtsova*, 1: 148; and Feoktistov, pp. 248–9. By this date, Tolstoi had received some of the governors' replies to his July circular, including those of Ushakov and Zubov.

Tolstoi allegedly justified allowing the commission to continue its work on the grounds "that it is better to prepare beforehand even for more or less radical reforms of the domestic administration in Russia than to create new institutions out of the blue." Meshcherskii quotes him to this effect in *Moi vospominaniia*, 3: 231.

junction with his bid to take control of government policy making, he arranged for the commission's dismissal on the ground that it had failed to accomplish its objective.

The debate in the Kakhanov Commission and the conservative gentry counterattack

The final period of the Kakhanov Commission's activity, which lasted until 1 May 1885, began in October 1884 with the convocation of the full commission. If the previous work of the commission seemed to take place in a political vacuum, the debates in the full commission were, in contrast, a microcosm of the conflicts that raged within ministerial circles and the landed gentry during the mid-1880s. Diverse interest groups within the commission sought to use the debates as a forum to arouse government support for their concerns, whether it be the economic and political future of the gentry or the usefulness of an independent judiciary in Russia; and such discussions implicitly (and on occasion explicitly) dealt with the ministerial power balance in the countryside. Although it is difficult to make generalizations about the conference bureaucrats, governors, ministerial representatives, zemstvo leaders, and gentry marshals who comprised the full commission, one thing is clear: These various factions, with the exception of the conference bureaucrats, generally displayed more concern for their own prerogatives and needs than for a systematic reorganization, or simply the administrative efficiency, of local government. Political power increasingly became the issue, and in this respect commission members foreshadowed the attitude of higher officials toward local government reform several years later.

Historians as diverse as B. B. Veselovskii and P. A. Zaionchkovskii contend that the local experts split into two camps over the Special Conference's proposals, with the gentry marshals opposing them and zemstvo leaders supporting them.[52] Actually, such a clear-cut delineation oversimplifies the situation. Gentry marshals often served as zemstvo board chairmen, as illustrated by Pazukhin, N. A. Chaplin (Bezhets District, Tver' Province), M. A. Konstantinovich, and Prince L. N. Gagarin; and gentry such as Konstantinovich, Chaplin, and I. A. Gorchakov (the chairman of the St. Petersburg provincial zemstvo board) campaigned in the debates for the participation of all social estates in the village and *volost'* administration. In short, these gentry regarded themselves primarily as zemstvo leaders and identified with zemstvo interests, in contrast to a few gentry marshals who openly opposed the abolition of separate peasant administration as a threat to the privileged status of the gentry. Rather, the nature and tradition of zemstvo activity in their home provinces was generally more influential than social origins in determining the attitudes of local officials toward all-estate

---

[52]Veselovskii, *Istoriia zemstva*, 3: 317; and Zaionchkovskii, *Rossiiskoe samoderzhavie*, pp. 219, 227.

village and *volost'* administration.[53] For instance, the advocates of these reforms, such as Chaplin, Gorchakov, and D. A. Naumov (the zemstvo chairman in Moscow province), came from provinces with active institutions that for two decades had favored abolishing estate distinctions between peasants and nonpeasants. In contrast, their adversaries represented provinces in which zemstvo activity suffered from a high rate of delegate absenteeism (Voronezh, Tambov, Simbirsk, Penza), or in which there was a history of conflict between governors and zemstvos (Orel, Perm).

Other prominent local experts in the debates besides those noted above included S. S. Bekhteev, the gentry marshal of Elets District (Orel); Prince A. D. Obolenskii, the gentry marshal of Penza Province; A. E. Zarin, the marshal of Pskov Province; and A. K. Anastas'ev, the governor of Perm Province. In addition, Tolstoi and Kakhanov appointed eleven officials, in most cases deputies of the various ministers, to participate with the Special Conference members and local experts in the debates. In particular, A. Ia. von Giubbenet, deputy minister of transportation and communication, and N. G. Printts, an official in the Ministry of Justice with experience in zemstvo affairs, took an active part in criticizing the conference's proposals.[54]

With twenty-six new members in the full commission, the Special Conference faced an uphill battle persuading the full commission to accept their reform proposals. Their task became even more difficult when Kakhanov, in his desire to be fair and thorough, had forty copies of the survey of governors' opinions hastily distributed to commission members prior to the first meeting on 5 October 1884.[55] Little did he foresee how damaging this

---

[53]The one exception perhaps involved gentry marshals who were elected by assemblies dominated by the middle and upper gentry and who defended their interests against the petty gentry and nongentry elements. The cases of gentry marshals Pazukhin, A. D. Obolenskii, and S. S. Bekhteev, as analyzed in this chapter, would fit this pattern. However, it should be noted that those three marshals came from areas in which zemstvos had administrative and fiscal problems, and that the diverse backgrounds and interests of gentry marshals, according to Hamburg, make it risky to generalize about them as a group. Hamburg, *Politics*, pp. 49–52.

[54]The full commission consisted of the following members (identifications given for those not previously mentioned in the text):

a. Chairman – M. S. Kakhanov.

b. Special Conference members – S. A. Mordvinov; F. L. Barykov; N. A. Vaganov; I. E. Andreevskii; G. P. Galagan; P. P. Semenov; and I. N. Durnovo. Senator M. E. Kovalevskii died on 31 January 1884, eight months before the full sessions began.

c. Invited local experts – A. V. Bogdanovich (governor of Voronezh); S. N. Gudim-Levkovich (governor of Kovno province); A. K. Anastas'ev; G. V. Kondoidi (gentry marshal of Tambov province); A. E. Zarin; Prince A. D. Obolenskii; S. S. Bekhteev; A. D. Pazukhin; N. A. Chaplin; I. A. Gorchakov; Prince L. N. Gagarin (gentry marshal and provincial board chairman in Riazan' province); M. A. Konstantinovich; P. A. Karpov (zemstvo delegate, Ekaterinoslav province); and E. N. Dubenskii.

d. Bureaucrats appointed to the commission – I. I. Shamshin; Maj.-Gen. M. A. Domontovich (official in the War Ministry); Count P. A. Shuvalov; Count K. I. Pahlen; T. I. Filippov (deputy state controller); A. Ia. von Giubbenet; Prince M. S. Volkonskii (deputy minister of education); N. G. Printts; P. N. Nikolaev (deputy minister of finance); V. I. Veshniakov (deputy minister of state properties); P. A. Markov (senator, deputy minister of justice); F. M. Markus (member of the State Council and deputy director of the Law Codification Section); A. Ol'khin (former *zemets*); and A. I. Kislinskii (former *zemets*).

[55]See Kakhanov's 28 August 1884 letter to Deputy Minister of Internal Affairs Durnovo in TsGIA. *f.*

brief catalogue of criticisms would be to the conference's proposals. Moreover, by giving commission members unusual latitude in their discussions, Kakhanov unwittingly allowed such critics as gentry marshals Bekhteev, Pazukhin, and Prince Obolenskii to dominate commission meetings. From the first meeting on, they scorned the conference proposals as impractical and, as one powerful interest group in the commission, directed the thrust of their estatist attack against Professor Andreevskii.[56] No doubt past frustrations in dealing with peasant officials and peasant delegates in the zemstvo assembly accounted in part for their opposition to the conference proposals. But, as gentry spokesmen, their main aim was state protection of the elite landed gentry (or the aristocratic element of the gentry, as Solov'ev calls it)[57] from the kulaks and "intelligentsia" – the groups, in their view, favored by the conference's program. The three marshals made their case during the climax of the "aristocracy's" campaign in 1884 and, like their counterparts outside the commission, called for state recognition of past gentry service; the leadership of an independent landed gentry in local administration (much as in England), reorganized along estatist (*soslovnyi*) lines; and the establishment of a Gentry Land Bank to make low interest loans available to the gentry in order to pay off their mortgages and hold on to their estates. Alexander III himself expressed sympathy for these concerns in 1883–4, going so far as to endorse a memorandum from O. B. Rikhter, chief of the Main Imperial Residence, that praised the gentry as the fundamental support of the crown, and establishing commissions that produced the imperial rescript to the gentry (21 April 1885) and a Gentry Land Bank (3 June 1885).[58]

Moreover, as the journals of the full commission meetings reveal, the gentry faction of Bekhteev, Obolenskii, and Pazukhin used many of the arguments of Katkov and Meshcherskii, the pro-aristocratic publicists who stood close to the throne, to defend the traditional estates order. Several months before the full commission met, Meshcherskii outlined the essence of the estatist argument used in the commission when he wrote Alexander III (11 June 1884):

Kantseliariia MVD, *op.* 2, *d.* 15, *l.* 412. The late date of the request left conference members little time to prepare their response.

[56] TsGAOR, *f.* Aleksandr III, 1884–1885, *op.* 1, *d.* 108, *l.* 79; Golovin, *Moi vospominaniia*, 2: 78; and *Dnevnik sekretaria A. A. Polovtsova*, 1: 259.

[57] On the stratification of the gentry into aristocratic, middle, and petty categories, and the political problems this posed for the gentry in the 1880s, see Solov'ev, pp. 169–71, 195–200; and Hamburg, *Politics*, pp. 59–68. Pazukhin's role in this campaign has frequently confused historians (for instance, Tvardovskaia, *Ideologiia poreformennogo samoderzhaviia*, pp. 234, 236), who acknowledge his collaboration with Katkov and later Tolstoi, yet argue that Katkov favored the "aristocratic gentry" while Tolstoi's counterreform proposals were aimed at the "middle gentry." As we shall see, it was Pazukhin who altered his arguments to suit Tolstoi (who had a very different view of the landed gentry's purpose than Katkov), rather than vice versa.

[58] Solov'ev, pp. 165–9, 172–4. The Taneev Commission (1883–5) helped in preparing Alexander III's rescript to the gentry and reviewed the criteria for earning gentry status, whereas a special commission chaired by Finance Minister Bunge, and including gentry marshals Bekhteev and Obolenskii, drew up proposals for the Gentry Land Bank. Hamburg, *Politics*, pp. 108–16.

Imperceptively a theory is coming forth that it is very easy to proceed from the theory of peasant welfare (*schast'e*) and of a public (*vsesoslovnoe*) or zemstvo economy to the theory of the gentry's demise, and to move from that theory to the equalization of all estates on the basis of education; it is but one step from that theory to the theory of autocracy's uselessness. This step has almost been made.[59]

Although the three marshals would ultimately fall out with each other (and with Meshcherskii) over the means of aiding the landed gentry, in the fall 1884 commission meetings they agreed that the conference's program, in ending separate peasant administration, would eventually oust the gentry from leadership in local self-government in favor of peasants groomed for this role by the gentry. This would undermine the raison d'être of a separate gentry estate and remove once and for all their claim to special imperial favor. Even though the government had not taken this claim seriously for several decades, particularly in the realm of local government (as the debate over the counterreforms would again reveal), at this point Bekhteev and Pazukhin presumed that the government could be induced to strengthen the gentry's position as a means of establishing order in the provinces. The reorganization of local self-government along social estate lines, they contended, was the key to gentry control and state security in this area.

In contrast, the bureaucrats appointed to the full commission comprised another interest group. Their goal in the impending commission debates was to protect the interests of their respective ministries. They, too, couched their objections to the conference proposals in terms of pragmatism and the administrative and fiscal needs of the government, but ministerial interests were their foremost concern. For example, M. S. Volkonskii, the deputy minister of education, was typical of the deputy ministers who attacked the proposed increase in zemstvo authority at the expense of their ministries. Although a son of the Decembrist S. G. Volkonskii, the deputy minister was no friend of the zemstvo. He had gained notoriety by making false promises to local zemstvos in order to raise money for the Griazi-Tsaritsyn railroad.[60] Thus, he claimed to have no objections to letting the Bureau of District Administration manage district school affairs, but he did oppose expanding zemstvo jurisdiction in the area of elementary public education. His arguments reflected the position of Tolstoi and Delianov, the minister of education (1882–97), who tolerated no interference in the state's control over public education. Consequently, Volkonskii agreed that the Bureau of District Administration could decide school-related questions on three conditions: (1) In such matters the district marshal (as ex officio chairman and as a government representative under the Laws of 13 June 1867) would retain the rights and obligations he currently possessed as chairman of the district school council; (2) all business under the jurisdiction of the school councils

---

[59]Quoted in Solov'ev, p. 171. Katkov made similar arguments in his editorials in the *Moscow News* from 1881 on.
[60]Volkonskii was nicknamed "dirty" (*griaznyi*) because of his involvement in this episode (1871). See the passage for 1 January 1890 in *Dnevnik sekretaria Polovtsova*, 2: 255.

would be transferred to the newly formed bureau; and (3) zemstvo jurisdiction in public education would be confined strictly to the areas defined by current legislation.[61] The commission's subsequent decision in late January 1885 to make the district marshal the ex officio chairman of the bureau and to give him the right to appeal its decision to a Bureau of Provincial Administration constituted a serious blow to the decentralists' plan for zemstvo control.[62]

Although the conference, gentry, and ministerial factions in the full commission clashed over almost all areas under discussion, two issues eventually dictated the nature of the full commission's recommendations. These were the proposal for an all-estate, that is, public village administration, and the Bekhteev–Pazukhin counterproject for section chiefs. The debate in the full commission began with the Bekhteev–Pazukhin faction criticizing the conference members for being inconsistent in article one, because they proposed a peasant *obshchina* and an all-estate village community and, in their opinion, the uneducated peasant would not comprehend the difference between the two. Printts and Shamshin also made a fiscal case against the proposal, claiming that by maintaining a separate peasant *obshchina*, the village community would be left with no property or means of support.[63] Taken aback by the outspoken opposition to the first issue under discussion, Kakhanov convinced the members to postpone a vote on this matter and to consider the social composition of the village administration. This was a crucial error in judgment on his part, because the composition of the village community was a much more explosive issue. Bekhteev's party correctly perceived Kakhanov's action as a delaying tactic in order to vote on article one at a more propitious moment.[64] Thus, the opposition unleashed equally severe criticism of the proposed all-estate village community in the second article. Galagan defected from the conference majority and joined Bekhteev, Anastas'ev, Printts, and Obolenskii in assailing the proposal. They explained that only two groups lived in the countryside – landlords and peasants – and that the latter had dwelled in their own communities for more than a thousand years. There was no evidence that they desired outsiders to administer the village with them; on the contrary, according to the Bekhteev faction, it was imperative to protect peasants from corrupt and alien *raznochintsy* (in this case educated people of nongentry status), a fact recognized by the architects of the 1861 statute. Bekhteev ridiculed the conference majority for alleging that the peasants were isolated from the regular administrative apparatus; it was absurd, he scoffed, to talk about the isolation of 80 percent of Russia's population. This bit of reverse logic confused some of the commission members and played on the conservative tendencies of the deputy ministers within

---

[61]*Zhurnal Osoboi Komissii*, no. 9, p. 12.
[62]Ibid., p. 99
[63]Ibid., no. 4, pp. 10–12.
[64]See Meshcherskii's comments in TsGAOR, *f.* Aleksandr III, *op.* 1, *d.* 108, *l.* 84 *ob.*

the commission who were hesitant about an immediate reform involving four-fifths of the nation's population.[65]

The Bekhteev party offered its own solutions to eradicate the problems of peasant administration. First, all residents who enjoyed the services of the village administration should pay for them, regardless of their estate affiliation. Bekhteev emphasized that this already was the practice in his district, and that it should be written into law. Second, it was necessary to free peasant officials from police functions and to put them under the firm personal supervision of an official elected by the zemstvo or appointed by the government.[66] Not surprisingly, in order to perpetuate the political control of the gentry landlords over the peasants, and thus preserve a source of cheap labor for the land magnates, Bekhteev and Pazukhin insisted that the zemstvo, the overwhelming majority of which were under gentry control, elect these supervisory officials. Their willingness to put gentry designs above the needs of state cost them the support of half of their faction, who split ranks and advocated state-appointed supervisory officials along the lines recommended by the governors.

The spokesmen for uniform village administration retaliated on this issue. Chaplin pointed out that many villages of peasants and nonpeasants lacked any administration, and referred to communities in Moscow, St. Petersburg, and his own Tver' Province. Citing the findings of the late senatorial inspector Kovalevskii, Kakhanov claimed that Ufa and Orenburg provinces contained many villages of resettled peasants and factory workers with no administration.[67] Naumov argued for the conference proposals on fiscal grounds, emphasizing that in Moscow Province alone one out of every five village residents was not a peasant, and hence was exempt from communal taxes. For all their merit, however, these were essentially the same arguments for all-estate village administration that were developed in the memorandum attached to the conference's proposals. No wonder they had little effect in winning over undecided members in the full commission. Among the decentralists, only Naumov introduced a new point in favor of all-estate village administration when he emphasized that nonpeasants living in the village currently showed no respect for peasant officials, because by law the resolutions of the village assembly were not binding on them.[68]

The showdown occurred at the seventh session on 27 October, when members voted on whether or not nonpeasants in the village should (1) pay taxes for the village administration, (2) be considered residents of the village if they owned property there, and (3) have the right to elect village community officials. In the first two cases, the proponents of an all-estate village community were outvoted by narrow margins, because they lost the support

[65]*Zhurnal Osoboi Komissii*, no. 4, pp. 21–4.
[66]Ibid., pp. 23–6.
[67]Ibid., pp. 27–8.
[68]Ibid., pp. 29, 53.

of some deputy ministers appointed to the commission. When the issue of the village administration first came up in mid-October, the commission split 10–10 in a preliminary vote over whether or not to support the conference's position.[69] Yet two weeks later the majority of the deputy ministers concluded, on the basis of the arguments presented in the debate, that the conference's proposal was premature although ultimately desirable. Bekhteev's arguments had persuaded them that the peasants lacked sufficient education and experience to participate with nonpeasants in governing the village on the basis of general civil law rather than peasant customs.

The advocates of an all-estate village community suffered defeat on the third issue by an even larger count (19–10). Kakhanov shocked his associates of the Special Conference by voting against them on this matter. Commission journals offer no explanation for Kakhanov's defection from the decentralist faction on this point. It seems probable, however, that the strong reaction of the local experts against the conference's project embarrassed the chairman and sowed doubts in him about the wisdom of organizing public self-government in the village in the immediate future. The consequences of this defeat and Kakhanov's defection were nevertheless immediately apparent. The decentralists within the commission split over the issue of whether or not to establish an all-estate *volost'* with or without a *votostel'*, thereby allowing the commission members in favor of maintaining the peasant *volost'* to prevail on this point. With no leader for their cause and no coherent plan for a counteroffensive in the wake of their defeat on the village and *volost'* administration, the cornerstone of their reform plan, the decentralists faced the prospect of being routed completely in the debate.[70]

Thus, Tolstoi's Trojan horse strategy to undermine the conference's reform plan of public village self-government paid handsome dividends. On 27 October, Meshcherskii enthusiastically wrote Alexander about the "victory of common sense and practice over theory," and noted that the local experts had vowed "to battle the bureaucrats, theoreticians, and intelligentsia who reigned in the original Kakhanov Commission." He credited Tolstoi with inviting local experts such as Pazukhin and Bekhteev.[71] Besides flattering Tolstoi, the statement provided an accurate assessment of the minister's views on the Special Conference.[72] Tolstoi told Meshcherskii, "I know provincial life better than the Lycurguses of the Kakhanov Commission, and as long as I hold my post, I will not allow the implementation of those liberal innovations and undertakings, which without a doubt are contrary to the needs of provincial life."[73] These comments in late 1884 reflected Tolstoi's

[69]Zaionchkovskii, *Rossiiskoe samoderzhavie*, p. 227.

[70]*Zhurnal Osoboi Komissii*, no. 4, pp. 53–5, 33–4.

[71]TsGAOR, *f*. Aleksandr III, 1885 [sic.], *op*. 1, *d*. 113, *ll*. 11–11 *ob*.; and Meshcherskii, *Moi vospominaniia*, 3: 183–4.

[72]TsGAOR, *f*. Aleksandr III, *op*. 1, *d*. 109, *ll*. 79 *ob*.-80.

[73]Meshcherskii, *Moi vospominaniia*, 3: 145.

Gessen argues that the emphasis on practical experience was merely a ploy of the opponents of the conference's proposals in order to attack the projects. He criticizes the conference members because

growing impatience with and criticism of the Kakhanov Commission, as well as his plans to take control in top official circles by ousting the "liberal" retinue of Loris-Melikov, whom he considered political foes of the autocracy. Up to this point in the debate, the majority of commission members displayed little inclination to abandon the local institutions created in the 1860s. Their evaluation of the Bekhteev–Pazukhin counterproject to create section chiefs with administrative and judicial powers revealed no deviation from this pattern. This controversial proposal prompted even hitherto lethargic members such as Veshniakov, Kislinskii, and Markov to take an active part in the discussions, for these sessions constituted a debate over the benefits and shortcomings of the Peasant, Zemstvo, and Judicial Reforms of the 1860s. Beyond that, the discussions raised even larger issues, including Russia's relationship to the West in terms of political development. Bekhteev and Pazukhin made their most elaborate case for *soslovnost'* (that is, gentry privilege) in the November 1884 sessions of the Kakhanov Commission, and Pazukhin reiterated much of it in his article "The Current State of Russia and the Estates Question," the core of which may well have been written in 1881–2. Katkov published the article in his *Russian Herald* (1885) as a means of gaining Tolstoi's support.[74]

In both the commission and the article, Pazukhin admitted that the abolition of serfdom was just and met the administrative needs of the state, as demonstrated by the success of this reform. At the same time, the Peasant, Zemstvo, and Judicial Statutes had violated Russia's traditional estates order and had replaced the landlord's authority over the peasants with many new

---

they fell for the trick and debated with their adversaries over practical needs, rather than sticking to "principles." Gessen, pp. 168–9. Yet given the pervasiveness of this argument in St. Petersburg in 1883–4, as we have already noted, it is quite possible that Tolstoi encouraged the "local experts" to make this point (thus reaffirming what many governors had written); such an action certainly fit in with Tolstoi's plans to orchestrate the defeat of the Special Conference's program.

[74]Whether Katkov used Pazukhin to attract Tolstoi's support (as suggested by Solov'ev, p. 181; Tvardovskaia, *Ideologiia poreformennogo samoderzhaviia*, p. 233; and Becker, p. 58) or Pazukhin used his ties with Katkov and Meshcherskii to attract Tolstoi's attention (as argued by Taranovski, "Politics of Counter-Reform," p. 388), it is clear that in 1884 Katkov and Pazukhin had very similar views on the elite gentry's role and the importance of the estate principle (*soslovnost'*) in local administration – ideas that, as detailed especially in Chapter 5, conflicted on key points with Tolstoi's bureaucratic centralism. Similarly, Becker's claim that Katkov "went on to arrange for Pazukhin's appointment as director of chancellery under Minister of Internal Affairs Tolstoi" (p. 58) is based more on supposition than hard evidence; after all, as detailed in the last section of this chapter, Katkov and Tolstoi did not always hold similar views on administration, personnel appointments, and gentry needs.

Alfred Rieber points out in his *Merchants and Entrepreneurs in Imperial Russia* (Chapel Hill, N.C., 1982), p. 95, that in 1882 (?) Pazukhin sent a proposal to the Kakhanov Commission that was published in revised form by Katkov in the *Russian Herald*; Rieber found the original proposal in the archive of Alexander III [TsGAOR, f. Aleksandr III, *op.* 1, *d.* 617, dated by archivists 1881–1882 (?)]. Pazukhin's proposal (which I have not seen), like his article, assailed the growing influence of the urban intelligentsia in the zemstvo and urged that the latter be reorganized along social estate lines. As Rieber notes, the internal history of Pazukhin's proposal and the publication of his article (in January 1885, not January 1884 as Rieber claims) is unclear; however, the delay in Pazukhin's rise to prominence in 1885–6 would suggest that his arguments were not especially novel or influential in the early 1880s, nor did Katkov have control over Tolstoi or the emperor.

authorities – the peasant village and *volost'* officials, the zemstvos, the justices of the peace, the peace arbitrators, and later the district bureaus – and all of these institutions, with their overlapping jurisdictions, confused the peasants. In other words, Pazukhin argued that paternalistic gentry control of the countryside was the key to the welfare of the state and the peasantry, and thus concluded that only the reestablishment of personal supervision over the peasants in the form of zemstvo-elected section chiefs with broad powers would bring order to peasant self-government. Pazukhin did not advocate a return to the arbitrary landlord control of the prereform period over the peasantry, but rather the reinstitution of autonomous peace arbitrators who obeyed laws and supervised peasants in their efforts at self-rule.[75]

Bekhteev cited more concrete reasons for tightening gentry control over the peasants and for giving section chiefs broad administrative and judicial powers. Unlike the conference's *volostel'*, the section chiefs first and foremost would provide immediate supervision over the peasantry, which alone would correct the current shortcomings of peasant administration. They would cost at least 50 percent less than the *volostel'*, because each official would supervise two to three *volosti*. Moreover, Bekhteev proposed the abolition of the justices of the peace, whose functions in petty justice would be transferred to the section chiefs. This would guarantee that the required number of educated and experienced personnel would be available for the new post and would reduce the expenses of the zemstvo.[76] Yet his contention that the section chief would be more accessible to the local population for their legal needs was mere rhetoric, because the territory under his jurisdiction would not be much smaller than that under the justices' jurisdiction. The gentry marshal concluded:

This combination [of powers] in any case will lead quickly to the elimination of (or even eradicate immediately) important and widely recognized shortcomings of local administration such as the excessive number of institutions, the absence of supervisory authority over peasant self-government, the peasants' vulnerability to harmful elements in the person of exploiters and predators in their communities who take advantage of their low level of intellectual and moral development, and so forth. Only the proposed combination of powers will lead to the simplicity in local administration that at present is one of the most desirable aspects of reform.[77]

The Bekhteev–Pazukhin counterproject evoked a torrent of criticism within the commission, because many members were committed to the separation of administrative and judicial powers established by the reforms of the 1860s. Kakhanov and twenty-one others insisted that administrative and judicial functions by nature were so different that no official could handle both responsibly. Whereas the courts, they explained, rendered decisions on

---

[75] A. D. Pazukhin, *Sovremennoe sostoianie Rossii i soslovnyi vopros* (Moscow, 1886), pp. 6–12. Pazukhin's brochure (published by Katkov's press) is an exact replica of the article that appeared in *The Russian Herald (Russkii vestnik)*, vol. 175 (January 1885), pp. 5–58.

[76] *Zhurnal Osoboi Komissii*, no. 5, pp. 9–12.

[77] Quoted from ibid., p. 24.

the basis of law, officials were directed by considerations of expediency in introducing measures. In short, the adoption of the counterproject would mean not only a reorganization of local officials, but, more important, a complete repudiation of the concept of administrative law and separation of powers that had guided Russian administrative development since the 1860s. No one recognized this more than Deputy Minister of Justice Markov, who emphasized that the judicial decisions of section chiefs accountable only to the Ministry of Internal Affairs would be outside the law.[78] Indeed, the counterproject posed the same threat to the justices of the peace and an independent judiciary within the commission that the attacks of Tolstoi and Pobedonostsev against Justice Minister Nabokov in 1884–5 were causing outside it. No wonder Markov used every argument he could – for example, the physical impossibility of supervising peasant administration conscientiously and of hearing petty litigation – in order to turn conservative officials in the Kakhanov Commission against the counterproject.[79]

Some commission members spoke out against the counterproject not so much from self-interest, but mainly because of their political philosophy. The adoption of the Bekhteev–Pazukhin proposal, they declared, would negate the main achievements of Alexander II's reign and remove Russia from the ranks of civilized nations. In working out the provisions of the Judicial and Zemstvo Reforms, Russian officials in the early 1860s had repudiated the notion that Russia's administrative development and institutions had to be distinct from the Western pattern.[80] The opponents of the counterproject stressed that the experience of the past two decades had demonstrated that Western concepts, such as the existence of a judiciary independent of the administration and public participation in local administration, had helped to curb the abuses that characterized police justice in prereform Russia. They outlined the historical pattern that all modern nations including Russia followed in their administrative development:

History shows that in all nations during the first stage of their development there is no separation of powers. As long as the needs of society are few in number, the government's activity, which aims at satisfying these needs, is not complicated. The fulfillment of all administrative needs depends on one person, who is able to handle them without any adverse effect. But the development of the state leads to new needs, the satisfaction of which exceeds the capability of individuals or separate groups, and *government activity* develops as a result. Various branches of administration begin to become distinct, and separate institutions are established to manage them. As the state recognizes public needs more clearly and increases its resources for

[78]Ibid., pp. 29–30.
[79]Ibid., pp. 28–9. For state legislation dealing with the shortcomings of the justices and the mass of petty litigation see *PSZ*, 2d ser, vol. 55, 61221, 15 July 1880 and 3d ser., vol. 6, 3613, 7 April 1886; and V. B., "Ukaz senata o mirovykh sud'iakh (Vnutrennee obozrenie)," *Russkoe bogatstvo*, no. 9 (1886): 186–7.
[80]Wortman, p. 259.

meeting them, the principle of separation of powers plays a greater role in state administration.[81]

In short, the majority of commission members concluded rather simplistically that the Judicial and Zemstvo Reforms had marked Russia's transition from a backward, despotic state to a civilized nation with a professional, specialized administrative structure. Such a view illustrated how tsarist officials were inclined to think in narrow terms, namely legislative development, rather than to consider the standards of educational development, political maturity, economic independence, and social mobility that constituted the benchmarks of contemporary Western civilization. Curiously, both sides cited local government practices in England to substantiate their arguments. Bekhteev and Pazukhin asserted that the English justices of the peace proved that officials discharging both administrative and judicial functions could be found in an advanced nation, whereas their opponents claimed that England was a special case because of her island status and tradition of decentralized self-government. They emphasized that English justices of the peace were above all judges who based their decisions on law rather than administrative expediency. Thus, spokesmen in the commission for public self-government such as Gorchakov and Chaplin, defeated in their quest for an all-estate *volost'*, pushed hard for the rejection of the Bekhteev–Pazukhin counterproject. With good reason, they feared that its adoption would preclude any self-government – either public or peasant – in the *volost'* in favor of arbitrary gentry control over the local population. In concluding the debate on the counterproject, they reminded commission members that virtually all zemstvo assemblies, including those in Pazukhin's home province, had rejected similar proposals for officials with administrative and judicial powers, and they urged the commission to do the same.[82]

On 24 November the commission voted 22–10 to reject the Bekhteev–Pazukhin counterproject. The vote attested to the commission's commitment to self-government and the autonomous judicial institutions introduced by the Peasant, Zemstvo, Judicial, and Municipal Statutes. Significantly, all three groups in the commission – the Special Conference members, the local experts, and the invited bureaucrats – voted against the counterproject; in fact, two out of every three local experts (including two governors and two gentry marshals) cast ballots against it. Instead, the commission decided to limit its recommendations to the establishment of a section chief elected by

---

[81]Quoted from *Zhurnal Osoboi Komissii*, no. 5, pp. 31–2.

[82]Ibid.; and Gessen, p. 184. The commission majority overlooked an unusual similarity between England and Russia that accounted for officials with combined administrative and judicial powers. In both nations there were not enough qualified personnel by the end of the nineteenth century to staff both the provincial bureaucracy and judiciary; in England, of course, this problem stemmed from the fact that justices of the peace customarily served without pay, and few individuals outside the country gentry could afford to hold these positions.

the zemstvo in order to supervise peasant self-government and, as a secondary responsibility, to implement government and zemstvo decisions.[83]

Thus, on this issue, like so many others, the commission cautiously followed a middle road and came out against a major reform of current local self-governing institutions. It is not surprising that their deliberations yielded this result. After all, the conference members and the invited local experts, headed by the gentry spokesmen, for the most part canceled out each other in the voting, thus leaving the ministerial delegates appointed to the commission with the balance of power. Unwilling to approve any reforms that could restrict their own jurisdictions, and still wedded in some cases to the ideology of the Great Reforms, officials such as Prince Volkonskii, Markov, Nikolaev, and von Giubbenet found it easier to criticize the short-comings of both the conference program and the counterproject than to suggest concrete solutions. Thus, as the commission moved into the sessions of January and February 1885, it made fewer decisions, restricted the scope of its activity, increasingly watered down its recommendations, and lost whatever momentum it had after the governors' criticisms in 1883–4. By early 1885 this inertia profoundly disturbed Tolstoi who, in his desire to unify ministerial government by asserting his leadership within it, concluded that local self-government required more substantive reform than minor adjustments in the existing mechanism.

New developments in ministerial politics: from gentry paternalism to bureaucratic paternalism

Why did Tolstoi call for the dismissal of the Kakhanov Commission on 28 February 1885? Reduced to its basics, the traditional interpretation holds that Pazukhin's attack against the zemstvo and judicial reforms in the January 1885 issue of the *Russian Herald* served as a manifesto of "gentry reaction" and provided the passive Tolstoi, who previously relied on Katkov and Pobedonostsev for political direction, with the impetus and ideas for the land captain and zemstvo counterreforms.[84] It depicts Tolstoi as part of a

---

[83]*Zhurnal Osoboi Komissii*, no. 5, p. 34.

[84]See S. N. Valk, "Vnutrenniaia politika tsarizma," *Istoriia SSSR*, vol. 2: *1861–1917 gg.*, pp. 238, 240; Kornilov, *Krest'ianskaia reforma*, pp. 236–8; Gessen, p. 199; Veselovskii, *Istoriia zemstva.* 3: 318–19; Zaionchkovskii, *Rossiiskoe samoderzhavie*, pp. 71, 366; Zakharova, *Zemskaia kontrreforma*, p. 77; Solov'ev, p. 184; Korelin, *Dvorianstvo v poreformennoi Rossii*, p. 196; Pirumova, pp. 38–9; Becker, pp. 131, 205; Yaney, *Urge to Mobilize*, p. 71; Whelan, pp. 175–6; and Taranovski, "Politics of Counter-Reform," pp. 375, 386, 424–5. Tvardovskaia contends that in 1884 Pazukhin, on Tolstoi's instructions, produced a memorandum calling for a reorganization of local government and zemstvo representation along estatist lines that circulated among top officials. She makes the claim to show that Pazukhin personally changed the course of state policy, although she fails to cite a source for this information or specify whether this was the earlier memorandum Pazukhin allegedly wrote (see note 75 above) or some other document. See Tvardovskaia, *Ideologiia*, p. 233. The mere existence of this memorandum alone does not prove Tolstoi's commitment to Pazukhin's views. Given Tolstoi's skill in manipulating Kakhanov Commission debates, as shown above, Pazukhin's "memorandum" may well have served Tolstoi as

"Kitchen Cabinet" including Pobedonostsev, Katkov, and Meshcherskii that, notwithstanding their personal differences, agreed on a reactionary "new course" that linked the survival of autocracy to that of the elite landed gentry as a separate estate (*soslovie*); and it views the dismissal of the Kakhanov Commission on 1 May 1885 as another sign of the government's pro-gentry course, heralded by the imperial rescript to the gentry ten days earlier, which recognized past gentry services in local administration and exhorted them to continue in this work.

Yet, given our analysis of the Kakhanov Commission's development and the crucial role that the governors and then Tolstoi played in its activity, there is reason to question many aspects of the traditional interpretation. After all, if Tolstoi was a pliant, career-minded minister who acted only under the influence of others, why did he allow the commission to remain open despite intense pressure from Katkov and Pobedonostsev to close it in 1882–3 (when Tolstoi was presumably more vulnerable) and despite the governors' repudiation of the conference project? As shown in the preceding section, a number of governors and other eminent local leaders made clear-cut suggestions concerning ways to reorganize local government well before 1885. Moreover, if Tolstoi's counterreform policies were merely the result of gentry pressure (and his desire to establish gentry control over local self-government), why, in the face of the pro-gentry (aristocracy) campaign orchestrated by Katkov and Meshcherskii in 1881–2 did he wait until 1885 to act? Even more, why did he allow the Pazukhin–Bekhteev counterproject to suffer defeat in the full commission? These and other questions (including the survival of what most historians regard as a "lame duck" commission for three years) suggest that Pazukhin was not the main force in the genesis of the counterreforms in local self-government from 1883 to 1890, whatever his collaboration with Tolstoi in devising them. Rather, Tolstoi's development as a politician in ministerial circles and the Kakhanov Commission's increasing lack of productivity accounted for his policy toward the commission in 1884–5.

The interpretation of Tolstoi as a passive minister derived largely from reports of his reliance as minister of education on Katkov in the late 1860s and early 1870s, and from the memoirs of top officials, particularly Feoktistov.[85] Yet if Tolstoi as minister of internal affairs had ever enjoyed good relations with Katkov, or for that matter with his patron, Pobedonostsev, they soon evaporated. In January 1883, Katkov already was attacking Tolstoi for being "too careful," meaning that Tolstoi was not immediately imple-

---

another means to sabotage the Special Conference program and, as shown below, mobilize gentry support for his own counterreform plans.

[85]Feoktistov, pp. 180–1, 222, 249; and *Dnevnik sekretaria Polovtsova*, 2: 190.

Sinel claims that in the 1870s Tolstoi and Katkov influenced each other and cooperated in carrying through educational reforms. After 1874, their relationship grew strained and Katkov began to attack Tolstoi for not devising a new university reform fast enough. Allen Sinel, *The Classroom and the Chancellery: State Educational Reform in Russia under Count Dmitry Tolstoi* (Cambridge, Mass., 1973), pp. 169–70, 253–4.

menting Katkov's program for assisting the landed gentry.[86] As relations between Tolstoi and Katkov rapidly deteriorated from late 1882 on, Feoktistov (whom Tolstoi named as head of the Main Bureau on Press Affairs in 1883) grew critical of his superior and, in his admiration for Katkov, wrote the latter that Tolstoi was incapable of independent action or of "finding an ally [read: Katkov] [and] forming a party."[87] For his part, Tolstoi in 1884 considered Katkov to be "the sort of swine I don't admit to my presence," as he confided to Polovtsov.[88] Meanwhile, synod chief Pobedonostsev clashed with Tolstoi over the role of the Orthodox Church in elementary education and over certain provisions of the new university reform.[89] Granted, a certain amount of personal acrimony is to be expected in the private correspondence of top state officials, especially in an autocratic regime that invited ministers to intrigue against each other; but there were more than enough personal and political conflicts in 1882–3 to show that Tolstoi was not the subservient minister that Pobedonostsev or Katkov had in mind in recommending his appointment to Alexander III.[90] In short, from the beginning of his tenure as minister of internal affairs Tolstoi trusted no one completely, and even though later he was personally impressed by Pazukhin, it would have been highly out of character for him to withdraw from the process of local self-government reform and to allow Pazukhin to dictate the provisions of these measures.

Rather, the years 1883–7 marked the period in which Tolstoi evolved from a bureaucrat who simply executed his sovereign's will to a politician who sought to mold it by establishing his control over central policy making and by creating local administrative order and efficiency. His rise in power not only engaged him in a power struggle with several ministers having ties to Loris-Melikov, including Judicial Minister Nabokov and Finance Minister Bunge, but along with his own administrative experience and conflict with Katkov, it changed his view on the gentry's role in local self-government and on the usefulness of the Kakhanov Commission. For instance, Tolstoi did not dismiss the Kakhanov Commission in 1882 or 1883 because he possessed neither the power nor an alternative plan of local government reform that he could see through to the end. When Alexander III asked him to become minister in 1882, he replied that he was extremely unpopular in educated circles as a result of his policies as minister of education, but that

---

[86]See A. A. Kireev's comment in Solov'ev, p. 107.

[87]Feoktistov, p. 179. By late 1882, Katkov was repeatedly expressing disappointment over Tolstoi's appointment as minister.

[88]See Polovtsov's diary entry for 10 December 1884, as quoted in Whelan, p. 60. Tolstoi on numerous occasions complained about Katkov's meddling in state politics. On their strained relations, see particularly Feoktistov's letter of 16 October 1882 to Katkov in ORGBL, *f.* Katkov, 1882, *k.* 12, *d.* 24, *l.* 8; and Feoktistov, pp. 212–13.

[89]See ibid., pp. 224–5; and ORGBL, *f.* Katkov, 1884, *k.* 12, *d.* 27, *l.* 12 *ob.*

[90]On the differences between Tolstoi, Pobedonostsev, Katkov, and Meshcherskii (who, according to Whelan, "enjoyed the contempt of virtually all St. Petersburg with the singular major exception of the tsar himself"), see Whelan, pp. 59–79; Solov'ev, pp. 105–9; and Yaney, *Urge to Mobilize*, pp. 75–7.

he would serve if the tsar so desired. More important, Tolstoi pointed out that he could not act in accord with Alexander II's reforms and that rather than entrust local administration to competing ministerial agents, it would be far better to rely on paternalistic gentry control over peasant administration and zemstvos. Despite this affirmation of faith in the landed gentry and autocracy, Tolstoi acknowledged that he had no concrete plans for reform.[91] Shortly thereafter, he told Prussian Ambassador H. L. von Schweinitz that his primary concern was order.[92] Thus, during 1882 and 1883, Tolstoi confined his work to enforcing the Temporary Regulations of 1881 introduced by Ignat'ev in the area of censorship, working with Minister of Education Delianov on a counterreform proposal for the universities, and learning the duties of his new post. As for the Kakhanov Commission, he told Polovtsov in late 1883 that, despite his opposition to the Special Conference's proposals he had not interfered because he did not want to be accused of preventing the commission from accomplishing anything worthwhile.[93] Actually, sensitivity to public criticism was of little concern to Tolstoi; on the contrary, he deliberately allowed the Kakhanov Commission to meet because he believed he could learn from it while devoting most of his time to the ministerial debate over the university counterreform.

By late 1884, however, Tolstoi's influence in ministerial circles and his opinion of gentry control over local self-government had changed significantly, as the Kakhanov Commission would soon discover firsthand. In getting Alexander III to ratify the university counterreform (officially sponsored by Delianov) on 15 August 1884, Tolstoi not only prevailed over a majority in the State Council, but he also replaced Pobedonostsev as the most powerful minister in St. Petersburg. The new university statute eliminated the autonomy granted to universities under the 1863 statute by placing them under state-appointed curators directly accountable to the Ministry of Education (Tolstoi's objective from 1879 on), and it introduced general state examinations to regulate the type of students admitted to the universities as well as the content of faculty lectures.[94] No official spoke more critically against the examinations than Pobedonostsev, who asserted that the educated public would regard them as a punitive measure. But Tolstoi, who had

---

[91]See Polovtsov's diary entry for June 1882, which summarizes Count Shuvalov's version of Tolstoi's conversation with Alexander III in TsGAOR, f. Polovtsov, op. 1, d. 20, ll. 78 ob.–79; and Golovnin's letter of 11 August 1883 to D. A. Miliutin in ORGBL, f. D. A. Miliutin, 1883, p. 61, d. 39, l. 39 ob.

[92]See H. L. von Schweinitz, *Denkwuerdigkeiten des Botschafters H. L. von Schweinitz* (2 vols.; Berlin, 1927), 2:203, as taken from Whelan, p. 69.

[93]See the passage for 16 November 1883 in *Dnevnik sekretaria Polovtsova*, 1: 148. Tolstoi added that, as soon as the results of its work were known, he intended to close the commission and to blot out all traces of its work. However, Tolstoi's actions over the next fifteen months clearly contradicted his stated intentions. Feoktistov, pp. 248–9.

[94]On the university counterreform and Tolstoi's role in its enactment, see Shchetinina, pp. 110–45; Zaionchkovskii, *Rossiiskoe samoderzhavie*, pp. 309–30. The State Council debate and Pobedonostsev's conflict with Tolstoi can be followed in Feoktistov's letters to Katkov in ORGBL, f. Katkov, 1883, k. 12, d. 26, ll. 1–2 ob., 10–10 ob.; and ibid., 1884, k. 12, d. 27, ll. 1, 3–4, 14 ob.

Katkov's support on this matter, persuaded Alexander III to side with him on all aspects of the university counterreform – a clear sign that the emperor had confidence in his minister of internal affairs as a man of action and in his policy of state control.

Meanwhile Tolstoi, given his growing power, came under attack from Katkov and Meshcherskii because he showed too little concern in getting low-interest state loans for gentry landowners and because he prevented an assembly of gentry marshals from convening in Moscow in November 1884 (in conjunction with the Taneev Commission's work on the forthcoming rescript to the gentry). Katkov, who stood at the zenith of his influence at this point, complained that Tolstoi showed little enthusiasm for gentry interests.[95] Tolstoi's view of the gentry and its role in local administration is analyzed in Chapter 5. The important point here is that by late 1884 he had little reason to use state subsidies to turn the gentry into a privileged, parasitic "aristocracy," closed off to new blood, as Katkov and Meshcherskii insisted he should. In a move away from his position of two years earlier, he no longer supported their attacks against bureaucratic interference in local administration. Rather, like the governors, he argued that reform of local administration was the state's prerogative alone and that the first estate existed to serve autocracy, not vice versa. By spring 1885, Tolstoi had so fallen out of Katkov's favor that, following the 21 April 1885 rescript to the gentry, the editor of the *Moscow News* sought unsuccessfully to have Tolstoi replaced as minister by Ostrovskii on the pretext of Tolstoi's poor health.[96]

However, the proof that Alexander III had raised Tolstoi to the status of *primus inter pares* among ministers, and that he supported his program of bureaucratization, came with the judicial counterreforms in 1884–5. Whereas Pobedonostsev failed to offer constructive alternatives to the reforms of the previous reign, the tsar found in Tolstoi an advocate of state control who, in his view, would undertake substantive measures to establish order in the courts, schools, and provinces. Thus, he complained to Tolstoi in 1884 and 1885 about the shortcomings of the judicial system and about Nabokov's procrastination in drafting proposals that would abolish jury trials and would subject judges to dismissal for rendering verdicts that displeased the government.[97] The fact that Alexander III initially authorized Tolstoi

---

[95] Solov'ev, pp. 169–70, 177–78, 193; and Tvardovskaia, *Ideologiia poreformennogo samoderzhaviia*, pp. 232–5.

Because of Tolstoi's refusal to allow the meeting, A. V. Meshcherskii, gentry marshal in Poltava province, asked Katkov to intervene and complained that "our friend D. A. Tolstoi is taken for a terrible contrabandist."

[96] Solov'ev, pp. 179–80. Katkov (who along with Ostrovskii and perhaps Pobedonostsev wrote the rescript) hailed it as a turning point in state policy that united the autocracy and gentry. See ibid., p. 177; *PSZ*, 3d ser. vol. 5, no. 2882, 21 April 1885; and *K. P. Pobedonostsev i ego korrespondenty*, vol. 1, pt. 2, pp. 538–40. By contrast, Polovtsov noted that although he approved of the rescript, it was no reason to get overexcited, and Ivan Alekseevich Shestakov (naval minister) and even Meshcherskii himself dismissed the document as an empty, ceremonial gesture. Solov'ev, p. 180.

[97] Zaionchkovskii, *Rossiiskoe samoderzhavie*, p. 234.

to reorganize the courts rather than Pobedonostsev, who was a legal specialist, is clear evidence that the emperor was willing to abandon the current ministerial system and support a unified government under Tolstoi's leadership.

Seizing the chance to discredit a ministerial rival, Tolstoi gave Katkov and Meshcherskii wide latitude in denouncing Nabokov and the judiciary in their editorials in 1884. The justice minister sought to cut his losses by making certain concessions, for instance, on the types of disciplinary action that could be brought against "negligent" judges.[98] By late 1885, the emperor, as well as Tolstoi and Pobedonostsev, had grown impatient with Nabokov's stalling tactics. Shortly after Pobedonostsev presented a project to abolish public trials, trial by jury, and the concept that judges could not be dismissed, Alexander III replaced Nabokov (5 November 1885) with Nikolai Avksent'evich Manasein, a career official in the Ministry of Justice who had made a good impression with his thorough inspection of the Baltic provinces in 1883–4.[99] Perceived as more compliant and pragmatic than Nabokov, Manasein, as events would show, proved to be a stubborn opponent of Tolstoi's proposals. For the time being, however, top officials interpreted the ministerial change (as well as Bunge's replacement as finance minister in 1887 by Ivan Alekseevich Vyshnegradskii) as a new direction in state policy. Not without reason, Nikolai Karlovich Girs, the minister of foreign affairs, ruefully concluded that no official with ties to the previous reign was secure in his position.[100]

In short, by early 1885 there was little doubt that Tolstoi had the imperial support necessary to undertake the reform of local self-government. In fact, Alexander III gave Tolstoi the chance to close down the Kakhanov Commission in November 1884, but the minister declined on the grounds that the outcome of its work was not clear. He believed that his newest appointees to the commission, Count Pahlen and Count Shuvalov, could paralyze the program of the Special Conference and persuade the full commission to make practical recommendations strengthening central control.[101] They failed in this task. Thus, three months later Tolstoi was convinced that the Kakhanov Commission had outlived its usefulness, and its activity from 11 to 23 February 1885 certainly supported this view. During that period, the commission postponed a final decision on the zemstvo role in public education, deferred indefinitely any reconsideration of judicial powers for the section chiefs, and referred the Bekhteev–Pazukhin counterproject on zemstvo reform to a special subcommission. The counterproject advocated reorganization of

---

[98]For an incisive account of Nabokov's tactics, see Whelan, pp. 160–7.

[99]See Golovnin's letter of 10 November 1885 to Miliutin in ORGBL, f. D. A. Miliutin, p. 62, d. 2, ll. 24–24 ob.; Pobedonostsev's letters of 15 May and 6 November 1885 to Alexander III in *Pis'ma Pobedonostseva k Aleksandru III*, 2: 74–7, 91–2; Alexander III's reply on 6 November in *K. P. Pobedonostsev i ego korrespondenty*, vol. 1, pt. 2, p. 495; and Zaionchkovskii, *Rossiiskoe samoderzhavie*, pp. 237–46. Pobedonostsev's 24 October memorandum containing his proposal for judicial reform is found in *K. P. Pobedonostsev i ego korrespondenty*, vol. 1, pt. 2, pp. 508–14.

[100]*Dnevnik sekretaria Polovtsova*, 1: 347

[101]See entry for 6 November 1884 in ibid., p. 256.

zemstvo representation along estate lines in order to minimize the participation of kulaks, merchants, and other nongentry landlords who, according to Bekhteev and Pazukhin, were dislodging the gentry from the assemblies. The two marshals indeed exaggerated the extent of this process in order to induce the government to implement local government reforms in the gentry's interests. By replacing property holdings with estate affiliation as the basis for zemstvo participation in one of four estate categories (gentry, urban commercial groups, the *meshchane*, and the peasantry), they obviously hoped to avert the political and economic decline of the gentry. Yet this was not their sole consideration. They truly believed that such a reform would lead to more orderly assemblies and would rekindle peasant interest in zemstvo representation, because peasants would be allowed to elect only peasants as delegates, and not private landlords.[102]

Consequently, the Bekhteev–Pazukhin counterproject and the Pazukhin article in the *Russian Herald* were significant not because they provided Tolstoi with new ideas and methods of local government reform. On the contrary, the minister was well aware of many of these ideas, including estate-based zemstvo representation prior to 1885 through the governors' reports and zemstvo addresses.[103] Rather, the February counterproject, along with the delays in other aspects of the commission's work, provided him with the pretext for recommending the dismissal of the commission. In early February 1885, he asked the emperor to accept his resignation, but the latter refused.[104] Bolstered by this expression of imperial confidence, Tolstoi ordered Kakhanov to prepare for the tsar a summary of the commission's activity from 19 January to 19 February, and the chairman's report clearly illustrated how little had been accomplished.[105] At the top of the report, Alexander III noted: "It seems to me that the Kakhanov Commission is working without results. All these questions should come from the Ministry of Internal Affairs and are too important to allow such an enormous commission to discuss them. Isn't it time to think of a way to halt its activity?"[106]

The tsar was particularly annoyed with the Kakhanov Commission's proposal to expand zemstvo jurisdiction in the district.[107] Tolstoi, however,

---

[102]*Zhurnal Osoboi Komissii*, no. 17, *prilozhenie*, pp. 18–19.

[103]For instance, see Kaluga Governor K. N. Zhukov's response to Tolstoi's 1883 circular in TsGIA, *f.* Kakhanovskaia komissiia, *op.* 1, *d.* 106, *l.* 86.

[104]See V. M. Golitsyn's diary entry for 12 February 1885 in ORGBL, *fond* V. M. Golitsyn, *delo* 13, *l.* 137

[105]TsGIA, *f.* Kantseliariia MVD, 1885, *op.* 1, *d.* 1190, *ll.* 228–34 *ob.*

[106]Quoted from ibid., *l.* 228.

According to Meshcherskii, Alexander III closely followed the debates of the Kakhanov Commission. The tsar stated that there were many valuable ideas in its reform projects but also many that were untimely and inappropriate. He was also disturbed by the difference in views between intelligent St. Petersburg officials and the local experts in the commission – a line, as we have seen, fed to the emperor by Tolstoi, Katkov, Meshcherskii, Pobedonostsev, and others. Meshcherskii wrote that he tried to convince Alexander to close the commission because its activity had aroused rumors among St. Petersburg liberals about reform, but the tsar did not heed his advice. Meshcherskii, *Moi vospominaniia*, 3: 196–8.

[107]Zaionchkovskii, *Rossiiskoe samoderzhavie*, p. 232.

was not so particular in his criticisms of its work in a subsequent evaluation of its activity (1885). He attacked nearly all the proposals as impractical and contended that a comprehensive and simultaneous reform of local administration based on abstract Western political theory — in short, local self-government outside the control of his ministry — was no solution to the mismanagement in peasant and district administration, which required immediate reform. Thus he concluded:

A study [of the Kakhanov Commission's work] leads to the conviction that the commission was *mainly* concerned with the wholesale introduction into our legislation of certain abstract principles considered appropriate by Western European theory, such as decentralization, the separation of administrative and judicial powers, and the autonomy of public institutions. Under such conditions, the satisfaction of urgent, practical needs evidently was to be relegated to second place.[108]

Tolstoi's remarks show that by mid-1885 he already had committed himself to the piecemeal, practical reforms of local administration that are the subject of Chapters 5–6. From the end of July 1885 on, Pazukhin worked under Tolstoi in this effort as director of the Ministry's chancellery.[109] Although Meshcherskii recommended that Pazukhin assist Tolstoi in his 29 April 1885 diary letter to Alexander III,[110] there are several compelling reasons why Tolstoi himself selected the gentry marshal for the post. On the one hand, the minister spent almost the entire spring and summer of 1885 in the Crimea because of poor health, and relied on subordinates to do almost all his work at the ministry.[111] In Pazukhin he found an energetic assistant familiar enough with the materials of the Kakhanov Commission to draft reform projects quickly. For Pazukhin, an outsider in St. Petersburg circles in 1885, the arrangement had benefits, because by doing Tolstoi's bidding he attained a prestigious foothold in Russian state service.[112]

More important, however, Pazukhin's counterproject and his article provided Tolstoi with an eloquent attack against the 1864 judicial and zemstvo legislation and the district bureaus, and the minister calculated that the marshal's collaboration might well mobilize gentry support for his bureaucratic aims, because Pazukhin, despite billing himself as a pragmatist, was a theorist.[113] Thus, Tolstoi could choose those aspects of Pazukhin's plan

---

[108]Quoted from TsGIA, *f*. Kakhanovskaia komissiia, *op*. 1, *d*. 119, *ll*. 3–3 *ob*.

[109]See S. A. Rachinskii's letter of 1 August 1885 to Pobedonostsev in ORGBL, *f*. Pobedonostsev, 1885, *k*. 4412, *d*. 2, *l*. 81; and Golitsyn's diary entry for 14 August 1885 in ibid., *f*. Golitsyn, *d*. 13, *l*. 329.

[110]TsGAOR, *f*. Aleksandr III, *op*. 1, *d*. 109, *l*. 8.

[111]Feoktistov, pp. 250–1; TsGAOR, *f*. Aleksandr III, *op*. 1, *d*. 109, *ll*. 4 *ob*., 6, 8 *ob*., 19; and ORGBL, *f*. D. A. Miliutin, p. 61, *d*. 44, *l*. 18.

[112]See Tolstoi's letter of 2 June 1886 to Pobedonostsev in *K. P. Pobedonostsev i ego korrespondenty*, vol. 1, pt. 2, p. 584; and Feoktistov's corroboration as quoted in Taranovski, "Politics of Counter-Reform," p. 443. Although Taranovski argues that Tolstoi was initially influenced by Pazukhin to propose purely gentry estate legislation, he maintains that by late 1886 it was Pazukhin who was espousing Tolstoi's statist position. Ibid., pp. 407, 424–31.

[113]Golovin, *Moi vospominaniia*, 2: 100–1.

for a gentry-dominated peasant and zemstvo administration that meshed with his theory of state control over local institutions, while discarding key concepts, for example, gentry control and the election principle, that did not. Although Pazukhin did almost all of the manual work in drafting the projects, the key ideas were Tolstoi's, and the proposals show that it was Pazukhin who embraced Tolstoi's viewpoint. Indeed, the stamp of bureaucratization left on the counterreform projects by Tolstoi was so obvious that Bekhteev and Prince Obolenskii (who continued to toe Katkov's line) could scarcely believe that Pazukhin had helped draft them.[114] K. F. Golovin, a conservative journalist and official, spoke for many gentry in lamenting Pazukhin's volte face when, reflecting on a letter from Pazukhin to the *Herald of Europe* (1888) regarding the proposed land captains, he concluded: "I did not want to believe that elected judges, simultaneously becoming guardians of village self-government, had lost their previous autonomy and had become simple protégés of the governors. It became clear where the path would lead."[115]

In summary, this chapter has traced the activity of the Kakhanov Commission and the ministerial and interest group politics surrounding it from 1881 to 1885. Although the commission ended its work with a whimper rather than a flourish, prompting Tolstoi to remark that three and a half years of activity produced no practical results,[116] we have seen that, on the contrary, it played a pivotal role in the process of local self-government reform. Its systematic work despite numerous ministerial changes underlined the government's commitment to reorganize local self-government and arrest the breakdown of authority in the countryside. Even Tolstoi himself implicitly acknowledged by other comments made in his 1887 report that the Kakhanov Commission had made significant contributions to his own proposals on local self-government reform. He credited it with rejecting the idea of a simultaneous, comprehensive reform as inconsistent with the material collected in the provinces and with recommending that a separate peasant administration be

---

[114]Ibid., p. 102. Whelan also draws this distinction between Pazukhin's original views and Tolstoi's. In her words, "Pazukhin's intention, in contrast to Tolstoi's, was in fact to spearhead a gentry reaction. Pazukhin made no secret of his desire to see a reassertion of gentry privilege and prerogative – and specifically gentry – that is, the landowning *pomeshchiki* – rather than nobiliar – which would include the despised bureaucrats in the higher ranks . . . His notion that some kind of gentry-cum-autocracy dyarchy could be reestablished along the lines of what had existed – at least in fond memory – under Catherine was quaint if not downright quixotic, but it was widely known (Pazukhin published a long article on this and others of his ideas both in Katkov's *Russian Messenger {Russkii vestnik}* and as a separate brochure)." Whelan, pp. 184–5. In contrast, Yaney maintains that Pazukhin was not acting out of gentry interests in calling for gentry section chiefs (land captains), but rather because he believed that the gentry were political leaders with practical experience; thus, Tolstoi was attracted to Pazukhin's ideas. Yaney, *Urge to Mobilize*, p. 73. Yaney does not see any change in Pazukhin's views before and after his work with Tolstoi. As shown in Chapter 5, Tolstoi made use of Pazukhin's "pro-gentry" program, as opposed to the more aristocratic (nobiliar) plans of Katkov, precisely because they suited his centralist aims.

[115]Quoted from Golovin, *Moi vospominaniia*, 2: 103.

[116]See Tolstoi's reply of 30 November 1887 to Kakhanov in TsGIA, *f*. Departament zakonov G. S., *op*. t. 11, *d*. 44, *l*. 476.

preserved. Nor did he deny that many of his ideas for peasant and zemstvo administration reform resulted from the governors' criticisms of the proposals put forth at the Special Conference.[117] Tolstoi's political adversaries also emphasized the Kakhanov Commission's importance in the reform process by collecting information on local institutions requiring reform, identifying their shortcomings, drafting concrete reform proposals, and providing an arena for the free exchange of gentry, zemstvo, and government views on reform methods.[118] The *Herald of Europe* predicted accurately in October 1885 that the work of the Kakhanov Commission would be the warehouse from which Tolstoi would draw the general plan and data for his anticipated reform.[119] As subsequent events revealed, Tolstoi not only drew greatly on the governors' and local experts' criticisms of the conference program in outlining his own bureaucratic proposals for local self-government reform (after arranging for the dismissal of the Kakhanov Commission); ironically, many of the Special Conference's arguments for decentralization and comprehensive reform would be resurrected by opponents of Tolstoi's land captain projects in the State Council debate in 1887–9.

Equally important, however, the fate of the Kakhanov Commission illustrated that political and institutional interests, more than practical administrative experience (even with all the talk about the latter), usually governed the position taken particularly by the ministerial participants in the debate over local self-government reform. To be sure, administrative ideology (decentralization versus state control) and the legacy of Alexander II's reforms served as focal points of discussion, just as the practical experience of the local experts had a major bearing on the outcome of the debates. But commission members understood that the political conservatism of tsarism and its limited personnel and funds ruled out more radical options such as genuine public self-government or, conversely, its complete eradication. The problem for autocracy in the 1880s, as in previous decades, was controlling the tempo of administrative and social change in the countryside – in other words, devising a strategy for rural development and control without sacrificing the traditional social estates order. As the Kakhanov Commission showed, deputy ministers, governors, zemstvo spokesmen, and gentry (not to mention nongentry groups) had very different ideas on how to do it. Moreover, the commission's experience proved once again that ministerial unity and order in St. Petersburg was a precondition for establishing effective, systematic local administration. Having begun its work auspiciously with the approval of the Committee of Ministers, the Kakhanov Commission never enjoyed real imperial support or interministerial unity. By early 1885 Tolstoi, having learned from and manipulated the commission and established himself as Alexander III's chief minister, decided to close it down and

---

[117]Ibid., *ll.* 470, 477–477 *ob*.

[118]This point was made at the time by Golovnin in his 25 March 1885 letter to Miliutin in ORGBL, *f.* D. A. Miliutin, 1885, *p.* 61, *d.* 44, *l.* 24 *ob*.

[119]"Vnutrennee obozrenie," *Vestnik evropy*, no. 5 (1885), p. 806.

introduce his own policy of local self-government reform. In short, the dependence of state policy making on the will of the tsar, the rivalry between ministers and, in some cases, between central and local officials — these realities of autocratic politics helped doom the Kakhanov Commission, just as they contributed to the isolation of the imperial government from its rural population. As the next two chapters will show, such problems did not disappear with the dismissal of the Kakhanov Commission.

CHAPTER 5

State control over local initiative: the Land Captain Statute of 1889

During the years of the Kakhanov Commission's activity, the reform of local self-government was not the primary concern of top officials. Ministers and members of the State Council, as we have seen, were more preoccupied with the debate over the university counterreform and the power struggle in ministerial circles over the direction of the judicial counterreforms. But from 1886 to 1890, local self-government reform, particularly the establishment of Tolstoi's land captains (*zemskie nachal'niki*), constituted the most significant and controversial issue in government circles. This was the issue on which Tolstoi sought to overcome bureaucratic inertia and establish his control over the government. Although Governor V. M. Golitsyn of Moscow doubtlessly exaggerated in calling the Land Captain Statute "no less significant and extensive than the peasant reform" of 1861,[1] contemporary officials of diverse views readily acknowledged that it was the legislative benchmark of Alexander III's reign and the cornerstone in Tolstoi's centralization policy, which was designed to create autocratic order by his control of the countryside.

The debates in ministerial circles in 1886–9 revealed that nearly all officials recognized the need for personal supervision of peasant self-government and agreed that continued anarchy in village administration could bring the collapse of the imperial regime itself. Yet Tolstoi's land captains project, which proposed to create effective rural administration and order by providing state supervision, evoked a torrent of criticism from various ministers and State Council members for almost three years. The reason is that other officials rightly saw it as a first step in Tolstoi's comprehensive policy of centralization, the goal of which was to bring central and local (elected and, in key cases,

---

[1]ORGBL, *f*. V. M. Golitsyn, 1889, *d*. 15, *l*. 421. Diary passage for 31 August 1889. Golitsyn added that the Land Captain Statute represented "the first step in putting back in order and restoring what [authority] has been shaken loose and demolished over the past twenty-five years."

appointed) officials under the purview of the minister of internal affairs. Whatever his real designs concerning ministerial reorganization, Tolstoi's plan to systematize his control over the bureaucracy hinted at the establishment of a "first minister" in the person of the minister of internal affairs. No wonder the project came under a scathing attack from other ministers who resisted any infringements on their jurisdiction or any institutional changes that would reduce them to the status of second-rank ministers.

In addition, the project encountered extensive opposition in the State Council because it signified a complete repudiation of the provisions of the Judicial and Zemstvo Reforms that many council members had helped draw up and implement. Firm believers in the supremacy of law over administration and in the State Council's indispensable role in the legislative process, these officials claimed that land captains with judicial powers would herald a return to the arbitrary and abusive control of the landed gentry over their serfs in prereform Russia. Although this was not Tolstoi's aim, a fact that most of Tolstoi's opponents recognized, this argument nonetheless prompted a majority in the State Council to vote against him in favor of a counter-proposal that would establish supervision over all social estates at the district level and would maintain the separation of administrative and judicial authority. This landmark decision severely damaged the council's standing with the tsar who, defying legislative custom, rejected both the majority and minority recommendations and wrote a new resolution in accord with Tolstoi's wishes.[2]

Hence, the debate over the land captain reform illuminates the problems that hampered the government in directing political, social, and economic reform in Russia – the bureaucratic inertia toward any change, the refusal of top officials to sacrifice any of their powers even in the interests of administrative efficiency, and the ideological divisions within the government over the direction of Russia's political development. In the midst of these problems, the government, by virtue of the Land Captain Statute, assumed the additional burden of providing efficient local administration and meeting local peasant needs without public assistance. This commitment set Russia apart from other European nations that also had decentralized their administrations and devolved local government authority in the 1860s and 1870s, and once again pointed up the challenge facing Russian officials in the late

---

[2]Whelan maintains that while Alexander III and his ministers attacked the State Council because it opposed the counterreforms, institutional tradition and the tsar's own desire for bureaucratic system compelled them to submit legislative projects to the State Council. Conversely, the jurists in the State Council, notwithstanding their desire for government based on law, lacked the institutional authority to defy the tsar's will on any important matter. As a result, the tsar and State Council could thwart one another, but neither could govern effectively. Whelan, pp. 198–203. Although this interpretation accurately characterizes the dilemmas of the tsar and the State Council, it suggests that Alexander III's ministers were a more united faction on counterreform proposals, vis à vis the State Council, than was the case. As shown in Chapters 5–6, polarization, intrigue, and inertia characterized relations between Alexander III's ministers, as well as the State Council's relationship with the tsar. Thus, the tsarist regime's capacity to govern in the 1880s was more limited than even Whelan suggests.

nineteenth century – namely, how to maintain a static system of autocratic control in a nation where, owing to influences from the West, dynamic forces of economic and social change were already at work, eroding the traditional order.[3]

Tolstoi's ideology of state control and the land captains project

The case for centralization. The work of elaborating and pushing through a plan for local government under state control required an energetic administrator with centralist views, and Tolstoi, a conservative bureaucrat by vocation and a historian in his spare time, more than adequately fulfilled these criteria. It is therefore appropriate to analyze his thought and policy here because only after the Kakhanov Commission's dismissal did he direct the preparation of local government reform. In fact, the years 1885 to 1889 were the period in which Tolstoi unveiled his plans for the systematic bureaucratization of local self-government and in which he displayed his considerable skills as a politician in defending his program against the attacks of other officials.

Tolstoi's views were the fruit of almost half a century in state service, including three top-level positions from 1865 to 1889 – ober prokuror of the Holy Synod, minister of education, and minister of internal affairs. Past experience in dealing with various branches of administration and his in-depth study of Russian and Western institutional history convinced him of the need for some means of coordinating state policy making in Russia.[4] Along with other young bureaucrats who attained high positions in the government in the 1840s and 1850s, he shared a common belief in the predominance of state interests over all others.[5] Yet Tolstoi parted ways with many of his friends in the government and in Grand Duke Konstantin Nikolaevich's "circle" in the mid-1850s over the issue of peasant reform. During subsequent decades he consistently opposed any dilution of autocratic authority, a fact that earned him the appreciation of Alexander II as well as the enmity of other ministers. Significantly, while his landholdings and

---

[3]Binkley, p. 149. Nor did Russia fit the Chinese pattern either. In nineteenth-century China, the government sought merely to tighten its control over the provinces by intermittently expanding its network of police officials. On this policy and the implications of its failure, see Kung-Chuan Hsiao, *Rural China: Imperial Control in the Nineteenth Century* (paperback ed., Seattle, 1967), pp. 49–56, 501, 504. See also Skocpol, pp. 150–3.

[4]Tolstoi wrote many historical works and had the reputation of a scholar. From 1882 to 1889 he served as president of the Imperial Academy of Sciences. His monographs, which reflect his statist ideology, include *Istoriia finansovykh uchrezhdenii Rossii so vremeni osnovaniia gosudarstva do konchiny Imperatritsy Ekateriny II* (St. Peterburg, 1848); *Akademicheskaia gimnaziia v XVIII stoletii; po rukopisnym dokumentam arkhiva Akademii nauk* (2 vols.; St. Petersburg, 1885); and *Rimskii Katolitsizm v Rossii* (2 vols.; St. Petersburg, 1876). On his Riazan' estate, he owned a huge library of over 40,000 foreign books in German, French, English, and Latin, with a concentration of works on education, Catherine II's reign, and non-Orthodox religions. See Feoktistov, p. 279; and Sinel, pp. 47, 49.

[5]On the service careers and personal backgrounds of these officials see Pintner, "Russian Civil Service on the Eve of the Great Reforms," pp. 55–65.

lineage placed Tolstoi in the elite landed gentry, friends and foes alike regarded him above all as the consummate state bureaucrat.[6] Out of bureaucratic loyalty, Tolstoi sublimated his criticism of the reforms of the 1860s and dutifully executed his sovereign's wishes. Such loyalty stemmed not only from his bureaucratic background, but also from the influence of Count D. N. Tolstoi, the deeply religious and nationalistic uncle who brought him up. Thus, his boldness in the 1880s in attacking the Western ideas introduced in Russia two decades earlier attested to Tolstoi's transformation from bureaucrat to politician and to his conviction that only reforms congruent with Russia's historical heritage could prove fruitful and enduring.

In the various arguments and provisions of his counterreforms program (1886), Tolstoi's ideology of centralization surfaced time and time again. First, like most government officials of his era, he believed that Western European monarchies were in a process of disintegration, the result of previous political concessions by European rulers to the church and people. By the nineteenth century, sovereign power in Western European states had been diffused among several bodies, effectively precluding absolute rule by the king. One such institution was the Roman Catholic church, which Tolstoi maligned because it pursued secular as well as religious goals. In contrast, in Russia the state brought the Orthodox church under its authority in the late seventeenth and early eighteenth centuries, thus preventing the fragmentation of authority that prevailed in Western Europe. At several points in his historical work, he reproached Catherine II and Alexander I not only for tolerating the Jesuit presence in Belorussia, but even more for debasing autocratic authority and patronizing the Latin clergy.[7] On the contrary, Tolstoi lauded the Russian state's control over the Orthodox church and practiced it as ober prokuror of the synod. In his view the clergy were "nothing more or less than a force which should be subordinated to the government, and which an intelligent government may skillfully use for its own purposes."[8]

The ideas expressed by Tolstoi on developments in the West are similar to those found in the writings of other contemporary Russian conservatives,

---

[6]As developed in this chapter, Tolstoi saw himself in similar terms. Polovtsov pointed out that Tolstoi was a typical St. Petersburg official except that he possessed a remarkable, historically oriented mind. See his passage for 25 April 1889 in *Dnevnik sekretaria Polovtsova*, 2: 190. Chicherin described Tolstoi as "an intelligent man with a firm character, but a bureaucrat from head to toe, narrow-minded and stubborn. He saw nothing besides St. Petersburg, hated any form of autonomy, and any manifestation of freedom." B. N. Chicherin, *Vospominaniia* (3 vols.; Moscow, 1929–34), 1: 192–3. For similar characterizations of Tolstoi, see V. N. Lamzdorf, *Dnevnik (1886–1890)*, ed. F. A. Rotshtein (Moscow-Leningrad, 1926), p. 195; Sinel, p. 52; Zaionchkovskii, *Rossiiskoe samoderzhavie*, pp. 61–5; Whelan, pp. 64–7; and Bunge's assessment, quoted in Taranovski, "Politics of Counter-Reform," pp. 386–7.
[7]D. A. Tolstoi, *Romanism in Russia: An Historical Study*, trans. by Mrs. M'Kibbin (2 vols.; reprint; New York, 1971), 1; 425; and ibid., 2: 367, 378. This study was originally published in French in 1863–4 under the title *Le Catholicisme romain en Russie* and earned Tolstoi a doctorate from the University of Leipzig. It was translated into English in 1874 and into Russian in 1876. Sinel, p. 50.
[8]Feoktistov, p. 169. Tolstoi's work as ober prokuror is detailed in Gregory L. Freeze, *The Parish Clergy in Nineteenth-Century Russia: Crisis, Reform, Counter-reform* (Princeton, 1983), pp. 298–347.

although his criticism of Western European institutions, while pungent, avoided the fanatical moralistic condemnations found, for instance, in Pobedonostsev's tracts. Tolstoi was not a great conservative ideologue or polemicist. Unlike Katkov or Pobedonostsev, his belief in the inappropriateness of Western ideas for Russia resulted from his past frustrations in working with the new self-governing institutions. And although his view that the local population should counsel the government on local needs without receiving any political power in return was consistent with Slavophile tradition, he was not a true Slavophile who on principle rejected all Western concepts and models as unsuitable for Russia. In fact, as minister of education he relied on the Prussian secondary schools as a model for his Secondary School Statute in 1874 because their organization provided for a greater degree of central control and their classical curriculum would help keep politically unreliable students out of the *gimnaziia*.

Rather, Tolstoi prided himself on being a pragmatist (he even called his work pragmatic history)[9] unfettered by any ideology and able to mold a variety of different ideas and institutions into a workable system. Committed to an exact official routine (he was renowned for holding office hours once a week and giving each visitor two minutes to state his business)[10] and obsessed with such administrative details as cost, institutional performance, and accountability, Tolstoi showed himself to be a bureaucratic manager rather than a political theorist.[11] But Tolstoi had his own ideological blind spots, not the least of which was his unquestioning belief that autocracy and its officials were always right. His suspicious attitude toward self-government (in the postreform period), bolstered by his reflections on history, led him to conclude in 1886 that Russia and Europe had followed a roughly similar course of political development until political revolutions (especially the French Revolution) occurred in the West.[12] The quickest way for autocracy to undermine its rule would be to take steps voluntarily that occurred in the West as a result of revolutions, specifically to abolish social estate distinctions and to allow national political representation for the public.

Such arguments brought credit on Tolstoi as a politician but not as a historian. At times he deviated from the standards of historical accuracy to make a political point. For instance, he contended that in Russia the people

---

[9]Tolstoi, *Istoriia finansovykh uchrezhdenii*, p. v.

[10]Sinel notes the experience of Meshcherskii, who found himself subject to this treatment. Although Tolstoi made no notes during the brief interview, he fulfilled Meshcherskii's request within five days, leading Meshcherskii to quip that never before had he really understood the meaning of the phrase "times [sic] is money." Sinel, p. 53.

[11]In his monographs, Tolstoi exhibited the same qualities; for instance, in writing about state taxation in the pre-Petrine and Petrine eras, he criticized the absence of organization, system, and equity in tax collection, and argued that elected officials rather than legislation would improve the process. Tolstoi, *Istoriia finansovykh uchrezhdenii*, pp. 18, 35–6, 45–8, 251–7. Besides providing rare evidence of Tolstoi's confidence in elected officials, this study (like his others) showed his preference for factual detail over theory or analysis; his belief in the paternalistic role of the state (and the subordination of all social estates); and his desire for administrative system (with as little red tape as possible).

[12]TsGIA, *f.* Departament zakonov G. S., 1887, *op.* t. 11, *d.* 44, *l.* 467.

did not aspire to participate in government, and that the peasant and zemstvo reforms had forced this function upon them with calamitous results. Although peasant apathy toward elected officials provided some justification for that view, Tolstoi obviously forgot about the significant number of landed gentry in the 1850s and 1860s who clamored for participation in government at both the local and national levels, just as he underestimated the resentment that the educated public would feel toward the government for retracting the autonomy of public self-government twenty-five years later.

Not surprisingly, the main object of Tolstoi's attack was the election principle, which, he contended, had no place in Russia. Elected officials during the past twenty-five years, he felt, had never enjoyed the respect or prestige of government officials.[13] Yet ignoring Russia's past was not the only mistake of the legislators of the 1860s; according to Tolstoi, they asssumed naively that in five years political institutions and attitudes that had developed in the West over centuries could take root in Russia. With deliberate exaggeration he asserted that these same individuals intended to ruin Russia completely by abolishing social estate distinctions and establishing public control over the countryside, as illustrated by their recommendations in the Kakhanov Commission.[14] They desired nothing short of a constitutional monarchy in Russia, with the tsar's prerogatives limited by law and public participation in government. As we shall see later, Tolstoi employed this tactic of exaggeration frequently with success because it played on Alexander's long-standing, indiscriminate hatred for constitutional governments. Thus, Tolstoi could get away with portraying autonomous public self-government as a stepping stone to constitutional monarchy and any and all critics of his proposal as opponents of autocracy.

Tolstoi's belief in autocracy as the instrument of change, progress, and unity in Russia followed logically from his conception of Russia's distinctiveness, and constituted a second postulate of his ideology of state control. He cited geographical, cultural, as well as historical reasons for autocratic control over local government:

The sparse population of Russia spread out over an immense territory, the inevitable remoteness from the courts that results from this, the low economic level of the public welfare and the patriarchical customs of our agrarian class — these are the conditions that demand the establishment of authority which, in its activity, will not be hampered by excessive formalism, an authority capable of restoring order promptly and correcting violations of the population's rights and interests as quickly as possible.[15]

Tolstoi argued that Russia was too large and undeveloped, and its population too uneducated to govern themselves on the basis of law. Only an educated population could comprehend and voluntarily obey written statutes

---

[13]Ibid., *f.* Departament obshchikh del MVD, 1886, *op.* 241, *d.* 51, *l.* 6 *ob.*
[14]Ibid., *l.* 5 *ob.*
[15]Quoted from ibid., *ll.* 20–20 *ob.*

and administer their affairs responsibly. But "the dark people have no concept of the separation of powers," he wrote, and they simply "are seeking an authority to protect them or at least tell them what to do."[16] Since the peasants lacked the moral and intellectual qualities to govern themselves, government-appointed supervisory officials were the only recourse for establishing an orderly and efficient village administration. Unlike the Great Reforms, Tolstoi emphasized, this measure would work in practice because it would be congruent with Russia's autocratic system and traditions, and would not create public institutions to challenge the state's authority:

> The first and most important prerequisite for the success and fruitfulness of the proposed reform is that all changes in local institutions be consistent with the basic principle of our government – imperial, autocratic authority. . . . The authority of Russian autocrats is the foundation of our state life, and all organs of administration should be subject to and coordinated with it. The history of our country shows that autocracy possesses strength and creative force, and that only such [state] institutions are known for their permanence and vitality, thus enabling autocracy to exert a free and proper influence on the lives of the people.[17]

But Tolstoi did not advocate central control over local government merely to eliminate opposition within the state or fulfill his own desire for power. Looking back at the record of public self-government, he genuinely believed that such control would be in the interests of the peasants themselves (however unflattering his view of the *narod*), because it would provide direction for peasant officials, assist them in fulfilling local needs, and protect the majority of peasants in their relations with local industrialists and kulaks. There was a note of benevolent paternalism in Tolstoi's concept of state control that went beyond merely maintaining provincial order. Indeed, he truly felt that the autocracy could turn the nation's backwardness to its advantage by reasserting its leadership in rural administrative and economic development, all of which would cultivate peasant support for tsarism while raising living standards in the village. He wanted local officials under the Ministry of Internal Affairs to take the initiative in meeting local administrative needs. This practical system would provide land captains with the discretionary authority to act quickly on particular local needs and situations that could not be legislated nationwide or even anticipated in some cases (Yaney, referring to the Weberian model, calls this line-over-staff authority).[18] With such extraordinary latitude in powers, the land captains, as Yaney correctly notes, were not conventional police officials (*stanovye*) or petty ministerial clerks; yet in contrast to the case with the peace arbitrators of the 1860s, Tolstoi intended to supervise the land captains closely and hold them ac-

---

[16]Ibid., *f.* Kantseliariia MVD, 1887, *op.* 2, *d.* 17, *l.* 330 *ob.*
[17]Quoted from ibid., *f.* Departament obshchikh del MVD, *op.* 241, *d.* 51, *ll.* 13–14.
[18]See TsGIA, *f.* Departament zakonov G. S., *op.* t. 11, *d.* 44, *ll.* 641 *ob.*-642 *ob.*; ibid., *f.* Departament obshchikh del, *op.* 241, *d.* 51, *ll.* 9 *ob.*-10; Kataev, *Mestnye krest'ianskie uchrezhdeniia*, pt. 3, p. 30; and Yaney, *Urge to Mobilize*, pp. 54–8, 84–5.

countable for their actions, because he recognized that lawlessness on their part would undermine order, the goal of his reforms.[19]

The root of lawlessness in local self-government, according to the minister, was the legislation of the 1860s and 1870s. Curiously, in this respect he agreed with the Kakhanov Commission decentralists, whom he scorned for believing that precise laws alone could guarantee efficient government in the village and district. These reforms, especially the Judicial Statutes and the 27 June 1874 statute, all diffused decision-making authority at the local level (*mnogovlastie*) and caused confusion among peasants accustomed to the supervision of their gentry landlords and later of the peace arbitrators. Tolstoi argued that the peasants had nothing in common with the justices of the peace and their formal procedures of judicial review, and the Ministry of Internal Affairs had no power to reform institutions outside its hierarchy. The zemstvo and municipal reforms were just as premature in creating local self-governing institutions isolated from the regular administrative apparatus. Thus, governors exercised no real control over these organs in the state's interests but were limited to formal procedures of appealing zemstvo and duma legislation.[20] Tolstoi's arguments in these areas closely paralleled the contention of the centralist-minded governors in 1883–4. He rarely questioned their attitudes and after 1883–4 almost always gave them the benefit of the doubt. On the other hand, in all fairness it must be added that he was not the only minister to accept the governors' views as gospel. The Committee of Ministers and Alexander III himself almost always sided with them in clashes with the zemstvo.[21]

Despite the adverse effect of the legislation of 1864, it was the abolition of the peace arbitrators in most provinces in 1874 that above all cleared the way for the corruption and disorder that characterized peasant self-government at the end of the 1870s and in the 1880s. Tolstoi pointed out that in one province alone from 1875 to 1880, 720 village officials were responsible for the loss of 226,715 rubles in village funds.[22] The final straw came in 1882 when, in conjunction with the abolition of the Main Committee for Rural Welfare, the Senate, rather than the Ministry of Internal Affairs, received the right to review complaints against decisions of the Provincial Bureau of Peasant Affairs. This law in effect eliminated any semblance of ministerial control over peasant administration. Overwhelmed by the mass of petty litigation, the Senate fell behind in resolving appeals and invariably rendered decisions on the basis of a strict interpretation of the law; and in most cases the decisions went against the governors, a fact that infuriated

---

[19]Yaney suggests, on the contrary, that Tolstoi was little concerned about accountability and gave little thought to policing the land captains.

[20]TsGIA, *f.* Departament obshchikh del MVD, *op.* 241, *d.* 51, *ll.* 15–16 *ob.*

[21]Seredonin, 4: 310–13, 319–20, 328–30. For specific cases, see TsGIA, *f.* Komitet ministrov, 1884, *op.* 1, *d.* 4396, *ll.* 146–147 *ob.*, 149–50; *d.* 4394, *ll.* 145–50; 1883, *op.* l, *d.* 4336, *ll.* 106 *ob.*-110; 1884, *op.* l, *d.* 4405, *ll.* 96 *ob.*-97 *ob.*; and 1888, *op.* l, *d.* 4665, *ll.* 124–5, 224 *ob.*-226

[22]TsGIA *f.* Kantseliariia MVD, *op.* 2, *d.* 17, *l.* 332.

Tolstoi. He demanded that since the Minister of Internal Affairs was responsible for peasant administration and state security in the provinces, he should possess the right to appoint all supervisory officials for peasant affairs.[23] Equally important, he called for a reduction in the number of separate institutions in local administration by granting land captains the functions of permanent members of district bureaus and of the justices of the peace. Tolstoi urged Alexander III not to delay any longer in eradicating Western administrative institutions and principles in Russia which, rather than arouse respect for law and enthusiasm for self-government, had influenced peasants to distrust all authority:

Many years of experience have shown completely the inappropriateness in our country of a system of local administration based on a strict division of administrative and judicial functions at the lowest levels, and the inevitable absence in such conditions of strong administrative authority in the district. The adverse consequences of anarchy for the village community that everyone recognizes indicate the urgent need for reestablishing administrative supervision over the village population in general, and especially over the peasant administration.[24]

Tolstoi's proposals on behalf of central control pointed to a desire to establish his preeminence in ministerial circles by bringing all local institutions under his authority. Of course, he was not so explicit in stating such objectives for fear of triggering widespread ministerial opposition against him. Yet there is little question that this was his goal, in the light of his recent participation in effecting ministerial changes, the degree of centralization in local government proposed in his projects, and the pains he took to convince Alexander III that his program constituted the best method to coordinate state policy and renovate the autocracy. In short, he proposed to create unity within the government by establishing under his direction a system of paternal control over its various agencies and over the local population as a whole. Of particular concern to Tolstoi was the establishment of a reliable system of justice for the peasant population. He emphasized that land captains with judicial powers would eliminate the pernicious influence of the country lawyers, whom he labeled "the worst poison of our countryside." This harmful Western institution exploited the peasants' illiterate condition and ignorance of the law, and interfered in every peasant dispute. In fact, their actions had sown so much discord among peasant families and village communes, the traditional bulwarks of government control over the peasants, that in 1886 Tolstoi introduced a separate proposal in the State Council to ban country lawyers.[25]

The disorder in peasant self-government had a profound impact on the gentry and state as well, as Tolstoi stressed in his proposals. It was no

---

[23] Ibid., *ll.* 375–375 *ob.*; and ibid., *f.* Departament obshchikh del MVD, *op.* 241, *d.* 51, *ll.* 21 *ob.*– 22

[24] Quoted from ibid., *f.* Kantseliariia MVD, *op.* 2, *d.* 17, *l.* 335 *ob.*

[25] Ibid., *l.* 331.

accident that Tolstoi made this point. After all, Alexander III had recently demonstrated his concern over the gentry's economic plight in his 1885 rescript to the gentry, and the minister felt that his proposal stood a greater chance of imperial ratification if the tsar saw it as a boon for the gentry. Thus, he pointed out that their economic interests were tied directly to those of the peasants (who made up the labor force in the fields and factories). In addition, the entire state suffered from the escalating arrears in peasant tax payments, compelling evidence in itself that the reorganization of peasant administration and the creation of order within it were matters of the highest priority for the government.[26]

Tolstoi proposed to accomplish this according to the following guidelines. Government-appointment supervisory agents would replace the collegial bureaus and the few remaining peace arbitrators and would oversee peasant affairs. These officials would be under the control of the provincial governors, who would act as his ministry's chief agents in the countryside. The zemstvos and municipal institutions were to be incorporated into the hierarchy of state institutions, with a system of government appointment to replace elections wherever possible in filling local offices. Recognizing that the success of land captains would largely hinge on the participation of the most educated, experienced, and loyal members of the local population, Tolstoi publicly advocated a greater role for the gentry in local administration. Litigation concerning petty village offenses would be decided by land captains, thus voiding the separation of powers. In short, these guidelines were to increase the control of the minister of internal affairs over the selection and activity of all local officials.[27]

The view of Russian development as distinct from the West, the emphasis on the role of autocracy in Russian history, and the belief that good government depended more on individuals than on laws – these were tenets of nineteenth-century Russian conservative thought from Karamzin on. Hence, it is easy to dismiss Tolstoi's arguments as nothing more than a desire to return Russia to her prereform status, in which the landed gentry controlled local administration and exercised unrestrained police powers over their serfs. However, viewed in the context of his bureaucratic pragmatism and of the shortcomings of peasant and zemstvo self-government, Tolstoi indeed expressed some very different ideas than his conservative predecessors (and counterparts) concerning the relationship between the state and social estates. He did not equate state control over local government with gentry control. Nor did he wish to reestablish the prereform system of administration in the countryside. Whereas Karamzin, Katkov, and the gentry opponents of the emancipation viewed the gentry as permanent partners of the state, governing together in the form of a dyarchy, Tolstoi regarded the gentry above all as the government's instrument, and a temporary one at that, in

---

[26]Ibid., *l.* 332 *ob.*
[27]Ibid., *f.* Departament obshchikh del MVD, *op.* 241, *d.* 51, *ll.* 27 *ob.*-28 *ob.*

the process of establishing state control over the village. The land captains, consisting of state-appointed officials, would be merely a transitional step toward the systematic establishment of bureaucratic control in the country-side. Once this had been accomplished, he implied, there would be no need to preserve the gentry estate distinctions of that office, and a separate gentry estate might well prove dispensable.[28] Tolstoi's willingness to use the gentry for the narrow designs of the state frequently put him in conflict with other conservatives such as Meshcherskii and Katkov, who demanded that the government show more appreciation for the gentry's past services and elevate their position above all by economic measures to increase their landholdings. Katkov in fact wanted the gentry to enjoy the autonomous position in local government that characterized their English counterparts, whereas Tolstoi, like Pobedonostsev, valued the gentry only for their direct service to the state.[29]

It is also clear that Tolstoi did not wish to recreate local administration in its prereform condition. He did not criticize the abolition of serfdom, which he considered in the economic interests of all concerned (a change of view perhaps brought about by Pazukhin). As for local administration, the prereform gentry were apathetic toward elected service and often despotic in the treatment of their serfs, and these conditions had contributed to peasant unrest under Nicholas I. Tolstoi's objective, on the contrary, was to eliminate abuses by local officials, which even during the postreform era had victimized the peasant population and jeopardized domestic tranquility. This he intended to accomplish by instituting a network of local officials under the firm control of the minister of internal affairs – a bureaucratic solution born of Tolstoi's political distrust of public initiative, his reverence

[28]TsGIA, f. Departament zakonov G. S., op. t. 11, d. 44, ll. 4, 222.

On Karamzin's view, see Richard Pipes' introductory essay in Karamzin's *Memoir on Ancient and Modern Russia*, trans. Richard Pipes (paperback ed.; New York, 1969), p. 60. Karamzin's own view that good people alone determined fair and efficient government is stated in ibid., pp. 190–5. According to Karamzin's theory, Tolstoi's concept of Russian government would probably place Russia in the category of a despotic state, in which authority resided in the autocrat, and the state, in choosing to govern by itself, paid no attention to the rights of social estates. Tolstoi's ideology fit under the category of bureaucratic conservatism, as defined by Pipes in "Russian Conservatism in the Second Half of the Nineteenth Century," *Slavic Review* 30, no. 1, (1971): 121–8

The idea of the land captains as agents of bureaucratic control in the provinces is elaborated in Yaney, *Systematization*, pp. 368–76. To my knowledge, Yaney was the first historian to characterize the land captains as state agents rather than as a new edition of gentry serfowners.

[29]Katkov's views are described in Edward C. Thaden, *Conservative Nationalism in Nineteenth Century Russia* (Seattle, 1964), pp. 45–6. Meshcherskii explained his differences with Tolstoi over ways to improve the gentry's position in the provinces in his 4 November 1884 diary-letter to Alexander III in TsGAOR, f. Aleksandr III, 1884–1885, op. l, d. 108, ll. 93 ob.–94.

Although Tolstoi and Pobedonostsev concurred on the role of the gentry as state servants, they disagreed over the viability of the gentry to assume this function in the 1880s. The doctrinaire Pobedonostsev maintained that the gentry were in a state of economic and moral decline and had outlived their usefulness to the state. Typically, he proposed no changes in the current situation. In contrast, Tolstoi argued that even though the gentry were decreasing in numbers and commanding less and less respect, they still could perform one last service to the state as land captains. Pobedonostsev explained his position in his 26 February 1884 letter to Alexander III in *Pis'ma Pobedonostseva k Aleksandru III*, 2: 46–8; and *Pobedonostsev i ego korrespondenty*, vol. 1, pt. 1, pp. 68–9.

of autocracy, and his past experience with public self-government.[30] Tolstoi believed that with local self-government and central policy making under his direction, at last Russia's administrative needs could be fulfilled in accordance with her political traditions, and that his proposed legislation could bring order, authority, and life to the tsarist regime. Yet he clearly overestimated the capabilities of the tsarist government, in terms of personnel and fiscal and technological resources, to supervise personally its local officials, and to carry out all functions of local administration. In effect, his proposals aimed at creating a type of *Polizeistaat* to harness society and protect autocracy by uprooting the seeds of pluralism sown in Russia by the Great Reforms.[31] Certainly, a system of central control over local self-government would be in line with Russia's autocratic tradition; few officials disputed this point. But could such a system function fairly and effectively and prevent even greater disorder? By emphasizing such issues, Tolstoi's opponents indeed raised doubts about the viability of autocracy in Russia in the future.

The land captains project. The land captains project that Tolstoi submitted to the State Council in February 1887 was not the original proposal drafted by Pazukhin in early 1886. Since the original draft is no longer extant in state archives, it is necessary to rely on the testimony of other officials for information on its content. According to Pobedonostsev, who participated in a preliminary review of the project in early April 1886, the most significant reforms entailed the appointment of land captains with administrative and judicial powers to decide elementary legal disputes between peasants; the reorganization of zemstvo representation according to social estates; and the replacement of elected zemstvo boards with bureaus for zemstvo affairs composed of local state representatives and two appointed zemstvo delegates. Other details of the project (especially on the procedures for appointing land captains) demonstrated that, in accordance with Tolstoi's instructions, Pazukhin had substituted state control for gentry control.[32]

The proposals evoked strong criticism from the participants at the session, who included Pobedonostsev, Ostrovskii, and Manasein. The latter, especially, attacked Tolstoi for proposing to abolish the justices of the peace and to grant judicial authority to the land captains. Rather than promote ministerial support for the project, the session united these ministers against it and prompted Pazukhin to solicit Katkov's help in persuading Pobedonostsev to support the project. Following the session, a dejected Tolstoi threatened

---

[30]See *Dnevnik sekretaria Polovtsova*, 2: 191; TsGIA, f. Departament zakonov G. S., *op.* t. 11, *d.* 44, *l.* 216 *ob.*; ibid., f. Kantseliariia MVD, *op.* 2, *d.* 17, *l.* 326; Golovin, *Moi vospominaniia*, 2: 53.

[31]In contrast, Pipes treats Russia in the 1880s as a developing modern police state in *Russia under the Old Regime* (New York, 1974), pp. 302–16. Pipes is concerned primarily with tsarist police measures against the revolutionaries and gives little attention to the development of state control in other areas of administration.

[32]See Pobedonostsev's letter of 18 April 1886 in *Pis'ma Pobedonostseva k Aleksandru III*, 2: 105; and Meshcherskii's diary entries for 6 and 9 May 1886 in TsGAOR, f. Aleksandr III, *op.* l, *d.* 108, *ll.* 111–14 *ob.* The meeting occurred on 2 April 1886.

to resign if Pobedonostsev's support was not forthcoming, although, in light of Tolstoi's influence over Alexander III and subsequent events, this was empty rhetoric more than anything else.[33] There is no evidence that Katkov ever attempted to win over Pobedonostsev, and Tolstoi subsequently made the "fatal concession," according to Prince Meshcherskii, of amending his project so that justices of the peace would exist alongside land captains.[34]

The project underwent further revisions, mainly in its wording, in a special subcommission handpicked by Tolstoi. It met in the fall of 1886 under the chairmanship of Deputy Minister Prince K. D. Gagarin and included Pazukhin as a member. There is no need to describe their work in detail here; suffice it to note that the subcommission, convened to rubber-stamp Tolstoi's proposal, clashed over two provisions of the project that foreshadowed the more volatile debate later in the State Council. In regard to the first provision, Prince A. R. Shidlovskii, marshal of the Khar'kov provincial gentry, objected to the broad judicial powers proposed for land captains. Such a measure would encourage arbitrariness, he remarked, and no country in the world contained officials or even bureaus with such extensive powers. Besides, the peasants would have little litigation to submit to the land captains, because the *volost'* court handled almost all their legal affairs. But the other nine members rejected Shidlovskii's proposal to restrict the judicial authority of land captains to lawsuits involving property damages, contract violations, and the like. They also vetoed his suggestion that complaints against the decisions of the Provincial Bureau for Village Affairs (a new institution proposed by Tolstoi) be referred to the Senate instead of the minister of internal affairs. Shidlovskii declared that the Senate was the supreme guardian of the rights of private citizens, and that no institution possessed more experience, competence, or public esteem in resolving legal disputes. In essence, even in Tolstoi's own commission the concept of bureaucratic control as a replacement for legal control was challenged, proof indeed that the fundamental change proposed by Tolstoi concerned the bureaucracy's relationship to local self-governing institutions and not the fact that the gentry would staff them. However, the other members agreed with Tolstoi's aim of overturning the law of 1882 and eliminating Senate interference in matters under the ministry's responsibility.[35]

---

[33] See *Pis'ma Pobedonostseva k Aleksandru III*, 2: 106; Pazukhin's letters of 31 March, 6 April, and 7 June 1886 to Katkov in ORGBL, *f.* Katkov, *p.* 19, *ll.* 101 *ob.*–103; and N. Liubimov's letter of 6 April 1886 to Katkov in ibid., *l.* 138 *ob.*

[34] See Meshcherskii's letter [between 18 October and 3 November 1888] to Alexander III in TsGAOR, *f.* Aleksandr III, *op.* 1, *d.* 897, *l.* 62 *ob.*; and Meshcherskii, *Vospominaniia*, 3: 279–80.

In his 18 February 1887 letter to Katkov, Pazukhin assailed Manasein and reemphasized the need for land captains to possess complete judicial control in the countryside. This, he argued, was the foundation of the project, and Tolstoi would make no concessions on this point. Meanwhile, as Whelan notes, Meshcherskii blamed Pobedonostsev for turning Manasein against the proposal; Whelan, p. 177. In fact, Manasein had his own ministerial interests in opposing the project and Tolstoi, as illustrated by his 5 February 1887 presentation to the State Council, already had made significant concessions to Manasein concerning the justices. ORGBL, *f.* Katkov, *p.* 19, *ll.* 105–105 *ob.*

[35] TsGIA, *f.* Kantseliariia MVD, *op.* 2, *d.* 1838, *ll.* 403, 420–421 *ob.*, 456 *ob.*-458. Besides Prince

The revised land captains project stipulated the establishment of a land captain in each section (*uchastok*) of a district, and a district assembly of land captains presided over by the district marshal. Overseeing both these institutions would be a Provincial Bureau for Village Affairs under the chairmanship of the governor. This body would review complaints against the activity of land captains and would assist the governor in supervising their activity. The minister of internal affairs would appoint land captains from a list of candidates submitted by the governors who would make their nominations after consulting with local gentry marshals. Tolstoi assumed naively that the land captains would enjoy greater respect among the local population because, unlike publicly elected officials, they would wear the uniform of the Ministry of Internal Affairs, hold rank VI in the Table of Ranks (the equivalent of the district marshal), and would receive a lucrative salary of 2,500 rubles annually. Apparently recent cases in which the peasants had disobeyed the orders of local police officials and even the district police chiefs slipped his mind.[36] Even more telling, he noted that the peace arbitrators had not worn uniforms owing to the temporary nature of their offices and the desire to discourage "bureaucratism." However, the situation was entirely different with the land captains: "In order to organize the new officials properly, it is necessary to include them in the regular system of state institutions. Thus, the government agents, managing such an important branch of administration as peasant affairs, will enjoy without question all the regular privileges customarily associated with state service."[37]

In defining the qualifications for this office, Tolstoi insisted on the need for a gentry estate requirement. The gentry as a whole constituted the most educated, experienced, and loyal element in the empire. He contended that there was no other reservoir competent for the government to draw upon regularly, and only the gentry estate requirement would guarantee that an individual possessed the background and aptitude to discharge the functions of land captains. Tolstoi pointed out that the Russian gentry never resembled the privileged caste found in China or the feudal aristocracies of Western Europe, but rather developed as a state institution, created by the state to serve its needs. True, this view largely ignored the development of the gentry after their emancipation from obligatory service in 1762. But Tolstoi did not bother with details; he wanted only to make an argument for reestablishing state authority over the gentry. Nor did an estate requirement (*soslov-*

Gagarin and Pazukhin (the dominant figure at the meetings), the subcommission included four governors – N. P. Dolgovo-Saburov (Simbirsk), I. M. Sudienko (Vladimir), V. V. Kalachev (Kostroma), and A. F. Anis'in (Viatka); and four provincial gentry marshals – A. E. Zarin (Pskov), P. A. Krivskii (Saratov), G. V. Kondoidi (Tambov), and Shidlovskii. Yaney contends that their practical experience helped shape Tolstoi's "line-over-staff" vision for land captains at this late date (Yaney, *Urge to Mobilize*, pp. 81–2), yet as we have already observed, the minister's basic approach to local self-government reform was well defined by early 1885 (even before the dismissal of the Kakhanov Commission).

[36] For example, see *Krest'ianskoe dvizhenie v Rossii v 1881–1889 gg.*, pp. 421–2, 424–31, 435–6, 448–59, 475–7, 491–2, 494–6.

[37] Quoted from TsGIA, *f.* Kantseliariia MVD, *op.* 2, *d.* 17, *ll.* 345–345 *ob.*

nyi tsenz), in his view, constitute a real change in postreform local self-government. The landed gentry had held a virtual monopoly on the offices of peace arbitrators, permanent members, and justices of the peace. With the numbers of gentry in the provinces dwindling year by year, Tolstoi declared that the government would have to act immediately if it hoped to establish its control over the village.[38] He told Meshcherskii that the current moment was most propitious for making use of the landed gentry remaining in the countryside.[39]

Thus, practical considerations, more than gentry class interests, seem to have accounted for Tolstoi's proposal of a gentry estate requirement as the main criterion for land captain service. He also stipulated that the candidate fulfill one of three other requirements (three or more years of experience as a peace arbitrator, district marshal, permanent member or justice of the peace; a secondary education; and immovable property worth at least 15,000 rubles). With the abolition of, or at least a sharp reduction in, the number of justices of the peace, Tolstoi envisioned no difficulty in finding qualified gentry, preferably from the middle and upper ranks, to serve as the 1,200–2,000 land captains proposed under the reform. In provinces without gentry representation, the minister of internal affairs would appoint land captains. In order to raise the prestige and security of the office, Tolstoi proposed that land captains should serve for an indefinite period.[40] Yet without close government supervision, such a situation was ripe for the abuses by land captains that Tolstoi did not want. In short, he anticipated that the gentry would step forward and serve enthusiastically as land captains, subjecting themselves to the regimen of bureaucratic activity, and that they would discharge their responsibilities conscientiously and judiciously. These were steep demands to make of a class in material decline, few in numbers, and with a less than brilliant record in local service. But given his distrust of local public initiative, Tolstoi had no other options for reforming local administration.

In the area of jurisdiction, Tolstoi claimed that the land captains would parallel the original peace arbitrators in terms of their responsibilities and authority. In fact, this argument was another ploy designed to promote his project with the landed gentry and the state officials who had helped prepare the reforms of the 1860s and who held high opinions of the original peace

---

[38]Ibid., *ll.* 337 *ob.*, 342–342 *ob.*

[39]Meshcherskii, *Vospominaniia*, 3: 291–2.

[40]TsGIA, *f.* Kantseliariia MVD, *op.* 2, *d.* 17, *ll.* 342 *ob.*, 344 *ob.*; and ibid., *f.* Departament zakonov G. S., *op.* t. 11, *d.* 44, *l.* 208.

George Yaney argues that Tolstoi subscribed to the myth of gentry virtue, and thus insisted on the gentry estate requirement. Actually, there was little mythical about it. Like most top officials, Tolstoi recognized that the gentry, despite their past shortcomings in local service, possessed the "special qualities" most desirable in local officials, namely a tradition of service and personal nobility. He attached even more importance to the gentry's superior education and service experience vis à vis other groups. Thus, a gentry estate requirement for land captains, in conjunction with the other criteria for office, would produce competent officials without bogging down the government in the prolonged process of selection. Ibid., *d.* 20, *ll.* 31–5, 41. For Yaney's argument, see *Systematization*, p. 373.

arbitrators. His argument was unconvincing for several reasons. The arbitrators (as he had admitted earlier) were landowners first and officials second, selected specifically to implement the peasant reform and to mediate land settlement disputes between peasants and their former landlords. They were chosen and dismissed by the Senate and thus outside the control of the minister of internal affairs; and they had very limited jurisdiction over the judicial affairs of peasants even after the legislation of 1866 increased their authority in this respect. In contrast, as Kakhanov and others pointed out, land captains were permanent agents of the ministry with substantially different functions and broader powers than the arbitrators.[41] Thus, Tolstoi's maneuver deceived no one, but on the contrary intensified his opponents' hostility toward the measure, as evidenced by the amount of ministerial criticism on this point.

Tolstoi could afford to draw parallels between the arbitrators and his land captains because the latter would perform many of the arbitrators' functions in supervising peasant self-government – among them inspecting peasant officials and institutions, disciplining and even dismissing unethical *volost'* scribes. But broader supervisory powers were more necessary in the 1880s than in the 1860s in order to curb the nearly endemic drunkenness and lawlessness that ostensibly devastated the rural government and economy. Thus, land captains would have the authority to protest decisions of village or *volost'* assemblies that violated the law or interests of the community – in other words, decisions made under the influence of bribes and green wine. Despite Tolstoi's claims, this stipulation was tantamount to nullifying peasant self-government in the event the land captain chose to exercise it, because in all likelihood the land captains in the district assembly would uphold his protest.[42] Not surprisingly, this stipulation was one that caused the loudest uproar among partisans of the Great Reforms tradition and the liberal press.

Administrative expediency alone, however, did not induce Tolstoi to propose judicial authority for the land captains. The minister asserted that the government was at a critical juncture in defining its relationship to the peasantry. It could either ignore the needs of the village estate and economy and risk letting peasants take matters into their own hands (with all the adverse consequences for the state); or it could ensure that the peasant community receive legal protection from country lawyers and factory employers by establishing state officials in peasant society to resolve petty legal disputes and rectify criminal offenses. In political terms, Tolstoi's proposal was intended to gain the peasants' respect for autocracy. He considered them potentially the most conservative group in the empire and a natural ally of the government, given their agrarian ties, their traditional faith in the tsar, and their distrust of the urban intelligentsia. However, the situation would

---

[41]TsGIA, *f*. Departament zakonov G. S., *op*. t. 11, *d*. 44, *ll*. 632–3 *ob*.
[42]Ibid., *f*. Kantseliariia MVD, *op*. 2, *d*. 17, *ll*. 350–350 *ob*. This was exactly what happened in the 1890s, according to Robbins, "Viceroys," chap. 8

change if traditional estate distinctions continued to break down and confusion prevailed in peasant administration and justice. The peasants might well curse the tsar for afflicting them with peasant self-government. Hence, to restore order and authority in the village, Tolstoi proposed to assign land captains jurisdiction over all civil suits involving personal contracts, obligations, and losses for amounts up to 300 rubles, and over criminal offenses committed by peasants in which damages totaled less than 300 rubles. To win the support of Pobedonostsev and Manasein for his project, Tolstoi amended it so that justices of the peace would hear cases concerning violations of federal statutes, larceny, fraud, and all civil suits from 300 to 500 rubles in value.[43]

If the legislators of the 1860s can be accused of unfounded optimism in the peasants' ability to govern themselves, it is equally fair to criticize Tolstoi for underestimating the sensitivity of some peasants to state control two decades later. The minister justified punitive powers for his land captains (that included a five-ruble fine or seven days' detention for peasants, *meshchane*, and other nonprivileged elements) on the grounds that punishments would halt disorder and prevent its recurrence only when administered immediately on the spot. Thus, they had the advantage of expediency and practicality in comparison with the formal review of violations by justices of the peace, a process that often occurred weeks after the offense. Following such delays, significant fines levied by the justices generally went unpaid, and long terms of detention contributed little to the moral rehabilitation of the offenders, while having a deleterious effect on the material welfare of their families.[44] This provision understandably aroused more resentment among peasants than any others.

Yet this system of state-directed change, which Tolstoi claimed could protect the peasantry, in fact paved the way for their abusive treatment by some land captains. The procedure for appealing a judicial decision of the land captains was enough to intimidate the peasant, who would be required to submit his protest to the land captain who rendered the decision. Such an act was indeed a risk, in view of the land captain's extensive punitive powers over the peasants. Consequently, the Provincial Bureaus for Village Affairs and the governors served as the only checks on the activity of land captains, and for geographical reasons alone, they were too remote from the scene of the abuse.

Nonetheless, Tolstoi himself claimed that the Ministry of Internal Affairs could exert more effective control over the land captains than the formal laws or public had in the past with respect to local officials. He was probably right in this assumption, provided he had enough officials available to supervise the land captains. By virtue of direct dismissal, demotion, or dis-

[43]TsGIA, *f.* Kantseliariia MVD, *d.* 17, *ll.* 359 *ob.*-360
[44]Ibid., *f.* Departament zakonov G. S., *op.* t. 11, *d.* 44, *l.* 498 *ob.*

ciplining of land captains, the ministry could indeed set an example for the local population in dealing with negligent or abusive officials. Yet the pitfall in Tolstoi's proposal consisted in the fact that he imposed these responsibilities entirely on the governors.[45] No matter how conscientious these thirty-four governors were, they could not possibly provide the close supervision over some 2,000 land captains (plus assume new responsibilities vis à vis the zemstvo envisioned in the proposed zemstvo legislation) that would prevent the land captains from abusing their discretionary powers. Consequently, the effectiveness of the land captain reform, as with previous reforms of local government, would depend largely on whether or not the "best people" would assume the burdens of the new office. No wonder Tolstoi urged the government and conservative press to portray this office, the mainspring of his policy of rural administrative control, as an honor and as a reward, when in fact the conditions surrounding its establishment revealed clearly the government's dissatisfaction with the gentry's past performance in public self-government.

Ministerial opposition to the land captains project

Background to the ministerial opposition: some personal and institutional factors. Given the proposed investiture of both administrative and judicial powers in the land captains and the bureaucratization of local self-government under the minister of internal affairs, it is no surprise that the land captains project came under widespread criticism. It generated more conflict in official circles than the university counterreform of 1884, the judicial counterreforms of 1887 and 1889, or, for that matter, any other piece of legislation during Alexander III's reign. Yet to appreciate the extent of and reasons for this opposition, it is necessary to consider briefly the background of these officials, their institutional loyalties, and their political ideologies.

The ramifications of Tolstoi's counterreform policy for the system of ministerial politics that generally had prevailed from Alexander II on were certainly sufficient grounds for the opposition of many high officials; and as noted earlier, by the mid-1880s Tolstoi had already begun to change this system. He used his favored status with Alexander III to pass important control measures, including the law (1886) limiting family property repartitions in the village (over the objections of Finance Minister Bunge),[46] the law on hiring village workers (1885), and the statute on factory supervision.[47]

---

[45]Ibid., *f.* Kantseliariia MVD, *op.* 2. *d.* 17, *l.* 376 *ob.*; ibid., *f.* Departament zakonov G. S., *op.* t. 11, *d.* 44, *l.* 238; and Yaney, *Urge to Mobilize*, pp. 84–5.

[46]Solov'ev, pp. 85–6.

[47]*Dnevnik sekretaria Polovtsova*, 1: 355–6, 413, 531–2, 540–1, and Kataev, *Mestnye krest'ianskie uzhrezhdeniia*, pt. 3, p. 10. The factory supervision statue (1886), which Tolstoi drafted in response to factory strikes of the previous year, is further evidence that Tolstoi subordinated "class interests" to state aims in his government control policy. After inspecting the factories, he concluded that the factory owners were largely to blame for labor unrest because of deplorable working conditions in the factories. The

All three measures were enacted despite stiff opposition from several ministers and jurists in the State Council who were determined to uphold Alexander II's reforms and the principles they embodied. As Whelan has shown in her account of the State Council, by Alexander III's reign such council members as Baron Nikolai and Kakhanov were part of a professionally oriented, highly educated corps of jurists who passed on their service values and political convictions to their sons. Wedded to the concept of *zakonnost'*, they ideologically opposed counterreforms that substituted expediency for legality and emphasized personal discretionary authority (in the manner of a *Polizeistaat*, as Taranovski has argued) and the rule of imperial favorites.[48]

However, because Alexander III's disdain for the State Council jurists was no secret, the State Council had little chance on its own of thwarting Tolstoi's plans or the counterreform policies in general. Rather, the more threatening and disconcerting opposition came from the tsar's ministers, many of whom were appointed through the influence of Tolstoi or Pobedonostsev, because they attacked the proposed land captains and zemstvo legislation for personal and political, as well as ideological, reasons – in a manner reminiscent of previous ministerial conflicts over local self-government. Indeed, the nature of ministerial appointments under Alexander III greatly complicated Tolstoi's task. On the one hand, Tolstoi's main ministerial foes on the land captain and zemstvo counterreforms (Manasein, Vyshnegradskii) were on the average ten years younger than Tolstoi. Given the turbulent events and changes of the previous thirty years, they represented a different generation of officials than Tolstoi, and as such saw themselves as beneficiaries, not critics, of the Great Reforms ideology and the realignment of ministerial power. Having attained top positions in government through hard work and expertise, these ministers were not about to take a back seat to Tolstoi in state policy making. They were loyal to the ministry that brought them professional prestige and rank; yet in their dealings at court these career bureaucrats were also more dependent than ever on retaining the tsar's favor (as the independently wealthy Polovtsov complained, "[our] officials think only about pleasing higher authority, without worrying whether their business is proceeding truly satisfactorily").[49]

---

statute (pushed through despite resistance from the finance minister) outlined regulations for concluding and terminating labor contracts; set up a schedule of wage payments; increased the penalties for striking; and, in accordance with Tolstoi's concept of the paternalistic state, created factory bureaus consisting of crown officials, factory inspectors, and representatives of the judiciary, zemstvos, and municipalities to resolve employer-workers' disputes. The law heralded the state's incursion into the sphere of factory management, which in most cases was in the hands of wealthy industrialists and gentry. *PSZ*, 3d ser., vol. 6, no. 4769, 3 June 1886.

[48]Whelan, pp. 155–6; Taranovski, "Politics of Counter-Reform," pp. 289–91. In her analysis of the social composition of Alexander III's State Council, Whelan notes that 72 percent of the members had a higher or elite education and 28 percent were jurists (the single largest subcategory of officials, despite Alexander III's intense dislike for them). She adds, however, that the State Council was clearly a gerontocracy and that many members played a passive role at important council sessions. Whelan, pp. 140–1, 145–6.

[49]Diary entry of 3 June 1889 in *Dnevnik sekretaria Polovtsova*, 2: 205. The data on the various ministers

On the other hand, unlike the wealthy gentry, who held most of the highest state offices in previous reigns, almost half of the top officials in Alexander III's reign possessed no property aside from the lands they received as rewards for state service. Many of these officials were sons of clergy (for example, Vyshnegradskii and Pobedonostsev) or of merchants (Ostrovskii). Of the eighty-three officials who made up the second rank in the Table of Ranks (including court officials, State Council members, and ministers), nearly 46 percent had no land at all, whereas only 31 percent had family estates; and the corresponding figures for officials of the third rank were 56 percent and 30 percent, respectively. In fact, only 31 percent of all these servitors had enough land (at least 1,000 *desiatiny*) to be considered independently wealthy, as in the cases of Delianov and Tolstoi, who belonged to the landed gentry and derived a significant income from their landholdings. In contrast, Pobedonostsev, Bunge, Vyshnegradskii, and Sol'skii had no land at all, while Nabokov, Ostrovskii, and Girs acquired only estates through service. In short, without an independent source of income, most of the arrivé officials (or "homines novi" as they were sometimes sarcastically called) viewed state service not only as their raison d'être, but also as the sole source of their livelihood and prestige.[50]

To be sure, other historians have pointed to the professionalizaton of the elite bureaucracy under Alexander III and argued that, notwithstanding the personalized authority of the tsarist system, the rise of such official talent and a distinct bureaucratic stratum enhanced the imperial regime's chances of directing the social and economic transformation occurring in postreform Russia. Many of Alexander III's ministers had spent a considerable period as deputy ministers in their particular ministries (in sharp contrast to the situation under Nicholas I and Alexander II) – for instance, Girs in Foreign Affairs, Bunge in Finance, Delianov in Education, German Egorovich Pauker and Giubbenet in Transportation and Communications, and (later) Durnovo in Internal Affairs. Manasein was a lifelong official in the Ministry of Justice; Ostrovskii spent over a decade as deputy state comptroller and as a member of the Department of State Economy (both appropriate training for the Ministry of State Properties); and Vyshnegradskii was a scholar reputed for his talents as a financier.

Far from acting as a unified bloc against the State Council along ideological lines, however, Alexander III's ministerial specialists identified their own career interests with those of their ministry and regarded any diminution in

(found in the appropriate volumes of *Russkii biograficheskii slovar'*) shows that Tolstoi was of the same generation as many of the liberals in the State Council who, as examples of the "enlightened bureaucrats" of the Great Reforms, defended the principles of *zakonnost'* and *glasnost'* and the reform institutions themselves. For an argument that emphasizes Alexander III's tendency to pick "outsiders" as his ministers (for instance, Vyshnegradskii, Witte, and N. V. Murav'ev, the justice minister in 1894–1905), see Taranovski, "Murav'ev Commission," p. 165.

[50]See Zaionchkovskii, *Rossiiskoe samoderzhavie*, pp. 113–16; idem, *Pravitel'stvennyi apparat*, pp. 197–208; Orlovsky, "High Officials in the Ministry of Internal Affairs," pp. 279–82; Whelan, pp. 148–52; and Bennett, pp. 162ff.

their jurisdiction in a reorganization of local self-government – the need for which was patently clear – as a personal affront. Hence, even more than their predecessors, they judged administrative reform projects in terms of their career and ministerial interests and, like tsarist officials in general, seemed oblivious to virtually everything outside St. Petersburg.[51] After all, besides Tolstoi, none of the ministers in power in the late 1880s had held a ministerial-level post other than the current one and few had firsthand acquaintance with the vast network of provincial officials (both state and elected). Without direct pressure from Alexander III (his actions will be explained in due course), these officials could hardly be expected to subordinate their authority in the interests of administrative unity and the establishment of leadership in state circles, the need for which was apparent to other officials.[52]

For these reasons, the arrivé official was a persistent opponent of any institutional reorganization rather than a proponent of counterreforms.[53] These officials intended to solidify the old ministerial order and their privileged status that developed under Alexander II, thus adding their weight to the State Council opposition; or, as in the case of Justice Minister Manasein, to reestablish it. Hence, we have the unusual case of ministers who attacked Tolstoi's proposal even though many of them, for ideological and pragmatic reasons, supported the concept of state control. For example, within his own ministry, Manasein pushed through a series of judicial counterreforms in 1887 and 1889 that strengthened his control over the local judiciary. He received the power to order the doors closed to the public for any trial that, in his opinion, could disturb social tranquility if its proceedings were made public. He also enforced an earlier law (1885) requiring judges to explain decisions to the minister of justice in the event the latter questioned the findings.[54] But in matters outside his ministry, as shown below with Tolstoi's project, there were few officials more resolutely opposed to state control than Manasein, because such a reform would cut deeply into the authority of the local judiciary. In short, for the ministers themselves, institutional interests and political ambitions were usually more important than ideological considerations (*Rechtsstaat* versus *Polizeistaat*) in determining their response to counterreform proposals made by their peers. Only with

---

[51]For official accounts of the polarization, self-interest, and drift in ministerial circles in the 1880s, see Solov'ev, pp. 56–8, 76–8, 113–15. The importance of these ministerial accounts lies not so much in their critical evaluation of fellow ministers, but in their common note of alarm over the absence of any unified state policy or purpose, and the relatively few, unimaginative suggestions on how to achieve such unity.

[52]See Golovnin's 11 August 1883 letter to Miliutin in ORGBL, *f.* D. A. Miliutin, *p.* 61, *d.* 39, *l.* 39; and Polovtsov's diary entries for 29 January, 14 March, 17 March, and 5 May 1882, and even for 1 March 1887 in TsGAOR, *f.* Polovtsov, *op.* 1, *d.* 20, *ll.* 45 *ob.*, 59 *ob.*-60, 61 *ob.*-62, 63, 75–76 *ob.*; and *Dnevnik sekretaria Polovtsova*, 2: 31.

[53]For a similar view, see Whelan, p. 229; the opposite argument is made in Bennett, pp. 170, 172–6, yet the author fails to draw the connection between the *raznochintsy* officials and the reactionary legislation of Alexander III.

[54]Wagner, pp. 375–6, 385; and Zaionchkovskii, *Rossiiskoe samoderzhavie*, pp. 255–6.

this in mind can we comprehend the unusual coalition of ministers and State Council members who, crossing generations and ideological lines, vehemently attacked the land captain reform and rendered the government increasingly unable to coordinate and systematize its ministerial apparatus.

Official criticism of the land captain project. The official criticism of the land captain project provides a good reminder of the need to question source materials critically. After all, nearly all officials who commented on Tolstoi's project claimed to support its main ideas (*osnovaniia*). However, this was not the case, for their replies constituted a severe attack against the proposed combination of administrative and judicial powers, the continued isolation of peasant administration, and the creation of bureaucratic plenopotentiaries of the Ministry of Internal Affairs to supervise the peasants – in essence, the very foundations of the project, according to Pazukhin and Tolstoi. Thus, all the claims by these officials about agreeing with the proposal amounted only to the fact that they acknowledged the political dangers associated with the breakdown of rural administration and the need to supervise peasants, although they had radically different views on who should supervise and what powers these officials should have.

By early 1887, Tolstoi already faced widespread opposition to his land captains proposal. His earlier concessions to Manasein and Pobedonostsev in the wake of the April 1886 meeting had altogether backfired. Manasein subsequently boasted to Polovtsov that "he [was] an opponent of the project from beginning to end," and that he planned to write a long refutation to it.[55] Nor was he the only official to submit detailed memoranda highly critical of the project in the spring of 1887. Five top officials attacked its key provisions – the bureaucratic nature of the land captains, the gentry estate requirement, the combination of powers, and the cost to implement the measures – and their replies raised even larger questions. How would the peasants react to bureaucratic control in the countryside? Would the landed gentry accept the bureaucratic regimen of land captain service? Should Russia follow a Western model of administrative development or not? And could the local population shoulder the additional cost of land captains without jeopardizing the flow of tax revenues to the central government and, accordingly, state plans to balance the budget and initiate a program of heavy industrialization?

Some officials, including Ostrovskii and State Comptroller Sol'skii, devoted little time, much less serious thought, to their comments. Yet even the latter decried the more blatant aspects of bureaucratization, prophetically asserting that the ministry's uniform and the subordination of the land captains to the local hierarchy would dissuade more intelligent local residents from serving.[56] But the strongest criticism of land captains appointed by and subject to the Ministry of Internal Affairs came from Kakhanov and

[55] Passage for 23 February 1887 in *Dnevnik sekretaria Polovtsova*, 2: 28.
[56] TsGIA, *f.* Departament zakonov G. S., *op.* t. 11, *d.* 44, *l.* 247.

Manasein. Both claimed to be committed to the process of devolution of power and diffusion of ministerial authority, and hence advocated zemstvo-elected officials to supervise peasant administration. Yet Manasein's support for zemstvo election reflected his desire to keep such supervisors outside Tolstoi's exclusive control. Both Kakhanov and Manasein prophetically warned that under a system of state-appointed land captains the government would be held directly responsible for the failings of these officials. In the event the land captains neglected their functions or abused their powers, the local population not only would not obey government authority, but might well turn against it;[57] and the numerous peasant disturbances in Ekaterinoslav, Simbirsk, and Orel provinces in 1892 due to the peasants' harsh treatment by land captains indeed substantiated these fears.[58]

Tolstoi's adversaries advanced several weighty arguments against gentry estate affiliation as the primary requirement for appointment as a land captain. For instance, Baron Nikolai, chairman of the combined departments of the State Council, was sparing but penetrating in his criticism. He claimed that this requirement would bind the government in its appointment of candidates, an obligation made all the more difficult by the steadily decreasing numbers of gentry. There was also no reason to think that peasants would obey gentry land captains any more than nongentry assigned to that office. In fact, he cautioned, the appointment of gentry alone might lead peasants to think that the government intended to reestablish serfdom. Baron Nikolai acknowledged that this was not Tolstoi's aim, but he feared that peasants might misconstrue the goal of the measure, and local gendarme officials attributed some episodes of peasant unrest in the early 1890s to precisely this factor.[59] Thus, Nikolai sided with Kakhanov and Manasein in declaring that property and education requirements similar to those for election to the zemstvo assembly were enough. The three officials, as well as Boris Pavlovich Mansurov, a State Council member who submitted two commentaries on Tolstoi's proposal in 1888, contended that the gentry's previous record in local administration left much to be desired, and that recent changes in zemstvo representation had proved that they had lost interest in this area.[60]

The virulent nature of these arguments proved once again that Russian officials in the 1880s were more adept at tearing down any proposals than in devising positive reform suggestions. Even Tolstoi, whom Witte called a "prominent person" in contrast to other officials,[61] was at his best in attacking the views of others. He rebuked Kakhanov and Manasein for

[57]Ibid., *l.* 174 *ob.*
[58]See *Krest'ianskoe dvizhenie v Rossii v 1890–1900 gg. Sbornik dokumentov*, ed. A. V. Shapkarin (Moscow, 1959), pp. 36–9, 88–91, 180–2, 191–5, 199–203.
[59]Ibid., pp. 43–4.
[60]See TsGIA, *f.* Departament zakonov G. S., *op.* t. 11, *d.* 44, *ll.* 511–12 *ob.*; for Manasein, ibid., *ll.* 146–47 *ob.*; for Kakhanov, ibid., *ll.* 174–5; for Mansurov, ibid., *ll.* 767–767 *ob.*
[61]S. Iu. Vitte, *Vospominaniia* (3 vols.; Moscow, 1960), 1: 298.

suggesting that land captains be elected on the grounds that such a change would only lead to "the ruin and demoralization in all branches of local administration that is inevitably associated with zemstvo elections."[62] As for the gentry estate requirement, Tolstoi took pains to erase any doubts about the purpose of the counterreform. While revealing that he was not averse to improving the status of the gentry, his replies intended to show once again that the needs of state were uppermost in his mind and that the gentry were the only group with the requisite education and experience to translate the objectives of government control into reality. He told Kakhanov:

There is no doubt that such a measure should raise the significance and spirits of the gentry. . . . But to conclude on this basis that the government is handing over local administration to one estate would be as incorrect as assuming that in 1861 the government refrained from directing the peasant reform. In as much as the peasant emancipation was carried out successfully by the government with the help of the gentry, we should expect that the reform of local administration undertaken in the same manner will turn out successfully. But the responsibility for local administration now, as then, will belong completely to the government, since local administration will remain in its hands. The landed gentry will participate in this matter not as an independent political force or as a corporate estate, but only as a class of servitors who, under the direction of the governor and the supervision of the Ministry, can successfully carry out His Majesty's objectives in local areas.[63]

Here in a nutshell was Tolstoi's political philosophy of local self-government. The gentry would function as government agents in establishing order and tranquility in peasant villages. He dismissed any comparisons between the land captains and prereform serfowners with the remark, "The radical distinction between the *votchina* police powers which each landowner had over the serfs on his estate and the administrative functions that the land captains, under the direct administrative control of higher officials, will have over peasants and *meshchane* is so pronounced and obvious that it will be clear to everyone."[64]

Yet without such government control over land captains in practice that Tolstoi desired, their distinction from prereform serfowners would not appear so obvious. Indeed, Tolstoi won the argument in semantics, but overlooked the implications of the criticism. Even his opponents recognized that the reform aimed primarily at eliminating administrative confusion and conflict in the countryside, and was not merely a pretext for increasing the gentry's political power. What they objected to was handcuffing the government in its selection of candidates and, in essence, relying exclusively on a class that was in a process of economic and political decline.[65] They emphasized that the government should recruit new elements, especially the educated youth

[62]Quoted from TsGIA, *f*. Departament zakonov G. S., *op*. t. 11, *d*. 44, *l*. 483. See also ibid., *f*. Kantseliariia MVD, 1887, *op*. 2, *d*. 20, *ll*. 28 *ob*.–29

[63]Quoted from ibid., *l*. 41 *ob*.

[64]Quoted from ibid., *ll*. 41–42 *ob*. Yaney makes the same point in *Urge to Mobilize*, p. 79.

[65]Ibid., *f*. Departament zakonov G. S., *op*. t. 11, *d*. 44, *ll*. 175 *ob*., 510 *ob*.-511.

of all estates, to fill the ranks and revitalize the ever-expanding local administrations. Like the decentralists of the Kakhanov Commission earlier, they contended that the government could no longer rely on the same personnel and antiquated methods to administer the empire, and they advanced an ideological argument for general public participation in government if it hoped to run more efficiently. The sclerotic system of autocratic rule, even with the centralization of all local officials under one ministry, lacked the flexibility to adjust to the current economic and social changes throughout the empire. And with the preservation of the justices of the peace under the revised project, they concluded, there would not be enough qualified gentry to fill the minimum 2,000 land captain posts.[66]

Even certain gentry leaders acknowledged that gentry interests were not Tolstoi's major concern, judging by their reaction to different drafts of the Land Captain Statute. The most famous case occurred in December 1887, when the Saratov provincial gentry objected to the conditions of service defined in the project. They submitted a report also asking Tolstoi to consider "the gentry's apprehensions over the fact that the introduction of a gentry estate requirement [for] land captains would make the gentry responsible for the success of the entire [reform] business, and could arouse the hatred of the peasants and envy of other estates against them."[67] They preferred to continue living independently and harmoniously with their peasant neighbors. Their unenthusiastic response to the new office likewise confirmed the predictions of Manasein and Kakhanov, among others, that many local gentry leaders, proud of their roles as public servants, would refuse to become a police force for the Ministry of Internal Affairs. Those inclined to state service opted for the cultured and comfortable life of St. Petersburg. Consequently, governors in several agrarian and industrial provinces (including Moscow, Tula, and Riazan') were forced to look beyond the hereditary landed gentry to fill the offices and appointed retired military officers lacking a secondary education to one out of every four positions.[68] In the light of these considerations and Tolstoi's proclaimed goals, the customary interpretation of this statute as gentry legislation must be seriously questioned.

Yet the issue that triggered the longest and most scorching attacks from high officials was the proposed combination of administrative and judicial

---

[66]Ibid., *l.* 765.

[67]Quoted from Kataev, *Mestnye krest'ianskie uchrezhdeniia*, pt. 3, p. 28. For similar gentry criticisms see Becker, p. 132.

Governor Golitsyn of Moscow recognized the limitations of the reform on the gentry's independence, claiming that it would bind them as local agents of the government. See ORGBL, *f.* Golitsyn, 1886, *d.* 13, *l.* 590.

[68]In six provinces where the landed gentry were relatively numerous, 36 of the initial 285 land captains had to be directly appointed by the state, given the absence of enough interested gentry candidates. See Yaney, *Urge to Mobilize*, p. 98; Golovin, *Moi vospominaniia*, 2: 146, 182, 184–6; and TsGIA, *f.* Departament zakonov G. S., *op.* t. 11, *d.* 44, *ll.* 147 *ob.*-148, 768 *ob.* The prominent Slavophile General A. A. Kireev wrote in his diary that the land captain legislation would be successful only if the gentry forgot about their "rights" and assumed the new "obligations" conferred on them. ORGBL, *fond* A. A. Kireev, 1889, *karton* 11, *l.* 98.

powers. Like no other issue in the debate over land captains, it welded the ideological and institutional opponents of centralization into a powerful coalition. Not only would this provision infringe on Manasein's local authority by limiting the number of justices of the peace and their powers (thereby setting a precedent that disturbed other ministers); in addition, it would signify a repudiation of the Great Reforms and damage Russia's image in the West (so claimed the ministerial opposition). Not surprisingly, Manasein devoted the major part of his critique of Tolstoi's project to this issue and asserted that land captains with administrative and judicial functions, contrary to Tolstoi's intention, would reduce the respect of the local populace for authority. But he really got to the heart of his objections when he complained that the measure would deprive the justices of the peace and all other district institutions of power and prestige, because their functions would be sharply curtailed. The courts (and, by implication, the Ministry of Justice) would be subordinated to the land captains, the judicial branch would lose its independence with respect to the administration, and the law and individual rights would be compromised by the new officials in their efforts to keep pace with all the petty litigation. In short, he concluded with some exaggeration, the proposal, if adopted, would destroy all respect for the law in the provinces.[69]

Rather than overturn the previous legislation, which had provided peasants with legal equality and eliminated the abuses of police justice, Manasein and Kakhanov recommended a reorganization of the justices of the peace in order to expedite the review of judicial cases and to bring the courts closer to the population (a process already begun by the 3 June 1886 Senate edict). Granting judicial powers to the land captains, in contrast, would only increase the number of judicial institutions in the provinces, add to the peasants' confusion over who would review their litigation, and distract the land captains from their main function of supervision. Such criticisms were effective if not unexpected, because Tolstoi insisted that practical considerations be the focus of his reform. His legalist opponents, who proceeded from the Western view that administrative and judicial powers were incompatible by nature, nonetheless were quite adept at exposing the practical shortcomings of the project.[70]

Manasein's opposition to such a combination of powers for land captains reflected the views not only of a minister intent on preserving his authority, but also of a professional jurist cognizant of the special knowledge needed to understand and to apply the law. He ridiculed Tolstoi for assuming that land captains without formal legal training could decide petty litigation in a fair manner. Most of the civil cases Tolstoi intended to transfer to the land captains in fact required a detailed knowledge of the law and had no relation to peasant administration. How could a land captain resolve a civil suit over

---

[69]TsGIA, *f.* Departament zakonov G. S., *op.* t. 11, *d.* 44, *l.* 148 *ob.*
[70]Ibid., *ll.* 150 *ob.*-151, 186.

property when he lacked a knowledge of torts and of the laws on punishment and compensation?[71] And, as Mansurov rightly observed, the land captains project itself offered no guidance on this matter. Its vagueness concerning the land captains' legal jurisdiction prompted Mansurov to question whether any of its compilers could pass an examination on this subject.[72] Thus, for various reasons, the land captain, an administrator devoting only part of his time to judicial affairs, would probably be even less effective than the justices of the peace in coping with peasant litigation. Rather than administrative order, argued these critics, Tolstoi's project, if enacted, promised only arbitrariness and wrongdoing by land captains.[73]

There was much substance to these criticisms. The judicial caseload alone would overwhelm the land captain and cause him to seek shortcuts, a problem compounded by the fact that, with the abrogation of the adversary principle, the land captain would have to collect the evidence. Nor did the project provide the local populace with any real legal recourse to protect themselves against the ministry's agents. Kakhanov and Manasein sifted through the bulk of proposed regulations on land captains, only to conclude that the appellate system was so complex on paper that uneducated peasants would not know where to begin in submitting appeals. Here they pinpointed a major flaw in the project and complained that it created a number of formal authorities over the land captains – for instance, the district assembly of the land captains, the district marshal, the governors, and the Provincial Bureau – but provided no real supervision. All of the aforementioned officials, for one reason or another, would have little time or inclination to check up on the land captains.[74] In short, the proposal portended a marked increase in paperwork, which Tolstoi claimed to oppose, while allowing the new officials wide latitude to abuse their authority. Kakhanov quipped that Tolstoi's cure for *bezvlastie* in peasant self-government might well prove worse than the

---

[71]Ibid., *ll.* 143, 152–3.

[72]Ibid., *l.* 569 *ob.*

[73]Ibid., *ll.* 639 *ob.*, 640. Yaney argues that Tolstoi and Pazukhin orginally planned for land captains to supervise all estates (*sosloviia*) at the subdistrict level, but that Manasein's opposition in 1886 forced them to limit the land captain's supervision to peasant self-government. Yaney, *Urge to Mobilize*, pp. 88–9, 90, 92. This claim seems puzzling, given Tolstoi's proclaimed goal (in 1885–6) of dealing separately with peasant administration through piecemeal reform (the land captain legislation): Pazukhin's defense of a separate estates administration throughout the 1880s; the access of the nonpeasant estates to the state courts; and Manasein's goal of preserving the justices of the peace and his ministry's local interests in criticizing Tolstoi's proposal. In this respect, see Whelan, pp. 183–4. Rather, Manasein and other top officials opposed Tolstoi's project because, in their view, it threatened to make permanent the isolated status of peasants in postreform Russia, thereby denying them a role in governing 80 percent of the population, and because it ran counter to the social and economic trends at work in the empire.

[74]TsGIA, *f.* Departament zakonov G. S., *op.* t. 11, *d.* 44, *ll.* 144–45 *ob.*, 157 *ob.*-159, 184–5, 197 *ob.*-198, 201–4, 252 *ob.*

On the other hand, a number of gentry marshals acknowledged in an anonymous memorandum to Tolstoi that the Land Captain Statute spelled out the jurisdiction of these officials. Perhaps they believed what they said, although it is likely that if the opposite were true, they would not have encouraged Tolstoi to impose more control over them. Ibid., *fond* D. S. Sipiagin, 1889–1890, *opis'* 2, *delo* 99, *ll.* 1–1 *ob.*

malady itself, as land captains, like their serfowning predecessors, would rule by fear rather than by law.[75] Mansurov summarized the views of the opposition when he asserted:

It is completely obvious that article 39 [concerning the appellate procedure] contains three juridical heresies – the violation of the basic principle *non bis in idem*; allowing an administrative official to determine the jurisdiction of a case at his own discretion; and authorizing him to sentence the offender not to the punishment prescribed by law, but to a stiffer punishment.[76]

A judicial system organized on such principles, he concluded, was intolerable in any civilized nation, and he recommended rejection of the provision that Tolstoi called the cornerstone of his project.[77]

Along with the jurisdictional and ideological concerns of ministers, fiscal expediency was a major factor throughout the postreform era in determining the fate of a measure, and in this respect the land captains proposal provided no exception. Finance Minister Vyshnegradskii was the main critic of the project in this area, because his fiscal policy aimed at reducing state expenditures and balancing the budget in order to enhance Russian credit in foreign money markets and to attract foreign investment. He abandoned Bunge's policy of reducing the tax burden and economic hardships of the peasantry (as evidenced by the easing of redemption payments in 1883 and the abolition of the poll tax in 1886) and demanded full collection of taxes and exportation of Russian grain in order to reduce her unfavorable balance of payments – an enterprise that, along with foreign policy matters, occupied much of Alexander III's attention in 1887. Vyshnegradskii worried that the land captains proposal would jeopardize his efforts at budget balancing by costing more to implement than the current institutions for supervising peasant administration. The measure would entail an additional 2.75 million rubles in zemstvo taxes that the peasants, already taxed to the limit, could not pay. His greatest fear, and a very valid one, was that a tax increase would strain the peasant economy to the breaking point and impede the flow of state tax revenues. Consequently, he concluded that Tolstoi's proposal would be acceptable only if salaries for land captains were reduced to 1,500 rubles.[78] Thus, Vyshnegradskii, at least in the area of peasant administration, did not oppose state control in principle; in fact, he intended to increase his own control over his tax inspectors and the village savings and loan institutions established in 1885 in order to cut down on peasant arrears. But when Tolstoi proposed to hand over supervision of these bodies to his land captains, the lines were drawn for a ministerial conflict between Vyshnegradskii and Tolstoi that lasted from 1887 until the latter's death two years

---

[75]TsGIA, *f.* Departament zakonov G. S., *op.* t. 11, *d.* 44, *ll.* 178, 189 *ob.*, 516 *ob.*
[76]Ibid., *l.* 567 *ob.*
[77]Ibid., *f.* Kantseliariia MVD, *op.* 2, *d.* 20, *l.* 31.
[78]Ibid., *f.* Departament zakonov G. S., *op.* t. 11, *d.* 44, *ll.* 250–250 *ob.*

later.[79] Kakhanov and Baron Nikolai went even further than Vyshnegradskii and insisted that the fiscal drawbacks of the proposal warranted its rejection.[80]

Realizing that opposition based on fiscal grounds could well scuttle his project, Tolstoi did some fast recalculations. He argued that land captains would cost only 1.5 million rubles per year more than the current institutions, or less than 4 percent of the annual budget for the zemstvos. These estimates led him to conclude:

This addition to the zemstvo budget will seem insignificant compared with the primary state need, in the fullest sense of the word, that the proposed reform will fulfill, and with the material benefits – the guarantee of order and the organization of public services – that it will bring to zemstvo taxpayers. Moreover, it should be noted that the additional expense will probably be made up by the savings foreseen with the proposed zemstvo reform.[81]

But for all his eloquence, Tolstoi failed to persuade Vyshnegradskii and other opponents that the reform would be financially sound. To a large degree, this stemmed from their view that Tolstoi's system, aside from burdening peasants beyond their limits, would force local residents to pay higher zemstvo taxes for state officials (land captains) over whom they had no control, and such taxes were already extremely unpopular with the peasants. In a sense, these critics subscribed to the Western concept that the public should have some voice over the disposal of funds levied by self-governing institutions. But Tolstoi never entertained such a notion, because he distrusted public institutions, and because he feared that, given Vyshnegradskii's commitment to a balanced budget, his proposal would arouse much sharper criticism in ministerial circles if he recommended that the state pay for the land captains.

As a result of extensive criticisms submitted by ministers and State Council members, the State Council postponed its review of the project until 1888. The decision infuriated Tolstoi for good reason; having led the tsar to believe that the ministers firmly supported the project in order to intimidate the opposition in the ministries and State Council, the embarrassed Tolstoi now resorted to denouncing State Council members almost daily in his reports to Alexander III.[82] The sovereign expressed equal displeasure over this turn of events and ordered the ministers affected by the reform to hold a series of meetings to reach an agreement. Although Tolstoi made some additional concessions on the land captains' judicial powers at these sessions in January and March 1888, Manasein and Vyshnegradskii still refused to endorse the project. The latter swore that he would never vote for the measure as long as each land captain received 2,500 rubles a year.[83] Far from creating a

---

[79]Ibid., *ll.* 253 *ob.*-254; and ibid., *l.* 234 *ob.*

[80]Ibid., *ll.* 207 *ob.*, 521 *ob.*-522.

[81]Quoted from ibid., *l.* 237 *ob.*

[82]Whelan, p. 179.

[83]See the 28 March 1888 passage in *Dnevnik sekretaria Polovtsova,* 2: 96–7.

   Other sources on these sessions include ibid., pp. 72, 74, 95, 476, 480; Feoktistov, p. 273; ORGBL,

consensus, the sessions aroused the hopes of Tolstoi's opponents, who left the meetings more convinced than ever that they could outlast Tolstoi and make a shambles of the project. The ministers agreed only to postpone review of the project in the State Council until the end of the year.

In sum, the official attacks levied against the project from early 1887 to mid-1888 illustrated that Tolstoi's project encountered extensive and deep-seated opposition in ministerial circles. Of all the ministers, only Delianov expressed his commitment to Tolstoi's project well before the debate over it began in the State Council. Many of Tolstoi's other erstwhile allies – for example, Pobedonostsev, Manasein, and Ostrovskii – either attacked the proposal from its inception or, as in the latter case, remained uncommitted toward it. Yet little did Tolstoi realize in the spring of 1888 that even more serious challenges lay ahead in the fall, when his opponents, capitalizing on Alexander III's detachment from the reform process, would rally together to present a counterproject.

Confrontation and climax: the State Council debate over the land captains proposal

The counterproject of Count Vorontsov-Dashkov. With Tolstoi's submission of the land captains project to the State Council in late fall 1888, the ministerial conflict over the measure took on a new guise marked by the increase in the number of opponents as well as a change in the tactics of opposition. Heretofore the regular ministers tried to derail the project by emphasizing practical shortcomings of Tolstoi's control policy (particularly as it concerned them), all the while assuring the emperor that they, too, desired a strong autocracy. Tolstoi had attempted to take advantage of these reassurances by emphasizing to the tsar that the other ministers admitted their support for the main ideas of his project, in contrast to the State Council. However, the minister himself belied his claims by intermittently denouncing his colleagues to Alexander III in moments of frustration, for example, following the ad hoc conferences the previous spring.

The counterproposal for a systematic overhaul of district administration submitted in late September 1888 by Count Illarion Ivanovich Vorontsov-Dashkov, the minister of the imperial household, constituted a new tactic employed by the steadily growing coalition of Tolstoi's opponents. The ideas in it did not originate with Vorontsov-Dashkov. Rather, they were an elaboration of the criticisms and recommendations submitted earlier by Kakhanov and especially by Egor Pavlovich Staritskii, chairman of the Department of Laws in the State Council and a participant in the compilation of the Judicial Statutes of 1864. Many ideas in the counterproject also reflected the views of the Special Conference of the Kakhanov Commission, although historians

f. Kireev, *k.* 11, *ll.* 49 *ob.*–50; and TsGIA, *f.* Departament zakonov G. S., *op.* t. 11, *d.* 44, *ll.* 493–506, 552a–552zh.

have not pointed out this connection. With its emphasis on decentralization and the elimination of a separate peasant administration, the counterproposal challenged the very goal of Tolstoi's project – namely, direct control of the Ministry of Internal Affairs over the peasantry.

To understand the significance of Vorontsov-Dashkov's memorandum, it is necessary to analyze briefly the ideas of Kakhanov and Staritskii. The fact that Kakhanov advocated a program of comprehensive, coordinated reforms in local government came as no shock. On the basis of his service as governor of Pskov and the work of his commission, Kakhanov concluded that Tolstoi's land captains would only compound the disjointed nature of local government. What was surprising, however, was his recommendation for changes outside the sphere of administration. Abandoning the narrow approach toward administrative reform followed by his fellow officials (and even himself earlier), Kakhanov pinpointed the impoverished condition of peasants and their dependence on wealthier neighbors (landlords, kulaks) as the source of all other problems in the village. He proposed to raise the intellectual and moral standards of peasants by reviving trade (even if considerable government investment in the countryside was necessary to stimulate development) and by facilitating procedures for peasant resettlement.[84] In short, Kakhanov was the only official during the debate to draw a relationship, albeit in general terms, between peasant economy and administration, and his proposals in this area anticipated Witte's industrialization policy and the approach of the turn-of-the-century agrarian specialists, who advocated the development of the market economy, the initiative of the individual peasant producer, and the removal of traditional communal restraints.[85] A simultaneous, comprehensive reorganization of local administration, argued Kakhanov, would elevate the peasantry to equal status with other classes and produce the changes in administrative structure and official attitudes necessary to make worthwhile government investment in rural economic development.

Staritskii submitted the blueprint for Vorontsov-Dashkov's district administration reform counterproject in April 1887. It was significant because it provided Tolstoi's opponents in the State Council with a concrete counterplan. Staritskii attributed the disunity in local administration to the absence of any official at the district level to coordinate the activity of all local institutions. The district gentry marshal, who presided over the district assemblies and bureaus, was an official elected by and beholden to one estate and thus not responsible for the activities of state or zemstvo institutions. Thus, although not directly advocating all-estate village government, Staritskii, by questioning the usefulness of the marshal, implied that separate estate institutions were obsolete, particularly in light of the diminishing

---

[84]Ibid., *ll.* 181 *ob.*, 635 *ob.*–636.

[85]The work of these agrarian experts, and their contribution to the Stolypin reforms, are analyzed in Macey, pp. 44–54, 56–81. The author likens these officials to the "enlightened bureaucrats" of the 1860s.

numbers of landed gentry in the countryside.[86] His proposal enabled the State Council opposition to resurrect the Kakhanov Commission's arguments for all-estate self-government in a final effort to block Tolstoi's control measures, to impress upon Alexander the need for decentralization and, in the process, to defend the ministerial power balance and the legacy of Alexander II's reforms.

Under Staritskii's plan, a government-appointed district chief would coordinate rather than dictate the activity of various district institutions. The models for such district officials existed in nearly all European countries, for instance, the subprefects in France and the noble commissioners (*Landräte*) in Prussia, and had been introduced recently in the Polish kingdom, the Caucasus, and Turkestan. These officials were even more necessary in European Russia, Staritskii contended, in view of the large size of some districts and the need for intermediate authority between the village and provincial levels. They would preside over the zemstvo assembly and a Bureau for District Administration, organized according to the Kakhanov Commission's proposal. Staritskii tried to convince Tolstoi of the benefits of his plan, which would provide the state with an official to guide zemstvo activity and to guarantee that zemstvo decisions would be enforced. But to Tolstoi the entire plan smacked of zemstvo control. Particularly significant was the fact that the district chief and bureau would have administrative, but not judicial, authority over all social estates and all institutions in the district.[87]

Why did Tolstoi oppose Staritskii's reform, which ostensibly would have created an agent of Ministry of Internal Affairs at the district level? Several factors were important here, among them his political views and his administrative experience. By the spring of 1888 Tolstoi was fed up with the stalling tactics of his adversaries, especially since the delays in the State Council's consideration of the project proved an embarrassing sign of weakness in his efforts to control ministerial activity. Tolstoi correctly perceived that Staritskii's proposal and Vorontsov-Dashkov's counterproject later aimed more at derailing the implementation of the land captains – and reducing the preeminence of his ministry – than introducing a concrete reform project. It was another manifestation of bureaucratic inertia that prevailed among many top officials, most prominently Pobedonostsev. Thus, his success in getting his project adopted attested not only to his stubbornness, but likewise to Alexander III's appreciation of the seriousness of the problems in local self-government.

Besides political reasons, Tolstoi opposed district chiefs because such officials had no precedent in Russian administrative history and similar Western institutions, in his mind, were irrelevant to the issue. Unlike his provincial governors, the district chiefs would have to work with, rather than control,

---

[86]TsGIA, *f*. D. S. Sipiagin, 1887, *op*. 2, *d*. 257, *ll*. 1–2.
   The original copy is in ibid., *f*. Departament zakonov G.S., *op*. t. 11, *d*. 44, *ll*. 259–68.
[87]Ibid., *f*. D. S. Sipiagin, *op*. 2, *d*. 257, *ll*. 2 *ob*.–3, 4 *ob*.: Yaney, *Urge to Mobilize*, p. 86.

the independent zemstvo, the *status in statu*, and Tolstoi feared, with some reason, that such contact would inevitably lead to slowness and further division in government. For practical purposes, the district was too large and contained too many villages for the district chief to handle day-to-day problems of peasant administration; indeed, under Staritskii's plan, according to Tolstoi, peasants would see little evidence of autocracy's concern for them, Thus, officials of his ministry at the subdistrict level would still be needed. Since peasant administration was the area of greatest concern to the government, all efforts, he insisted, should be directed to establishing land captains.[88]

But Tolstoi's refusal to accept Staritskii's recommendations galvanized his opponents in the State Council. The subsequent battle that unfolded between the State Council and the minister of internal affairs had a twofold significance. Besides determining the future of public self-government in Russia and the fate of the zemstvo and judicial legislation of the 1860s, the debate, as Whelan's study reveals, had critical importance for the State Council as a legislative-advisory institution in the government.[89] As shown earlier, this body had achieved its greatest prestige and responsibility in state policy making under Alexander II, when the tsar took the initial steps to decentralize and diffuse ministerial power, to involve the populace in public life, and to introduce rational procedures to direct the bureaucracy. By the late 1870s, State Council members, as a matter of regular legislative procedure, expected to be consulted on all significant legislation, and they regarded ministerial interference in the State Council's deliberations as improper.[90] Yet such ministerial intrusions in the council's role and attempts to bypass the council became frequent practices under Alexander III, especially in debates over counterreform legislation, because ministers feared the opposition of the jurists who made up a fourth of the fifty-plus members in the State Council and had lifetime membership in it.[91] Thus, given the need for at least appearances of legal procedure, ministers submitted projects to the council, and then pleaded with the emperor to ignore its criticisms and support their measures. In nineteen of fifty-nine cases, Alexander approved the minority opinion of the State Council, and on one occasion he ignored the opposition of every council member except War Minister Petr Semenovich Vannovski and ratified a project that the latter had submitted.[92] Yaney rightly notes

[88]TsGIA, *f*. Departament zakonov G. S., *op.* t. 11, *d.* 44, *ll.* 461 *ob.*-462, 464–464 *ob.*, 466.

[89]Whelan, pp. 186–7.

[90]Yaney, *Systematization*, pp. 261–2, 270.

[91]Whelan, pp. 141–2.

For examples of such proposals, see the Temporary Regulations on Jews and the 14 August 1881 Statute on Measures for Preserving State Security described in Zaionchkovskii, *Rossiiskoe samoderzhavie*, pp. 98–9; and S. P. Pokrovskii, *Ministerskaia vlast' v Rossii: Istoriko-iuridicheskoe issledovanie* (Iaroslavl', 1906), pp. 437–8. In January 1887, Pobedonostsev complained to Alexander about the "legalistic" views of the State Council concerning the judicial counterreform projects. Yet Pobedonostsev himself attacked Tolstoi's project from precisely this standpoint. *Pis'ma Pobedonostseva k Aleksandru III*, 2: 128.

[92]See the 11 November 1888 entry in *Dnevnik sekretaria Polovtsova*, 2: 102.

that such a situation did not "favor the development of a legal administrative system even by tsarist standards."[93]

Hence, State Council members (who were not ministers) saw in the land captains issue a chance to reassert their role in the legislative process and to convince Alexander III of the serious consequences of disrupting rational, regular government by supporting minority measures. By submitting a counterproposal, they felt they had provided the emperor with a face-saving alternative to another confrontation with his State Council. When Polovtsov failed to persuade Pobedonostsev to compile a counterproject in November 1888, he began to consolidate support for Vorontsov-Dashkov's counterproposal submitted two months earlier – a step that jeopardized his own close relationship with the tsar. Yet, as secretary of the State Council, he respected its legislative-consultative function in government, and, in addition, he was one of many officials who feared that Tolstoi's control system would extend the central government beyond its capacity to govern effectively.

Why did Polovtsov select Vorontsov-Dashkov's plan as the basis for the State Council's opposition? Certainly, it contained no new ideas and in some areas, Polovtsov admitted, it reiterated Staritskii's arguments poorly. Vorontsov-Dashkov was no expert on local administration but mainly a figurehead who, according to Alexander III, had no independent views of his own. However, as Tolstoi's ministerial opponents saw it, the latter point made him a good choice to submit a counterproject, for he could not be suspected of having ulterior motives. He was a high-ranking minister on excellent terms with the tsar, an official who had expressed no serious opposition to his sovereign in the past. Also, he was a wealthy landowner from a distinguished family and thus could not be accused of disloyalty to the state or gentry.[94] By uniting behind Vorontsov-Dashkov's counterproject, the opposition in the State Council hoped to demonstrate their support for both and persuade Alexander that his approval of Tolstoi's project, with its bureaucratization, would be tantamount to repudiating his confidence in the State Council, in his minister of the imperial household, and in the landed gentry.

The most striking aspect of Vorontsov-Dashkov's counterproject was its similarity in many areas to the proposals of the Kakhanov Commission decentralists. For example, it called for a Bureau of District Administration consisting largely of representatives from elected public institutions, proof that public control over the district government was the goal of the counterproject. Because it adhered to the spirit of the reforms of the 1860s, it

---

[93] Yaney, *Systematization*, p. 271.

[94] See *Dnevnik sekretaria Polovtsova*, 2: 151: and TsGIA, *f.* Departament zakonov G. S., *op.* t. 11, *d.* 44, *ll.* 588 *ob.*–590 *ob.* Vorontsov-Dashkov owned a huge estate in Tambov province and claimed to have some familiarity with the problems of peasant administration and their effect on the economy of peasants and landed gentry. Still, he was not considered especially knowledgeable on the subject, and Alexander only read the counterproject two months after it was submitted. See the entry for 13 November 1888 in *Dnevnik sekretaria Polovtsova*, 2:104.

received nearly unanimous support from the "old reformers" in the State Council (including nine of the twelve members who were ministers under Alexander II). Vorontsov-Dashkov's proposal to establish section chiefs to supervise villages had some important ramifications as well, as Tolstoi was quick to point out. Unlike the land captains, Vorontsov-Dashkov's section chiefs would have jurisdiction over all estates of the realm, a provision that Tolstoi felt would herald the establishment of all-estate village self-government, further diffuse ministerial authority in the countryside, and set in motion forces of change, such as urbanization, social mobility, and the breakdown of collective responsibility that would lead to anarchy among uneducated peasants.

Even worse, in Tolstoi's opinion, Vorontsov-Dashkov's section chiefs would have none of the judicial competence of the justices of the peace. They would be simply administrative officials elected by the district gentry assembly from among local gentry meeting the property and education/service requirements. Historians have generally overlooked the fact that the counterproject favored the gentry more than the land captain proposal because it consigned peasant administration wholly to gentry control (as opposed to state-appointed land captains selected from gentry ranks) and specified no means of bureaucratic or legal supervision over the section chiefs.[95] The State Council's support for the counterproject revealed that many top officials still considered public control over provincial administration to be just as appropriate in Russia as in the West.

Systematic decentralization or central control by one ministry, comprehensive reform or reestablishing authority over the peasants – these were the watchwords of official debate on the land captains. All of Tolstoi's efforts during the previous two years to win over his opponents to the project had proved fruitless. Consequently, in late November 1888 he faced the opposition of nearly the entire State Council, united behind a counterproject that would decentralize rather than consolidate state control. Nevertheless, it is significant that Tolstoi never contemplated withdrawing his project from discussion in the State Council. As a major piece of legislation, he insisted on introducing the reform project through regular legislative channels in order to give it the stamp of legitimacy and the seal of permanence. Such considerations were all the more important because, as both sides recognized, the outcome of the proposal would determine the direction of future political development in Russia.

The debate in the State Council and Alexander III's decision. The opposing sides in the land captains issue came face to face for the first time in sessions of the combined departments of the State Council in December 1888. The three sessions were not noteworthy for their cordiality. Debate on the issue reached such a fever pitch and members interrupted each other so frequently

[95]TsGIA, *f.* Departament zakonov G. S., *op.* t. 11, *d.* 44, *ll.* 611–15.

that at times the State Council resembled the chaotic peasant assemblies that they unanimously condemned. No doubt Tolstoi's personal defense of his project in the State Council, in defiance of his physician's orders, contributed greatly to the explosive atmosphere. Recognizing the uphill fight he faced, he told his deputy ministers that "I may die defending the project, but I will not allow anyone to take my place in the battle in the State Council."[96] But such bravado did not enhance the chances for his project. During the debate he often became confused, contradicted himself, and failed to refute the criticisms of his opponents – all in all a pitiful performance for a minister who prided himself on his mastery of administrative detail.[97] In a pathetic scene that demonstrated the temper of the proceedings, the emaciated Tolstoi, infuriated by Mansurov's demands for comprehensive reform of local government, pulled out a bottle of heart medicine, poured several drops into a glass of water, and remarked facetiously: "Boris Pavlovich, I drink to your health."[98] Tolstoi's antics not only stunned the council members, but, much more important, made a painful impression on Alexander III, who began to doubt that his minister could bring his project to a successful legislative conclusion.

A minority of officials in the combined departments reiterated Tolstoi's multiple objections to a comprehensive reform. Tolstoi, on his part, confined his argument to two points. First, the peasants themselves wanted the government to establish firm control over the village as quickly as possible. The minister based his assertions on information received from the governors, many of whom claimed that the peasants had never had any faith in self-government. Yet Tolstoi presented no new evidence in the State Council to show that peasants wanted land captain–type officials, either. Second, the promulgation of a comprehensive reform would entail a long delay and increase significantly the prospects of peasant unrest in the coming summer. Tolstoi refused to make any concessions at all on the land captains' powers or to relinquish any of his control over them, even after Peretts organized a meeting to iron out differences between the two factions. Confident of Alexander's support, he had no reason to make any more concessions to his opponents or even to bother making a strong case for his project at the general assembly session in mid-January 1889; as events soon proved, Tolstoi had convinced the tsar that the bureaucratization of local self-government was a precondition for strengthening autocracy and that only his ministry could direct the process.[99]

[96]Meshcherskii, *Moi vospominaniia*, 3: 281.

[97]Feoktistov, p. 279.

[98]This story is told in Meshcherskii, *Moi vospominaniia*, 3: 281.

 Although Polovtsov did not mention this episode specifically, he noted several tense exchanges between Mansurov and Tolstoi. See the passage for 10 December 1888 in *Dnevnik sekretaria Polovtsova*, 2: 126.

[99]See the entries for 29 March, 23 November, 7 and 10 December 1888, and 16 January 1889 in ibid., pp. 97, 113, 123, 126, 146; Pobedonostsev's letter of 29 December 1888 to Alexander III in Pobe-

The fact that the combined departments and the general assembly adopted the counterproject by overwhelming margins (18–7 and 39–13, respectively) was no surprise in the light of the composition of the State Council. Nine members with backgrounds in law (either as officials in the Ministry of Justice or participants in the 1864 Judicial Reform) voted against Tolstoi's proposal to give land captains both administrative and judicial authority. These officials, including Mansurov, Staritskii, and N. I. Stoianovskii, led the attack against Tolstoi primarily for not devising a system of legal control over land captains. The majority of the State Council did concede, however, that supervision over the peasants was imperative and that section chiefs could be introduced without first drafting a plan for district administration reform, but only on the condition that comprehensive reforms integrating the peasantry into the regular administrative structure would follow.[100]

It is more difficult to explain why several of Tolstoi's ministerial foes in the past, especially Vyshnegradskii, Ostrovskii, Pobedonostsev, and Manasein, voted in favor of the land captains. No doubt the submission of Vorontsov-Dashkov's counterproject was an important factor in their decision. Vyshnegradskii apparently regarded Tolstoi's proposal as the lesser of two evils. Calculating that the establishment of both district chiefs and section chiefs under Vorontsov-Dashkov's plan would entail heavier tax burdens for the peasantry and would threaten to disrupt the peasant economy even more than Tolstoi's measure, he shifted to Tolstoi's side, but only in December 1888.

Ostrovskii by no means defended the project with enthusiasm, either. Although he declared his intention to back Tolstoi in early November, this announcement represented a calculated effort to ingratiate himself with Alexander III (who he felt would support Tolstoi) and pave the way for the tsar to appoint him as Tolstoi's successor. More to the point, Pobedonostsev and Ostrovskii both predicted that Tolstoi would never live to implement his project. Consequently, his successor would be able to reorganize the district administration along the lines proposed by Staritskii, and Ostrovskii was confident that he would succeed Tolstoi. Thus, personal ambitions were likely the main reason for Ostrovskii's vote.[101]

Personal and political considerations likewise influenced Pobedonostsev to vote for the land captains. In his 29 December 1888 letter to Alexander III, Pobedonostsev emphasized the need for policelike officials to curb the dominance of kulaks and "loudmouths" in the peasant assembly.[102] Yet a day earlier he joined with Ostrovskii in assailing Tolstoi's project as an insig-

---

donostsev, *Pis'ma Pobedonostseva k Aleksandru III*, 2: 204; and TsGIA, *f*. Departament zakonov G. S., *op*. t. 11, *d*. 44, *ll*. 776–776 *ob*., 787.

[100]See TsGIA, *f*. Departament zakonov G. S., *op*. t. 11, *d*. 44, *ll*. 840 *ob*.-842, 845, 847–847 *ob*.; and *Dnevnik sekretaria Polovtsova*, 2: 145–6.

[101]See the entries for 12 November and 28 December 1888 and 9 January 1889 in *Dnevnik sekretaria Polovtsova*, 2: 103–4, 136–7, 143.

[102]Pobedonostsev, *Pis'ma Pobedonostseva k Aleksandru III*, 2: 206.

nificant step toward an immediate overhaul of district administration. Pobedonostsev's vote represented an attempt to regain the exclusive confidence of his former pupil that Tolstoi now enjoyed. He spoke of his waning influence in the late 1880s in correspondence and conversations with friends, and the sharp drop in the number of his letters to the tsar during this period in contrast with the early 1880s indeed attested to his decline.[103] His vote in the State Council for the creation of a representative of strong autocratic authority was probably no coincidence; after all, his staunch defense of autocracy eight years earlier following Alexander II's assassination had catapulted him to the pinnacle of his power.

Manasein's vote for Tolstoi's project is the most perplexing of all in view of his previous severe attacks against it. Tolstoi's opponents counted on his support during the State Council debates and Manasein even fulminated against the judicial powers of the land captains during the sessions. On the other hand, in a diary passage for 22 November 1888 Kireev mentioned an agreement between Tolstoi and Manasein, but did not elaborate on it.[104] These intrigues notwithstanding, it is significant to recall that by late 1888 Tolstoi had made substantive concessions in his project so that justices of the peace would retain much of their jurisdiction. According to a table prepared for the Ministry of Internal Affairs in December 1888, the justices would maintain jurisdiction over 56 percent of all criminal cases and 75 percent of all civil disputes that they currently handled.[105] At the same time, Manasein was confident that the State Council would vote down Tolstoi's proposal, thereby preserving the justices of the peace while affording him the luxury of appearing as a loyal supporter of autocracy. Like Ostrovskii, he harbored ambitions to become the new minister of internal affairs, clear evidence of the prestige and importance that top officials attached to that post.[106] Yet when Alexander III declared himself in favor of land captains and the abolition of the justices, Manasein threw caution to the wind and tried to sabotage the implementation of the land captains and protect his justices (and his ministry). Rather than devise the regulations for establishing investigating officers (to assist the land captains), as the tsar ordered, Manasein in spring 1889 submitted a project that would have perpetuated the justices under a different name, thus leading Alexander to grumble that "the proposals of the Minister of Justice have been unsatisfactory to such a degree that I assumed his intention was to destroy the entire project."[107]

[103]Zaionchkovskii notes that these letters increasingly focused on affairs of the Holy Synod and contained fewer comments on various state issues, in contrast to his letters earlier in the decade. Zaionchkovskii, *Rossiiskoe samoderzhavie*, p. 59. See also similar comments of contemporaries in ORGBL, *f.* Kireev, *k.* 11, *l.* 149; Meshcherskii, *Moi vospominaniia*, 3: 334–5, 337; Pobedonostsev, *Pis'ma Pobedonostseva k Aleksandru III*, 2: and *Dnevnik sekretaria Polovtsova*, 2: 220, 271.

[104]ORGBL, *f.* Kireev,*k.* 11, *l.* 85 *ob.*

[105]TsGIA, *f.* Departament zakonov G. S., *op.* t. 11, *d.* 44, *ll.* 692 *ob.*-695.

[106]ORGBL, *f.* Golitsyn, *d.* 15, *l.* 147; and TsGAOR, *f.* Aleksandr III, *op.* 1, *d.* 108, *l.* 117.

[107]See the tsar's comments to Polovtsov on 17 July 1889 in *Dnevnik sekretaria Polovtsova*, 2: 226. Manasein, who acknowledged on several occasions that this was his goal indeed, failed in his efforts.

In short, Tolstoi had even less support in the State Council than the 39–13 vote in the general assembly might indicate; and without imperial intervention there appeared virtually no chance that the proposed land captains would see the light of day. In this context, the State Council's vote was all the more significant because its members assumed that the tsar would support Tolstoi, although on the basis of Polovtsov's discussions with Alexander, they hoped that their views would receive serious consideration. Hence, in atypical fashion, they courted a confrontation with the tsar. There was little basis for such sanguine hopes. Convinced by Tolstoi that further delays in the establishment of land captains would mean peasant riots the following summer, the emperor felt that state control could no longer be delayed. According to Zaionchkovskii, Tolstoi himself did not believe peasant unrest was imminent, and statistics for 1888 and the first half of 1889 revealed that not one large-scale peasant disturbance had occurred.[108] Still, the argument impressed Alexander, as did Tolstoi's assertion that the State Council consisted of quasi constitutionalists intent on limiting the autocrat's authority. Mere ignorance did not account for Alexander's willingness to accept Tolstoi's claims. While possessing limited intelligence, he was generally an astute judge of character. He had come to respect Tolstoi's frankness and his determination to take control of the reform process and bring order and unity to the government. Tired of the prolonged State Council debate and disturbed by concessions made by Tolstoi during the course of it, he decided to side with Tolstoi, "*le dernier des mohicans* in support of the principle of monarchy."[109]

But the final imperial decision on the land captains issue shocked friends and foes of the measure alike. Rather than approve either the majority or minority opinion, as was legislative custom, Alexander III appended his own resolution to the minority report, which substantially altered its content. He prescribed that justices of the peace be abolished in order to make available qualified personnel to serve as land captains and to ease the tax burden on the local population. The land captains and *volost'* courts would take on the larger share of cases previously decided by the justices.[110] In essence, the tsar returned to the ideas expressed in the original land captains project and ignored three years of official discussions on the measure. Such action evoked tears of gratitude from Tolstoi and protests of indignation from Polovtsov and other State Council members. However, the reason for the tsar's decision was clear enough. Not only did he want to show that he, as autocrat, would dictate such important matters; in addition, he felt that Tolstoi's watered-

---

[108]Ibid., p. 483. See also the passage for 22 December 1888, in which Alexander III mentioned the possibility of peasant riots. He apparently based his opinion on the predictions of several governors. Ibid., p. 132.

[109]This was the tsar's phrase, quoted in the entry for 25 January 1889 in ibid., p. 151. See also ibid., pp. 137–8, 148; Feoktistov, p. 274; Meshcherskii, *Moi vospominaniia*, 3: 285; and the passage for 25 December 1888 in ORGBL, *f.* Golitsyn, *d.* 15, *l.* 163.

[110]TsGIA, *f.* Departament zakonov G. S., *op.* t. 11, *d.* 44, *l.* 853.

down project, if enacted, would have rendered the land captains ineffective in controlling peasant administration.[111]

Hence, contrary to the traditional view, Alexander III's resolution was neither a total victory for Tolstoi nor a death-bed concession in view of his deteriorating health.[112] Rather, several months before Tolstoi's death (on 25 April 1889), Alexander introduced his own variant of the reform because of Tolstoi's poor performance in the State Council debates. Ironically, the emperor's decision was another example of imperial arbitrariness in central policy making that Tolstoi himself was trying to minimize by establishing a clear system of central control under the direction of the minister of internal affairs. Tolstoi wanted the tsar to approve only proposals that had the imprimatur of the minister of internal affairs. But despite all the talk of rational, systematic bureaucratic procedure, the land captain decision reaffirmed that in the end only the autocrat's view mattered. Personalized autocracy and systematized, legal administration could coexist only if the autocrat set the example, consistently required his officials to adhere to laws and standard procedures of government, and, to facilitate the latter, established a set hierarchy of ministers. However, Alexander III, like his predecessors and son, invariably sacrificed systematization in favor of autocratic prerogative (control). The tsar's exalted position above the law was as old as autocracy itself, but the reaffirmation of this truth in 1889 nevertheless wounded the *amour propre* of officials in the State Council, who cherished the thought that the reforms of the 1860s had put Russia on the path of Western political development. His resolution was a direct slap at the State Council and its role in the legislative process. It provided new impetus for ministers to avoid seeking the State Council's endorsement for their projects, to intrigue against one another, and to curry the favor of the tsar or persons close to him. Such developments could not but discredit autocracy further in the eyes of educated society.[113]

Alexander III cryptically dismissed Polovtsov's protest that his decision violated legislative tradition. The emperor replied that he had the power to write law and that the State Council was to blame for betraying imperial

---

[111]In his memoirs, Meshcherskii claimed to play the main role in persuading Alexander to abolish the justices of the peace, and Whelan (pp. 180–1) presents circumstantial evidence to support this claim. Meshcherskii did write the tsar with such advice between 17 October and 3 November 1888, and he cooperated with A. A. Tatishchev, former governor of Penza and current member of the State Council, in sending a memorandum to Alexander on the same issue. See TsGAOR, *f.* Aleksandr III, *op.* 1, *d.* 897, *ll.* 62 *ob.*-64; and Meshcherskii, *Moi vospominaniia*, 3: 287. Although Meshcherskii's claim cannot be ruled out, the evidence is too fragmentary to conclude that Meshcherskii was the decisive influence on the tsar in this matter, especially given his penchant for exaggerating his impact on domestic policymaking. In fact, in his 1 December [1888?] letter to Alexander, Meshcherskii admitted that the tsar did not express his views to him, and thus it was necessary to guess about the tsar's feelings. TsGAOR, *f.* Aleksandr III, *op.* 1, *d.* 897, *l.* 126.

[112]For instance, see Zaionchkovskii, *Rossiiskoe samoderzhavie*, p. 395.

[113]These ideas are expressed in *Dnevnik sekretaria Polovtsova*, 2: 278–9. For the text of the Land Captain Statute, see *PSZ*, 3d ser., vol. 9, no. 6196, 12 July 1889; and for the other measures adopted in conjunction with the Land Captain Statute (the Judicial Powers of Land Captains, the Reform of the *Volost'* Courts) see TsGIA, *f.* Departament zakonov G. S., *op.* t. 11, *d.* 44, *ll.* 908–14, 1064–1132.

confidence in it and defying his wishes. However, the subsequent deterioration in relations between the State Council and the tsar in the spring of 1889, the result of the Council's deliberately slow and detailed review of Tolstoi's project, was no laughing matter, not even to Alexander; by May the government was in a full-blown constitutional crisis.[114] When Baron Nikolai asked for dismissal as chairman of the combined departments, Polovtsov wondered out loud why the other members of the State Council had not submitted similar requests. The State Council's position, he surmised, was intolerable as long as the autocrat adhered to Tolstoi's opinion of it as "a mob of freethinkers."[115]

In sum, the State Council members sustained a double defeat on the land captain project. Not only did they fail to block Tolstoi's policy of centralization and control of his ministry over the peasant administration; they also found their role in the legislative process and their efforts to create rational government in Russia undermined. The combination of powers vested in the land captains, the continued isolation of the peasant estate and administration (under the Ministry of Internal Affairs), and the tsar's decision to legislate by autocratic prerogative – these trends were vivid proof of the realities of Russian politics, notwithstanding the talk about bureaucratic system and administrative order. Polovtsov hoped to minimize the nature of the defeat by suggesting that a cabinet system of ministerial government be organized. It would help eliminate the interministerial rivalries that had exerted such a paralyzing influence on the land captains debate.[116] Other ministers hoped that Tolstoi's death and the revisions in the zemstvo counterreform project under debate might still enable them to maintain their local authority. But in the summer of 1889 Alexander III was in no mood for a reform that could lead to limitations on his powers. On the contrary, he had elected to impose unrestricted state control over local administration in order to achieve unity by force.

Implementation and impact of the land captains

Although the debate in ministerial circles over the land captains subsided after 12 July 1889, the government's work in this area did not end with the promulgation of the new law. Its implementation in thirty-six provinces in European Russia was a task no less demanding than the elaboration of the counterreform. This responsibility fell on the Minister of Internal Affairs and the governors, who were to provide personal supervision over the land

---

[114]See *Dnevnik sekretaria Polovtsova*, 2: 178–9, 193. Whelan (p. 186) is correct in arguing that the State Council had no power base to organize a rebellion or constitutional challenge against the tsar; still, that did not prevent many council members from believing after the tsar's 29 January 1889 resolution that tsarism's days were numbered, given the inability of the government to develop a unified, coherent state policy.

[115]Entry for 16 May 1889 in *Dnevnik sekretaria Polovtsova*, 2: 199–200.

[116]Passage for 17 July 1889 in ibid., p. 227.

captains, and on the gentry, who were to fill the new office.[117] While an in-depth analysis of the land captains' activity after 1890 is beyond the scope of this study,[118] a few words here about the implementation and impact of the land captains are necessary to draw our conclusions later about autocratic politics and the effects of Tolstoi's centralization policy.

From the outset, ministerial control over the land captains was never fully established owing to several factors. First, Tolstoi died before the land captains project was even promulgated. As this chapter has shown, the land captains legislation was *Tolstoi's* project, as evident by its bureaucratic thrust, his visible role in the ministerial debate and intrigues on the matter (despite his infirmity), and his skill in convincing Alexander III to repudiate the State Council and legislative tradition by introducing land captains with full judicial powers. Tolstoi's activity in 1887–9 demonstrated his belief that rural administrative order and efficiency were vital to the survival of autocracy, and that his ministry's control over peasant and zemstvo administration were preconditions for establishing that order. Although Tolstoi's death was not unexpected, it disrupted the process of preparing the land captains legislation for implementation. It placed Ivan Nikolaevich Durnovo, an official less competent and less committed to central control, in charge of this process. Durnovo had participated in the reform considerations and had supported Tolstoi's reforms, and hence Alexander III appointed him minister of internal affairs. But, by all accounts, Durnovo lacked the energy, firm will, and political stature of his predecessor; he had little use for Pazukhin (whose influence in administrative reform vanished following the death of his patron),[119] and he made no real effort to force governors to discipline and/or remove inefficient land captains.[120]

Without constant prodding from St. Petersburg, many of the governors clearly let up in supervising the land captains because they were overburdened with other obligations. As head of the provincial police, supervisor of the local zemstvos, provincial and district institutions, and chairman of several provincial bureaus, the governor had little time to watch over the 50–100 land captains in his province. Their burdens were not alleviated by the fact that no formal supervisory procedures (for example, regular inspection periods) were introduced as part of the land captains legislation. Consequently, some governors concluded in the 1890s, contrary to Tolstoi's original intention, that land captains were outside their chain of command and subordinate directly to the Ministry of Internal Affairs, which in effect meant

---

[117]See the entries for 5 and 11 December 1889 in V. P. Meshcherskii, *Dnevnik kniazia V. P. Meshcherskogo za 1889 (noiabr'i dekabr') i za 1890 god (ianvar', fevral', i mart)* (St. Petersburg, 1890), pp. 36, 55–6.

[118]For the best treatment, see Mandel, "Paternalistic Authority," chaps. 5–8.

[119]Pazukhin's "disappearance" from elite circles is noted by Feoktistov in Solov'ev, p. 198, and by Durnovo himself, in a letter he sent on 27 August 1889 to State Comptroller Sol'skii. Cf. TsGIA, f. D. M. Sol'skii, 1889, *op.* 2, *d.* 145, *l.* 1 *ob.* Pazukhin died on 27 January 1891.

[120]See the letter of 4 May 1889 from Alexander III to Pobedonostsev in *Pobedonostsev i ego korrespondenty,* vol. 1, pt. 2. pp. 900, 908; Meshcherskii, *Moi vospominaniia,* 3: 353–4; ORGBL, f. Kireev, *k.* 11, *ll.* 116–116 *ob.*; ibid., f. Golitsyn, *d.* 15, *l.* 293.

subject to no real control. Nor did the district assemblies of the land captains or the provincial bureaus for peasant affairs (presided over by the governors) police the land captains in a conscientious fashion.[121] The result was that governors such as Golitsyn of Moscow, who recognized the significance of the land captains legislation and took their supervisory functions seriously, despaired over the implementation of the land captains.[122] As Robbins shows in his probing study of Russian governors from 1880 to 1917, the solution for most of them was to report routinely on the successful work of the land captains, while actually ignoring their activity.[123]

The initial problem facing the governors was finding the best people to serve as land captains, a difficult task even after the tsar's decision to abolish the justices of the peace. Although the reluctance of some gentry to volunteer their services was understandable, given the bad publicity that the office had received in the higher echelons of the government and in the press, the backlash against the legislation was perhaps most pronounced among the traditionalist gentry (soslovniki). Their criticism of the bureaucratic land captains revealed that the legislation, far from marshalling gentry support for the government as Tolstoi had intended, had antagonized these groups with its emphasis on regulation and its implicit attack on past gentry service. To be sure, much of the gentry's bitterness stemmed from the agrarian crises caused by Witte's industrialization policy and the government's apparent insensitivity to gentry needs (entail, long-term credit, protection of privilege). But the traditionalist gentry campaign took dead aim at the counterreform legislation, as illustrated by the writings of F. D. Samarin (gentry marshal in Bogorodsk District, Moscow Province) and A. A. Planson (a district gentry marshal in Ufa Province).[124] As early as 1893, Meshcherskii's Citizen ridiculed the land captains as "chinovniki, automatons, living from day to day, reading official guberniia circulars, scribbling away, filing their busy work in the proper places."[125]

Faced with the difficulty of finding sufficient gentry volunteers, Alexander III, on the advice of the governors, abolished the education requirement for land captains in late 1889 in order to increase the number of eligible gentry. Unfortunately, this decision in no small way lowered the overall caliber of

---

[121]Robbins, "Viceroys," chap. 8; Mandel, "Paternalistic Authority," chap. 6.

[122]See the passages for 16 October 1888, and 5 August and 7 November 1889 in ORGBL, f. Golitsyn, d. 15, ll. 87, 395, 491–2. In December 1889, Golitsyn wrote in his diary that Durnovo was not competent to supervise the implementation of the land captains, unlike his predecessor. Ibid., l. 520. See also Weissman, pp. 26–7.

[123]Robbins, "Viceroys," chap 8; and Seredonin, 4: 330. According to Khizhniakov, Chernigov governor Anastas'ev went even further to suppress the truth. When peasants visited him to complain about their land captains during his tour of the provinces, he ordered the peasants flogged until they admitted that they were happy with the land captains. Khizhniakov, p. 166.

[124]Becker, pp. 58, 132, 153ff.

[125]Quoted from ibid., p. 133. The resentment of the more moderate gentry (active in zemstvo service) over the counterreforms, with their "smoke screen of exaggerated praise for the political preeminence of Russia's traditional 'leading estate,' " is discussed in Roberta T. Manning, The Crisis of the Old Order in Russia: Gentry and Government (Princeton, 1982), pp. 47–57.

the land captains of the 1890s. According to one report from the Ministry of Internal Affairs to the State Council (1902), only 20 percent of the land captains met the ministry's optimal requirements of having prior experience in local administration and owning their own local estates. It concluded that less than half of the officeholders had the pertinent experience to hold their posts.[126] In short, despite Alexander III's edicts and state efforts to enhance the status of land captains, the office, for personal, political, and economic reasons, remained unattractive to many gentry.[127] Some governors acknowledged this implicitly when they urged Alexander III in 1891–2 to raise the salary of land captains, ostensibly in recognition for their meritorious work despite low wages. But their comments really attested to the problem of locating suitable candidates. It was not uncommon to find land captains with little experience in or knowledge of village affairs, as V. G. Korolenko, a noted writer and public leader, described with respect to famine relief in the early 1890s:

The land captain is an investigator, master, guardian [and] philanthropist. He draws up the lists, he verifies, he organizes the grain stores, he gives them out. Now imagine in that position a man who knows the village and its ways as much as a person may know it who first studied in a *gymnasium* or a *korpus*, then in a military school, an academy or university. The countryside, that's a vacation or a dacha for the summer months. And with such a preparation, a man finds himself grappling with the most vital and complex questions of rural life.[128]

But inexperience was only one of several shortcomings of the land captains, especially as perceived by Russia's educated public. Overwhelmed by obligations and unrestrained by superiors, some land captains resorted liberally to their discretionary powers to punish peasants for insubordination under article 61 in order to force them to obey their orders. In Tula Province alone from 1891 to 1899, the land captains employed this article over 2,000 times a year, a fact that convinced some key officials and public leaders that it served as a weapon to exploit peasants rather than as a vehicle to ensure that their legal demands were fulfilled.[129] Such sensationalized incidents so stigmatized the land captains that, following the 1905 Revolution, the Ministry of Internal Affairs attacked them for abusing their powers. After 1906, the Land Section of the ministry stepped up inspections of these officials, and the land captains lost their judicial powers (at least on paper) in 1912, although that measure was not implemented in most provinces prior to the outbreak of World War I.[130] Still, the worst problem, according to a gov-

---

[126]Weisman, p. 28; and A. A. Liberman, "Sostav instituta zemskikh nachal'nikov," *Voprosy istorii*, no. 8 (1976), 204.

[127]*Dnevnik sekretaria Polovtsova*, 2: 235–6, 245, 495; and Golovin, *Moi vospominaniia*, 2: 183.

[128]Quoted in Robbins, *Famine in Russia 1891–1892: The Imperial Government Responds to a Crisis* (New York, 1975), p. 232. On the land captains' unfamiliarity with peasant custom and rural administration see A. I. Novikov, *Zapiski zemskogo nachal'nika* (St. Petersburg, 1899), pp. 26–7, 99–100; and Robbins, "Viceroys," chap. 8.

[129]Pokrovskii, *Ministerskaia vlast'*, pp. 451–2.

[130]Yaney, *Urge to Mobilize*, pp. 104–5.

ernment commission investigating the countryside (1905), was simple inefficiency and laziness of the land captains.[131]

Under such conditions, uniform, efficient administration of the village was no closer to reality in the late 1890s than in the previous three decades. Although Western scholars disagree over the significance of the land captains' work in the 1890s, there is little doubt that they were perceived by peasants and nonpeasants alike as one more step in the bureaucratization of the countryside.[132] This process was already under way at the *volost'* level in the early 1880s, and the extension of state control over the peasant village in the 1890s had positive as well as negative consequences for the state. On the one hand, the land captains' control over the *volost'* elder made the latter more vigilant in state tax and arrears collection, often to the distress of the village community. Unfortunately, these efforts did little to arrest the massive growth of redemption and tax arrears by the end of the century. In addition, by using its *volost'* and in some cases village agents, the government had the means to discourage ruinous land repartitions in the village, although the frequency and economic effects of such communal repartitions is a topic that requires further study.

On the other hand, the accounts of various land captains and correspondents who surveyed peasant communities in European Russia for Prince V. N. Tenishev found that, far from correcting the abuses of peasant officials, land captains realized that as outsiders they had few means of direct persuasion over the peasants (besides punitive authority, which could be counterproductive if used indiscriminately), and that their own work depended on the cooperation of the *volost'* elder and scribe. Hence, in a number of cases they ignored the petty abuses of peasant officials provided that the latter carried out land captain directives on tax collection and other vital matters. Similarly, the land captains, according to these sources, had little success in raising the peasants' social consciousness by organizing village welfare and charity organizations, or orphanages.[133] On the contrary, land captains who sought to regiment village life ran the risk of engendering antigovernment feelings among the peasants, as Saratov Governor B. B. Meshcherskii warned in 1895.[134] Likewise, such bureaucratic measures did little to rectify the real ills in peasant administration, for instance, the unmanageable size of many village communities; the unwillingness of peasants to hold elected office, owing to the economic hardship and personal risks of such duty; the cor-

[131]Solov'ev, p. 191; V. I. Gurko, *Features and Figures of the Past: Government and Opinion in the Reign of Nicholas II*, trans. Laura Matveev, ed. J. E. Wallace Sterling, Xenia Joukoff Eudin, and H. H. Fisher (Stanford, 1939), pp. 146–7; and Weissman, p. 28.

[132]For instance, see Astyrev, *V volostnykh pisariakh*, pp. 31–4; Novikov, pp. 35–8, 96–7; S. T. Sememov, *Dvadtsat' piat' let v derevne* (Moscow, 1915), pp. 86–7, 158–9.

[133]Mandel, pp. 252–300; Novikov, pp. 31–4; V. V. Tenishev, *Administrativnoe polozhenie russkogo krest'ianina* (St. Petersburg, 1908), pp. 32–6.

[134]Robbins, "Viceroys," chap. 8. In fact, peasants usually responded to the land captains' regulation by a number of means, ranging from compliance to deceit and passive disobedience. Incidents of open defiance were relatively rare.

ruption of peasant officials; and the growing poverty of the villages in general.[135] Although the main state efforts to address these problems came after the turn of the century in the form of the Witte Conference on Rural Agriculture and the Editing Commission under A. S. Stishinskii (deputy minister of internal affairs), it is worth emphasizing that the shortcomings of peasant officialdom under the land captains' tutelage had already come under the scrutiny of the minister of internal affairs in 1893–4. Over the next five years that ministry collected testimony from various provincial conferences and officials on the inadequacies of the legislation dealing with peasant self-government as well as recommendations for change, although the proposals here stopped well short of the changes recommended in 1903 by the Witte Conference (the majority advocated reorganizing the village community on the all-estate principle and linking its activity more directly to the local zemstvo).[136]

Here, it is sufficient to conclude that Tolstoi's system of state-controlled peasant administration did not develop in practice as he had planned. Nor did his successors maintain the preeminent position of the ministry that would have enabled them to introduce additional reforms to expand the state control apparatus. Rather, the 1890s were a period of rapid industrialization and the precipitous rise of Witte, the new finance minister. During these years, Alexander III and his successor shifted their priorities and concentrated on catching up to the West in industrial development and finding an ally (France) to replace Germany as the source of credit and security. This meant the rejection of Tolstoi's notion that Russia should adhere to a different, agrarian-based path of economic and social development. But in changing course, Alexander III, Nicholas II, and their ministers unleashed dynamic forces of economic and social change that challenged the system of autocratic control, and the tensions between the two nurtured the political unrest of the early twentieth century. Before we consider the implications of these processes for Russia's later development, it is necessary to analyze Tolstoi's control policy for the zemstvo – the other mainspring of his counterreform legislation.

---

[135]Weissman, p. 29; Novikov, pp. 28–34.

[136]See *Svod zakliuchenii gubernskikh soveshchanii po voprosam otnosiashchimsia k peresmotru zakonodatel'stva o krest'ianakh*, vol. 1: *Sel'skoe i volostnoe upravlenie* (St. Petersburg, 1897), pp. 1–150, 321–67, 607–792: and *Trudy redaktsionnoi kommissii po peresmotru zakonopolozhenii o krest'ianakh*, ed. A. A. Rittikh (6 vols.; St. Petersburg, 1903–4). See also Simonova, pp. 178–9; and *Krizis samoderzhaviia v Rossii 1895–1917*, pp. 46–7. The chief result of this work prior to 1900 was the publication of a collection of civil regulations regarding the village population under the auspices of the Ministry of Internal Affairs. See *Sbornik postanovlenii otnosivshikhsia k grazhdanskomu pravu lits sel'skogo sostoianiia* (St. Petersburg, 1898).

CHAPTER 6

The politics of the zemstvo counterreform, 1888–90

Although the land captains legislation constituted the nucleus of Tolstoi's policy to bureaucratize local self-government, as we have seen, historians have devoted much more attention to the Zemstvo Statute of 1890. Such concern is not surprising. On the one hand, more than other self-governing institutions, the zemstvo involved the educated public and was identified by defenders and critics alike with the constitutional development of the tsarist regime. On the other hand, the very changes that the zemstvo counterreform project underwent from 1888 to 1890 have spawned controversy and led historians to interpret the final legislation diversely as "a complete distortion of the 1864 Statute" and as "nothing more than a second, much worse variant" of its predecessor.[1] Even Tolstoi's motives for drafting the zemstvo legislation have aroused scholarly debate, with most historians depicting Tolstoi as a clear-cut reactionary whose policy consisted of responding

[1] For the first interpretation see Kornilov, *Kurs istorii Rossii XIX v.*, p. 302; for the second, see Tseitlin, "Zemskoe samoupravlenie i reforma 1890 g. (1865–1890)," *Istoriia Rossii v XIX veke*, 5: 138. Scholars expressing views similar to Tseitlin include Veselovskii, *Istoriia zemstva*, 3: 318; Korkunov, 2: 397; Vitte, *Samoderzhavie i zemstvo*, p. 145; Zaionchkovskii, *Rossiiskoe samoderzhavie*, p. 410; Zakharova (who argues that the 1890 legislation, for all of its bureaucratic features, was a pale shadow of the original Tolstoi-Pazukhin project), *Zemskaia kontrreforma*, pp. 150, 161; Whelan, pp. 195–6; Kermit E. McKenzie, "Zemstvo Organization and Role within the Administrative Structure," *The Zemstvo in Russia*, pp. 31, 37, 54, 57–9, 64. Like the other accounts above, McKenzie regards the 1890 legislation as the unfortunate triumph of the state theory of self-government over the societal (public) theory that was embodied in the 1864 statute, although throughout his essay he suggests that the 1890 counterreform provided the framework for more effective zemstvo work (especially at the provincial level) in establishing public schools and health. This point is made more forcefully by Yaney, who calls the 1890 statute an improvement over the 1864 reform because the government replaced the gentry as the directing force in zemstvo activity. Yaney, *Systematization*, p. 247. Yaney, however, provides little data on the results of the government's activity in this sphere. Eklof views 1890 as a turning point in zemstvo work to develop rural primary education, although he credits the change not simply to the 1890 legislation but rather to a "specific political conjuncture" that marked the first time that "the old socialist dreams of 'going to the people' coalesced in practice with the ideals of small deeds liberalism." Also, the shock of the famine of 1891–2 provided impetus for the new zemstvo efforts in primary education. Eklof, p. 97.

to exogenous political forces of the period, be they the "constitutionalist" demands of zemstvo leaders or gentry class interests.[2] The reasons for this are clear enough. The limitations on zemstvo autonomy and the increase in gentry representation were truly the most visible effects of the 1890 statute.

Yet if we look beyond the usual state–society paradigm (that has led historians to contrast the zemstvo's status under the legislation of 1864 and 1890) and search for the connecting threads between the land captains and zemstvo proposals, a different picture of Tolstoi emerges. The minister was convinced by experience that strong, efficient local government responsive to the needs of the population offered the best hope for order and public support in the provinces. To be sure, Tolstoi's instinctive distrust of elected officials predisposed him against zemstvo initiatives in local economic and administrative development. Like his governors, Tolstoi believed that zemstvos and state institutions frequently and needlessly clashed in providing local public services. The resulting conflicts not only made elected office unattractive to the most educated and wealthy local residents, but in general lowered public respect for all authorities. Yet, his political prejudices notwithstanding, Tolstoi had administrative reasons to rewrite the zemstvo statute. The pervasive absenteeism in zemstvo assemblies, the burgeoning zemstvo expenditures at a time of agrarian distress, the indifference and occasional hostility of peasants toward the zemstvo, and the influx of incompetent, self-centered petty landowners, bureaucrats, and peasants into zemstvo affairs – all of these factors explained why many zemstvos were short of revenues and rural public support in the early 1880s.

Tolstoi's solution to these problems was to transform the self-governing zemstvo into a regular state institution (bureaucratization) under the direct control of the Ministry of Internal Affairs. His methods to crown his system of paternalistic bureaucratic control over the countryside were innovative and radical. He proposed to appoint zemstvo board officials, to make zemstvo service an obligation for elected delegates, and to grant governors (and in select cases the minister of internal affairs) the authority to review all zemstvo resolutions. These measures, and not the reorganization of zemstvo representation along estate lines, were the principal and most controversial aspects of Tolstoi's program to bring the zemstvo under state control. The plan for reorganizing zemstvo representation worked out by Pazukhin suited Tolstoi's state control purposes, because it guaranteed that the gentry, the most enlightened and loyal group in the provinces, would predominate in the district and provincial assemblies. With these inducements, he presumed, the gentry would support the government's program of local economic development. At the same time, Tolstoi's proposals for state-controlled zem-

---

[2] Cf. Zakharova, *Zemskaia kontrreforma*, pp. 100, 111; Zaionchkovskii, *Rossiiskoe samoderzhavie*, pp. 83, 439; Pirumova, pp. 37–40; Tvardovskaia, *Ideologiia poreformennogo samoderzhaviia*, pp. 232–8; Solov'ev, pp. 188–92; Korelin, *Dvorianstvo v poreformennoi Rossii*, pp. 214–15; Tseitlin, "Zemskoe samoupravlenie i reforma 1890 g.," p. 126; A.A. Kizevetter, *Na rubezhe dvukh stoletii (Vospominaniia 1881–1914)* (Prague, 1929), p. 146; and, recently, Becker, pp. 131–2, 134–6.

stvos and his view of zemstvo service as an obligation for elected delegates showed his distrust of independent gentry work in this area.

Tolstoi's zemstvo counterreform proposal met opposition from some gentry, who as public servants valued their independence from bureaucratic control and resented the minister's betrayal of confidence in them. Above all, however, the proposal was assailed by rival ministers, who believed its implementation would give Tolstoi overall control over local economic development and clear predominance in ministerial circles. Largely out of personal and institutional interests, his major adversaries, Vyshnegradskii and Manasein, contended that precise laws rather than broad discretionary powers for governors would make zemstvo officials more responsible and efficient. In the long run, Vyshnegradskii's attacks against Tolstoi ushered in a decade of conflict between the ministers of finance and of internal affairs for control over zemstvo policy making, especially in the realm of zemstvo taxation; in the short term, the opponents of centralization forced Tolstoi's successor Durnovo, beginning in 1889, to yield on key points under discussion and within the year to abandon the course of bureaucratic control over the zemstvo. Durnovo's policy in this respect resulted primarily from his weak position as a newcomer in ministerial circles.

In any event, Alexander III's ratification of the State Council's opinion marked a victory for Tolstoi's ministerial opponents and the traditional ministerial power balance, because it preserved the zemstvo outside the exclusive control of the minister of internal affairs and enabled other ministers to influence central policy on the zemstvo. Far from becoming the transmission belts of state authority that Tolstoi had envisioned, the zemstvos, as a result of the 1890 statute, remained relatively autonomous institutions that became cells of political opposition to the autocracy while continuing to be a source of frequent ministerial conflicts.

The bureaucratization of the zemstvo: proponents and opponents

On 8 January 1888, Tolstoi submitted his zemstvo reform project to the State Council, over a year after he and Pazukhin had drafted it. Tolstoi's fear that opponents of the land captains project and of the zemstvo reform proposal would team up against him if both were considered together accounted for the delay in the presentation of the latter. Not without reason, he suspected that the zemstvo project would arouse even more criticism than the land captains project, in view of its applicability to all groups in Russia. But in this case Tolstoi underestimated the extent of the opposition to land captains. When it became clear that official debate over the land captains might last indefinitely, he immediately submitted his zemstvo project.

Tolstoi's zemstvo counterreform proposal of 1888 was designed first and foremost to put his ideas of centralization and government-dictated social development into practice. Witte, who had very similar views on the need for strong autocracy and change introduced from the top, later described Tolstoi as the architect of the zemstvo counterreform, with its regimentation and bureaucratization of local self-government.[3] Pazukhin's proposal (1884–5) to give the gentry control in the zemstvo by establishing representation along estate lines was an insufficient guarantee of state control for Tolstoi. After all, in many provinces gentry delegates were the leading zemstvo critics of the autocracy, demanding an end to government interference in local economic affairs, and standing at the forefront of liberal movements in Russia.[4] Rather, the thrust of his recommendations for integrating the zemstvo into the hierarchy of state institutions – namely, government-appointed zemstvo officials and increased gubernatorial control – were taken from suggestions made by governors in their annual reports and in response to Kakhanov Commission proposals.

The governors' criticisms of zemstvo activity in the mid–1880s had enormous significance for Tolstoi's legislative projects on the zemstvo, not only because they pinpointed the "irresponsible people" who were taking control of zemstvo affairs, but also because their comments on excessive zemstvo expenses and taxation perturbed the parsimonious Tolstoi.[5] Although the minister, not surprisingly, was sympathetic to the governors' complaint that they had little control over the zemstvos, he particularly bristled over reports from the governors of Perm, Poltava, Chernigov, and Penza provinces on rising zemstvo taxes coupled with cutbacks in public services available in the villages. Unnecessary expenditures were bad enough, but excessive zemstvo taxes jeopardized the already unstable rural economy as well as the flow of state revenues. Under these circumstances, he feared, the peasants might well turn against all authorities. Consequently, Tolstoi and Alexander III paid much attention to the governors' demands for more control over zemstvo finances in European Russia to protect the local population.[6] Impressed with their complaints, and seizing upon the plan for zemstvo reorganization outlined by Pazukhin and Bekhteev, Tolstoi came up with a program for ministerial control over the zemstvo. His approach was reminiscent of his policy as minister of education, the goals of which were "to tighten his control over everything already under his jurisdiction, to emasculate those institu-

[3]Vitte, Vospominaniia, 1: 300.

[4]Solov'ev, pp. 192–3.

Soviet specialists on the topic regard Tolstoi's proposals as nothing more than an official regurgitation of Pazukhin's ideas because of the reorganization of zemstvo representation along estate lines that Pazukhin had long advocated. See ibid., pp. 190, 197; Zaionchkovskii, Rossiiskoe samoderzhavie, p. 65; and Zakharova, Zemskaia kontrreforma, pp. 91–3.

[5]Zaionchkovskii, Rossiiskoe samoderzhavie, pp. 61–2; and Sinel, p. 49.

[6]Zaionchkovskii, Rossiiskoe samoderzhavie, pp. 207–8, 214; and the 1884 report of Perm Governor Lukoshkov in TsGIA, f. Departament obshchikh del MVD, op. 223, d. 165, l. 6. The governor observed that although the majority of zemstvo expenditures were earmarked for local needs, the heavy tax burden on the local population had exhausted them economically and had undermined efforts to improve the local economy. Ibid., l. 6 ob. It should be noted that Alexander III was the first ruler to have the governors' annual reports printed and distributed in full to all state ministers. Yaney, Systematization, p. 299.

tions he could not manipulate, to dominate previously independent bodies, and to prevent any outside interference in ministry affairs."[7]

Perhaps more than any other single incident, the Cherepovets zemstvo affair (Novgorod Province) from 1884 to 1888 induced Tolstoi to propose legislation to restrict zemstvo self-government. The episode illustrated dramatically the difficulties encountered by state officials attempting to correct the wrongdoings of zemstvo officials in compliance with the 1864 statute. In 1885, Novgorod Governor Mosolov complained that the Cherepovets District board had refused to obey his orders and those of the local police, judiciary, and public school inspectors. They had encouraged district residents to ignore these regulations over the past decade, and had tried to attain exclusive influence over the population. Besides arousing public disrespect for government officials by their own example, claimed Mosolov, the district board members made excessive expenditures without any consideration for local taxpayers. The result was zemstvo tax arrears more than double the annual tax rate. The district economy was in ruin. When Mosolov protested these expenses in the interests of the local residents, the district board contemptuously mocked his decision.[8] The governor did not explain why the local population would heed zemstvo officials who oppressed them with zemstvo taxes instead of government officials, and many other details of the episode remained unclear. Nonetheless, the report upset Alexander III so much that he scrawled on it: *"What measures has the government taken against this disorder?"*[9]

Tolstoi needed no further prodding. He dispatched a team of three officials (from separate ministries) to investigate conditions in Cherepovets District, and they recommended that the chairman and three zemstvo board members be exiled from Novgorod Province by administrative order. Although confirming Mosolov's allegations, they deliberately did not overreact to the situation. The officials advised that a temporary commission be attached to the district board in order to audit zemstvo accounts annually and that the district zemstvo be barred temporarily from local school affairs. But Mosolov complained that such a punishment was too lenient, and Tolstoi, capitalizing on this chance to exert central control, supported the governor's proposal to replace the district board with an appointed Temporary District Administration for Zemstvo Affairs until a new Zemstvo Statute was promulgated. Under the governor's direct supervision, this new four-man bureau would straighten out zemstvo affairs in the district and, above all, draw up guidelines for more equitable zemstvo taxation of property.[10]

[7]These are Sinel's words in *Classroom and the Chancellery*, p. 56.

[8]TsGIA, *f.* Departament obshchikh del MVD, 1886, *op.* 223, *d.* 193, *ll.* 12–13; ibid., *d.* 183, *l.* 10 *ob.*; and ibid., *f.* Komitet ministrov, 1888, *op.* 1, *d.* 4657, *ll.* 7–7 *ob.* Mosolov noted that the Cherepovets district board spent over 70 percent of its annual budget on nonmandatory expenses (zemstvo administration, public education, public health, and the like), an unusually high figure for a district zemstvo. Ibid., *l.* 105.

[9]Quoted from Seredonin, 4: 320. Emphasis found in Seredonin.

[10]TsGIA, *f.* Komitet ministrov, *op.* 1, *d.* 4657, *ll.* 6 *ob.*, 8 *ob.*-9 *ob.*, 10 *ob.*-12.

It is hardly surprising that this proposal met with stiff opposition in early 1888 in the Committee of Ministers. After all, it would flagrantly violate the provisions of the Zemstvo Statute of 1864 and would replace public self-government in Cherepovets District with a bureau directly subordinate to Tolstoi, who by implication would have the authority to select justices of the peace and other local officials outside the Ministry of Internal Affairs. Nevertheless, the Cherepovets affair provoked enough concern in official circles that Tolstoi managed to steer the proposal through the committee, despite severe criticism from legalists such as Baron Nikolai and Stoianovskii, and from former Finance Ministers Bunge and Abaza. His opponents succeeded in imposing a three-year limit on the new temporary bureau, during which the Cherepovets zemstvo board and assembly could not meet.[11] In short, even though the Cherepovets incident was the only clash between government and zemstvo of such magnitude, the outcome of it boded ill for the zemstvo. It showed that the minister of internal affairs would go to any lengths to bring local economic administration under his control; and it proved to Tolstoi that bold, quick action by the government would be effective in eradicating disorder in zemstvo administration and economy.[12] By the same token, it foreshadowed the official resistance that would arise from Tolstoi's efforts to make government agencies of the zemstvos.

More than anything else, the Cherepovets affair demonstrated the confusion and conflict among local officials that could result from the separate zemstvo and state institutions in the provinces carrying out the same functions. Tolstoi summed up the situation when he declared: "Many years of experience in the implementation of this system, based on the principle that the state and zemstvo had completely different interests, already has shown fully that such division of authority (*dvoevlastie*), such dualism in local administration in practice can lead only to the most unfavorable results in the political, administrative, and economic respect."[13] He was not the first official to regard the separate status of the zemstvo as the primary cause of disorder in local administration; but unlike those in the Kakhanov Commission, Tolstoi emphasized the concrete administrative problems created by such dualism – the waste of funds, the duplication of functions (for example, of zemstvo and state physicians), the failure of zemstvos to meet their obligations in food supply and road repair, and the bureaucratic discord. He even allowed that gubernatorial interference was in part to blame for zemstvo mismanagement. But rather than delineate the governors' authority over the

---

[11]Zaionchkovskii, *Rossiiskoe samoderzhavie*, p. 213; Seredonin, 4: 321.

[12]Zaionchkovskii, *Rossiiskoe samoderzhavie*, p. 214. The Cherepovets affair was not the only case of zemstvo officials who irritated Tolstoi. For other examples, see ibid., pp. 209–10; Khizhniakov, pp. 170–4; and, on the Pfeifer affair in Moscow district in the late 1880s, ORGBL, *f.* V. M. Golitsyn, *d.* 15, *l.* 321; and TsGIA, *f.* Kantseliariia MVD, *op.* 2, *d.* 1835, *ll.* 18–19 *ob.*, 32–7. Significantly, however, between 1865 and 1890 only five persons elected as zemstvo board chairmen were not confirmed in office by the government, as opposed to 80 such cases between 1891 and 1909. McKenzie, "Zemstvo Organization and Role," p. 50.

[13]Quoted from TsGIA, *f.* Kantseliariia MVD, *op.* 2, *d.* 1838, *l.* 307.

zemstvo to prevent such conflicts, he proposed the more expedient solution of complete gubernatorial control.

Next to order and unity in local government, fiscal concerns were the most important of Tolstoi's considerations for reform. The existence of separate zemstvo and state physicians, veterinarians, teachers, surveyors, architects, and statisticians meant a heavier tax burden on the local population. Even though he did not estimate the amount that his proposal would save, Tolstoi regarded economy as a key point in his favor, as evidenced by his lengthy arguments on the subject. He emphasized that during the past decade many provinces had experienced a rapid inflation in zemstvo salaries and expenses as well as a slowdown in zemstvo construction of hospitals, schools, clinics, and food supply warehouses. In Tolstoi's mind, these developments and the growing number of zemstvo officials indicted for embezzlement of public funds since the mid–1870s were closely related phenomena, and clear proof of his contention that individuals less devoted to local public services were gaining control of elected offices.[14] More than anywhere else, Tolstoi here appropriated the arguments of such centralist governors as Mosolov and A. A. Tatishchev of Penza; in an undated letter to Pazukhin (written between 1885 and 1887), Tatishchev articulated views that formed the framework for Tolstoi's zemstvo counterreform project of 1888:

In short, complete anarchy prevails in zemstvo self-government and it is utterly impossible to leave matters in such a state. In my opinion, the government, having given the population the right of self-government, cannot remain a detached observer of the chaos resulting from it. Seeing that the population does not exercise and cannot make use of this unusual right artificially conferred on them, [the government] should take measures to eliminate this abnormal course of affairs, which is harmful for the entire state. It seems to me that there is only one way out of this anomaly – to subordinate zemstvo assembly resolutions to government control, not from a formal standpoint, but in reality. Instead of delegates whom the zemstvo does not want and cannot elect properly, the government should appoint [board] representatives, and the zemstvo assemblies should have the right to evaluate their activity and to present their conclusions to the government for decisions.[15]

Furthermore, Tatishchev advised his friend Tolstoi that, considering the burdensome zemstvo taxes and the intrigues in zemstvo elections, it was no wonder that "the population regards the self-government granted to them

---

[14]Ibid., *ll.* 307 *ob.*, 309. Tolstoi's criticism of growing zemstvo expenditures had some merit; for example, in Tver' the zemstvo budget doubled between 1868 and 1890 (reaching 1,298,000 rubles) without corresponding increases in zemstvo revenues. Although the discrepancy in Tver' stemmed from an especially active zemstvo, that was not the case in other provinces, and in any case the overextended zemstvos in the 1880s and 1890s borrowed state funds to meet operating expenses. Zemstvo indebtedness led the government to take over some mandatory expenses of the zemstvo (for instance, payment for land captains and the provincial statistical committees under the 1 June 1895 law). Veselovskii, *Istoriia zemstva,* 1: 241–3.

[15]Quoted from TsGIA, *f.* Kantseliariia MVD, *d.* 1834, *ll.* 24–24 *ob.* Mosolov made similar remarks in his report for 1886 in ibid., *f.* Departament obshchikh del MVD, *op.* 223, *d.* 183, *ll.* 5 *ob.*-6.

with indifference and finds itself in the hands of a few people who dispose of zemstvo funds to their own advantage."[16]

Tolstoi's intention of rewriting the entire Zemstvo Statute of 1864 in response to these exaggerated claims brought him under the attacks of liberals such as V. Iu. Skalon in the *Russian News* and the *Northern Herald*. Yet such criticism did not faze him at all.[17] Ironically, at one time or another these same critics had favored some increase in state control over the zemstvo as a means of raising public respect for that body. Still, they insisted on autonomous elected self-government that Tolstoi intended to do away with through a three-part program: the appointment of zemstvo executive officials by the governor (and by the minister of internal affairs in the case of the chairman); the submission of every zemstvo resolution to the governor or minister for approval; and the redefinition of elected zemstvo service as an obligation to the state. Such a plan had the advantages of allowing the government to determine who would serve in zemstvo offices and what their economic and social programs in the countryside would be. It would reinforce the land captains with additional government representatives in the districts to restore public respect for autocracy and, by means of the elected zemstvo assemblies, provide the government with the counsel of those knowledgeable on local economic affairs.

Such control-minded governors as Mosolov and Lukoshkov had long advocated state-appointed zemstvo officials and, following the Cherepovets affair, Tolstoi drafted legislation to this effect. This was the most important change in the government's effort to control zemstvo activity. Contrary to the wording of the 1864 statute, zemstvo board officials did not simply enforce the assembly's decisions, but in fact drew up proposals that the assembly ratified during their brief sessions each year. Thus, Tolstoi correctly reasoned that the government could not establish its control over the zemstvo unless it dictated who would serve on the zemstvo bureaus, the name that Tolstoi proposed to give the boards. He insisted:

State affairs can be entrusted only to state institutions dependent on the governors. ... No matter what measures are taken regarding elected zemstvo boards, they always will be directed in their activity by the will of the zemstvo assemblies alone. Thus, in the event the election concept is retained in order to fill the offices of the zemstvo executive organs, *the main objective of the proposed reform – the incorporation of zemstvo institutions into the regular structure of the state administration –* will remain unaccomplished. If elected boards are preserved, then no legislative measures will eliminate the isolated status of the zemstvos.[18]

Under Tolstoi's system the government would appoint rather than approve the election of chairmen and members of the zemstvo bureau from among

---

[16]Quoted from ibid., *f.* Kantseliariia MVD, *d.* 1834, *ll.* 22–22 *ob.* Tatishchev's ties with Tolstoi and Meshcherskii are noted in Whelan, pp. 180, 235.

[17]Zakharova, *Zemskaia kontrreforma*, pp. 122–3.

[18]Quoted from TsGIA, *f.* Departament obshchikh del MVD, *op.* 241, *d.* 51, *l.* 141. Emphasis is mine.

the most qualified local residents enjoying the confidence of the local population. The fact that the government would use the same criteria in naming zemstvo bureau officials that it used for appointing land captains ensured that politically reliable people, in general, the wealthier landed gentry, would be selected.[19] But more significant, the bureaucratic nature of the new zemstvo bureaus, the new state service regulations that these officials would follow, the salaries, and the uniforms of the Ministry of Internal Affairs they would wear would erase any doubts about their identity as state officials rather than public servants.

Tolstoi did not satisfy himself with these changes in the zemstvo bureau structure. He demanded that all zemstvo assembly resolutions, including those on budgetary appropriations and tax reform, require government approval (in most cases by the governors) before enactment. This measure opened the door for the governors' interference in zemstvo finance, an area in which the zemstvos cherished the autonomy granted them in 1864. However, the proposal had some merit to it. The Cherepovets district zemstvo was not the only institution to abuse its taxation powers; and in some areas the gentry landowners in control of the zemstvo refused to vote appropriations for public charities, hospitals, and schools because they wanted to hold down their zemstvo taxes.[20] In other areas, the inequitable apportionment of the tax burden had ruined the peasants and other classes of the local population. Such a reform would give the minister of internal affairs, through the governors, considerable influence in national fiscal policy making by allowing him to lobby for a reduction in property taxes of certain groups. Naturally, the finance minister bitterly opposed Tolstoi's intentions to give governors rather than Finance Ministry representatives such authority, although both officials agreed that a maximum rate for zemstvo taxes on immovable property, similar to the regulation in the 1870 Municipal Statute, was absolutely essential.

Besides unrestricted veto powers (which governors were to use if zemstvo enactments in their judgment violated the law, state interests, or the welfare of local inhabitants), Tolstoi's proposal gave governors the right to initiate discussions in and to submit their own proposals to the zemstvo assemblies on measures to improve the local economy.[21] The latter stipulation had the potential advantage of establishing cooperation and coordination between the zemstvo and other government institutions by involving the governor in daily work of the zemstvo, and by making him more responsible for its successes and failures. No longer would the governor be able to disclaim any responsibility for zemstvo inefficiency on the grounds that the law, by

---

[19]Zakharova, *Zemskaia kontrreforma*, p. 105; TsGIA, *f.* Kantseliariia MVD, *op.* 2, *d.* 1833, *l.* 16 *ob.*; and ibid., d. 1838, *l.* 320.

[20]Ibid., *l.* 322 *ob.* Veselovskii and Yaney argue that in many districts the sole desire of the gentry delegates was keeping their taxes at a minimum and imposing extraordinarily heavy taxes on merchants and industrialists. Veselovskii, *Istoriia zemstva*, 3: 289–312; and Yaney, *Systematization*, p. 352.

[21]TsGIA, *f.* Kantseliariia MVD, *op,* 2, *d.* 1838, *l.* 320 *ob.*

limiting him to vetoes on statutory grounds, tied his hands in this matter. Conversely, a capricious governor determined to thwart the zemstvo could wreak havoc on the local economy (as exemplified by P. V. Nekliudov, who was removed as governor of Orel in the mid–1890s because of his floggings of peasants).[22] Such conflicts occurred often enough after 1890 that one of Tolstoi's successors admitted that food supply and taxation matters were handled more smoothly and satisfactorily in provinces without zemstvo institutions. Finally, as in the case of the Land Captain Reform, the Senate would be virtually eliminated from local administration, because the minister of internal affairs would resolve almost all conflicts between the governors and zemstvos.[23]

Absenteeism of assembly delegates and the general indifference of the wealthy gentry toward public service were major obstacles to efficient zemstvo activity. Tolstoi proposed to rectify these problems by requiring persons elected as zemstvo delegates to serve or face stiff punishment. Participation in zemstvo assemblies no longer would be a political right in the Western sense, to be exercised by those desiring to serve the public. Rather, telegraphing his intent to the first estate, Tolstoi stressed that

With the recognition of zemstvo affairs as the business of the government, the obligations of the delegates will acquire the significance of service to the state and the nature of a duty, the execution of which should be mandatory for all those persons who hold the public trust and are elected to the assembly. If the government, in taking on the management of the zemstvo economy as a branch of the state economy, deems it useful to invite local estate representatives to participate along with the administration in this important work, then it is obvious there can be no talk about voluntary participation as a *right* of the population. The notion of such a right is pertinent only in the realm of private, civil intercourse; but in the sphere of state activity, every right is imposed as an obligation on the persons to whom it is extended. That is why zemstvo representation, under the proposed new status of zemstvo affairs, should not be regarded as a right, but rather an *obligation* of the local population, the conscientious execution of which, in necessary cases, will be guaranteed by appropriate punitive measures.[24]

Punishments for absenteeism would be severe, with a fine of ten to a hundred rubles for the first absence, thirty to three hundred rubles for the second,

---

[22]Fallows, p. 186.

[23]TsGIA, *f.* Kantseliariia MVD, *d.* 1838, *ll.* 323–323 *ob.* For the views of Ivan Logginovich Goremykin, Minister of Internal Affairs from 1895 to 1898, on clashes between governors and zemstvos, and Witte's commentary on them, see Vitte, *Samoderzhavie i zemstvo*, p. 156.

[24]Quoted from TsGIA, *f.* Kantseliariia MVD, *d.* 1838, *ll.* 319–319 *ob.* Emphasis in the original. See also *l.* 303. There were a few exceptions to the rule. Persons sixty years of age or older, those who had served at least two previous three-year terms in a district or provincial or zemstvo assembly, and those who were delegates in another provincial or district assembly were not required to attend. In certain cases spelled out in an appendix to the project, individuals in state service were exempt from the obligation. Still, the article shows that the measure was intended to crack down on negligent delegates who claimed that their bureaucratic superiors would not let them out of work to attend the assemblies. Tolstoi ordered all of these officials to give their subordinates paid leave to attend the annual zemstvo assemblies. Ibid., *d.* 1833, *l.* 15.

and legal prosecution as well as a suspension of three to nine years from participation in local administration offices for additional offenses.[25]

On no other point did Tolstoi reveal so clearly his views on the differences between Russian and Western administrative development. In Russia, the people served the state, and all administrative institutions rightfully should be state organs, whereas in the West government activity was dictated by public will. Even the model of the Prussian *Landräte* who became increasingly bureaucratized in the nineteenth century was not completely pertinent to Russia because, as Tolstoi recognized, the Russian gentry as a group had not displayed the junkers' enthusiasm for and initiative in local government, much less their sense of corporate responsibility.[26] Whereas the use of privileges, regulation, and punishments to force public participation in the zemstvo might seem barbaric to the West and to Western-oriented Russians, Tolstoi argued that it was consistent with Russia's autocratic tradition. Experience had proven to him beyond doubt the apathy of Russians for self-government, most of whom were too ignorant and uncivilized to discharge this function properly. Had he looked beyond his centralist bias in evaluating the record of public self-government, however, he would have recognized that the establishment of public self-government on terms dictated by the state, as shown earlier, was a major cause for public indifference in this area.

Although he was mindful of Russia's tradition of state-dictated development, however, Tolstoi did not want to turn back the clock, nor did he believe that autocratic rule and an educated population were by definition incompatible. Despite his fear of change, he realized that Russia could not return to her preindustrial, servile past. The autocracy's function was to control, rather than to impede change. In this respect, the government, by taking over the vast network of local public institutions created in the 1860s and by resurrecting the traditional concepts of state-controlled change and the values of state service, had an unprecedented opportunity to establish its authority over all aspects of Russian life at a minimum expense. Hence, Tolstoi's centralization program for local self-government derived more from his political goals than from a simple desire to eradicate the constitutionalist demands of zemstvo leaders in the late 1870s or to prop up a decaying gentry for its own sake. Valuev scorned Tolstoi's project for precisely these reasons and called it a true monument to his talents.[27] Yet nowhere in his project did Tolstoi call for the abolition of zemstvo institutions; in fact, he emphasized their potential usefulness to the government. In his 1888 report, he pointed out that cases of constitutionalist or federalist demands of zemstvos

---

[25]Ibid., *l.* 22 *ob.* According to Veselovskii, between 1891 and 1909 only 38 zemstvo delegates were punished under this provision (36 were reprimanded, 2 were fined). Veselovskii, *Istoriia zemstva*, 3: 353–4.

[26]On the *Landräte* and bureaucracy in Prussia, see Lysbeth W. Muncy, *The Junker in Prussian Administration under William II, 1888–1914* (reprint; New York, 1970), pp. 175–96, 224–6; and John R. Gillis, *The Prussian Bureaucracy in Crisis 1840–1860; Origins of an Administrative Ethos* (Stanford, 1971), pp. 31, 211–12.

[27]Zakharova, *Zemskaia kontrreforma*, p. 111.

in the past were exceptions and not the reason for his counterreform proposal. This statement should not be taken at face value, because he actually saw such demands as an abuse of the autonomy granted to these institutions in 1864. Nonetheless, such incidents were not the main reason for the counterreform.[28] The zemstvos had made no political demands of this nature since 1881, and, judging by the general inertia of the central bureaucracy, it is highly unlikely that political aspirations voiced a decade earlier would be sufficient impetus for the promulgation of a counterreform.

What disturbed Tolstoi in particular were the signs of and persistent complaints against chaotic and irresponsible zemstvo activity in the 1880s, and these prompted him to submit his counterreform proposal. The concrete problems associated with past zemstvo activity – specifically the public apathy, the high taxes, and the exploitation of zemstvo office for personal gain – were his justification for central control over these institutions.[29] He criticized the reformers of the 1860s because they assumed that the local population was prepared to assume the responsibilities of self-government, an attitude that, he claimed, ignored the fact that the preform gentry had not governed their affairs without state direction. Indeed, Tolstoi's proposal for central control over the zemstvo was considerably different from the gentry-dominated local administration prior to 1861. The regular state appointment of zemstvo officials, the obligatory nature of zemstvo service, the preservation of zemstvo institutions themselves, and the representation of all social estates had no counterparts in preform local government, which relied heavily on the voluntary services of the gentry. Whereas Pazukhin favored a return to the Nicholaevian system of local administration, in which, under the myth of centralization, the gentry had relative autonomy in local government, Tolstoi advocated bureaucratization to a degree far beyond that proposed by Valuev, Timashev, or Shuvalov. He wanted to manipulate rather than destroy the zemstvos because, he maintained, bureaucratized zemstvos could discharge valuable services for the government. In his view,

The abolition of zemstvo representation does not at all enter into this task. The government cannot refuse the assistance of the population in managing the local economy and goods and services. The historical example of all countries and nations convincingly shows that the activity of merely bureaucratic agencies and control of

---

[28]Scholars who emphasize this factor as the principal motive in Tolstoi's proposals include ibid., p. 161; Tseitlin, "Zemskoe samoupravlenie i reforma 1890 g.," p. 101; Avinov, "Glavnye cherty v istorii zakonodatel'stva," p. 21; and Pokrovskii, *Ministerskaia vlast'*, p. 454. Yet as Manning persuasively argues, the zemstvo oppositional movement did not really take shape until 1894–1905, when seventy-one provincial zemstvo assemblies adopted resolutions with constitutionalist demands (for instance, calling for zemstvo participation in a national legislative process, or for a constitutional government with guarantees of civil rights). In contrast, from 1865 to 1890 only ten provincial assemblies passed oppositionist resolutions, nine of which (in 1878–81) called for a constitution in Russia similar to that given to Bulgaria. Roberta T. Manning, "The Zemstvo and Politics, 1864–1914," *The Zemstvo in Russia*, pp. 136–8. Although Tolstoi was not one to ignore the constitutional implications of public self-government, his zemstvo project stemmed from his desire to eliminate local state-zemstvo conflicts and create a system conducive to effective local administration.
[29]TsGIA, *f.* Kantseliariia MVD, *op.*, 2, *d.* 1838, *l.* 307 *ob.*

representatives of the local population, has never proved fruitful [sic!]. . . . Even under normal circumstances, can we expect useful results in securing public food supply and protecting public health from the activity of state agents alone, who have no ties with the locality and, by the very nature of their obligations, are inclined to resort to routine methods?[30]

Naturally, Tolstoi's project, with its redefinition of the status of zemstvo institutions and of the relationship between state and gentry, generated controversy. His adversaries in official circles did not question the reorganization of zemstvo representation along estate lines (and presumably the increase in gentry control) that were proposed in the project. But they did repudiate his brazen attempts to bureaucratize the zemstvos and thereby extend his control over all local self-government. Hence, it is difficult to agree with Zakharova that the ministerial debate was little more than a conflict over details of the project between two groups of reactionary ministers representing different strata of the gentry.[31] With the exception of Minister of Education Delianov and of K. P. Pos'et, the former minister of transportation and communications, the ministers commenting on Tolstoi's proposals in fact lashed out against its main provisions.

Several factors probably accounted for the fervor of their criticism and their outspoken defense of public self-government. First, most of Tolstoi's opponents saw his project as an effort to minimize or eliminate altogether the influence of other ministers, particularly finance and justice, over the development of the local economy and justice (through their tax inspectors and justices of the peace). In fact, this clash pointed up the larger conflict between the ministers of internal affairs and of finance over the general direction and tempo of rural economic development. Tolstoi defended the traditional agrarian society and favored a controlled pace of industrial development in order to minimize and to deal with the disruptive effects of that process. But Vyshnegradskii and especially his successor Witte pressed for a rapid, forced pace of industrialization. The debate over local self-government reform was an issue that could decide which ministry would have the upper hand in this important matter. No wonder Vyshnegradskii and Manasein eloquently defended zemstvo autonomy; in the light of their views on fiscal control and judicial counterreform noted earlier, their arguments cannot simply be attributed to their belief in the value of decentralization and local public autonomy.

In addition, for all its shortcomings, the zemstvo was a better and more publicized example of public self-government in action than local peasant officials. It was one of the milestones of the Great Reforms era and of Russia's emergence as a modern state. These officials could argue in good conscience

[30]Quoted from ibid., *l.* 312.
[31]Zakharova, *Zemskaia kontrreforma*, p. 165.
    In other sections of her work, she contradicts this generalization and refers to a conflict between bureaucratic "liberals" and reactionaries. Ibid., p. 139.

and in the manner of the Kakhanov Commission decentralists that government interference had caused past problems between state and zemstvo institutions, and represented no solution. Finally, by mid–1888 Tolstoi's opponents had rallied against him on the land captains project, and this feeling carried over to the zemstvo measure. Instead of individually recommending changes in the project, as was customary during reviews by the various ministers, Tolstoi's foes actively campaigned and sought to change the minds of officials supporting it.

Most shocking to Tolstoi was Vyshnegradskii's reply. The latter's refusal to grant the minister of internal affairs exclusive control over zemstvo taxation blocked Tolstoi's success in this area, and later would enable Finance Minister Witte to direct government policy toward the zemstvo in the late 1890s. Such ministerial infighting was a significant obstacle to coordinated state policy, especially under the weak Nicholas II, who succeeded as tsar in 1894. Yet Vyshnegradskii had political motives for defending public self-government in September 1888. More secure in his position than a year earlier and in charge of the Commission to Review Legislation on Zemstvo Taxation (established in 1886), he was beginning to draft his own proposals on tax reform. He shuddered at the thought of Tolstoi's governors ignoring the local welfare and whimsically ordering huge zemstvo expenditures, with their ramifications for his budget-balancing efforts; and Tolstoi's proposal to increase the governor's authority in this area might well preempt his own reform plans. Thus, he demanded that, rather than the governor, a bureau with representatives of the Ministry of Finance (specifically, the director of the Provincial Financial Board and tax inspectors) and of the Ministry of Internal Affairs decide on the feasibility of zemstvo tax measures.[32] Even though the zemstvos repeatedly had abused their right of taxation, he felt the control of the minister of internal affairs over the local economy posed even greater dangers. Not to be outdone in terms of "bureaucratic paternalism" and interests of state, Vyshnegradskii defended the existing ministerial power balance in the countryside in warning

If, in accordance with the project of the Minister of Internal Affairs, the Finance Ministry were removed completely from participating in zemstvo affairs, inasmuch as they concern fiscal interests, then the state would be depriving itself of the assistance of the agencies most qualified in this area. . . . The direct and responsible participation of the directors of the Provincial Financial Boards in the provinces and of the tax inspectors in the district in resolving issues of taxes and expenses can effectively protect the taxpayers from being overwhelmed by local taxes at the expense of state interests. [It] can lead to the establishment of uniform methods in apportioning zemstvo and state taxes, and to equitable taxation and proper assessment of land, and all of these no doubt comprise the primary conditions necessary for the proper activity of the entire economy.[33]

[32]TsGIA, f. Kantseliariia MVD, op. 2, d. 1836, ll. 119–20, 126.
[33]Quoted from ibid., l. 120.

To enlist support for his view, Vyshnegradskii made an impassioned plea for exact legislation to regulate the autonomous zemstvo. He even invoked the memory of Baron Korf, the champion of autonomous public self-government during the State Council debate in 1863, in order to prove the long-recognized need for precise laws:

The fears expressed by Baron Korf have been justified in practice and his arguments not only have not lost their validity, but now are even more pertinent. . . . So that the new institutions can carry out the task conferred on them with greater success than those currently existing, it is necessary above all that their activity be regulated to the appropriate degree by precise and defined laws. Decentralization and increasing the rights of local institutions can be of genuine benefit without violating the unity in administration necessary for state interests only when the general guidelines for their activity are established by exact and clear laws.[34]

Hence, Vyshnegradskii sided with the legalists in the State Council who advocated the rule of law over the use of discretionary powers in local administration. In the event the governors received authority over the zemstvo budget, he insisted that the law stipulate what areas and how much control over these expenses they could exercise.[35] Such criticism demonstrated Vyshnegradskii's desire to bury Tolstoi's project in a debate over principles in the State Council more than his support for the ideas and institutions introduced by the zemstvo reform of 1864.

More outspoken on behalf of autonomous public self-government was Minister of Justice Manasein who, along with State Comptroller Sol'skii, attacked Tolstoi for not providing factual evidence to support his criticisms of zemstvo activity, and for relying on ministerial control, rather than on a comprehensive reform program, to integrate the zemstvo into the government apparatus.[36] Many of Manasein's arguments reiterated the views of the decentralists in the Kakhanov Commission, especially his support for elected zemstvo boards instead of appointed zemstvo bureaus. While admitting that some unreliable and incompetent people had gained election to these offices, he insisted that elections had numerous advantages over government appointment. How could an appointed zemstvo bureau be expected to enforce the resolutions of a zemstvo assembly that had no control over it?[37] Or, as Sol'skii maintained, what assurance was there that the government would appoint better people from among the delegates in the assembly? Such a solution ostensibly would perpetuate the dualism in local administration that Tolstoi wished to eliminate. By subordinating the zemstvo bureau to the Ministry of Internal Affairs, Ostrovskii warned, "the government only will arouse disenchantment in the local population for zemstvo activity and zemstvo interests, and will achieve results completely contrary to what the

---

[34]Quoted from ibid., *l.* 116.
[35]Ibid., *ll.* 127 *ob.*–128.
[36]Ibid., *ll.* 136–7, and *d.* 1838, *ll.* 520–520 *ob.*
[37]Ibid., *d.* 1836, *l.* 139.

Minister expects from the reform."[38] Along with Manasein, Vyshnegradskii, and Sol'skii, Ostrovskii mistakenly viewed the proposal as a return to the prereform system of provincial committees that even Tolstoi criticized. Instead, he recommended more precise laws on zemstvo jurisdiction and increasing the governors' supervision over elected zemstvo boards.[39] In short, these ministers were able to use effectively the arguments developed by the Kakhanov Commission decentralists to protect their own ministerial interests without having to devise a counterplan in order to undermine many key provisions in Tolstoi's program of state-controlled zemstvos.

No stipulation provided better proof that the zemstvos were to be state institutions than the notion of zemstvo service as an obligation to the state. For this reason, it was assailed by nearly all ministers, including those like Pobedonostsev, who claimed to support the project as a whole. He agreed on the need to prevent the election of politically unreliable people as delegates and to increase state supervision over the zemstvo. But true to his nature, he rejected some of Tolstoi's proposals as too radical, and asserted:

I see no direct need or benefit from changing the basic principle in the organization of zemstvo institutions by incorporating them into the regular hierarchy of government institutions with a bureaucratic service nature. . . . That is why I expect no benefit from changing the boards into zemstvo bureaus which, according to the project, indisputably will lend them a bureaucratic character.[40]

Thus, Pobedonostsev subscribed to the main idea of the Zemstvo Statute of 1864 — that the zemstvo was an institution of public self-government, fundamentally different from regular government institutions, and that local residents had the freedom to decline election to the assembly. Such views clearly distinguished him from Tolstoi, the centralist-minded statesman who understood the need to implement sweeping if unpopular control measures in order to create his bureaucratized system in the countryside.

Unlike Pobedonostsev, who opposed institutional reform on general principle, Manasein, Vyshnegradskii, and Sol'skii recognized the need for some alternatives to bureaucratization in order to reinvigorate the zemstvos. They invariably concluded that further decentralization through a comprehensive district reform was probably the only solution. Indeed, Sol'skii was a good example of an official who became more outspoken in support of the Great Reform legislation the longer these issues were debated in official circles. Nearly silent in the early stages of the land captains debate, he attacked Tolstoi's entire zemstvo project, especially the obligatory nature of zemstvo service, which he termed a gross violation of the gentry's corporate rights. Besides unfairly burdening the gentry appointed by the government with all responsibility for zemstvo affairs, the project, with its threat of punishments for not attending zemstvo assemblies and its limitations on zemstvo

---

[38]Ibid., *d.* 1838, *l.* 531 *ob.*
[39]Ibid., *ll.* 467 *ob.*; Zakharova, *Zemskaia kontrreforma*, pp. 131–4.
[40]Quoted from TsGIA, *f.* Kantseliariia MVD, *op.* 2, *d.* 1836, *l.* 96 *ob.*

jurisdiction, was an insult to the gentry and other representatives who took public service seriously. Sol'skii and Ostrovskii predicted that Tolstoi's project, if enacted, would only increase zemstvo expenses and public indifference for elected service.[41] Yet no one made a more elaborate argument for public self-government (with the typical comparisons of prereform and postreform life) than Manasein, when he proclaimed:

I consider it my duty to state that the cause of the shortcomings in our public [zemstvo] activity is not, in my opinion, rooted in the principle of self-government itself. By comparing the current conditions of district life with those preceding the creation of zemstvo institutions, there is hardly any basis for denying the useful results of [zemstvo] activity in many respects, the best representatives of whom conscientiously attend to the fulfillment of the important tasks conferred on them. If selfish or generally unreliable people are found among zemstvo members, the prevention of their harmful influence on zemstvo affairs where it takes on a criminal nature, or at least a substantial diminution of such offensive behavior (which is not unknown in other spheres of public and even government service), can be attained on the one hand by authorizing the government to inspect zemstvo boards, and on the other by perfecting the current procedures for bringing prosecution against zemstvo members for offenses in office.[42]

Thus, precise laws, stronger legal measures to prevent the misuse of zemstvo funds, public elections, and voluntary public service – these were the rudiments of public self-government that Tolstoi's opponents defended. They did not quibble over details, but in fact challenged his assumptions about the feasibility and benefits of state-controlled zemstvos. They pinpointed the unrealistic aspects of Tolstoi's arguments, for instance, his belief that the "best" gentry would be willing to abandon military service careers, civil service in St. Petersburg, or, in some cases, their freedom as public servants for regimented bureaucratic work in the new zemstvo. Under these conditions, zemstvo assemblies might well become meetings of disgruntled delegates who would spend their time criticizing government proposals – a situation that Tolstoi wanted to avoid.

For all their arguments in favor of public self-government, decentralization and comprehensive reform, it is important to remember that these ministers were critics and not the initiators of local administration reform. As such, their arguments had only a paralyzing effect on Tolstoi's proposals, and did not result in concrete legislation to decentralize decision-making authority even further or to systematize local government as a whole. Defenders of public initiative in local administration primarily as a safeguard for their ministerial interests, they showed little inclination to formulate plans to expand public autonomy in zemstvo affairs. Such conditions produced stagnation and not ingenuity in a government attempting to resolve complex administrative problems in a period of social and economic diversification.

---

[41]Ibid., d. 1838, ll. 519, 530 ob.-531.
[42]Quoted from ibid., d. 1836, ll. 139–139 ob.

The reorganization of zemstvo representation. In the second part of his zemstvo counterreform proposal, Tolstoi unveiled his ideas for reorganizing zemstvo representation in accordance with the three traditional estates of the realm. At first glance, this plan seems to be nothing more than a concession to gentry class demands for estate representation and gentry control of the zemstvo, a view no doubt stemming from the fact that Pazukhin drafted the original project and in it reiterated his claim that, beginning in the late 1870s, nongentry elements were displacing the gentry (*vytesnenie dvorianstva*) from the district zemstvo assemblies. Moreover, in 1885–7 gentry assemblies in Tula, Smolensk, Poltava, Kaluga, Pskov, and Simbirsk provinces petitioned for similar changes;[43] and, as we have seen, the government did take some substantial economic measures to stave off the demise of the gentry (a primary base of its social support) as rural landowners.[44] Yet other factors – for instance, the nature of Tolstoi's other proposals and the fact that the gentry, according to statistics and official reports, predominated in an overwhelming majority of zemstvo institutions from 1865 to 1890 – suggest that gentry class interests were unlikely to be the chief reason for the counterreform. Although the increase in gentry representation was the most obvious feature of the 1890 statute (mainly because the plan of reorganization survived the State Council debate intact), it was but another component in Tolstoi's plan to make state institutions out of the zemstvos, and to enlist the gentry's services to that end.

In this section of the project, Tolstoi sought to improve the quality of zemstvo officials elected by reorganizing the current electoral assemblies into separate gentry, urban, and peasant estate curiae. He also proposed to prohibit peasants from electing gentry landlords or any other nonpeasants as their delegates, because such individuals rarely defended peasant interests in the zemstvo assemblies.[45] Tolstoi regarded the participation of such conservative elements as the middle and prominent gentry in large numbers as a precondition for effective zemstvo administration under state control. Why else would he point to the factional conflicts in the zemstvo assemblies and the mismanagement of the zemstvo boards in the 1870s, the period that prominent landlords began to withdraw in large numbers from zemstvo

---

[43]Korelin, *Dvorianstvo v poreformennoi Rossii*, p. 214.

[44]Solov'ev, p. 198. Other accounts adhering to this view are Zakharova, *Zemskaia kontrreforma*, pp. 27, 100, 161; Pokrovskii, *Ministerskaia vlast'*, p. 455; and Zaionchkovskii in *Dnevnik sekretaria Polovtsova*, 2: 500. Korelin attributes the proposed reorganization to the government's desire (not gentry pressure) to eradicate the oppositionist tendencies of the zemstvos. Korelin, *Dvorianstvo v poreformennoi Rossii*, p. 214. In contrast, Witte and Whelan attach little importance to the increase in gentry representation and emphasize the establishment of government control over the zemstvo, yet neither relates the reorganization of zemstvo representation to Tolstoi's larger designs. See Vitte, *Samoderzhavie i zemstvo*; and Whelan, p. 189. Gentry landholdings in forty-seven provinces in European Russia did decline from 80.7 million *desiatiny* in 1872 to 71.2 million (in 1882) and to 62.9 million (in 1892), whereas during the same period peasant landholdings rose from 7.3 million *desiatiny* in 1872 to 10.7 million (1882) and to 16.3 million in 1892. N. P. Oganovskii, ed., *Sel'skoe khoziaistvo Rossii v XX veke. Sbornik statistiko-ekonomicheskikh svedenii za 1901–1922 gg.* (Mouton reprint, 1968; Moscow, 1923), pp. 60–1.

[45]TsGIA, *f.* Kantseliariia MVD, *op.* 2, *d.* 1838, *l.* 313.

affairs, yet well before the kulaks and intelligentsia had any influence?[46] To reverse this trend, he called for the apportionment of zemstvo delegates according to estates and for a reduction in the total number of delegates in order to weed out incompetent and unreliable participants and to increase gentry majorities in most provinces. Since the zemstvos would be state institutions, there was no need to follow the Western notion of equal representation for all estates. The new criterion for participation of various groups would be their usefulness to the state.

At the same time, Tolstoi recognized that the petty gentry were as guilty as certain merchants and kulaks of using zemstvo office to further personal interests, for instance, to get zemstvo loans and to supplement their income from their landed estates. To curb this practice, he proposed to raise the property requirement for indirect representation of petty landowners from 1/20 to 1/10 the full quota. Prominent landowners who owned at least thirty times the amount of the regular property requirement would be allowed to participate in the zemstvo assemblies without election.[47] This provision would apply to 1,121 landowners in thirty-four provinces, of whom 871 were gentry.[48]

Emphasizing that central control was the primary goal of the counterreform, Tolstoi insisted that the gentry, in keeping with their heritage of service to the tsars, were the only group who could give zemstvo work the aura of service to the state:

> The forthcoming zemstvo reform, which has the aim of incorporating the local organs managing the economy into the regular structure of our state institutions, requires appropriate changes in zemstvo representation. In order to make the procedure for electing delegates of the zemstvo assemblies congruent with the foundations of our state organization, it is necessary to establish this procedure on the estate principle, since the estates of the realm in Russia have always been and still remain the only historically established and properly organized social groups. Their assignment now as always is to fulfill various government obligations and, in this respect, to render direct assistance to the government in local administration.[49]

Consistency alone would require Tolstoi to abolish all-estate zemstvo elections and autonomous public self-government. Rarely in the past had public institutions cooperated with state officials in providing medical services, teachers, and famine relief to local residents. What promise of improvement would there be if state-appointed land captains were forced to deal in these

---

[46]Ibid., f. Departament zakonov G. S., op. t. 11, d. 23a, l. 596 ob.

[47]Ibid., f. Kantseliariia MVD, op. 2, d. 1838, ll. 315 ob.-316, 318–318 ob.

The subcommission under Prince Gagarin changed this provision so that prominent landowners could exercise this privilege only if they had resided at least ten years in the province. This was an attempt to prevent newly wealthy merchant landowners who had purchased gentry lands from wielding too much power in the zemstvo assemblies.

[48]Zakharova, Zemskaia kontrreforma, p. 102.

[49]Quoted from TsGIA, f. Kantseliariia MVD, op. 2, d. 1838, ll. 314 ob.-315. For an interpretation that emphasizes the strength of the landed gentry in the 1880s and the influence that Pazukhin's estatist arguments had on Tolstoi counterreforms, see Becker, pp. 134–6.

vital matters with independent zemstvo institutions? The subordination of the zemstvo to Tolstoi's authority thus became a corollary to the introduction of the land captains, and in the process he used many of Pazukhin's arguments to give the measure the appearance of progentry legislation in hopes of arousing the enthusiastic participation of prominent and middle gentry in zemstvo activity.

Statistics on gentry participation in the zemstvo assemblies and official commentaries on Tolstoi's proposal likewise suggest that, contrary to the claims of L. G. Zakharova and others, the minister had ulterior motives for introducing a reform that favored the gentry.[50] Two conclusions can be drawn on the basis of this evidence. First, the gentry were in firm control of zemstvo assemblies and boards at the district and provincial levels in the mid–1880s. This fact is illustrated by their domination of zemstvo board offices at the district and provincial levels and seats in the provincial assemblies (see Table 6.1).[51] Since these positions were filled by election in the district assemblies (and, in the case of board posts, carried a salary with them), we can assume that the gentry possessed the influence, in some cases disproportionate to the number of their delegates, to take control of zemstvo affairs if and when they chose to do so. Second, the electoral assembly system established in 1864, with its relatively fixed representation for various groups

---

[50]Zakharova challenges Veselovskii's contention that the 1890 statute produced no significant change in the gentry's control of zemstvo affairs (Veselovskii, *Istoriia zemstva*, 3: 351–2). Relying heavily on the claims of Pazukhin and other gentry publicists, she argues that the declining influence of gentry in local zemstvo assemblies and boards led the government to introduce the zemstvo counterreform; unlike Pazukhin, she cites data to show that from 1865 to 1886, especially in provinces of the central industrial region (for instance, Kostroma, Moscow, Vladimir), merchant landowners managed to increase their representation in the landowner's electoral assembly by two to three times, and in some cases they constituted one-third of the total number of participants. Under these circumstances, they were elected to zemstvo office, a development that had adverse consequences for local economic administration. Zakharova, *Zemskaia kontrreforma*, pp. 4, 17, 20, 23–4, 64. Yet elsewhere Zakharova herself acknowledges that the displacement of gentry in the district assemblies by nongentry landowners was not a widespread phenomenon, but a process that was only beginning in a few industrial provinces, and Tolstoi himself exaggerated the separate cases in which the gentry had lost their influence. Ibid., pp. 52, 100. Indeed Korelin contends that the representation of gentry and officials in the district zemstvo assemblies in thirty-four provinces *increased* from 41.7 percent in the mid–1870s to 42.4 percent (34.7 percent gentry, 7.7 percent officials) in 1883–6 – in other words, the gentry was solidifying its control over the zemstvos in the late 1870s and early 1880s (particularly if one excluded those districts where there was no gentry representation). Korelin, *Dvorianstvo v poreformennoi Rossii*, pp. 213–14. Solov'ev acknowledges that prior to 1890 the zemstvos were under the control of the middle landed gentry; Solov'ev, p. 192. Such qualifications seriously challenge the contention that Tolstoi's zemstvo counterreform was designed primarily so that the gentry could regain control of the zemstvo. If the gentry enjoyed commanding pluralities in the zemstvo assemblies of most provinces, why would relatively few exceptions result in a comprehensive reform of zemstvo institutions, instead of adjustments in property requirements for zemstvo participation in these provinces (as permitted under the 1864 legislation)? Furthermore, Pazukhin's claim about the influx of the "intelligentsia" into the zemstvos in the 1880s was precisely the kind of exaggerated argument that Katkov had been making since the mid–1860s in order to defend the traditional *soslovie* system. Becker, pp. 60, 206.

[51]McKenzie argues that in 1886 gentry and officials constituted 55.5 percent of the district board members (as opposed to 30.9 percent for the peasants) and 89.48 percent of the provincial board officials. McKenzie, p. 54. Korelin argues that the gentry/official membership on the district boards stood at 50 percent in 1883–6 – down from 66 percent in the mid–1870s. Korelin, *Dvorianstvo v poreformennoi Rossii*, p. 213.

Table 6.1. *Gentry members of district zemstvo boards and provincial assemblies, 1883–6*

Province	District zemstvo boards, gentry officials (%)	Provincial assembly, gentry officials (%)
I. Black Earth		
Kursk	87	94
Tula	78	94
Orel	78	91
Voronezh	76	82
Riazan'	63 (11 peasants, 25 merchants)[a]	88
Penza	61 (23 peasants, 13 merchants)	83
Tambov	43 (33 peasants, 24 merchants)	93
II. Southern Steppe		
Kherson	83	79
Ekaterinoslav	88	92
III. Southwest		
Khar'kov	76	93
Poltava	59 (41 peasants)	96
Chernigov	61 (33 peasants)	88
IV. Lower Volga		
Saratov	67	78
Samara	44 (48 peasants)	75
Simbirsk	42 (50 peasants)	83
V. Northwest		
Novgorod	63 (23 merchants)	80
Smolensk	63 (26 peasants)	98
Pskov	65 (27 peasants)	83
St. Petersburg	46 (17 peasants, 25 merchants)	88
VI. Central Industrial		
Tver'	73	85
Kostroma	58 (37 peasants)	83
Vladimir	53 (31 peasants)	66 (33 merchants)
Nizhnii Novgorod	43 (40 peasants, 14 merchants)	73
Kaluga	42 (31 peasants, 19 merchants)	80
Moscow	39 (44 peasants, 15 merchants)	67 (24 merchants)
Iaroslavl'	33 (50 peasants, 17 merchants)	73 (16 merchants)

Cumulative totals for 26 provinces

581 gentry/officials	(61.4)[b]		1,567 gentry/officials	(84.1)	
249 peasants	(26.3)		94 peasants	(5.1)	
106 merchants	(11.2)		179 merchants	(9.7)	
11 others	(1.6)		30 others	(1.6)	
947 (district zemstvo boards)			1,870 (provincial assembly)		

[a] Percentages of peasant and merchant members on district zemstvo boards are given in parentheses for provinces in which these groups had significant representation.
[b] Percentages given in parentheses.
Source: Compiled from *Statisticheskie tablitsy soderzhashchie dannye o sostave zemskogo predstavitel'stva v 34 guberniiakh Rossii*, appended to M. I. Sveshnikov, *Osnovy i predely samoupravleniia* (St. Petersburg, 1892).

and majorities for the landlords, had worked well in practice. Although the number of merchants and kulaks in the landowners' assemblies increased more than marginally in a small minority of provinces, on the whole the relative percentages of district electors and delegates of diverse social origins remained remarkably stable. In six provinces (Vologda, Viatka, Olonets, Perm, Tavrik, and Ufa), the peasants dominated the zemstvo assemblies in the mid–1880s as they had twenty years earlier. For the other twenty-eight provinces, gentry representation had increased from 42.4 percent to 44.5 percent.[52] Although the merchants increased their delegate representation in district assemblies from 7 percent to 16 percent in five central industrial provinces, many of these gains came at the expense of the clergy, whose participation in the landowners' assembly virtually ceased by 1883. Equally significant, the merchants in the landowners' assembly had much more difficulty electing their own delegates in provinces in which they formed a sizable segment of electors.[53] This phenomenon was hardly surprising, since merchant land magnates had no burning desire to participate in the zemstvo, preferring rather to elect delegates who promised not to raise their taxes.

Several other conclusions can be drawn from the statistics for gentry participation in zemstvo boards and provincial assemblies, keeping in mind the figure for gentry representation in the district assemblies (44.5 percent). First, in only six provinces (Tambov, Simbirsk, Nizhnii Novgorod, Moscow, Kaluga, and Iaroslavl') did the percentages of gentry on the zemstvo boards dip below the national average for their representation in the district assemblies, a sign that in most provinces nongentry groups were not usually a significant political force. In the other twenty provinces, the gentry controlled the elections of zemstvo board officials. During the previous two decades they monopolized these posts as well as the seats in the provincial assemblies.[54]

---

[52]Zakharova, *Zemskaia kontrreforma*, p. 171; and Tseitlin, "Zemskoe samoupravlenie i reforma 1890 g.," pp. 84–5. The most significant reductions in gentry representation in the district assembly occurred in the provinces of Tavrik (− 6.7 percent), Moscow (− 6.4 percent), Nizhnii Novgorod (− 6.4 percent), Kostroma (− 5.5 percent), Ekaterinoslav (− 5.4 percent), Pskov (− 5.1 percent) and Kaluga (− 4.2 percent). In six other provinces gentry losses amounted to less than 3 percent, an insignificant figure for twenty years. In contrast, gentry representation increased most noticeably in Kursk (+ 11.7 percent), Poltava (+ 9.5 percent), Chernigov (+ 9.4 percent), and Smolensk (+ 6.9 percent), and in seven other provinces it rose from 1 to 6 percent.

[53]Zakharova concurs that the merchants benefited from the decline in clergy participation; see Zakharova, *Zemskaia kontrreforma*, p. 17; and the various provincial election statistics in *Statisticheskie tablitsy*, appended to Sveshnikov, *Osnovy i predely samoupravleniia*.

[54]TsGIA, f. Kantseliariia MVD, 1888, *op.* 2, *d.* 1835, *ll.* 100–1, 105, 113–16, 121. This was a main problem, as Tolstoi realized. In 132 of 384 districts, gentry marshals served simultaneously as district zemstvo board chairmen − further proof that local self-government suffered from a shortage of qualified personnel and that many elected officials made sinecures of their posts. Veselovskii, *Istoriia zemstva*, 3: 219–23. Although in their writings Tolstoi and Pazukhin idealized the work of the gentry marshals in the zemstvos, largely to secure gentry involvement in these matters, Senator G. A. Evreinov charged in 1888 that over the previous two decades the district marshals, more than any other group, had embezzled zemstvo funds. Veselovskii, *Istoriia zemstva*, 3: pp. 333–4; and Becker, p. 227. Such perceptions likewise explain why Tolstoi wanted bureaucratic supervision of gentry officials, as opposed to delegating rural self-government to them entirely.

Second, in provinces such as Tambov, Poltava, Simbirsk, and Samara, the discrepancy between the small percentage of gentry and officials serving on the district boards and the higher figures for those in the provincial assemblies might be explained simply by the apathy of many gentry for zemstvo service. Rather than toil year-round on the district boards, the gentry in these provinces preferred the prestige and ease of being provincial assembly delegates. Their indifference toward zemstvo work was a constant problem. Judicial Minister Manasein emphasized this point in announcing that he would oppose any reorganization of zemstvo representation along estate lines until Tolstoi proved that apathy and absenteeism of the gentry were not the principal reasons for the unsatisfactory activity of the zemstvos;[55] and Tolstoi, not surprisingly, never denied this fact. Vyshnegradskii also saw through the Tolstoi–Pazukhin argument and contended that the zemstvo was increasingly in the hands of the petty gentry, who were making careers of zemstvo service. These individuals had no qualms about accepting bribes, making deals with kulaks and merchants, and using zemstvo contracts to increase their wealth, all of which produced disorder in the zemstvo administration. Tolstoi acknowledged that certain groups of gentry were indeed part of the problem when he recommended excluding 43,416 petty landlords eligible for zemstvo service – or 31.9 percent of all landlords in thirty-four provinces from 1883 to 1886.[56]

In essence, the main problem in zemstvo representation was not the displacement of gentry representatives by merchants and kulaks, but the apathy of the "best" members of the gentry, a fact recognized by Tolstoi and many of his ministerial colleagues.[57] Why else would he draft measures for obligatory zemstvo service under threat of punishment? As for the other ministers, they argued that reorganizing zemstvo elections according to social

[55]TsGIA, f. Kantseliariia MVD, d. 1836, ll. 140 ob.-141.
[56]See ibid., d. 1833, l. 13; and ibid., d. 1836, ll. 120 ob.-121.
    Tolstoi intended to limit the participation of petty gentry and give overwhelming majorities to the middle and prominent gentry in the gentry estate electoral assemblies. For instance, in the black earth and Lower Volga provinces, the petty gentry would comprise 22.1 percent and 15.9 percent of gentry electors, respectively. On the other hand, Tolstoi could not arrest the economic decline of the landed gentry, and despite significant reductions in the number of petty gentry eligible to participate, in the northwest and central industrial provinces they continued to play a great part in the gentry electoral assemblies after 1890. Thus, according to Tolstoi's projections, in the northwest region they would account for 25.9 percent of the electors, and in the central industrial region the figure would be 25.8 percent. Ibid., Departament zakonov G. S., op. t. 11, d. 23a, ll. 155 ob.-156.
[57]Manasein replied that, according to all the evidence, "the landlords' assembly is a genuine assembly of the district gentry since, with few exceptions, all the land is in their hands." He further warned that if the small number of kulaks were forced to participate in the peasants' electoral assembly, they would win election as delegates more easily and exert a harmful influence on zemstvo affairs. He maintained that the current system, which allowed new economic ties to develop among the district landowners of all estates, was far superior to Tolstoi's proposal. Ibid., f. Kantseliariia MVD, op. 2, d. 1836, ll. 140 ob.–141 ob. Apparently, the attacks of Manasein, Sol'skii, and Vyshnegradskii against Pazukhin's theory persuaded Durnovo to tone down this idea in the revised proposal. In his 27 August 1889 letter to Sol'skii, he acknowledged that the gentry already possessed the lion's share of representation in the zemstvo, but insisted nonetheless that the current election system discouraged the "best" gentry from participating. See ibid., f. D. M. Sol'skii, op. 2, d. 145, l. 3 ob.

estates would produce no substantive changes in current representation and therefore directed their attention to the controversial aspects of the project. Tolstoi's recommendation to make prominent landowners ex officio members of the provincial zemstvo assemblies regardless of their estate affiliation came under severe attack, because it was an artificial method of dealing with the shortcomings in zemstvo activity. Manasein and Vyshnegradskii opposed it on practical grounds, and argued that prominent gentry who were not members of district assemblies and lacked knowledge of local economic conditions would be of little value in the provincial assembly.[58] Pobedonostsev criticized the measure on principle, because it would allow unscrupulous merchant and peasant land magnates to wield greater influence in the zemstvo. He recommended instead that the government establish its control over the zemstvo by appointing a small number of provincial assembly delegates (up to one-fifth the total number), and Durnovo later inserted this change into his project.[59]

Along with the ministerial opposition, some of the leading spokesmen for the traditional estates order (*soslovniki*) likewise realized that Tolstoi, far from expressing confidence in the first estate, intended to police it through the bureaucratized zemstvo. Thus, unlike the gentry assemblies that in 1887 hailed the forthcoming zemstvo project (and in some cases favored the abolition of the zemstvo),[60] several gentry marshal "experts" in Tolstoi's own subcommission (under Prince Gagarin) spoke out against the reorganization of the zemstvos. Shidlovskii, Zarin and Krivskii – men whose gentry loyalties were beyond dispute – were most critical of provisions on the obligatory nature of zemstvo service; the gubernatorial control over all zemstvo affairs; and the establishment of zemstvo representation according to the three estates. According to Krivskii, the latter particularly would ruin the gentry because, in reassigning merchant landowners to the urban electoral assembly, it would undermine the local economic ties that were developing among landowners of a given district.[61] Krivskii minced no words in assailing the project as a brazen attempt to destroy the zemstvo:

Having reviewed all the articles of the project concerning the direct increase in the governor's authority, one must conclude that not only the control and supervision of zemstvo activity but even the direction of all zemstvo affairs is to be placed in

---

[58]Ibid., *f.* Kantseliariia MVD, *op.* 2, *d.* 1836, *ll.* 122, 143–143 *ob.*

[59]Cf. ibid., *l.* 95; and ibid., *d.* 1838, *l.* 539.

In accordance with Pobedonostsev's criticism, Durnovo also reduced the number of zemstvo delegates on the grounds that the fewer the number of delegates, the more reliable they would be. Whereas Tolstoi proposed 10,465 district and 1,948 provincial assembly delegates for thirty-four provinces, Durnovo recommended 8,905 and 1,103 as the appropriate figures. See ibid., *ll.* 543 *ob.*-544.

[60]Becker, pp. 134–5, who also notes that by the early 1890s the traditionalist gentry were abandoning the zemstvo institutions to their more liberal counterparts and devoting themselves to work in the corporate institutions where they led the defense of gentry privilege. Ibid., 141–2.

[61]For this and other criticisms from the three gentry marshals, see TsGIA, *f.* Kantseliariia MVD, *d.* 1833, *ll.* 66–71, 57 *ob.*-62 *ob.*, 110–13, 143–50, 157–60.

the governor's hands. Under these circumstances it would be fully consistent to abolish the zemstvo assemblies and to confer their obligations on the provincial and district zemstvo bureaus.[62]

The three marshals praised the record of public self-government and demanded that the ministry cease to depict the zemstvo project as a measure in the gentry's interest. If the government desired control of zemstvo affairs, they concluded, public self-government should be abolished and the local public should be allowed to devote themselves to their private concerns; but, Krivskii suggested, if the government truly had the gentry's welfare at heart and if it required public assistance in local economic administration, it should give the local population a free hand in this area.[63]

Such remarks were proof that public self-government had considerably more support among the gentry and central bureaucracy than Tolstoi imagined, and that a significant segment of the gentry took their commitment as public servants very seriously. From their vantage point, they refused (unlike Pazukhin) to become mere pawns of the minister of internal affairs. After all, over a century had passed since the gentry had been emancipated from obligatory state service, and their values and priorities had changed. Tolstoi assumed naively that he could regiment provincial society into cooperating with the government on the latter's terms without arousing rural dissatisfaction. But top officials and gentry who supported public self-government for ministerial or ideological reasons were in no mood for Tolstoi's control over their local economic affairs, despite the latter's professed concern for the landed gentry. None of these officials doubted that the gentry, as the most educated and experienced estate, should be the leaders in zemstvo affairs. But they did oppose artificial measures to ensure their leadership and implied that sooner or later nongentry elements would have to take over in this area, owing largely to the economic attrition of the landed gentry. Tolstoi's opponents did not speculate as to when this change would occur; indeed, their attentions centered on the fundamental issue of the project – whether the zemstvo would continue as a public self-governing institution or would become a state agency, a question far more explosive and of much greater implications for Russia's political future.

The power of criticism: the debate in the State Council and the Law of 12 June 1890

When the State Council began to review the revised zemstvo project in March 1890, the opponents of the zemstvo counterreform enjoyed two advantages that they did not have during the land captains debate. First and most important, their adversary was Durnovo, who, compared with the deceased Tolstoi, was unskilled in the methods of ministerial intrigue, less

---

[62]Ibid., *l.* 155 *ob.* [misnumbered *list* in *delo*].
[63]Ibid., *l.* 165.

committed to firm central control over local government, and inclined to yield to opponents in order not to alienate them. A. A. Abaza facetiously dubbed him "the false Dmitrii," and the publicist Golovin observed that the new minister, for all his pretensions of following in Tolstoi's footsteps, behaved like a hospitable gentry marshal willing to make lavish promises to other officials in order to maintain favor. Kireev even more bluntly regarded him as a "fool" (*durak*) and as Meshcherskii's protégé.[64] Personalities always played a crucial role in State Council debates, and this was especially true in its review of the zemstvo project, as Durnovo's opponents seemed more interested in how far they could push him than in approving a cohesive reform.[65] Second, time was definitely the ally of the opposition. The passage of the Land Captain Statute in 1889 and its implementation in 1890 made approval of the zemstvo project during the current session of the State Council all the more urgent. In fact, according to Polovtsov, Alexander III issued Durnovo a virtual ultimatum to achieve this, because he wanted to implement a cohesive program of state control at the same time.[66] Such pressure put Durnovo in a difficult position, to say the least. Unless the tsar intervened directly in the discussion, he would have to make revisions in accordance with the opposition's view in order to get the project through the State Council. On the other hand, his complaining to the tsar against ministers with greater seniority might easily be interpreted by Alexander III as a sign of weakness on Durnovo's part. Faced with this dilemma, he decided to try to solidify his status as minister by pushing the project through the State Council. Yet Durnovo was clearly not the man for such a struggle, and the result was an emasculated zemstvo statute without many of the state control provisions of the original project.

Given his experience in the Special Conference of the Kakhanov Commission, there might be reason to think that Durnovo revised the zemstvo counterproject because he adhered to the idea of decentralization. However, there is no evidence that he had firm convictions along these lines, and his reputation was that of an opportunist who changed his political views to maintain favor. The explanation for Durnovo's actions during this period is found above all in the maze of bureaucratic politics and power relationships in ministerial circles. The most important fact was that Durnovo did not have imperial support even close to the degree that Tolstoi enjoyed it. Indeed, Tolstoi died as the tsar's favored and most powerful minister, even if Alexander III had some doubts about

---

[64]For Abaza's characterization see Zakharova, *Zemskaia kontrreforma*, p. 139; and V. N. Lamzdorf, *Dnevnik 1891–1892*, ed. F. A. Rotshtein, trans. Iu. Ia. Solov'eva (Moscow-Leningrad, 1934), p. 105. Golovin's comment is found in Golovin, *Moi vospominaniia*, 2: 148; and for Kireev see Solov'ev, p. 65.

[65]See the observations of Gurko, pp. 24–5. The procedures and nature of the State Council meetings encouraged such behavior. Following speeches in favor of and against the project, council members were asked whether they were with or against the particular minister who introduced it. Council members, according to Gurko, often had no understanding of the issue under discussion, but voted against it because they had a score to settle with its sponsor.

[66]Passage for 19 April 1890 in *Dnevnik sekretaria Polovtsova*, 2: 276.

Tolstoi's effectiveness during the final months of the land captains debate. Thus, in a system with relatively equal ministers once again, ministerial peer pressure upon Durnovo became a powerful influence, especially in matters subject to bargaining. Durnovo's concessions on the zemstvo counterreform project to ministers who were his seniors in ministerial rank were truly a typical case of peer group pressure as a major force in bureaucratic power relations.[67] His willingness to appease opponents on the left and right proves that his sole purpose was to avoid a prolonged acrimonious debate in the State Council over zemstvo legislation that, by going against the tsar's wishes, would embarrass him. Such efforts to avoid jurisdictional conflicts with other ministers that might lead to censure by his peers was typical behavior for a new minister. It is sufficient to recall that Tolstoi formulated his control policy slowly and avoided ministerial confrontations over it until he was certain of Alexander's backing.

Under these circumstances, the conventional argument that the State Council alone whitewashed the zemstvo reforms of its "reactionary" provisions must be questioned.[68] Such a generalization overlooks not only the motives of the opponents of the reform, but also the fact that Durnovo yielded to his ministerial foes on some controversial points of the project months before the State Council sessions. In his 27 August 1889 letter to Sol'skii and in his 4 February 1890 revised project, for instance, he conceded that zemstvo executive officials should be elected. Otherwise, the public might lose interest in zemstvo affairs. Thus, in one sweeping statement Durnovo demonstrated his willingness to perpetuate the zemstvo as a separate institution of public self-government, the very object of Tolstoi's attack. He mistakenly took comfort in the knowledge that all elected candidates would require government approval, which, in his opinion, was sufficient guarantee of state control.[69] He retreated from the attacks against the obligatory nature of zemstvo service and proposed that this provision be toned down so that the law, in a manner like the Prussian District Statute (1872), would classify elected zemstvo service as an obligation, but would not spell out the punishments for absenteeism or refusal to serve.[70] No less important, he agreed to delineate by law the extent of the governors' powers concerning zemstvo resolutions on the grounds that they lacked the time to analyze each one. Consequently, in response to Vyshnegradskii's suggestion, he recommended

---

[67]Crozier, pp. 190–1.

[68]For the conventional view, see Avinov, "Glavnye cherty v istorii zakonodatel'stva," pp. 22–3; Vitte, *Samoderzhavie i zemstvo*, p. 143; Zakharova, *Zemskaia kontrreforma*, pp. 141–4, 150; and Kornilov, *Kurs istorii Rossii XIX v.*, 3: 302. In contrast, Tseitlin credits Durnovo with making many changes to weaken central authority over zemstvo executive institutions. Tseitlin, "Zemskoe samoupravlenie i reforma 1890 g.," p. 137.

[69]TsGIA, f. D. M. Sol'skii, *op.* 2, *d.* 145, *ll.* 6 *ob.*-7; and ibid., f. Kantseliarria MVD, *op.* 2, *d.* 1838, *ll.* 539 *ob.*–540.

[70]TsGIA, f. Kantseliariia MVD, *op.* 2, *d.* 1838, *l.* 535 *ob.*; and ibid., f. D. M. Sol'skii, *op.* 2, *d.* 145, *ll.* 4–5 *ob.*

creating a Provincial Bureau for Zemstvo Affairs under the chairmanship of the governor in order to review disputes between the zemstvo and administration over local economic affairs.[71]

Having pulled the teeth out of Tolstoi's policy of state control, Durnovo nonetheless predicted his project could reduce time-delaying conflicts between the government and zemstvo. And there was some truth to his claim. The Provincial Bureau for Zemstvo Affairs, proposed to provide the zemstvo with recourse in the event of conflict with the governor, could easily become his rubber stamp because, like the Provincial Bureau for Municipal Affairs, he had authority over all its members. For many years control-minded governors had advocated such an institution for this purpose, and it would play a vital role in coordinating zemstvo and government activity and improving zemstvo services in the 1890s. But Durnovo's arguments for coordinating state and public administration rather than controlling zemstvo activity proved that his project would not eradicate the dualism in local government. By perpetuating elected zemstvo boards and the de facto nature of voluntary zemstvo service, the revised project left the zemstvo as a public institution with a certain degree of autonomy. Not surprisingly, by the mid–1890s the zemstvos and governors were often protesting the interference of one another in local economic matters, especially pertaining to zemstvo taxation and budgets.[72] The government could prevent the zemstvo from taking certain measures more effectively than ever before; but, contrary to Tolstoi's wishes, it could not direct its activity.

The attack against Durnovo in the State Council led by Vyshnegradskii also centered on the issue of zemstvo taxation. The finance minister insisted that a representative from his ministry take part in the Provincial Bureau's review of such matters, presumably to protect the interests of the state and local population. Backed against a wall, Durnovo responded that zemstvo affairs were the concern of his ministry alone. Such bickering, which went against the State Council's code of conduct, prompted Polovtsov to lament that "every really important legislative issue in Russia boils down to the extent of personal jurisdiction [for individual ministers], and not to a matter of principle."[73] Polovtsov's observation was incisive. Although ministerial conflicts had occurred in the past on other issues, at the end of the 1880s central officials, as illustrated particularly by the debates over the land captains and zemstvo projects, were more concerned with the extent of their authority than with exercising it. The unity in central policy making that Tolstoi had desired was lacking. How could stability and order prevail in provincial administration when these qualities were absent in St. Petersburg?

The success of a state control policy hinged on the degree of authority

[71]Ibid., f. Kantseliariia MVD, d. 1838, ll. 534–5.

[72]Fallows, pp. 192–4, 199–200.

[73]Quoted from passage for 26 March 1890 in *Dnevnik sekretaria Polovtsova*, 2: 267. Durnovo compromised with Vyshnegradskii on this point and allowed the director of the Provincial Financial Board to submit his opinion on the feasibility of zemstvo tax proposals to the governor.

given to land captains and governors, the agents of the Ministry of Internal Affairs in the peasant and zemstvo administrations, respectively. In the light of the growing gubernatorial supervision over zemstvo affairs (that began in the late 1860s and was spelled out under the 1876 Code of Laws and in the resolutions of the Committee of Ministers), Durnovo's adversaries appreciated the need to block any further changes in this direction in order to safeguard their influence in local economic affairs. Reversing their earlier position, they maintained that the Provincial Bureau for Zemstvo Affairs alone could not protect the zemstvo against arbitrary governors, and demanded that the governors' veto power over zemstvo decisions be defined by law even more precisely than Durnovo had proposed. At this point, the latter balked and countered with Tolstoi's argument that governors should have the right to protest any zemstvo resolution.[74] When the discussions ended, the Committee of Ministers and Senate were authorized to resolve disputes between the governors and zemstvo assemblies – yet another triumph for the traditional ministerial system. Although governors by law could protest zemstvo resolutions that violated the law or state interests, or that were contrary to local economic welfare, they were deprived of the absolute control they were to have received under the original project.[75] In this respect, the project amended by the State Council differed little from current legislation, according to which a number of state institutions had responsibilities in the area of public self-government.

By early April 1890, the State Council and autocracy appeared to be on another collision course, the prospect of which alarmed Durnovo and Polovtsov. Durnovo feared that his adversaries might whittle away his project to nothing and postpone its passage indefinitely. Polovtsov, on his part, worried that the State Council would incur Alexander's wrath just as it had the year before, in the event Durnovo complained to the tsar. Yet only when Polovtsov went to reassure the tsar about discussions on the zemstvo project in the State Council did he discover that Durnovo had taken pains to convince Alexander that the council discussions were progressing smoothly.[76] And the tsar, who had grown impatient with the State Council in the past, was willing to accept this explanation provided the council finished the discussions before summer vacation. On no occasion did he suggest resolving the debate by tsarist fiat as he had done with the land captains project, and generally he concealed his views on the zemstvo legislation, a fact that led Polovtsov to conclude that the council lacked imperial confidence.[77] Yet the emperor's indifference probably stemmed from the fact that following Tolstoi's death, he turned his attention increasingly to other issues, primarily

---

[74]See passage for 10 March 1890 in ibid., p. 264.

[75]Ibid., pp. 265, 271, 285, 500; TsGIA, *f*. Departament zakonov G. S., *op*. t. 11, *d*. 23a, *ll*. 1145–6. For an analysis of the new burdens the legislation placed on the governors see Robbins, "Viceroys," chap. 7.

[76]See the passages for 2, 5, and 30 April in *Dnevnik sekretaria Polovtsova*, 2: 269, 272, 278.

[77]Ibid., pp. 278–9.

Russia's industrial development and the construction of the trans-Siberian railroad, and relied more heavily on his finance minister. In any event, Durnovo realized his objective and on 12 June 1890 Alexander III approved the journal of the State Council. The new law contained few traces of the state control measures envisioned by Tolstoi, but its promulgation did solidify Durnovo's position as minister of internal affairs.[78]

In many respects, the 1890 statute was as ambiguous as its predecessor, and, like the 1864 reform, it was acclaimed in nearly all quarters. To the "liberal" *Russian News* the legislation was a pleasant surprise, a mere shadow of the original proposal and a reaffirmation of the usefulness of public participation in local government. Conservative journalists were no less enthusiastic in their endorsement of it, with the *Moscow News* applauding the new statute as a guarantee that zemstvo officials would obey government officials in the future.[79] Within three years, however, its patchwork quality disappointed nearly everyone, as various political quarters realized it was neither Tolstoi's program of state control nor a reaffirmation of public self-government. Consequently, rather than quell the discussions over the status and powers of zemstvo institutions, it intensified them, especially in light of zemstvo activity in the early 1890s under the provisions of the new statute.

The implementation of the 1890 statute and its implications

Russian officials eager to evaluate the Zemstvo Statute of 1890 in practice did not have long to wait. No sooner did Alexander III sign the new law than the government and zemstvos faced the twin scourge of famine in twenty provinces in 1891–2 and a cholera epidemic in 1892–3. These disasters, which preceded the full implementation of the 1890 legislation, nevertheless provided an augury of the critical challenges that faced the bureaucracy and zemstvos in the 1890s. During this most fruitful decade of zemstvo work, among other impressive achievements, zemstvos built over 3,300 schools from 1895 to 1898, a figure surpassing the total constructed from 1878 to 1894, and from 1896 to 1901 they spent an average of 38,200 rubles per year on education in each province – far above the annual average of 5,900 rubles for 1881 to 1890.[80] They likewise formed provincial committees to recommend changes in the Food Supply Statute to the government; systematically collected data on peasant illiteracy for the first time; raised the number of village economy warehouses from 37 to 254 between 1890 and 1898; increased the number of zemstvo medical personnel (discounting physicians) in the provinces (from 6,778 to 8,546); and doubled the amount spent on voluntary services overall.[81]

---

[78]For the text of the statute see *PSZ*, 3d ser., vol. 10, no. 6927, 12 June 1890.
[79]Veselovskii, *Istoriia zemstva*, 3: 349–50.
[80]Ibid.: 389, 391; Zakharova, *Zemskaia kontrreforma*, p. 164. See also Eklof, pp. 286–314.
[81]Veselovskii, *Istoriia zemstva*, 3: 389, 391; and Robbins, *Famine in Russia*, p. 178. Jeffrey Brooks points out that according to the 1897 census, only 21 percent of the population of the Russian Empire was

Although historians have long recognized these zemstvo accomplishments, until recently few of them have suggested that the zemstvo counterreform had a favorable influence on zemstvo activity or on the revitalization of zemstvo work in the 1890s. Rather, prerevolutionary historians writing from the vantage point of the zemstvo oppositional movement generally attributed this activity to the role of the "third element" – physicians, teachers, statisticians and the like, who recognized the need to participate in the zemstvos following the famine of 1891–2. Soviet historians have also looked outside the 1890 legislation to explain the increase in zemstvo activity and, in most cases, have pointed out that new professional people displaced the gentry in the zemstvos in the 1890s. In marked contrast, Western scholars Yaney, Robbins, and a number of contributors to the recent work *The Zemstvo in Russia: An Experiment in Local Self-Government* (1982) have contended that the counterreform had a positive effect in coordinating the work of state and zemstvo officials and in making the zemstvo administration responsible to the central government.[82] Here, to bring this chapter to conclusion, we shall make a few observations on the impact of the zemstvo counterreform on zemstvo activity and zemstvo–government relations in the 1890s in order to assess the counterreform's significance for local self-government and for the ministerial conflict in this area.

Although the 1890 statute lacked the bureaucratic control features that Tolstoi deemed indispensable, even in its watered-down form it provided a framework for more effective zemstvo administration. Hence, from a strictly administrative standpoint it represented an improvement over the 1864 legislation. It attracted literate, more responsible people committed to public welfare rather than mere personal interests to serve in the zemstvos and, more significantly, it enabled the governor to take an active part in zemstvo affairs. In the first case, the statute restricted the participation of the petty landowners and peasants in the zemstvo and gave the landed gentry a two-to-one advantage in representation over the peasantry. The measure reduced the total number of district assembly delegates from 13,196 to 10,236, and of provincial assembly delegates from 2,284 to 1,618[83] – an expedient, albeit

literate (29 percent of the men, 13 percent of the women). Although zemstvo committees did much to reveal the extent of rural illiteracy, their efforts to form literacy schools in the 1890s were blocked by the government (1891), which turned these schools over to the church. Jeffrey Brooks, "The Zemstvo and the Education of the People," *The Zemstvo in Russia*, pp. 243, 264.

[82] For the prerevolutionary interpretation, see Veselovskii, *Istoriia zemstva*, 3: 363; Avinov, "Glavnye cherty v istorii zakonodatel'stve," p. 27; and Kizevetter, *Na rubezhe dvukh stoletii*, p. 147. For Soviet historians, see Zakharova, *Zemskaia kontrreforma*, p. 164; and Zaionchkovskii, *Rossiiskoe samoderzhavie*, p. 410. Pirumova, by contrast, plays down the significance of the "third element" in this zemstvo activity and the development of a liberal movement, and stresses the contribution of hereditary gentry and urban professionals as zemstvo activists. Pirumova, pp. 55, 125. The views of Yaney and Robbins are found, respectively, in *Systematization*, p. 249; and *Famine in Russia*, p. 29. See also the contributions of Fallows, McKenzie, Ramer, and Frieden in *The Zemstvo in Russia*.

[83] Zakharova, *Zemskaia kontrreforma*, pp. 145, 152; and TsGIA, *f.* Departament zakonov G. S., *op.* t. 11, *d.* 23a, *l.* 1141. According to Zakharova, more than half of the approximately 80,000 qualified voters in the 1883 zemstvo elections lost their voting rights under the new statute, the principal victims being peasants, the petty gentry, and other landowners who participated by indirect represen-

politically callous, response to the perennial shortage of qualified, reliable personnel for local self-government. Likewise, the decision to raise the number of delegates required for a quorum in the zemstvo assembly from one-third to one-half of those present revealed the government's determination to have zemstvos take their work seriously.[84] According to Veselovskii, these gentry-dominated zemstvos (unlike their pre–1890 predecessors) responded by looking beyond their personal or class interests. The famine had convinced many gentry that their fortunes were linked to those of the peasantry, and so they decided to improve the peasant economy and redistribute the zemstvo tax burden more equitably.[85]

Second, the 1890 statute provided a blueprint for the interaction of zemstvos and government officials, especially at the provincial level, that sparked the activity of the provincial zemstvos from the mid–1890s to 1905 (a period that saw a frequent crossover of officials serving in state and public institutions).[86] No longer did the provincial zemstvo remain isolated from its district counterparts, as it was prior to 1890; rather it began to coordinate their work. The benefits of provincial zemstvo leadership were felt in many areas, especially zemstvo medicine, where the provincial assemblies and boards introduced more uniform standards, assumed responsibility for the health of factory workers, appointed additional, more competent medical personnel (nonphysicians), and more willingly heeded the advice of professional physicians in organizing public health facilities.[87] Granted, significant problems remained in the area of zemstvo medicine and public health; for example, as late as 1910 only 8 districts (out of 359) had a physician–patient ratio of less than 1:10,000.[88] But in this and other areas of practical administration, the zemstvos had a clearer view of their role and more state resources available to them.

In this respect, the 1890 statute contributed most significantly to rural administrative improvements by mandating greater communication between zemstvos and governors. In the process, both parties (in most provinces) developed a clearer understanding of their respective functions in local economic administration that allowed zemstvos to concentrate more on public health and public education. Ironically, by taking over the mandatory food supply and cartage expenses of the zemstvos, owing to their indebtedness, the state allowed these institutions to increase their expenses on public health from 22.5 percent of their budget in 1890 to 27.6 percent in 1900, and on public education from 15.3 percent in 1890 to 17.6 percent.[89] The

tation. Zakharova, *Zemskaia kontrreforma*, pp. 151–2. The new law authorized the land captain to appoint peasant delegates from among nominees of the *volost'* assemblies, a provision that enhanced his control over peasant administration.

[84]McKenzie, p. 50.

[85]Veselovskii, *Istoriia zemstva*, 3: 372–3, 380. See also Hamburg, *Politics*, pp. 195–8.

[86]Fallows, p. 212.

[87]Nancy M. Frieden, "The Politics of Zemstvo Medicine," *The Zemstvo in Russia*, p. 320.

[88]Samuel C. Ramer, "The Zemstvo and Public Health," *The Zemstvo in Russia*, p. 306.

[89]Ibid., p. 307. On the governors' contribution, see Robbins, "Viceroys," chap. 7.

governors were active in this work because the new law held them responsible for the state of local economic administration (as part of the state economy). As the pivotal figure in Tolstoi's bureaucratized local self-government from the village level up, the governor under the zemstvo legislation was held accountable for zemstvo ordinances that were illegal or not in the interests of the state or local population and for zemstvo negligence in providing local facilities and services. Through the Provincial Bureau for Zemstvo Affairs the governors could personally see to the enforcement of zemstvo resolutions and the collection of zemstvo taxes and arrears by land captains and local police. Although zemstvo tax arrears remained a serious concern throughout the decade, zemstvo expenditures could not have doubled from 1890 to 1900 had governors not done their part to ensure a more regular flow of income.[90] The governors displayed their vigilance most in times of crisis, as in the famine of 1891–2, when they ordered land captains to work with zemstvos in public food relief and the collection of zemstvo taxes and insurance fees. In 1892, Governor V. P. Rokasovski of Tambov Province praised the effectiveness of the new organization of local self-government when he applauded the land captains for cooperating with all other elements in the famine relief campaign. He emphasized that "only the existence of a responsible administration [unit] close to the people, in the persons of the land captains, made it possible for the zemstvo to manage the difficult task of determining the needs of the population . . . [and] correctly and justly distributing the food and seed loans."[91]

However, as we have seen repeatedly with ministerial conflicts over local self-government, officials looked beyond their political differences during specific crises and worked toward a common goal. The same pattern applied to zemstvo–government relations in the 1890s. Although the 1890 statute provided a basis for zemstvo–government cooperation, and their collaboration in the famine and cholera relief efforts (1891–3) raised hopes on all sides, in a political sense the 1890 statute perpetuated a major flaw of its predecessor. Thanks to the efforts of Tolstoi's opponents in the ministries and State Council, the legislation neither granted the zemstvo full autonomy as a separate public institution with its own executive agents, nor did it incorporate it into the hierarchy of state institutions. It provided no definitive solution to the basic problem of conflict at the local level between state and public officials and in St. Petersburg and the provinces between various ministers over zemstvo activity. Collaborative efforts by these officials hence depended largely on the personalities of those involved, and the unreliability of such a system, as Tolstoi had warned in his proposals, had prevented uniformly efficient administration. Tolstoi's contention was again verified following the national crisis of 1891 to 1893. Moreover, as demonstrated

---

[90]Veselovskii, *Istoriia zemstva*, 1: 15–16, 203, 226. Still, in 1899 zemstvo tax arrears made up 65 percent of the fixed taxes budgeted for collection by the zemstvos, as opposed to 50 percent for 1883. Ibid., pp. 200–2; and Tseitlin, "Zemskoe samoupravlenie i reforma," p. 105.

[91]Robbins, *Famine in Russia*, p. 154.

by conflicts over zemstvo taxation and budgetary matters, the zemstvo counterreform held both zemstvos and the overburdened governors responsible for the welfare of provincial society. Where the personalities did not mesh, the result was frequently administrative conflicts that required senate adjudication (especially from 1897 to 1905).[92] Tragically, once the famine crisis had abated, at least temporarily, some governors viewed successful zemstvo operations as a potentially serious threat to autocracy and to their control over local affairs, and consequently in their reports denounced the shortcomings of the zemstvos in 1891–3. No doubt the zemstvos had made mistakes in the relief operations, but they were attributable in part to the unusual latitude and autonomy granted to them by governors at the time.[93]

More important, the 1890 legislation, contrary to Tolstoi's design, failed to muster political support for the monarchy. Indeed, most zemstvo assemblies, contrary to their earlier protests over the land captains legislation, hardly discussed the zemstvo counterreform at all, much less communicated their thoughts to the government.[94] But silence in this case did not necessarily mean consent. Quite the contrary, those aspects of Tolstoi's bureaucratization of local self-government that survived the counterreforms debate increased the friction between the conservative gentry (who resented their subordination to the regular bureaucracy) and state officials (who had few hereditary ties to the land). Despite this friction, Pleve, as minister of internal affairs (1902–4), attempted to go further than Tolstoi and bring the land captains and gentry marshals completely into the bureaucracy.[95] As for the liberal gentry and other active zemstvo members (*zemtsy*), their disillusionment with the government crystallized in 1895 following Nicholas II's blunt rejection of nine zemstvo petitions for national representation as "senseless dreams." It grew in the late 1890s as the tsar, adhering to Witte's policy of forced industrialization through foreign credit, neglected the agrarian interests of rural society and excluded the zemstvo from public food supply (1900) and other functions. Besides offending zemstvo leaders with curtailments of their jurisdiction, these actions placed on the ministries the awesome responsibility of fulfilling these local needs alone, and the government's failure in repeated cases (for instance, the famines in 1898 and 1901) were bound to make political enemies out of educated society. Perhaps worst of all, the 1890 legislation with its promises of orderly, responsive local government and paternalistic bureaucracy, failed to revive peasant faith in the zemstvo. Although the peasants stood to benefit from much of the zemstvo activity of 1890 to 1905 (despite the reduction in their representation in the assemblies), they (and the urban merchants) generally regarded the zemstvo as little more than another unwelcome tax to pay. In short, the 1890 zemstvo counterreform (and the land captain legislation) contributed greatly to the govern-

[92]Fallows, pp. 183–4, 186–7, 192–4.
[93]Robbins, *Famine in Russia*, p. 175.
[94]Pirumova, p. 47.
[95]Weissman, pp. 37, 87.

ment's isolation at the turn of the century and to the gentry's backlash against it after the 1905 Revolution.

Equally significant, with respect to the fate of autocracy, the Zemstvo Statute of 1890 intensified ministerial conflict over local self-government. The debate over local government reform in the 1880s and 1890s showed that even more than solutions to concrete administrative and fiscal problems, the government needed some institution or official at the top to coordinate state policy making in order to avoid paralyzing jurisdictional and ideological conflicts between ministers. But the 1890 statute not only failed to give the Ministry of Internal Affairs exclusive control over the zemstvo that Tolstoi desired; even more, it opened the door for other ministers to exercise control over these institutions, as Witte did at the turn of the century, and to assert their leadership in state policy making. During that period, Witte grappled with Ivan Logginovich Goremykin, minister of internal affairs, over zemstvo jurisdiction and implementation of these institutions in the Western provinces, and Witte's insistence on fiscal control over the zemstvo cast Goremykin in the unlikely role of their defender.[96] Under Tolstoi's system, such confrontations would have been inconceivable, but the revisions in the zemstvo legislation made by Durnovo opened up this possibility. The Statute of 1890 thus created the framework for more effective zemstvo administration, while perpetuating the political conflict between the government and zemstvo at the provincial level, and between various ministries in St. Petersburg. At best it was a palliative, a temporary measure, which prolonged ministerial conflict. At the same time, it drove the most educated forces of the local population into opposition to the autocracy by calling them to zemstvo service and then failing to ensure that they would have an active role in the process.

[96]*Krizis samoderzhaviia 1895–1917*, pp. 96–109.

CHAPTER 7

Conclusion

In enacting the Land Captain and Zemstvo statutes of 1889 and 1890, the government formally concluded more than twelve years of systematic work on rural self-government reform.[1] Likewise, the legislation closed a chapter in postreform Russian history that saw the introduction of self-government in the countryside in the early 1860s and the first serious state efforts to reorganize it over the next quarter century. During this period and increasingly in the 1890s, the Russian government faced a rural crisis marked by acute land and grain shortages, the breakup of traditional patriarchal ties, and the rapid swelling of tax and redemption arrears; in the latter case, direct tax arrears rose from 22 percent of the anticipated collection in 1876–80 to 119 percent in the years 1896–1900, and in 1903 redemption dues arrears hit 138 percent.[2] Amid these developments, Russian officialdom exhibited many characteristics of a government in crisis as it grappled with the problem of local self-government and other matters connected with state penetration of the provinces. Overwhelmed by the many tasks of rural administration and development and short of personnel and funds, the government nevertheless distrusted the self-governing institutions that it had created to assist it. Seeking an ideology of administration that could provide the right combination of local initiative and political control, the state repeatedly sought to reorganize local self-government. Yet each time its efforts at institutional renovation became bogged down in interest group politics, particularly when the debates reached the highest circles in St. Petersburg. Without imperial intervention, for better or for worse, the proposed legislation was buried under the weight of official opposition and inertia.

Here, our purpose is to relate the findings of our study to two larger

---

[1]Of course, in 1892 the government adopted a new Municipal Statute. Its major provisions adhered to the guidelines of the 1890 zemstvo counterreform.
[2]Rogger, *Russia*, pp. 77, 88; see also *Krizis samoderzhaviia 1895–1917*, chaps. 1–4.

questions. First, how do the evidence and arguments in this study add to or alter the conventional political interpretations of local self-government, especially concerning the origins of the counterreforms? Such a question, as we have seen, entails a reevaluation of the activity of local self-governing institutions, the role of various social and ministerial groups in the reform process, and the relationship between Pazukhin and Tolstoi in devising the program to bureaucratize local self-government. Second, what does our analysis of autocracy and local self-government tell us about the structure and functioning of tsarism and its ministerial apparatus at the end of the nineteenth century?

In this respect, our study points up a fateful irony of the government of late Imperial Russia that other accounts, focusing primarily on capital city politics or on rural administration, have overlooked. As the government grew more knowledgeable and concerned about its local self-governing institutions, and rural conditions generally in the 1870s and 1880s, it proved less capable of reforming them by legislative means. In essence, both administrative and political factors must be kept in mind in assessing autocracy's record on local self-government reform and its implications for the survival of the old order. Local self-government, as introduced in elected peasant, zemstvo, judicial, and municipal institutions, was no luxury for the tsars. Rather, it was necessary to compensate for the inadequacies of prereform administration and the lack of state personnel and fiscal resources to govern the provinces alone. But local self-government had important political and administrative ramifications for the entire government. Not only did it become a topic of ideological conflict between elite officials who advocated zakonnost' and greater public responsibility on the local level versus those who preferred more state control, but local self-government discharged administrative functions vital to the state ministries, which had their own local bureaucracies and sense of institutional mission in the countryside. Hence, the state repeatedly sought to balance local administrative initiative and political order – a challenge that frustrated Valuev, Tolstoi, and Pleve, their distant successor as minister of internal affairs, who in the period 1902–4 sought to reduce "excessive centralization" by decentralizing (deconcentrating) local administration while elevating the governors' leadership in local affairs.[3]

This perennial quest to activate public self-government and neutralize it politically proved in fact to be a curse of autocratic power. This was because in introducing administrative decentralization and public self-government, Alexander II – in what we have called his ministerial system – diffused responsibility for local administrative and economic development among numerous ministries. Besides promoting more effective and specialized ministerial activity at the local level, this arrangement established a ministerial

[3]Weissman, pp. 30–3, 37–8, 46–60.

power structure that left his personal authority intact.[4] For political reasons as well, he left the traditional social estates order fundamentally in place as he introduced public self-government, thereby ensuring that the experienced landed gentry, despite their past failings in local administration, would play the leading role in peasant and zemstvo self-government. Unfortunately, this policy that favored political control over public initiative had a number of adverse consequences for tsarism from 1861 to 1900. Besides failing to define local self-government as a truly public or state enterprise – in effect, leaving it unprotected by law or government authority – the policy also tied local self-government reform to ministerial government. Thus, local self-government reform served as a battleground for rival ideologies and interests and concerned many ministers, not merely successive ministers of internal affairs (the focus of most studies of the counterreforms). For similar reasons, it evoked intense conflict among zemstvo, gentry, and other rural spokesmen anxious to use the principles of decentralization and self-government to their own advantage. Hence, reform, never an easy process in tsarist Russia, became even more complicated and cumbersome under Alexander II and Alexander III, as special interests frequently transcended administrative needs of state.

More immediately, however, this system of public self-government bred administrative confusion and political dissatisfaction in the provinces and St. Petersburg. By the late 1870s, the state had compelling practical reasons for overhauling local self-government. The autocratic crisis, with its backdrop of revolutionary attacks on tsarism, had its roots in the breakdown of peasant and zemstvo administration, and it awakened top officials to the political dangers of mismanaged rural administration, sporadic zemstvo–bureaucratic conflict, and rapidly rising absenteeism in peasant and zemstvo assemblies. Significantly, from the late 1870s on elite officials were preoccupied with these problems because, unlike revolutionary terrorism, they did not diminish even temporarily following the end of the "crisis of autocracy" in 1882. Although reports of rural anarchy (*bezvlastie*), administrative confusion (*mnogovlastie*), official corruption, and apathy during this period were probably exaggerated – given the tendency of some conservative officials to equate "democracy" with "anarchy" – still, coming from many different sources and pinpointing many specific examples, they dispelled official illusions about the inherent democratic tendencies of peasants. They understood the ineffectiveness of peasant customary law in maintaining rural order and the inability of the *volost'* administration to handle peasant, zemstvo, and state needs.[5] Faced with nearly uniform criticism of peasant self-government, top

---

[4]For a similar view, see Taranovski, "Aborted Counter-Reform," p. 163.

[5]Mironov, drawing largely on a survey of 816 communes carried out in 1878–80 by the Free Economic Society and the Russian Geographic Society, provides insight into the organization and functions of the peasant communes and their elected officials and peasant respect for customary law (versus statutory law and bureaucratic authority). Although many of his findings corroborate the picture of peasant self-

officials naturally concluded that peasants left unsupervised by the district bureaus might lose their respect for all authorities. In this context, the sudden, massive growth in tax arrears disturbed the ministers and Alexander II, because such arrears, which were due to mismanaged tax collection and poor harvests, crippled zemstvo and state work and because, more than any other aspect of local self-government, they were the subject of peasant complaints.[6]

Under these circumstances, the government began the process of local self-government reform in 1879–80 – well before Pazukhin arrived in the capital in 1884 (where most political interpretations of the counterreforms begin). In tracing the development of the land captains legislation, we have seen that *all* factions in the reform debate from 1881 to 1890 favored establishing personal supervisory authority (*edinonachalie*) over peasant self-government and using the landed gentry in some fashion (elected, appointed) in this capacity. More important, this evidence of a rural administrative crisis, although by no means a complete or even true picture in all cases, convinced the government in 1880–81 that it could no longer afford to leave the provinces unsupervised, in the hands of elected officials who acted according to local custom or personal interest. True, Tolstoi later used the rural authority crisis and reports of zemstvo–government friction in the late 1870s and early 1880s to consolidate his political power and the social support of autocracy, but this should not obscure the main point. Even before the reaction following Alexander II's assassination began, the government committed itself to some basic concepts in local self-government reform that were introduced in the legislation of 1889–1890.

Given these priorities and the recurrent shortage of qualified local personnel and funds, the government debate focused on ideologies of administration, and not gentry interests, to the dismay of Katkov and Meshcherskii. As in the early 1860s, the reform discussions of the 1880s concentrated on the relationship between state and local public institutions and provided expression for two conflicting ideologies of state building – decentralization and centralization (which in its extreme form meant bureaucratization). There

government presented here in Chapters 3 and 4, he contends that commune peasants exhibited genuine enthusiasm for "democratic" self-government and their elected officials. Yet analysis of peasant statements in official reports in the late 1870s to early 1880s (which were more influential in shaping government perceptions) contradicts Mironov's claim that "elected [peasant] officials did not stand above the commune but operated under its authority, and all administrative and police measures in the commune were taken only with the consent of the village assembly." Moreover, in those villages in which Mironov's claim may have had some validity, the government could hardly feel reassured (given its dependence on peasant revenues and grain production), for as Mironov notes, commune officials at times joined with their neighbors in defying local bureaucratic authorities. Mironov, "The Peasant Commune," pp. 444–7.

[6]According to Rieber, fiscal concerns were far more important in state policy making than historians have generally recognized. He also shows that, from Alexander II's reign on, top ministers were reluctant to approve any measure that jeopardized the state's fiscal interests. Alexander II's government made its decisions on redemption policy, railroad construction, and industrialization with the state's fiscal stability, not its capitalist development, in mind. Rieber, "Alexander II: A Revisionist View," pp. 50–2.

were two reasons for this. On the one hand, both ideologies could be modified to fit the current political environment and the aspirations of various officials. Like other European nations in the late nineteenth century, the Russian government was neither completely centralized nor decentralized, but contained aspects of both centralization and decentralization.[7] Thus, the decentralists in the Kakhanov Commission favored ending peasant self-government and separate state and zemstvo institutions in the belief that the decentralization of the 1860s was too limited for the 1880s.

In their plans to reorganize local self-government, the decentralists and centralists not only put forth conflicting ideologies, but as the discussions at all levels of government revealed, they brought political issues concerning autocracy and the estates order to the forefront. Although both factions proclaimed their support for autocracy and gentry leadership in local self-government, they had very different views on Russia's political future and the state–gentry relationship. For administrative reasons, the Kakhanov Commission decentralists, more so than Tolstoi's ministerial foes in 1887–9, advocated comprehensive local government reform and a devolution of political authority beyond the Great Reforms, because they assumed that Russia belonged to the community of Western nations and should emulate their political evolution. Their proposals to give the zemstvo executive authority over peasant administration and to create zemstvo-controlled district bureaus revealed their commitment to the principles of Alexander II's reforms and the public service ideal that they embodied. They were convinced that the gentry, freed from bureaucratic interference in their roles as zemstvo officials and supervisors in an all-estate village and *volost'* administration, would educate peasants and establish genuine public self-government at all levels – a prospect that left the future of the traditional estates order in doubt. It was precisely that possibility that made this proposal so objectionable to Pazukhin and the other conservative gentry marshals that Tolstoi invited to the full commission debates.

Yet Tolstoi was even more determined to use the gentry as a vehicle in his administrative and political designs, even though traditional historiography has emphasized Pazukhin's influence on Tolstoi and treated the land captain and zemstvo counterreforms as part of the state's policy after 1881 to prop up the first estate. Certainly, Alexander III's government reaffirmed its support for the traditional estates and Tolstoi, conservative that he was, viewed autocracy and the estates order as inseparable. But it is misleading to conclude that the land captains and zemstvo counterreforms were due primarily to Tolstoi's desire for a new "pro-gentry course" or to gentry class pressure or interests. Such an interpretation not only overlooks the statist reasons for the legislation but, as an explanation for the counterreform, it is flawed in three ways. First, contrary to Pazukhin's celebrated argument in 1884–5, the gentry was not being displaced as leaders in local self-

[7]Levy, p. 55.

government by nongentry in the early 1880s, as Tolstoi and other officials readily acknowledged. The gentry indeed maintained its dominant role in local self-government as peace arbitrators, elected justices of the peace, permanent members of the district bureaus, and zemstvo assembly chairmen and executive officials. As Tolstoi saw it, the problem was that some gentry officials put their concept of public service above the state's welfare, while petty gentry and nongentry landowners ignored the needs of the state and local population in making careers out of elected office.

Second, although the *soslovie* system was remarkably durable as a legal order that allowed social groups to interact with state agencies, under Alexander III the elite bureaucracy developed more and more into a separate caste in Russian society with its own income, ethos, and ideologies.[8] Even Tolstoi, who was not one of the arrivés who worked his way into the ministries from the 1860s on, was renowned for subordinating all interests (even personal ones) to the needs of state. Heeding the advice of his governors, in 1883–4 he aimed to transform local gentry officials from elected rural guardians into his state agents, in effect impressing them into a distinct rural bureaucratic corps. True, Tolstoi wanted his officials to have wide discretionary powers to operate effectively in the villages, unencumbered by excessive regulation and intrusive supervision. But as Tolstoi and his opponents all recognized, the main issue in local self-government reform was the relationship between the state and local self-government, not whether the gentry would continue to play the leading role in this area. This point is substantiated by a third factor that challenges the view that the counterreforms were introduced mainly to suit the gentry. Far from signaling a new faith in the landed gentry, the legislation, with its bureaucratic regimen for land captains and its attack on previous gentry leadership, impressed Pazukhin's gentry *confrères* Krivskii, Bekhteev, Prince Obolenskii, and others, as an assault on the traditional *soslovie* system.

In essence, Tolstoi intended to have the gentry serve on his terms to restore administrative order and build rural support for autocracy. This distinguished him from such other conservatives as Pobedonostsev and Katkov, who merely spoke of a bond between tsar and *narod*. Although Tolstoi's program hinged on attracting the necessary gentry volunteers to hold these offices (hence, the value of Pazukhin's association and the gentry-bias of the legislation), it was no throwback to the prereform era of local gentry control. Nor was it a plan for the systematic mobilization of rural support and the modernization of rural society, a process that hit its stride with Stolypin's reforms (1906–11) and Soviet collectivization two decades later. Rather, Tolstoi's plan of bureaucratized local self-government gambled on harnessing rural society and, through his Ministry of Internal Affairs, on putting the

[8]See Freeze, "The *Soslovie* (Estate) Paradigm," pp. 25–6; Zaionchkovskii, *Pravitel'stvennyi apparat*, pp. 179–221; Whelan, pp. 138–56; and Taranovski, "The Politics of Counter-Reform," pp. 119–41.

state in control of rural development. Judging by the results of the 1890s, the plan (to the extent that it was introduced) failed to do either.

This point, of course, raises anew the larger issue of the systematization of Russian government and the question of whether the autocratic system was in crisis in the late nineteenth century. To be sure, Russian autocracy in the mid–1890s did not experience the type of *political* challenge to its rule, or crisis of survival, that occurred in 1878–82 and again in 1905 and 1917, and it would be overstating the case to argue that the problems of local self-government reform analyzed in this work led directly and inexorably to 1905. By 1900, few top officials anticipated the political upheavals that would soon occur. Indeed, certain developments in state circles boded well for the government. The provincial bureaucracy and zemstvos were in the hands of more experienced and specialized personnel, and top officials, more informed about rural conditions, were beginning to look beyond narrow administrative and fiscal interests and were devising strategies to modernize the rural economy, dismantle traditional peasant institutions, and bring the state bureaucracy into this process at the grass roots level. Some scholars have seen the establishment of the Ministry of Agriculture in 1894 and Witte's program for industrialization, among other things, as evidence of a "perceptual revolution" that took place in the thinking of key officials at the turn of the century.[9]

By the same token, many top officials in their writings presented a picture of a government in complete disarray and growing in disillusionment at the turn of the century. Although there was nothing new in their complaints about ministerial disunity and discord and the state's subversion of the landed gentry, the admission that many officials, not to mention public leaders, desired constitutional reform sounded an ominous note for tsarism.[10] More significantly, these officials as a group concurred that autocracy had failed to bring effective bureaucratic control to the provinces from 1861 to 1900. Despite the headway made through the counterreforms, as the nineteenth century drew to a close, the imperial government faced a greater crisis of "bureaucratic penetration" of the countryside than it did in the late 1870s, when the state first acknowledged that the Great Reforms had not produced the administrative control and rural development or the rural support that the government had in mind.

Indeed, if we look back at state efforts to reform local self-government from 1861 to 1900, it is clear that by the end of the century the imperial

---

[9]See particularly the argument of Macey, pp. 31, 44–5, 51–3, 148–9, 244, 249.

[10]See War Minister A. N. Kuropatkin's conversation with Witte (1 January 1902) as recorded in *Krizis samoderzhaviia 1895–1917*, p. 93; although Witte was not above exaggeration to marshal support for his zemstvo proposals, his statement that many elite officials favored political reform (and Kuropatkin's implicit concurrence) attested to growing official doubts about the viability of autocracy; on this theme, see also "Dnevnik A. A. Polovtsova [1901–1903]," *Krasnyi arkhiv*, vol. 3 (1923), pp. 95–6; the views of A. S. Ermolov in Rogger, *Russia*, p. 37; and Weissman and Solov'ev.

government suffered from three serious, if not fatal, weaknesses. First, the government arguably had less rural social support than it did in the 1860s, when it imposed a broad, and not altogether popular, program of reforms in the countryside that also aimed at propping up the traditional social order. At the time the enlightened bureaucrats were quite optimistic that local self-government would provide a vehicle to mobilize the support of the progressive landed gentry for the regime. Twenty-five years later, however, the situation was different. Given the diminishing numbers of landed gentry and the problems that gentry-led local self-government created for the state, Tolstoi decided to bureaucratize self-government in order to build peasant support for autocracy. In other words, fifteen years before the more celebrated and radical agrarian reforms of Stolypin, the government saw the peasantry as its most important and permanent base of rural support.

From the state's vantage point, there were some initial signs that land captains were succeeding in introducing law (*zakonnost'*) into the peasant village. By 1900, peasants were bringing increasing numbers of cases to the reorganized *volost'* courts, which, under the land captain's supervision, operated on the basis of the civil code rather than local customary law.[11] Yet such trends do not tell us much about peasant reaction to bureaucratization. On the contrary, published accounts largely suggest that the peasants viewed the land captains as state agents who acted according to personal authority rather than law. The intrusion of land captains into the villages did little to rekindle peasant enthusiasm for elected office; in fact, peasants and their officials regarded them as unwelcome interlopers much as colonized peoples have resented foreign protection.[12] Like peasants in developing nations they saw little connection between the taxes they paid and the state services provided, perhaps because in 1894 over 80 percent of all *volost'* expenditures went to administrative costs, versus 12 percent for public health and charity and only 3 percent to peasant agriculture.[13] In short, although it is risky to generalize about peasant attitudes toward the state, it is clear that the counterreforms did not have the administrative and political effect on the peasants that Tolstoi had in mind. In 1902, Minister of Internal Affairs Sipiagin admitted as much in attacking the corruption and collusion of peasant officials and village police and in contending that such officials occasionally participated in mass disorders.[14] Yet, significantly, the ministry's plan for peasant administrative reform consisted mainly of strengthening the punitive authority and bureaucratic duties of the village elder.[15]

If Tolstoi's bureaucratization of local self-government as a rule failed to generate peasant support for autocracy, it even more critically alien-

[11]Frierson, p. 57.
[12]Compare this with the nature of local self-government in French Morocco as described in Ashford, pp. 27, 48.
[13]See Riggs, pp. 367–8, and Weissman, p. 29.
[14]Ibid., p. 30. See also Novikov, pp. 117–18.
[15]*Trudy redaktsionnoi komissii* [1903–4], 1: 124–8. See also Simonova, pp. 221–3.

ated and polarized the landed gentry. The traditionalist faction, still bitter about and critical of the Great Reforms, in many instances attacked the counterreforms as they retreated to the strongholds of their corporate institutions, thereby adding to the fragmentation of local administration. They coalesced briefly with their liberal counterparts in the 1905 Revolution out of a common hatred for officialdom.[16] After 1905, the traditional gentry, feeling betrayed by the counterreform experience, did its best to derail Stolypin's legislation and the further extension of the bureaucracy into the countryside.[17] Meanwhile, the liberals' campaign for genuine public self-government, zemstvo autonomy, a zemstvo at the *volost'* level (*melkaia zemskaia edinitsa*), and constitutional reform circa 1900 drew from gentry ranks along with urban professionals and the Third Element. It pointed to the archaic nature of Tolstoi's bureaucratic paternalism, given the increasing urbanization, industrialization, and erosion of traditional class distinctions.[18] In effect, the counterreforms did mold public opinion, but not in the manner that Tolstoi envisioned. Rather, Russian officials, more isolated than ever, were in the precarious position of deriving little visible support from the countryside, and as such Russian officialdom in the late nineteenth century found itself reduced to small deeds in matters of rural administration and economic development — measures unlikely to build rural support in the short run.[19]

Ministerial fragmentation constituted a second important weakness of the late imperial regime and one directly connected, as we have seen, to the process of ministerial expansion in the provinces through local self-government reform. In tracing the crisis of late tsarist officialdom, we recognize that bureaucracies by nature have their conflicts, stress points, and professional identities. This was particularly true in tsarist Russia because all power

[16]Robbins, "Viceroys," chap. 7; Becker, pp. 156–61.

[17]Leopold H. Haimson, "Conclusion: Observations on the Politics of the Russian Countryside (1905–1914)," *The Politics of Rural Russia, 1905–1914*, ed. Leopold H. Haimson (Bloomington, Ind., 1979), p. 294.

[18]Weissman, pp. 31–2, 35–7.

[19]On the importance of the gulf between the bureaucracy and gentry, see Skocpol, pp. 85–90; she sees this as a major cause of the downfall of the old regime in ibid., pp. 110–11, 155–7. The connection between bureaucratic isolation and "small deeds" administration is suggested by Anthony Downs, who argues that bureaucratized states (or governments with large and tall bureaucracies, in his words) frequently suffer from an absence of good sources of information outside the government and a distortion of information within the government. This process, according to David Christian (who applies Downs' model to the tsarist/Soviet case), is "liable to be particularly severe when a bureaucracy is undergoing rapid change or for some other reason is rather unstable. Rapid changes in the hierarchy itself and its environment make it harder for the high command to keep abreast of events." Christian, pp. 80–3. Christian's work helps clarify why the tsarist government found it difficult to carry out even routine tasks of local administration, even though its bureaucracy was more specialized and attuned to rural problems. Similarly, Grew points out the political and social risks of bureaucratized local self-government in contending that "increased penetration without increased participation tends, as it did in Russia and Germany, to lead to an isolated elite and to institutional rigidity and inefficiency; for the state comes to depend upon a set of links with society that resists the formation of those new connections required as society changes." Grew, "Crises and Their Sequences," *Crises of Political Development*, p. 26.

revolved around the person of the emperor and because as an autocratic society the government functioned as the only legally sanctioned political arena up to the 1905 Revolution. Moreover, ministerial fragmentation was not a new phenomenon in Russia at the end of the nineteenth century. It existed in the prereform era, and clashes between the ministers of justice and of internal affairs in the 1860s were so commonplace that N. A. Miliutin labeled them "our constitution."[20]

Nonetheless, as this study shows, by the time of the counterreforms the central government was not only fragmented on ideological and institutional grounds, with the latter particularly dividing Alexander III's ministers; even more important, this absence of unity and direction in central policy making had critical ramifications for state efforts to direct rural development and mobilize rural support. By the 1880s, Alexander III's ministers, firmly rooted in the ministerial system and balance of power ethos inherited from their predecessors, proved quite effective in the tactics of procrastination, petty criticism, counterprojects and intrigue in their attempts to oppose Tolstoi's counterreforms. Accountable only to an autocrat who remained passive in most administrative matters, these ministers repeatedly resisted any changes and pressed for a quick return to normal bureaucratic routine following periods of national emergency, for instance, 1878–82. Such bureaucratic behavior in the aftermath of a government crisis was by no means unique to Russia in the 1880s. The increase in specialized administrators, the turnover in elite personnel, the emphasis on discipline and careerism, the intense fighting between top officials, and the desire to close off bureaucratic ranks to outsiders had many of the earmarks of the power struggle in the Prussian bureaucracy following the 1848 Revolution.[21] Whereas the Prussian bureaucracy of the 1850s and 1860s surrendered its corporate identity and autonomy and allied itself with the junkers, in Russia elite officials became more isolated from landed society and more dependent on the tsar. Each of the ministries involved with local administration and, ipso facto, local self-government, developed its own priorities for rural administrative and economic development. For these reasons, Tolstoi's counterreform projects, which attested to his "primacy" in ministerial circles and proposed to give him control over local administrative, fiscal, and judicial matters, came under attack as deviant impulses that invited severe sanctions from his bureaucratic peer group.[22] These ministers all realized that Tolstoi's plan to create his

[20]Taranovski, "Aborted Counter-Reform," pp. 163; he adds that several decades later a high official complained to Koni that such ministerial "altercations" were a type of Russian "Magna Charta liberatum."

[21]See Gillis, *The Prussian Bureaucracy*, pp. 148–52, 203–5, 209–14; and for evidence of similar attitudes of modern French officials, Crozier, p. 226. See also Merle Fainsod, "Bureaucracy and Modernization: The Russian and Soviet case," *Bureaucracy and Political Development*, ed. Joseph LaPalombara (Princeton, 1963), p. 236; and Raeff, "The Bureaucratic Phenomena," p. 405.

[22]Crozier, p. 191. The tables were turned in the late 1890s to 1902 when Minister of Internal Affairs Sipiagin led the attack against Witte's plan to abolish the mutual guarantee in the peasant *obshchina*. For details, see Vitte, *Vospominaniia*, 2: 184; and *Krizis samoderzhaviia 1895–1917*, pp. 58–60.

own corps of paternalistic state agents jeopardized their own power and that of their field agents.

Such ministerial fragmentation had adverse consequences in the provinces, too, not only in blocking other reform measures (for instance, Justice Minister Murav'ev's plan in the 1890s to extend the regular court system down to the district level),[23] but also in adding to the burdens of provincial officialdom. At the end of the nineteenth century, the twenty or so collegial bureaus representing the various ministries at the provincial level had no standardized procedures or integrated functions. In practice more than ever, the responsibility for ministerial policy execution fell on the governors and provincial administration became the scene of power struggles, especially between the ministers of finance and of internal affairs.[24] The administrative and political problems that this situation created become clearer when we compare the late tsarist rural administration with developments in the last three French Republics and in Soviet Russia. In the former case, local self-government (in the municipality and commune) had more restricted functions than its tsarist counterpart, yet it was also more protected by law. The French prefects who were subordinated to the Ministry of Interior signified centralized bureaucratic authority at the provincial level, but their powers were more limited geographically and more circumscribed by law. Similarly, as Armstrong and other scholars have noted in their comparisons of governors/prefects, the French and German governors received a more specialized legal education than their tsarist contemporaries.[25] By virtue of precise laws, self-governing institutions in France were usually (but not always) allowed more initiative to discharge their limited administrative functions (improving communal facilities, building schools). The French prefects and their subordinates handled largely police functions and enjoyed ministerial protection. Thus, in France self- governing institutions did (and do) not possess sovereign authority or constitute a political threat to the central bureaucracy.[26]

Soviet local officialdom (*oblast'* level and below) is likewise part of a more integrated governmental system, even though it does not operate according to the legalist principles of Western administration. Although local Soviet officials have lost much of the autonomy and authority that they held prior to the 1930s, even in recent times they have handled a variety of functions and have had "a span of control unparalleled in the Western world."[27] In

---

[23]The opposition here was led by Minister of Internal Affairs Durnovo who rejected Murav'ev's suggestion that some of the land captain's judicial authority be transferred to the district judge – a proposal that, given the burdens of land captains, made sense. But the Ministry of Internal Affairs refused to give ground and joined with other government officials who saw the proposal as too limited. Ultimately, the plans for the judicial counterreform died in commission. Taranovski, "Aborted Counter-Reform," pp. 169–74.

[24]Weissman, pp. 44–7.

[25]Armstrong, *European Administrative Elite*, pp. 255–7, 266–7; and Robbins, "Viceroys," chap. 10.

[26]David D. Bien and Raymond Grew, "France," *Crises of Political Development*, p. 252; Mark Kesselman, *The Ambiguous Consensus: A Study of Local Government in France* (New York, 1967), p. 66.

[27]Hough, pp. 3, 124; and Merle Fainsod, *Smolensk under Soviet Rule* (Cambridge, Mass., 1958), p. 149.

many respects – their personal style of governance, their patron–client relations (and the protection of networks of corruption) – local Soviet officials
in practice have assumed characteristics of the late tsarist paternalistic bureaucracy. But on paper the Soviet system remains far more integrated and
complex than its predecessor, and better able to manage local economic
initiative and party control. After all, it contains many more institutions
(but not those autonomous institutions and social groups that challenged
the imperial bureaucracy). In the party it has an ideology (democratic centralism) and an organization at all levels to resolve bureaucratic conflict,
make important professional assignments, mobilize and educate the population (*rukovodstvo* and *vospitanie*), and above all maintain political control
when administrative decentralization is desirable. Although the dual subordination of local officials to local party organs and their specialized ministries probably reduces the party's ability to influence lower officialdom,
nevertheless it enables the party to adapt its policies more effectively to the
needs of the moment (initiative versus stability).[28]

The tsarist government, however, lacked such unity, legal protection, or
human resources for its local self-government. Indeed, the ministerial conflict
over local self-government reform from 1861 to 1900 shows that tsarist
officials joined forces in opposing reform proposals much more readily than
in supporting any measure, whatever its objective. Although other works
on the institutional and ideological limits of reform have reached a similar
conclusion,[29] our study illustrates how much ministerial conflict over local
self-government reform over the long haul inhibited the development of rural
administration and central policy making. There were two reasons for this.
First, more than other areas (labor policy, agriculture, peasant resettlement)
that produced interministerial conflict, the expansion of ministerial power
into the provinces in the nineteenth century limited opportunities for public
participation in local administration, especially given the state's determination to monopolize political power.[30] Second, local self-government suffered because the ministerial opponents of Valuev, Loris-Melikov, Tolstoi,
and later Witte used local self-government as a means of protecting their
own local authority or defending the principles of the Great Reforms while
doing little to promote its development. Personality politics and ideological
conflict, not ministerial order, dictated reform legislation in Russia. Such
compartmentalized government and the attitudes it bred posed great difficulties for tsarism in years when, challenged by rapid population growth,
the appearance of new social groups, industrialization and agrarian crises,

---

[28]On the above, see Fainsod, "Bureaucracy and Modernization," pp. 258–60; Hough, pp. 92–124;
Robbins, "Viceroys," chap. 10. The party's imaginative use of ideology, propaganda, and mass organizations is detailed in Peter Kenez, *The Birth of the Propaganda State: Soviet Methods of Mass Mobilization,
1917–1929* (Cambridge, 1985).
[29]See particularly the works of Orlovsky, Taranovski, and Whelan.
[30]Weissman, p. 4.

and public criticism, the state had to make far-reaching changes in administrative personnel and procedures to survive.

Even with the expansion of ministerial power, rural Russia remained seriously undergoverned. This fact constituted a third weakness of the tsarist system in the late nineteenth century, and it was closely related to Russia's crisis of "bureaucratic penetration" and to the personalized nature of autocratic authority. On the one hand, Russia's "undergovernment," like that of nineteenth-century Spain and post-Risorgimento Italy, was the result of the country's economic backwardness. The tsarist government consistently lacked adequate resources to regulate social and economic affairs and provincial/regional administration.[31] For instance, in 1900, according to Weissman, the Ministry of Internal Affairs had only 1,582 constables and 6,874 police sergeants to administer a rural population of roughly 90,000,000, and personnel shortages were even more the rule in other branches of government.[32] By contrast, the more industrialized European states (Britain, France) had long established rural administrative networks, so that in the late nineteenth century they had fewer conflicts over rural jurisdictions of local state, corporate, and public institutions.

On the other hand, unlike Italy and Spain, Russia owed much of its "underinstitutionalized" status to the distinct nature of autocratic rule, which favored personal authority and discretionary action over formal regulations and a vastly increased bureaucracy. The personalized, paternalistic nature of autocracy had its champions in postreform Russia, who claimed that such rule was especially suited to governing the countryside with a minimum of personnel. The autocrat, his ministers, governors, and land captains could cut through red tape, circumvent "irrelevant" laws and procedures, and get to the heart of rural administrative problems. Unfortunately, however, such personalized authority without any organization to coordinate or prioritize policy invited ministerial infighting on major reform issues, especially because elite officials were more dependent than ever on retaining special imperial favor. On the local scene, such personal authority did little to promote cooperation between state and public officials, as zemstvo difficulties with rural police officials illustrated. In this respect, the assassination of Alexander II in 1881 did not produce the abrupt turnabout in tsarist administration that historians usually assume.[33] Rather, both Alexander II and his

---

[31]See Stanley G. Payne, "Spain and Portugal," *Crises of Political Development*, p. 211; and Raymond Grew, "Italy," *Crises of Political Development*, p. 289.

[32]Weissman, pp. 11, 23–4.

[33]Whelan maintains that Alexander III's reign saw the tsarist bureaucracy exercise decision-making authority on administrative matters, whereas under Alexander II a "tsarist autocratic administration" prevailed. This generalization (however awkward in terminology) is valid if one has in mind the ability of Alexander III's elite bureaucracy to resist reform and to take initiative vis à vis the tsar in daily administrative matters. Yet Alexander III's reign, as we (and Whelan have) noted, was filled with examples of when the tsar decided to intervene in the legislative process and personally alter the outcome of ministerial action in more disruptive fashion than his father. Whelan, p. 198.

successor refused to relinquish any personal power and instead made government decisions on what they considered to be the best interests of autocracy. In Alexander II's case, this meant reorganizing the ministerial power structure (initially at the expense of the Ministry of Internal Affairs), introducing comprehensive administrative reforms, and providing a greater role in the reform process for subordinate institutions (the ministries and State Council). The tsar's reliance on a variety of state agencies for initiative made such an impact on officials involved in reform preparations during his reign that, not surprisingly, twenty years later in the State Council debate over the land captains and zemstvo projects, many of these same officials exaggerated their role in policy making. They forgot that by the late 1870s the Ministry of Internal Affairs, with Alexander's firm backing, had begun to assert its own control over local officials from other ministries (for instance, the justices of the peace).

Unlike his father, Alexander III at first believed that no change at all would be in the best interests of autocracy, and that the tsar had a sacred duty not to be bound by law or to rely on subordinate agencies. When his anachronistic views failed to curb rural administrative conflicts and disorder, the tsar turned to Tolstoi's program of centralization (bureaucratizing local self-government), and to counterreforms in education and the judiciary. Yet even then Alexander III did not display the commitment to see the reform through to its conclusion, as did Alexander II, and with Tolstoi's death in 1889, the impulse for reforming local self-government slackened noticeably. In part, this irresolution had its roots in the way the tsars manipulated their ministers, for both Alexander II and his son flattered themselves as better judges of men than of proposals. Generally distrusting their officials, they never allowed any one minister to direct state policy (as primus inter pares) for more than several years, and ministers took advantage of that tendency. Although this system left the emperor in control of his court, it spread feelings of insecurity, powerlessness, and pessimism among ministers, who hesitated to propose controversial reforms that could embroil them in conflict with their colleagues and possibly lead to their dismissal. In view of the evidence in this study, it is clear that the tsar and his ministers were both manipulators and victims of this system of personalized authority.

In short, by the time of Nicholas II's reign (and indeed up to 1906) Russia remained an autocratic state in principle and fact, with all of the problems that such rule entailed. Like its prereform counterpart, the late imperial regime was overburdened with routine work, isolated from its subjects, and "had no time and energy left to think, plan, and conceive policies *de longue haleine.*"[34] The government, as illustrated by the history of local self-government reform, suffered because of the absence of an institution (a cabinet, for instance) or a permanent ministerial hierarchy to plan long-term administrative policy, set priorities, and coordinate state initiatives. As evident

---

[34]The phrase is Marc Raeff's in *Well-Ordered Police State*, p. 217.

from the reigns of Alexander II and Alexander III, the tsar was not able to handle these extensive, weighty responsibilities alone; indeed, top officials, ranging from Dmitrii Miliutin to Dmitrii Tolstoi, made precisely this point in the 1870s and 1880s in calling for an institution/hierarchy to provide direction in central policy making and local administration.[35] The turnover in imperial "favorites" in postreform Russia, each of whom had his own plan of local self-government reform, proved that no lasting reorganization of local government (or control over the steady development of rural society and economy) was possible without a fixed ministerial hierarchy or institutional structure in the capital to set policy priorities for officials.[36]

In a wider sense, the problems that the Russian government had with local self-government and local self-government reform seem relevant to transitional societies undergoing modernization, especially where autocratic regimes are involved. Although historical circumstances by their very nature are unique, the tsarist experience supports the argument that local self-government is vital to "developing" states, even if it has proved more successful in industrialized societies. As this study suggests, the greatest immediate problem with local self-government for autocracies is not the political risks that it poses but rather the difficulty of mobilizing rural support for it, especially in conditions of material poverty, illiteracy, and village parochialism.[37] In tsarist Russia, such traditional problems had roots in the *soslovie* organization that the government religiously defended up to the twentieth century. But Russia's experiment with local self-government likewise shows that unified central government and a clear delineation of the identity, role, and limits of local self-government are vital preconditions for the development of public self-government. In transitional societies, bureaucratic institutions provide the catalyst for rapid economic and social development; where boundaries between local state and public institutions are not clearly defined, jurisdictional conflict and public disenchantment are likely to follow. At the same time, this study points up the political risks that regimes face in bureaucratizing local self-government, particularly when the process is undertaken haphazardly, or as part of a political reaction. Under such conditions, local self-government may well become a vehicle of political opposition (as happened in Russia after 1900), especially if bureaucratized self-government should fail to deliver effective administration in

---

[35]According to Golovnin, Tolstoi, upon his appointment as minister of internal affairs, told Alexander III that the government lacked unity and that some type of ministerial hierarchy would lead to more orderly government. But at the time he was in no position to press his point. See Golovnin's 11 August 1883 letter to D. A. Miliutin in ORGBL, *f*. D. A. Miliutin, *d*. 39, *l*. 39 *ob*. Finance Minister Bunge also argued that the incomplete nature of the reforms of the 1860s, that is, the absence of a cabinetlike system, sowed disunity among the various ministries as well as between the government and public institutions. Seredonin, 4: 310–11.

[36]Levy, p. 58; Crozier, p. 163.

[37]See the discussion in Riggs, pp. 367–8, 373–4; and idem, "Bureaucrats and Political Development: A Paradoxical View," *Bureaucracy and Political Development*, pp. 121, 131–5; Shanin, pp. 72–4; Ashford, p. 100; and Pintner, "Russia," pp. 360–1, as opposed to Bien and Grew, "France," p. 253.

return for its rural costs. As the tsarist state discovered early in the twentieth century, the failure to mobilize public support and preserve rural order would open the door to more revolutionary approaches in matters of rural development and governance.

Select bibliography

The following bibliography does not pretend to be a comprehensive list of the voluminous source materials and literature on local self-government in the postreform period. The activity of the zemstvo institutions alone during this period is covered by a bibliography of over 130 pages in Volumes 2 and 4 of Veselovskii's *Istoriia zemstva za sorok let*. Rather, the following lists the archival *fondy* and published works that are cited in the notes of this study, as well as the general reference works that I found most useful in researching the topic.

I. UNPUBLISHED SOURCES: ARCHIVAL MATERIALS

Leningrad

Gosudarstvennaia publichnaia biblioteka imeni M.E.
Saltykova-Shchedrina. Otdel rukopisei.
Fond 600   A. A. Polovtsov.
Tsentral'nyi gosudarstvennyi istoricheskii arkhiv SSSR.
Fond 694   D. M. Sol'skii.
Fond 721   D. S. Sipiagin.
Fond 851   A. V. Golovnin.
Fond 908   P. A. Valuev.
Fond 1149   Departament zakonov Gosudarstvennogo Soveta.
Fond 1263   Komitet ministrov.
Fond 1282   Kantseliariia Ministerstva vnutrennikh del.
Fond 1284   Departament obshchikh del Ministerstva vnutrennikh del.
Fond 1317   Osobaia komissiia dlia sostavleniia proektov mestnogo upravleniia (Kakhanovskaia komissiia).
Fond 1391   Reviziia senatora I. I. Shamshina Saratovskoi i Samarskoi gubernii.

Moscow

Gosudarstvennaia biblioteka SSSR imeni V. I. Lenina. Otdel rukopisei.
Fond 75   V. M. Golitsyn.
Fond 120   M. N. Katkov.
Fond 126   A. A. Kireev.
Fond 169   D. A. Miliutin.
Fond 230   K. P. Pobedonostsev.
Tsentral'nyi gosudarstvennyi arkhiv Oktiabr'skoi revoliutsii, vysshikh organov gosudarstvennoi vlasti i gosudarstvennogo upravleniia SSSR.
Fond 569   M. T. Loris-Melikov.
Fond 583   A. A. Polovtsov.
Fond 677   Aleksandr III.
Fond 728   Zimnyi dvorets.
Fond 825   Bakuniny.
Fond 1099   T. I. Filippov.

I I.   G E N E R A L   R E F E R E N C E   W O R K S

Entsiklopedicheskii slovar'. 43 vols. Ed. I. E. Andreevskii and others. St. Petersburg-Leipzig, 1890–1907.
Gosudarstvennaia publichnaia biblioteka im. M. E. Saltykova-Shchedrina.
Katalog fonda revizii senatora A. A. Polovtsova Kievskoi i Chernigovskoi gubernii 1880–1881 gg. Comp. M. Ia. Stetskevich. Leningrad, 1960.
Kabuzan, V. M. *Izmeneniia v razmeshchenii naseleniia Rossii v XVIII-pervoi polovine XIX v.* Moscow, 1971.
Russkii biograficheskii slovar'. 25 vols. St. Petersburg, 1869–1918.
Sovetskaia istoricheskaia entsiklopediia. 16 vols. Ed. E. M. Zhukov and others. Moscow, 1961–76.
Vodarskii, Ia. E. *Naselenie Rossii za 400 let (XVI-nachalo XX vv.).* Moscow, 1973.
Zaionchkovskii, P. A., ed. *Istoriia dorevoliutsionnoi Rossii v dnevnikakh i vospominaniiakh. Annotirovannyi ukazatel' knig i publikatsii v zhurnalakh.* 4 vols. in 10 parts. Moscow, 1976–85.

I I I.   P U B L I S H E D   P R I M A R Y   S O U R C E S

A. Documents, contemporary brochures, newspapers

Arefa, N. I. *Polozhenie o gubernskikh i uezdnykh zemskikh uchrezhdeniiakh.* St. Petersburg, 1894.
Bermanskii, K. L. "Konstitutsionnye proekty tsarstvovaniia Aleksandra II." *Vestnik prava.* Vol. 35, bk. 9. 1905, pp. 223–91.
Garmiza, V. V. "Predlozheniia i proekty P. A. Valueva po voprosam vnutrennei politiki (1862–1866 gg)." *Istoricheskii arkhiv* 1 (1958): pp. 138–53.
Gosudarstvennyi sovet. *Otchet po Gosudarstvennomu sovetu.* 23 vols. St. Petersburg, 1870–92.

"Graf Loris-Melikov i imperator Aleksandr II o polozhenii Rossii v sentiabre 1880 g." *Byloe*, no. 4 (26) (1917): 34–8.

Islavin, M. V. *Obzor trudov Vysochaishei utverzhdennoi, pod predsedatel'stvom Stats-Sekretaria Kakhanova, Osoboi Komissii.* 2 pts. St. Petersburg, 1908.

Istoricheskaia zapiska o khode rabot po sostavleniiu i primeneniiu Polozheniia o zemskikh uchrezhdeniiakh. St. Petersburg, n.d.

Katkov, M. N. *Sobranie peredovykh statei iz "Moskovskikh vedomostei."* 1863: no. 140; 1864: no. 140; 1880: nos. 46, 47, 227; 1881: nos. 68, 71, 118, 119. Moscow, 1897.

"Konspekt rechi D. A. Miliutina: Mysli nabrosannye na sluchae novogo soveshchaniia." *Vsesoiuznaia biblioteka im. V. I. Lenina. Zapiski Otdela rukopisei.* Vol. 2. Moscow, 1939, pp. 26–9.

"Konstitutsiia grafa Loris-Melikova." *Byloe*, no. 4–5 (1918): 125–86.

"Konstitutsionnye proekty nachala 80-kh gg. XIX veka." *Krasnyi arkhiv*, 6 (31) (1928): 118–43.

[Kovalevskii, M. M.] *Konstitutsiia grafa Loris-Melikova i ego chastnye pis'ma.* Berlin, 1904.

Krest'ianskaia reforma v Rossii 1861 goda: Sbornik zakonodatel'nykh aktov. Comp. K. A. Sofronenko. Moscow, 1954.

Krest'ianskoe dvizhenie v Rossii v 1870–1880 gg. Sbornik dokumentov. Ed. P. A. Zaionchkovskii. Moscow, 1968.

Krest'ianskoe dvizhenie v Rossii v 1881–1889 gg. Sbornik dokumentov. Ed. A. V. Nifontov and B. V. Zlatoustovskii. Moscow, 1960.

Krest'ianskoe dvizhenie v Rossii v 1890–1900 gg. Sbornik dokumentov. Ed. A. V. Shapkarin. Moscow, 1959.

Materialy po preobrazovaniiu mestnogo upravleniia v guberniiakh dostavleny gubernatorami, zemstvom, i prisutstviiami po krest'ianskim delam. 3 vols. St. Petersburg, 1883–4.

Materialy po vysochaishe utverzhdennoi osoboi komissii dlia sostavleniia proektov mestnogo upravleniia. 10 vols. St. Petersburg, 1884.

Matthews, Mervyn, ed. *Soviet Government: A Selection of Official Documents on Internal Policies.* New York, 1974.

Ministerstvo vnutrennikh del. *Ministertvo vnutrennikh del. Istoricheskii ocherk.* St. Petersburg, 1901.

Sbornik tsirkuliarov Ministerstva vnutrennikh del za 1880–1884 gg. Comp. and ed. D. V. Chinchinadze. St. Petersburg, 1886.

Sistematicheskii ukazatel' k Sborniku tsirkuliarov i instruktsii Ministerstva vnutrennikh del za vremia s 1 ianvaria 1858 g. po 1 ianvaria 1880 g. s raspredeleniem tsirkuliarov i instruktsii po stat'iam Svoda zakonov izdaniia 1876 goda. Comp. D. Chukovskii. St. Petersburg, 1881.

Khoziaistvennyi departament. *Vysochaishe utverzhdennoe 12 iiunia 1890 goda polozhenie o gubernskikh i uezdnykh zemskikh uchrezhdeniiakh.* St. Petersburg, 1903.

Zemskii otdel. *Sbornik uzakonenii o krest'ianskikh i sudebnykh uchrezhdeniiakh, preobrazovannykh po zakonu 12-go iiulia 1889 goda.* St. Petersburg, 1890.

Oganovskii, N. P., ed. *Sel'skoe khoziaistvo Rossii v XX veke. Sbornik statistiko-ekonomicheskikh svedenii za 1901–1922 gg.* Mouton reprint. The Hague, 1968 [Moscow, 1923].

Otmena krepostnogo prava: Doklady ministrov vnutrennikh del o provedenii krest'ianskoi reformy 1861–1862. Ed. S. N. Valk. Moscow-Leningrad, 1950.

Pazukhin, A. D. *Sovremennoe sostoianie Rossii i soslovnyi vopros.* Moscow, 1886.

Petrunkevich, I. I. "Blizhaishie zadachi zemstva." *1864–1914: Iubileinyi zemskii sbornik.* Ed. B. B. Veselovskii and Z. G. Frenkel'. St. Petersburg, 1914, pp. 429–36.

Polnoe sobranie zakonov Rossiiskoi Imperii. 2d ser. 55 vols. St. Petersburg, 1825–81. 3d ser. 33 vols. St. Petersburg, 1885–1916.

Polozhenie o zemskikh uchrezhdeniiakh 12 iiunia 1890 goda so vsemi otnosiashchimisia k nemu uzakoneniiami. 4th ed. Comp. M. I. Mysh. St. Petersburg, 1908.

Pravitel'stvuiushchii senat. *Istoriia pravitel'stvuiushchego senata za dvesti let 1711–1911* gg. 5 vols. St. Petersburg, 1911.

Raeff, Marc, ed. *Plans for Political Reform in Imperial Russia, 1730–1905.* Englewood Cliffs, N.J., 1966.

Rzhevusskii, M. I. *Alfavitny svod opredelenii Senata po zemskim delam za 50 let.* Khar'kov, 1916.

Sbornik postanovlenii, otnosivshikhsia k grazhdanskomu pravu lits sel'skogo sostoianiia. St. Petersburg, 1898.

Sbornik pravitel'stvennykh rasporiazhenii po delam do zemskikh uchrezhdenii otnosiashchimsia (1864–1889). 13 vols. St. Petersburg, 1900–2.

4 vols. St. Petersburg, 1868–76.

Sbornik pravitel'stvennykh rasporiazhenii po delam do zemskikh uchrezhdenii otnosiashchimsia (za 1875–1876 gg.). St. Petersburg, n.d.

Sbornik uzakonenii otnosiashchikhsia do zemskikh uchrezhdenii (po Svodu zakonov i prodolzheniiam izdaniia 1876 goda) s vkliucheniem reshenii Pravitel'stvuiushchego senata i pravitel'stvennykh raziasnenii i s prilozheniem gorodovogo polozheniia. Novgorod, 1879.

"Senatorskie revizii 1880 goda." *Russkii arkhiv* 50 (1912): 417–29.

Shchetinina, G. I. "Novyi dokument po istorii vnutrennei politiki Rossii epokhi vtoroi revoliutsionnoi situatsii (Proekt A. A. Saburova–D. A. Miliutina)." *Problemy istochnikovedeniia.* Vol. 2. Moscow, 1961, pp. 3–14.

Svod zakliuchenii gubernskikh soveshchanii po voprosam otnosiashchimsia k peresmotru zakonodatel'stva o krest'ianakh. 3 vols. St. Petersburg, 1897.

Svod zakonov Rossiiskoi Imperii poveleniem Gosudaria Imperatora Nikolai Pavlovicha sostavlennyi. 3d ser. *Prodolzheniia.* St. Petersburg, 1858–1914.

Trudy komissii o gubernskikh i uezdnykh uchrezhdeniiakh. 6 vols. St. Petersburg, 1860–3.

Trudy redaktsionnoi kommissii po peresmotru zakonopolozhenii o krest'ianakh. 6 vols. St. Petersburg, 1903–4.

Valuev, P. A. "Duma russkogo vo vtoroi polovine 1855 goda." *Russkaia starina.* 24, no. 9 (1893): 503–14.

"Zapiska P. A. Valueva Aleksandru II o provedenii reformy 1861 g. (Publikatsiia i predislovie O. N. Shepelevoi)." *Istoricheskii arkhiv,* no. 1 (1961): 66–81.

"Vsepoddanneishii doklad gr. P. A. Valueva i dokumenty k Verkhovnoi Rasporiaditel'noi Komissii 1880 g. kasatel'nye." *Russkii arkhiv,* no. 11–12 (1915): pp. 216–48.

Vitte [Witte], S. Iu. *Samoderzhavie i zemstvo: Konfidentsial'naia zapiska Ministrov finansov Stats-Sekretaria S. Iu. Witte (1899 g.).* 2d ed. Stuttgart, 1903.

Zapiska po krest'ianskomu delu. St. Petersburg, 1904.

Zhurnal Vysochaishe uchrezhdennoi Osoboi Komissii dlia sostavleniia proektov mestnogo upravleniia. 19 nos. St. Petersburg, 1884–5.

B. Diaries

Dnevnik D. A. Miliutina. 4 vols. Ed. P. A. Zaionchkovskii. Moscow, 1947–50.

Dnevnik E. A. Perettsa, gosudarstvennogo sekretaria (1880–1883). Moscow-Leningrad, 1927.

Dnevnik gosudarstvennogo sekretaria A. A. Polovstova v dvukh tomakh (1883–1892). 2 vols. Ed. P. A. Zaionchkovskii. Moscow, 1966.

Dnevnik kniazia V. P. Meshcherskogo za 1889 god (noiabr' i dekabr') i za 1890 god (ianvar', fevral', i mart). St. Petersburg, 1890.

Lamzdorf, V. N. *Dnevnik 1886–1890.* Ed. F. A. Rotshtein. Moscow-Leningrad, 1926.

    Dnevnik 1891–1892. Trans. Iu. Ia. Solov'eva. Ed. F. A. Rotshtein. Moscow-Leningrad, 1934.

Nikitenko, A. V. *Dnevnik v trekh tomakh.* 3 vols. Ed. N. L. Brodskii. Leningrad, 1955.

Polovtsov, A. A. "Dnevnik mirovogo posrednika Aleksandra Andreevicha Polovtsova (Peterburgskoi gubernii, Luzhskogo uezda)." *Russkaia starina,* no. 1 (1914): 95–104.

    "Dnevnik A. A. Polovtsova [1901–1903]." *Krasnyi arkhiv* 3 (1923): 75–112.

    "Iz dnevnika A. A. Polovtsova (1877–1878 gg.]." *Krasnyi arkhiv* 2(33) (1929): 170–203.

    "Iz dnevnika A. A. Polovtsova [1895–1900 gg.]." *Krasnyi arkhiv* 46 (1931): 110–32.

    "Iz dnevnika A. A. Polovtsova [1894]." *Krasnyi arkhiv* 67 (1934): 168–86.

Valuev, P. A. *Dnevnik 1877–1884 gg.* Ed. V. Ia. Iakovlev-Bogucharskii and P. E. Shchegolev. Petrograd, 1919.

    Dnevnik P. A. Valueva, ministra vnutrennikh del 1861–1876 gg. Ed. P. A. Zaionchkovskii. 2 vols. Moscow, 1961.

C. Memoirs

Astyrev, N. M. *V volostnykh pisariakh. Ocherki krest'ianskogo samoupravleniia.* Moscow, 1886.

Aveskii, V. A. "Zemstvo i zhizn'. (Zapiski predsedatelia zemskoi upravy." *Istoricheskii vestnik* 127, no. 1 (1912): 156–86.

Belogolovyi, N. A. *Vospominaniia i drugie stat'i.* 4th ed. St. Petersburg, 1901.

Blinov, N. *Zemskaia sluzhba. Besedy glasnogo-krest'ianina Akima Prostoty.* St. Petersburg, 1881.

Chicherin, B. N. *Vospominaniia.* 3 vols. Moscow, 1929–34.

Feoktistov, E. M. *Vospominaniia E. M. Feoktistova. Za kulisami politiki i literatury 1848–1896.* Ed. Iu. G. Oksman. Leningrad, 1929.

Golovin, K. F. *Moi vospominaniia.* 2 vols. St. Petersburg, 1910.

"Gosudarstvennoe zasedanie 8 marta 1881 goda." *Russkii arkhiv,* no. 7 (1906): 445–8.

Grot, Ia. K. "Vospominanie o grafe M. A. Korf (Rodilsia 11-go sentiabria 1800, † 2-go ianvaria 1876 g.)." *Russkaia starina* 15 (1876): 422–5.

Gurko, V. I. *Features and Figures of the Past: Government and Opinion in the Reign of*

Nicholas II. Trans. Laura Matveev. Ed. J. E. Wallace Sterling, Xenia Joukoff Eudin, and H. H. Fisher. Stanford, 1939.

Khizhniakov, V M. *Vospominaniia zemskogo deiatelia.* Petrograd, 1916.

Kizevetter, A. A. *Na rubezhe dvukh stoletii (Vospominaniia, 1881–1914).* Prague, 1929.

Koni, A. F. *Na zhiznennom puti.* 2 vols. St. Petersburg, 1913.

Sobranie sochinenii v vos'mi tomakh. 8 vols. Ed. V. G. Bazanov, A. N. Smirnov, and K. I. Chukovskii. Moscow, 1966–9.

Koshelev, A. I. *Zapiski Aleksandra Ivanovicha Kosheleva (1812–1883 gody).* Berlin, 1884.

Meshcherskii, V. P. *Moi vospominaniia.* 3 vols. St. Petersburg, 1897–1912.

N. A. K. (pseud.). "Mirovye posredniki pervogo prizyva (Lichnye vospominaniia)." *Istoricheskii vestnik,* no. 7 (1904): 89–100.

Novikov, A. I. *Zapiski zemskogo nachal'nika Aleksandra Novikova.* St. Petersburg, 1899.

Petrunkevich, I. I. "Iz zapisok obshchestvennogo deiatelia: Vospominaniia." *Arkhiv russkoi revoliutsii* 21 (Berlin, 1934).

Semenov, S. T. *Dvadtsat' piat' let v derevne* (Moscow, 1915).

Shumakher, A. D. "Neskol'ko slov o g. A. E. Timasheve i otnoshenie ego k obshchestvennym uchrezhdeniiam." *Vestnik evropy* 27 (1892): 846–57.

"Pozdnye vospominaniia." *Vestnik evropy* 34 (1899): 695–728.

Tiutcheva, A. F. *Pri dvore dvukh imperatorov 1855–1882.* Moscow, 1928–9.

Vitte [Witte], S. Iu. *Vospominaniia.* 3 vols. Moscow, 1960.

D. Letters and correspondence

"Aleksandr Vasil'evich Golovnin v 1863 i 1881 gg.: Ego pis'ma" *Russkaia starina* 56 (1887): 507–15.

"Perepiska Aleksandra III s gr. M. T. Loris-Melikovym (1880–1881 gg.). *Krasnyi arkhiv* 8 (1925): 101–31.

"Perepiska ministra vnutrennikh del P. A. Valueva i gosudarstvennogo sekretaria S. N. Urusova v 1866 godu." *Istoriia SSSR,* no. 2 (1973): 115–27.

"Pervye nedeli tsarstvovaniia imperatora Aleksandra Tret'ego: Pis'ma K. P. Pobedonostseva iz Peterburga k Moskvu k E. F. Tiutchevoi, 1881." *Russkii arkhiv,* no. 5 (1907): 89–102.

Pobedonostsev, K. P. *K. P. Pobedonostsev i ego korrespondenty: Pis'ma i zapiski.* Vol. 1, 2 parts. Moscow-Petrograd, 1923.

Pis'ma K. P. Pobedonostseva k Aleksandru III. 2 vols. Moscow, 1925.

"Pis'ma K. P. Pobedonostseva k Aleksandru III." *Krasnyi arkhiv,* no. 4 (1923): 317–37.

"Pis'ma K. P. Pobedonostseva k gr. N. P. Ignat'evu." *Byloe,* no. 27–28 (1925): 50–89.

"Pis'mo K. P. Pobedonostseva k N. S. Abaze." *Golos minuvshego,* no. 6 (1914): 231–2.

Rieber, Alfred J., ed. *The Politics of Autocracy: Letters of Alexander II to Prince A. I. Bariatinskii,* with an historical essay by Alfred J. Rieber. The Hague, 1966.

Sobranie sochinenii R. A. Fadeeva. 3 vols. Ed. V. V. Komarova. St. Petersburg, 1889.

"Vozhd' reaktsii 60–80-kh godov (Pis'ma Katkova Aleksandru II i Aleksandru III)." *Byloe*, no. 4 (26) (1917): 3–32.

IV. SECONDARY WORKS

Abbott, Robert J. "Police Reform in Russia, 1858–1878." Unpublished Ph.D. Dissertation, Princeton University, 1971.

Abramov, Ia. V. *Chto sdelalo zemstvo i chto ono delaet (Obzor deiatel'nosti russkogo zemstva)*. St. Petersburg, 1889.

Akhun, M. "Istochniki dlia izucheniia istorii gosudarstvennykh uchrezhdenii tsarskoi Rossii (XIX-XX vv.)." *Arkhivnoe delo*, no. 1 (1939): 77–91.

Aleksandrov, V. A. *Obychnoe pravo krepostnoi derevni Rossii XVIII-nachalo XIX v.* Moscow, 1984.

Anderson, William, ed. *Local Government in Europe*. New York, 1939.

Anfimov, A. M. "Krest'ianskoe dvizhenie." *Rossiia v revoliutsionnoi situatsii na rubezhe 1870–1880-kh godov. Kollektivnaia monografiia*. Ed. B. S. Itenberg. Moscow, 1983, pp. 161–96.

Ekonomicheskoe polozhenie i klassovaia bor'ba krest'ian Evropeiskoi Rossii 1881–1904 gg. Moscow, 1984.

Anfimov, A. M., and A. M. Solov'eva. "Obostrenie nuzhdy i bedstvii ugnetennykh klassov." *Rossiia v revoliutsionnoi situatsii na rubezhe 1870–1880-kh godov. Kollektivnaia monografiia*. Ed. B. S. Itenberg. Moscow, 1983, pp. 135–60.

Armstrong, John A. "Tsarist and Soviet Elite Administrators." *Slavic Review* 36, no. 1 (March 1972): 1–28.

The European Administrative Elite. Princeton, 1973.

Arsen'ev, K. K. *Za chetvert' veka (1871–1894). Sbornik statei*. Petrograd, 1915.

Ashford, Douglas E. *National Development and Local Reform: Political Participation in Morocco, Tunisia, and Pakistan*. Princeton, 1967.

Atkinson, Dorothy. "The Zemstvo and the Peasantry." *The Zemstvo in Russia: An Experiment in Local Self-Government*. Ed. Terence Emmons and Wayne S. Vucinich. Cambridge, 1982, pp. 79–132.

The End of the Russian Land Commune 1905–1930. Stanford, 1983.

Avinov, N. N. "Graf Korf i zemskaia reforma 1864 goda (Iz istorii sostavleniia polozheniia o zemskikh uchrezhdeniiakh 1864 g.)." *Russkaia mysl'*, no. 2 (1904): 94–111.

Opyt programmy sistematicheskogo chteniia po voprosam zemskogo samoupravleniia. Moscow, 1905.

"Glavnye cherty v istorii zakonodatel'stva o zemskikh uchrezhdeniiakh." *1864–1914: Iubileinyi zemskii sbornik*, pp. 1–34.

Barraclough, Geoffrey. *An Introduction to Contemporary History*. Baltimore, 1967.

Basdevant-Gaudemet, Brigitte. *La Commission de décentralisation de 1870: Contribution a l'étude de la décentralisation en France au XIXe siècle*. Paris, 1973.

Becker, Seymour. *Nobility and Privilege in Late Imperial Russia*. DeKalb, Ill., 1985.

Belokonskii, I. P. *Zemstvo i konstitutsiia*. Moscow, 1910.

Bennett, Helju A. "The *Chin* System and the *Raznochintsy* in the Government of Alexander III, 1881–1894." Unpublished Ph.D. Dissertation, University of California at Berkeley, 1971.

Bezobrazov, V. P. "Zemskie uchrezhdeniia i samoupravlenie," *Russkii vestnik* 110, no. 4 (1874): 524–73.

Gosudarstvo i obshchestvo. Upravlenie, samoupravlenie i sudebnaia vlast': Stat'i. St. Petersburg, 1882.

Bien, David D., and Raymond Grew. "France." *Crises of Political Development in Europe and the United States.* Ed. Raymond Grew. Princeton, 1978, pp. 219–70.

Binkley, Robert C. *Realism and Nationalism*: 1852–1871. New York, 1935.

Black, C. E. *The Dynamics of Modernization: A Study in Comparative History.* New York, 1967.

Blank, P. "Vopros o gubernskikh zemskikh uchrezhdeniiakh." *Russkii vestnik* 98, no. 3 (1872): 171–201.

Bleklov, S. M. "Krest'ianskoe obshchestvennoe upravlenie." *Istoriia Rossii v XIX veke.* Vol. 5. St. Petersburg, n.d., pp. 139–64.

Blinov, I. A. *Otnosheniia senata k mestnym uchrezhdeniiam v XIX veke.* St. Petersburg, 1911.

Bol'shov, V. V. "Materialy senatorskikh revizii 1880–1881 gg. kak istochnik po istorii mestnogo upravleniia Rossii." *Vestnik Moskovskogo Universiteta.* Ser. 9. *Istoriia,* no. 4 (1976): 38–54.

Brooks, Jeffrey. "The Zemstvo and the Education of the People." *The Zemstvo in Russia: An Experiment in Local Self-Government.* Ed. Terence Emmons and Wayne S. Vucinich. Cambridge, 1982, pp. 243–78.

Byrnes, Robert F. *Pobedonostsev: His Life and Thought.* Bloomington, Ind., 1968.

Chernukha, V. G. "Pravitel'stvennaia politika i institut mirovykh posrednikov." *Vnutrenniaia politika tsarizma (seredina XVI-nachalo XX v.).* Ed. B. V. Anan'ich, S. N. Valk, and R. Sh. Ganelin. Leningrad, 1967, pp. 197–238.

"Problema politicheskoi reformy v pravitel'stvennykh krugakh Rossii v nachale 70-kh godov XIX v." *Problemy krest'ianskogo zemlevladeniia i vnutrennei politiki Rossii: Dooktiabr'skii period.* Ed. S. N. Valk and V. S. D'iakin. Leningrad, 1972, pp. 138–90.

Krest'ianskii vopros v pravitel'stvennoi politike Rossii (60–70 gody XIX v.). Leningrad, 1972.

Vnutrenniaia politika tsarizma s serediny 50-kh do nachala 80-kh gg. XIX v. Leningrad, 1978.

Christian, David. "The Supervisory Function in Russian and Soviet History." *Slavic Review* 41, no. 1 (Spring 1982): 73–90.

Crozier, Michel. *The Bureaucratic Phenomenon.* Chicago, 1964.

Czap, Jr., Peter A. "The Influence of Slavophile Ideology on the Formation of the *Volost'* Court of 1861 and the Practice of Peasant Self-Justice Between 1861 and 1889." Unpublished Ph.D. Dissertation, Cornell University, 1959.

"P. A. Valuev's Proposal for a *Vyt'* Administration, 1864." *Slavonic and East European Review* 45, no. 105 (1967): 391–410.

Daragan, D. *Mysli sel'skogo khoziaina po raznym zemskim voprosam. Sbornik statei po raznym voprosam, pomeshchennym v "Vestnike Pskovskogo Gubernskogo Zemstva."* St. Petersburg, 1884.

Demis, L. *Zemskie uchrezhdeniia.* 3d ed. St. Petersburg, 1865.

Druzhinin, N. M. "Senatorskie revizii 1860–1870-kh godov (K voprosu o realizatsii reformy 1861 g.)." *Istoricheskie zapiski* 79 (1966): 139–75.

"Glavnyi komitet ob ustroistve sel'skogo sostoianiia." *Issledovaniia po sotsial'no-politicheskoi istorii Rossii: Sbornik statei pamiati Borisa Aleksandrovicha Romanova.* Ed. N. E. Nosov and others. Leningrad, 1971, pp. 269–86.

Russkaia derevnia na perelome 1861–1880 gg. Moscow, 1978.

Dzhanshiev, G. A. *Epokha velikikh reform: Istoricheskie ocherki.* 8th ed. Moscow, 1900.

Eklof, Ben. *Russian Peasant Schools: Officialdom, Village Culture, and Popular Pedagogy, 1861–1914.* Berkeley, 1986.

Emmons, Terence. *The Russian Landed Gentry and the Peasant Emancipation of 1861.* Cambridge, 1968.

Eroshkin, N. P., Kulikov, Iu. V., and Chernov, A. V. *Istoriia gosudarstvennykh uchrezhdenii Rossii do velikoi oktiabr'skoi sotsialisticheskoi revoliutsii.* 2d ed. Moscow, 1965.

Evenchik, S. L. "Pobedonostsev i dvoriansko-krepostnicheskaia liniia samoderzhaviia v poreformennoi Rossii." *Uchenye zapiski No. 309. Kafedra istorii SSSR.* Moscow, 1969, pp. 52–338.

Evreinov, G. A. *Zametki o mestnoi reforme.* St. Petersburg, 1888.

Fainsod, Merle. *Smolensk under Soviet Rule.* Cambridge, Mass., 1958.

"Bureaucracy and Modernization: The Russian and Soviet Case." *Bureaucracy and Political Development.* Ed. Joseph LaPalombara. Princeton, 1963, pp. 233–67.

Fallows, Thomas. "The Zemstvo and the Bureaucracy, 1890–1914." *The Zemstvo in Russia: An Experiment in Local Self-Government.* Ed. Terence Emmons and Wayne S. Vucinich. Cambridge, 1982, pp. 177–242.

Field, Daniel. *The End of Serfdom: Nobility and Bureaucracy in Russia, 1855–1861.* Cambridge, Mass., 1976.

Fischer, George. *Russian Liberalism.* Cambridge, Mass., 1958.

Florinsky, Michael T. *Russia: A History and an Interpretation.* 2 vols. New York, 1947.

Freeze, Gregory L. *The Parish Clergy in Nineteenth-Century Russia: Crisis, Reform, Counter-reform.* Princeton, 1983.

"The *Soslovie* (Estate) Paradigm and Russian Social History." *American Historical Review* 91 (February 1986): 11–36.

Fried, Robert C. *The Italian Prefects: A Study in Administrative Politics.* New Haven, 1963.

Frieden, Nancy M. *Russian Physicians in an Era of Reform and Revolution, 1861–1905.* Princeton, 1981.

"The Politics of Zemstvo Medicine." *The Zemstvo in Russia: An Experiment in Local Self-Government.* Ed. Terence Emmons and Wayne S. Vucinich. Cambridge, 1982, pp. 315–42.

Frierson, Cathy. "Crime and Punishment in the Russian Village: Rural Concepts of Criminality at the End of the Nineteenth Century." *Slavic Review* 46, no. 1 (Spring 1987): 55–69.

Gantvoort, John G. "Relations between Government and Zemstvos under Valuev and Timashev, 1864–1876." Unpublished Ph.D. Dissertation, University of Illinois, 1971.

Garmiza, V. V. *Podgotovka zemskoi reformy 1864 goda.* Moscow, 1957.

"Zemskaia reforma i zemstvo v istoricheskoi literature." *Istoriia SSSR*, no. 5 (1960): 82–107.

Gessen, V. M. *Voprosy mestnogo upravleniia.* St. Petersburg, 1904.

Geyer, Dietrich. *Russian Imperialism: The Interaction of Domestic and Foreign Policy, 1860–1914*. Trans. Bruce Little. New Haven, 1987.

Gill, Graeme J. *Peasants and Government in the Russian Revolution*. New York, 1979.

Gillis, John R. *The Prussian Bureaucracy in Crisis 1840–1860: Origins of an Administrative Ethos*. Stanford, 1971.

"Germany." *Crises of Political Development in Europe and the United States*. Ed. Raymond Grew. Princeton, 1978, pp. 313–46.

Golovachev, A. A. *Desiat' let reform, 1861–1871*. St. Petersburg, 1872.

Golovin, K. F. *Nashe mestnoe upravlenie i mestnoe predstavitel'stvo*. St. Petersburg, 1884.

Gorfein, G. M. "Osnovnye istochniki po istorii vysshikh i tsentral'nykh uchrezhdenii XIX-nachala XX v." *Nekotorye voprosy izucheniia istoricheskikh dokumentov XIX-nachala XX v. Sbornik statei*. Ed. I. N. Firsov. Leningrad, 1967, pp. 73–108.

Got'e, Iu. V. *Istoriia oblastnogo upravleniia v Rossii ot Petra I do Ekateriny II*. 2 vols. Moscow, 1913.

"Pobedonostsev and Alexander III." *Slavonic and East European Review* 7, no. 19 (1928): 30–54.

"Bor'ba pravitel'stvennykh gruppirok i manifest 29 aprelia 1881 g." *Istoricheskie zapiski* 2 (1938): 240–99.

Gradovskii, A. D. *Sobranie sochinenii A. D. Gradovskogo*. 9 vols. St. Petersburg, 1899–1904.

Grant, Steven A. "*Obshchina* and *Mir*." *Slavic Review* 35, no. 4 (December 1976): 636–51.

Grew, Raymond. "The Crises and Their Sequences." *Crises of Political Development in Europe and the United States*. Ed. Raymond Grew. Princeton, 1978, pp. 3–40.

"Italy." *Crises of Political Development in Europe and the United States*. Ed. Raymond Grew. Princeton, 1978, pp. 271–312.

Haimson, Leopold H., ed. *The Politics of Rural Russia 1905–1914*. Bloomington, Ind., 1979.

Halevy, Elie. *England in 1815*. Trans. E. I. Watkin and D. A. Barker. Paperback ed. New York, 1961.

Hamburg, G. N. "Portrait of an Elite: Russian Marshals of the Nobility, 1861–1917." *Slavic Review* 40, no. 4 (Winter 1981): 585–602.

Politics of the Russian Nobility 1881–1905. New Brunswick, N.J., 1984.

Hamerow, Theodore S. *The Birth of a New Europe: State and Society in the Nineteenth Century*. Chapel Hill, N.C., 1983.

Haxthausen, Baron August von. *Studies on the Interior of Russia*. Trans. Eleanor L. M. Schmidt. Ed. with an introduction by S. Frederick Starr. Chicago, 1972.

Heilbronner, Hans. "The Administration of Loris-Melikov and Ignat'ev, 1880–1882." Unpublished Ph.D. Dissertation, University of Michigan, 1954.

"Alexander III and the Reform Plan of Loris-Melikov." *Journal of Modern History* 33, no. 4 (1961): 384–97.

"The Russian Plague of 1878–1879." *Slavic Review* 21, no. 1 (1962): 89–112.

Hood, Christopher. *The Limits of Administration*. London, 1976.

Hough, Jerry F. *The Soviet Prefects: The Local Party Organs in Industrial Decision-making*. Cambridge, Mass., 1969.

Hsiao, Kung-Chuan. *Rural China: Imperial Control in the Nineteenth Century*. Paperback ed. Seattle, 1967.

Iordanskii, N. I. *Konstitutsionnoe dvizhenie 60-kh godov*. St. Petersburg, 1906.

Istoriia SSSR. Vol. 2: *1861–1917 gg. Period kapitalizma.* Ed. L. M. Ivanov, A. L. Sidorov, and V. K. Iatsunskii. Moscow, 1959.

Itenberg, B. S. "Krizis samoderzhavnoi vlasti." *Rossiia v revoliutsionnoi situatsii na rubezhe 1870–1880-kh godov. Kollektivnaia monografiia.* Ed. B. S. Itenberg and others. Moscow, 1983, pp. 90–134.

Ivanovskii, V. V. *Opyt issledovaniia deiatel'nosti organov zemskogo samoupravleniia.* Kazan', 1881.

Jones, Robert E. *The Emancipation of the Russian Nobility 1762–1785.* Princeton, 1973.

Karamzin's Memoir on Ancient and Modern Russia: A Translation and an Analysis. Trans. Richard Pipes. Paperback ed. New York, 1969.

Karyshev, N. A. *Zemskie khodataistva 1865–1884 gg.* Moscow, 1900.

Kataev, I. M. *Doreformennaia biurokratiia: Po zapiskam, memuaram, i literature.* St. Petersburg, 1914.

Kataev, M. M. *Mestnye krest'ianskie uchrezhdeniia 1861, 1874 i 1889 gg. (Istoricheskii ocherk ikh obrazovaniia i norm deiatel'nosti).* 3 parts in one: St. Petersburg, 1911.

Kenez, Peter. *The Birth of the Propaganda State: Soviet Methods of Mass Mobilization, 1917–1929.* Cambridge, 1985.

Kesselman, Mark. *The Ambiguous Consensus: A Study of Local Government in France.* New York, 1967.

Kheifets, M. I. "Arkhivnye materialy M. T. Loris-Melikova (K istorii vtoroi revoliutsionnoi situatsii v Rossii)." *Istoricheskii arkhiv.* no. 1 (1959): 193–203.

Vtoraia revoliutsionnaia situatsiia v Rossii (konets 70-kh-nachalo 80-kh godov XIX veka). Krizis pravitel'stvennoi politiki. Moscow, 1963.

Kizevetter, A. A. "Nikolai Alekseevich Miliutin." *Istoricheskie otkliki.* Moscow, 1915, pp. 221–68.

Mestnoe samoupravlenie v Rossii, IX-XIX st.; Istoricheskii ocherk. 2d ed. Petrograd, 1917.

Korelin, A. P. "Dvorianstvo v poreformennoi Rossii (1861–1904 gg.)." *Istoricheskie zapiski* 87 (1971): 91–173.

Dvorianstvo v poreformennoi Rossii 1861–1904 gg.: Sostav, chislennost', korporativnaia organizatsiia. Moscow, 1979.

Korf, P. L. *Blizhaishie nuzhdy mestnogo upravleniia.* St. Petersburg, 1888.

Korf, S. A. *Dvorianstvo i ego soslovnoe upravlenie za stoletie 1762–1855 gg.* St. Petersburg, 1906.

Administrativnaia iustitsiia v Rossii. 2 vols. St. Petersburg, 1910.

Korkunov, N. M. *Russkoe gosudarstvennoe pravo.* 4th ed. 2 vols. St. Petersburg, 1903.

Kornilov, A. A. *Krest'ianskaia reforma.* St. Petersburg, 1905.

"Krest'ianskaia reforma 19 fevralia 1861 goda." *Krest'ianskii stroi: Sbornik statei A. A. Kornilova, A. A. Lappo-Danilevskogo, V. I. Semevskogo i I. M. Strakhovskogo.* Vol. 1: *Istoricheskaia chast'.* Ed. P. D. Dolgorukov and S. L. Tolstoi. St. Petersburg, 1905.

Obshchestvennoe dvizhenie pri Aleksandre II, 1855–1881; istoricheskie ocherki. Moscow, 1909.

"Deiatel'nost' mirovykh posrednikov." *Velikaia reforma. Russkoe obshchestvo i krest'ianskii vopros v proshlom i nastoiashchem. Iubileinoe izdanie.* Vol. 5. Ed. A. K. Dzhivelegov, S. P. Mel'gunov, and V. I. Picheta. Moscow, 1911, pp. 237–52.

"Krest'ianskoe samoupravlenie po Polozheniiu 19 fevralia." *Velikaia reforma.* Vol. 6, pp. 137–58.

"K istorii konstitutsionnogo dvizheniia kontsa 70-kh nachala 80-kh godov." *Russkaia mysl'.* Bk. 7. 1913, pp. 25–46.

Kurs istorii Rossii XIX v. 3 vols. St. Petersburg, 1914.

Krieger, Leonard. *The German Idea of Freedom: History of a Political Tradition.* Paperback ed. Chicago, 1972.

Krizis samoderzhaviia v Rossii 1895–1917. Ed. B. V. Anan'ich, R. Sh. Ganelin and others. Leningrad, 1984.

Kuz'min-Karavaev, V. D. "Krest'ianstvo i zemstvo." *Velikaia reforma.* Vol. 6, pp. 277–87.

LeDonne, John P. *Ruling Russia: Politics and Administration in the Age of Absolutism 1762–1796.* Princeton, 1984.

Leontovich, V. V. *Istoriia liberalizma v Rossii, 1762–1914.* Trans. Irina Ilovaiskaia. Paris, 1980.

Leroy-Beaulieu, Anatole. *Un Homme d'état russe (Nicolas Miliutine): d'après sa correspondance inédité.* Paris, 1884.

The Empire of the Tsars and the Russians. Trans. Zenaide A. Ragozin. 3 vols. New York, 1894.

Levin, Sh. M. *Obshchestvennoe dvizhenie v Rossii v 60–70e gody XIX veka.* Moscow, 1958.

Levy, Jr., Marion J. *Modernization and the Structure of Societies: A Setting for International Affairs.* Princeton, 1966.

Lewin, Moshe. *Russian Peasants and Soviet Power: A Study of Collectivization.* London, 1968.

Liberman, A. A. "Sostav instituta zemskikh nachal'nikov." *Voprosy istorii,* no. 8 (1976): 201–4.

Lincoln, W. Bruce. "Russia's 'Enlightened' Bureaucrats and the Problem of State Reform 1848–1856." *Cahiérs du monde russe et soviétique.* 12, no. 4 (October-December 1971): 410–21.

"N. A. Miliutin and the St. Petersburg Municipal Act of 1846: A Study in Reform under Nicholas I." *Slavic Review* 33, no. 1 (March 1974): 55–68.

In the Vanguard of Reform: Russia's Enlightened Bureaucrats 1825–1861. DeKalb, Ill., 1982.

Lokhvitskii, A. V. *Guberniia, ee zemskie i pravitel'stvennye uchrezhdeniia.* St. Petersburg, 1864.

Macey, David A. J. *Government and Peasant in Russia, 1861–1906: The Prehistory of the Stolypin Reforms.* DeKalb, Ill., 1987.

Malkova, Z. I., and M. A. Pliukhina. "Dokumenty vysshikh i tsentral'nykh uchrezhdenii XIX-nachala XX v. kak istochnik biograficheskikh svedenii." *Nekotorye voprosy izucheniia istoricheskikh dokumentov XIX-nachala XX v.,* pp. 204–28.

Malloy, Jr., James A. "The Zemstvo Reform of 1864: Its Historical Background and Significance in Tsarist Russia." Unpublished Ph.D. Dissertation, Ohio State University, 1965.

Mandel, James I. "Paternalistic Authority in the Russian Countryside, 1856–1906." Unpublished Ph.D. Dissertation, Columbia University, 1978.

Manning, Roberta T. *The Crisis of the Old Order in Russia: Gentry and Government.* Princeton, 1982.

"The Zemstvo and Politics, 1864–1914." *The Zemstvo in Russia: An Experiment in Local Self-Government*. Ed. Terence Emmons and Wayne S. Vucinich. Cambridge, 1982, pp. 133–76.

Mansurov, A. P. "Aleksandr Vasil'evich Golovnin v ego otnosheniiakh k zemstvu 1866–1874 gg." *Russkaia starina* 55 (1887): 441–5.

McKenzie, Kermit E. "Zemstvo Organization and Role within the Administrative Structure." *The Zemstvo in Russia: An Experiment in Local Self-Government*. Ed. Terence Emmons and Wayne S. Vucinich. Cambridge, 1982, pp. 31–78.

Mironov, Boris. "The Russian Peasant Commune after the Reforms of the 1860s." Trans. Gregory Freeze. *Slavic Review* 44, no. 3 (Fall 1985): 438–67.

Mordovtsev, D. I. *Desiatiletie russkogo zemstva, 1864–1875*. St. Petersburg, 1877.

Mosse, Werner E. "Russian Bureaucracy at the End of the *Ancien Régime*: The Imperial State Council, 1897–1915." *Slavic Review* 39, no. 4 (December 1980): 616–32.

Muncy, L. W. *The Junker in the Prussian Administration under William II: 1888–1914*. Reprint, New York, 1970.

Nevedenskii, S. *Katkov i ego vremia*. St. Petersburg, 1888.

Orlovsky, Daniel T. "Recent Studies on the Russian Bureaucracy." *Russian Review* 35, no. 4 (October 1976): 448–67.

"High Officials in the Ministry of Internal Affairs, 1855–1881." *Russian Officialdom: The Bureaucratization of Russian Society from the Seventeenth to the Twentieth Century*. Ed. Walter M. Pintner and Don Karl Rowney. Chapel Hill, N.C., 1980, pp. 250–82.

The Limits of Reform: The Ministry of Internal Affairs in Imperial Russia, 1802–1881. Cambridge, Mass., 1981.

Orzhekhovskii, I. V. *Iz istorii vnutrennei politiki samoderzhaviia v 60-70-kh godakh XIX veka*. Gor'kii, 1974.

Paina, E. S., "Senatorskie revizii i ikh arkhivnye materialy (XIX-nachalo XX v.)." *Nekotorye voprosy izucheniia istoricheskikh dokumentov XIX-nachala XX v.*, pp. 147–75.

Pavlova-Sil'vanskaia, M. P. "Sotsial'naia sushchnost' oblastnoi reformy." *Absoliutizm v Rossii: Sbornik statei k semidesiatiletiiu so dnia rozhdeniia i sorokapiatiletiiu nauchnoi i pedagogicheskoe deiatel'nosti B. B. Kafengauza*. Ed. N. M. Druzhinin, N. I. Pavlenko, and L. V. Cherepnin. Moscow, 1964, pp. 460–91.

Payne, Stanley G. "Spain and Portugal." *Crises of Political Development in Europe and the United States*. Ed. Raymond Grew. Princeton, 1978, pp. 197–218.

Pearson, Thomas S. "The Origins of Alexander III's Land Captains: A Reinterpretation." *Slavic Review* 40, no. 3 (Fall 1981): 384–403.

"Russian Law and Rural Justice: Activity and Problems of the Russian Justices of the Peace, 1865–1889." *Jahrbücher für Geschichte Osteuropas*, no. 1 (1984): 52–71.

Petrov, F. A. "Nelegal'nye obshchezemskie soveshchaniia i sezdy kontsa 70-kh-nachala 80-kh godov XIX veka." *Voprosy istorii*, no. 9 (1974): 33–44.

Pintner, Walter M. "The Social Characteristics of the Early Nineteenth Century Russian Bureaucracy." *Slavic Review* 29, no. 3 (September 1979): 429–43.

"Russian Civil Service on the Eve of the Great Reforms." *Journal of Social History* 8, no. 2 (Spring 1975): 55–65.

"Russia." *Crises of Political Development in Europe and the United States*. Ed. Raymond Grew. Princeton, 1978, pp. 347–82.

"Civil Officialdom and the Nobility in the 1850s." *Russian Officialdom: The Bureaucratization of Russian Society from the Seventeenth to the Twentieth Century.* Ed. Walter M. Pintner and Don Karl Rowney. Chapel Hill, N.C., 1980, pp. 227–49.

"The Evolution of Civil Officialdom, 1755–1855." *Russian Officialdom: The Bureaucratization of Russian Society from the Seventeenth to the Twentieth Century.* Ed. Walter M. Pintner and Don Karl Rowney, Chapel Hill, N.C., 1980, pp. 190–226.

Pipes, Richard. "Russian Conservatism in the Second Half of the Nineteenth Century." *Slavic Review* 30, 1(March 1971): 121–8.

Russia under the Old Regime. New York, 1974.

Pirumova, N. M. *Zemskoe liberal'noe dvizhenie: Sotsial'nye korni i evoliutsiia do nachala XX veka.* Moscow, 1977.

Pokrovskii, M. N. "Obshchaia politika pravitel'stva 1866–1892 g." *Istoriia Rossii v XIX veke.* Vol. 5, pp. 1–78.

Pokrovskii, S. P. *Ministerskaia vlast' v Rossii: Istoriko-iuridicheskoe issledovanie.* Iaroslavl', 1906.

Ponomarev, B. N., and others, eds. *Istoriia SSSR s drevneishikh vremen do nashikh dnei v dvukh seriiakh v dvenadtsati tomakh.* 1st ser. Vols. 4 and 5. Moscow, 1967–68.

Priklonskii, S. A. *Ocherki samoupravleniia zemskogo, gorodskogo i sel'skogo.* St. Petersburg, 1886.

Prokof'eva, L. S. *Krest'ianskaia obshchina v Rossii vo vtoroi polovine XVIII-pervoi polovine XIX v. (na materialakh votchin Sheremetevykh).* Ed. Iu. G. Alekseev. Leningrad, 1981.

Raeff, Marc. "The Russian Autocracy and Its Officials." *Harvard Slavic Studies* 4 (1957): 77–91.

"The Well-Ordered Police State and the Development of Modernity in Seventeenth- and Eighteenth-Century Europe: An Attempt at a Comparative Approach." *American Historical Review* 80 (December 1975): 1221–43.

"The Bureaucratic Phenomena of Imperial Russia, 1700–1905." *American Historical Review* 84 (April 1979): 399–411.

The Well-Ordered Police State: Social and Institutional Change through Law in the Germanies and Russia, 1600–1800. New Haven, 1983.

Understanding Imperial Russia: State and Society in the Old Regime. Trans. Arthur Goldhammer. New York, 1984.

Ramer, Samuel C. '"The Zemstvo and Public Health." *The Zemstvo in Russia: An Experiment in Local Self-Government.* Ed. Terence Emmons and Wayne S. Vucinich. Cambridge, 1982, pp. 279–314.

Rieber, Alfred J. "Alexander II: A Revisionist View." *Journal of Modern History* 43, no. 1 (1971): 42–58.

Merchants and Entrepreneurs in Imperial Russia. Chapel Hill, N.C., 1982.

Riggs, Fred W. "Bureaucracy and Political Development: A Paradoxical View." *Bureaucracy and Political Development.* Ed. Joseph LaPalombara. Princeton, 1963, pp. 120–67.

Administration in Developing Countries: The Theory of Prismatic Society. Boston, 1964.

Robbins, Richard G., Jr. *Famine in Russia: The Imperial Government Responds to a Crisis.* New York, 1975.

"The Tsar's Viceroys: Provincial Governors and Governance in the Last Years of the Empire." Unpublished manuscript.

Rogger, Hans. "Russian Ministers and the Jewish Question, 1881–1917." *California Slavic Studies*. Vol. 8. Ed. Nicholas V. Riasanovsky, Gleb Struve, and Thomas Eekman, 1975, pp. 15–76.

Russia in the Age of Modernisation and Revolution 1881–1917. London, 1983.

Romanovich-Slavatinskii, A. *Dvorianstvo v Rossii ot nachala XVIII veka do otmeny krepostnogo prava: Svod materiala i prigotovlennye etiudy dlia istoricheskogo issledovaniia*. St. Petersburg, 1870.

Rosenberg, Hans. *Bureaucracy, Aristocracy, and Autocracy: The Prussian Experience 1660–1815*. Boston, 1966.

Rostow, W. W. *Politics and the Stages of Growth*. Cambridge, 1971.

Sazonov, G. P. *Obzor deiatel'nosti zemstv po narodnomu prodovol'stviiu, 1865–1892 gg.* 2 vols. St. Petersburg, 1893.

Semenov, N. P. *Osvobozhdenie krest'ian v tsarstvovanie imperatora Aleksandra II: Khronika deiatel'nosti komissii po krest'ianskomu delu.* 3 vols. plus index. St. Petersburg, 1889–94.

Seredonin, S. M. comp. *Istoricheskii obzor deiatel'nosti Komiteta ministrov.* 5 vols. St. Petersburg, 1902.

Shanin, Teodor. *The Roots of Otherness: Russia's Turn of Century.* Vol. I: *Russia as a 'Developing Society'.* New Haven, 1985.

Shchetinina, G. I. *Universitety v Rossii i ustav 1884 goda.* Moscow, 1976.

Simonova, M. S. *Krizis agrarnoi politiki tsarizma nakanune pervoi Rossiiskoi revoliutsii.* Moscow, 1987.

Sinel, Allen. *The Classroom and the Chancellery: State Educational Reform in Russia under Count Dmitry Tolstoi.* Cambridge, Mass., 1973.

Sirinov, M. A. *Zemskie nalogi. Ocherki po khoziaistvu mestnykh samoupravlenii v Rossii.* Iur'ev, 1915.

Skalon, V. Iu. *Zemskie voprosy. Ocherki i obozreniia.* Moscow, 1882.

Mneniia zemskikh sobranii o sovremennom polozhenii Rossii. Berlin, 1883.

Zemskie vzgliady na reformu mestnogo upravleniia. Obzor zemskikh otzyvov i proektov. Moscow, 1884.

Skocpol, Theda. *States and Social Revolutions: A Comparative Analysis of France, Russia, and China.* Cambridge, 1979.

Sliozberg, G. B. *Dorevoliutsionnyi stroi Rossii.* Paris, 1933.

Slobozhanin, M. *Iz istorii i opyta zemskikh uchrezhdenii v Rossii.* St. Petersburg, 1913.

Solov'ev, Iu. B. *Samoderzhavie i dvorianstvo v kontse XIX veka.* Leningrad, 1973.

St- - -k, Ia. (pseud.) "Valuevskaia komissiia." *Russkaia mysl'.* Bk. 3 (1891): 1–22.

Starr, S. Frederick. *Decentralization and Self-Government in Russia, 1830–1870.* Princeton, 1972.

"Local Initiative in Russia Before the Zemstvo." *The Zemstvo in Russia: An Experiment in Local Self-Government.* Ed. Terence Emmons and Wayne S. Vucinich. Cambridge, 1982, pp. 5–30.

Stasov, V. V. "Graf Modest Andreevich Korf: Biograficheskii ocherk, 1800–1876." *Russkaia starina* 15 (1876): 402–21.

Strakhovskii, I. M. *Krest'ianskie prava i uchrezhdeniia.* St. Petersburg, 1903.

"Krest'ianskii vopros v zakonodatel'stve i v zakonosoveshchatel'nykh komissiiakh posle 1861 g." *Krest'ianskii stroi: Sbornik statei.* Vol. 1, pp. 371–455.

Svatikov, S. G. *Obshchestvennoe dvizhenie v Rossii 1700–1895.* 2 parts in one. Rostov-on-the-Don, 1905.

Sveshnikov, M. I. *Osnovy i predely samoupravleniia: Opyt kriticheskogo razbora osnovnykh voprosov mestnogo samoupravleniia v zakonodatel'stve vazhneishikh evropeiskikh gosudarstv.* St. Petersburg, 1892.

Taranovski, Theodore. "The Politics of Counter-Reform: Autocracy and Bureaucracy in the Reign of Alexander III 1881–1894." Unpublished Ph.D. Dissertation, Harvard University, 1976.

"The Aborted Counter-Reform: Murav'ev Commission and the Judicial Statutes of 1864." *Jahrbücher für Geschichte Osteuropas,* no. 2 (1981): 161–84.

Tatishchev, S. S. *Imperator Aleksandr II: Ego zhizn' i tsarstvovanie.* 2 vols. St. Petersburg, 1911.

Taub, Richard P. *Bureaucrats under Stress: Administrators and Administration in an Indian State.* Berkeley, 1969.

Tenishev, V. V. *Administrativnoe polozhenie russkogo krest'ianina.* St. Petersburg, 1908.

Thaden, Edward C. *Conservative Nationalism in Nineteenth-Century Russia.* Seattle, 1964.

Thomas, Keith. "The United Kingdom." *Crises of Political Development in Europe and the United States.* Ed. Raymond Grew. Princeton, 1978, pp. 40–98.

Timberlake, Charles E. "The Birth of Zemstvo Liberalism in Russia: Ivan Il'ich Petrunkevich in Chernigov." Unpublished Ph.D. Dissertation, University of Washington, 1968.

"Ivan Il'ich Petrunkevich: Russian Liberalism in Microcosm." *Essays in Russian Liberalism.* Ed. Charles E. Timberlake. Columbia, Mo., 1972, pp. 18–46.

Tolstoi, D. A. *Istoriia finansovykh uchrezhdenii Rossii so vremeni gosudarstva do konchiny Imperatritsy Ekateriny II.* St. Petersburg, 1848.

Akademicheskaia gimnaziia v XVIII stoletii; po rukopisym dokumentam arkhiva Akademii nauk. 2 vols. St. Petersburg, 1885.

Romanism in Russia: An Historical Study. 2 vols. Trans. Mrs. M'Kibbin. Reprint. New York, 1971.

Torke, Hans J. "Continuity and Change in the Relations Between Bureaucracy and Society in Russia, 1613–1861." *Canadian Slavic Studies* 5, no. 4 (Winter 1971): 457–76.

Tseitlin, S. Ia. "Zemskaia reforma." *Istoriia Rossii v XIX veke.* Vol. 3, pp. 179–231.

"Zemskoe samoupravlenie i reforma 1890 g. (1865–1890)." *Istoriia Rossii v XIX veke.* Vol. 5, pp. 79–138.

Tvardovskaia, V. A. *Ideologiia poreformennogo samoderzhaviia (M. N. Katkov i ego izdaniia).* Moscow, 1978.

Vasil'chikov, A. I. *O samoupravlenii: Sravnitel'nyi obzor russkikh i inostrannykh zemskikh i obshchestvennykh uchrezhdenii.* 2 vols. in one. St. Petersburg, 1872.

V. B. "Ukaz senata o mirovykh sud'iakh (Vnutrennee obozrenie)." *Russkoe bogatstvo,* no. 9 (1886): 186–7.

Venturi, Franco. *Roots of Revolution: A History of the Populist and Socialist Movements in Nineteenth-Century Russia.* Trans. Francis Haskell. New York, 1960.

Veselovskii, B. B. *Istoriia zemstva za sorok let.* 4 vols. St. Petersburg, 1909–11.

"Detsentralizatsiia upravleniia i zadachi zemstva." *1864–1914: Iubileinyi zemskii sbornik,* pp. 35–49.

Vinogradoff, Paul. *Self-Government in Russia.* London, 1915.

"Vnutrennee obozrenie: Vozobnovlenie zasedanii Kakhanovskoi komissii." *Vestnik evropy*, no. 6 (1884): 363–70.

"Vnutrennee obozrenie." *Vestnik evropy*, no. 5 (1885): 805–22.

Vorms, A., and Parenago, A. "Krest'ianskii sud i sudebno-administrativnye uchrezhdeniia." *Sudebnaia reforma 1864–1914*. Ed. N. V. Davydov and N. N. Polianskii. 2 vols. Moscow, 1915. Vol. 2, pp. 81–171.

Vucinich, Alexander. "The State and Local Community." *The Transformation of Russian Society: Aspects of Social Change since 1861*. Ed. Cyril E. Black. Cambridge, Mass., 1967, pp. 191–208.

Wagner, William G. "Tsarist Legal Policies at the End of the Nineteenth Century: A Study in Inconsistencies." *Slavonic and East European Review* 54, no. 3 (July 1976): 370–94.

Walkin, Jacob. *The Rise of Democracy in Prerevolutionary Russia: Political and Social Institutions under the Last Three Tsars*. New York, 1962.

Wallace, Donald Mackenzie. *Russia on the Eve of War and Revolution*. Ed. with an introduction by Cyril E. Black. Paperback ed. New York, 1961.

Weissman, Neil B. *Reform in Tsarist Russia: The State Bureaucracy and Local Government, 1900–1914*. New Brunswick, N.J., 1981.

Whelan, Heide W. *Alexander III and the State Council: Bureaucracy and Counter-Reform in Late Imperial Russia*. New Brunswick, N.J., 1982.

Wortman, Richard S. *The Development of a Russian Legal Consciousness*. Chicago, 1976.

Yaney, George L. *The Systematization of Russian Government: Social Evolution in the Domestic Administration of Imperial Russia, 1711–1905*. Urbana, Ill., 1973.

The Urge to Mobilize: Agrarian Reform in Russia, 1861–1930. Urbana, Ill., 1982.

Zaionchkovskii, P. A. "Verkhovnaia rasporiaditel'naia komissiia (K voprosu o 'krizise verkhov')." *Voprosy istorii sel'skogo khoziaistva, krest'ianstva, i revoliutsionnogo dvizheniia v Rossii: Sbornik statei k 75 letiiu akademika Nikolaia Mikhailovicha Druzhinina*. Moscow, 1961, pp. 254–71.

"Zakon o zemskikh nachal'nikakh 12 iiulia 1889 goda." *Nauchnye doklady vysshei shkoly. Istoricheskie nauki*, no. 2 (1961): 42–72.

Krizis samoderzhaviia na rubezhe 1870–1880-kh godov. Moscow, 1964.

Rossiiskoe samoderzhavie v kontse XIX stoletiia (Politicheskaia reaktsiia 80-kh-nachala 90-kh godov). Moscow, 1970.

"Vysshaia biurokratiia nakanune Krymskoi voiny." *Istoriia SSSR*, no. 4 (1974): 154–64.

Pravitel'stvennyi apparat samoderzhavnoi Rossii v XIX v. Moscow, 1979.

Zakharova, L. G. *Zemskaia kontrreforma 1890 g.* Moscow, 1968.

Samoderzhavie i otmena krepostnogo prava v Rossii 1856–1861. Moscow, 1984.

"Zemskie khodataistva v 1876 i 1877 g." *Vestnik evropy*, no. 6 (1880).

Zyrianov, P. N. "Sotsial'naia struktura mestnogo upravleniia kapitalisticheskoi Rossii (1861–1914 gg.)." *Istoricheskie zapiski* 107 (Moscow, 1982): 226–302.

Index

278

peace arbitrators (*mirovye posredniki*) (*cont.*) 173, 249; abolition of (1874), 34, 37–9; appointment of, 28–30; district assemblies of, 29; and land captains, 29n, 170, 177–9; in Tver' (1862), 32, 56
peasant land bank, 66
peasant resettlement, 66, 76, 126, 128, 147, 194
peasantry: emancipation of, 10, 21–23; illiteracy, 24–5, 81, 83, 85–7; land shortages of, 79, 83, 89n, 194; social stratification of, 81, 85, 89, 134; and state control, 179–80, 186, 190, 196, 199, 207–8, 252; under serfdom, 3, 22
peasant self-government, xii, 21–3, 26, 28–9, 57, 61, 63–6, 70, 89, 100–3, 113, 114, 125–30, 150, 153, 161–2, 179, 208–9, 247, 249, 252; apathy toward, 25, 84–6, 88, 137, 169; bribery in, 24–5, 27, 60, 81, 82, 85, 87–8; peasant disillusionment with, 24, 60, 81, 82–3, 84–6, 87, 99, 116–17, 139, 172, 199, 248, 252; fiscal mismanagement, 67–9, 75, 82, 116, 171; and village economy, 27, 60, 66, 75, 81, 84–5, 86, 91, 138, 180–2, 194, 208; *see also* district bureau for peasant affairs; ministry of internal affairs; peace arbitrators
peasant unrest, 89n, 116, 138, 177, 199, 202, 252
Penza, province and zemstvo, 76, 126, 127n, 143, 230t
Peretts, E. A., 102, 106, 109, 113, 115, 122n, 199
Perfil'ev, S. S., 108
Perfil'ev, V. S., 68
Perm, province and zemstvo, 68, 86, 143, 231
Peter I, 2, 3
Petrunkevich, I. I., 71, 72
Pirogov, N. I., 31
Planson, A. A., 206
Pleve, V. K., 243, 246
Pobedonostsev, K. P., 105, 110–15, 117, 134–5, 153–8, 168, 174, 175–6, 180, 182, 183, 185, 193, 195, 196n, 197, 200–1, 225, 233, 250
Polish insurrection (1863), 25, 48
Polizeistaat (well-ordered police state), xv, 3, 10, 19, 175, 182, 184
Polovtsov, A. A., 79, 81, 82, 83, 84, 88, 91n, 96–7, 100, 102, 122n, 123, 124, 135n, 157n, 167n, 182, 185, 197, 202, 204, 235, 237, 238
Poltava, province and zemstvo, 72, 230t, 231n
Pos'et, K. P., 222
Printts, N. G., 143, 146
proizvol, *see* bureaucracy, arbitrariness of
provincial administration, 2–5, 15, 133–4, 146, 223; shortcomings of, 1–3, 9, 12, 251, 255, 257; *see also* governors; ministry of internal affairs
provincial bureau for peasant affairs, 29, 83n, 171

provincial bureau for village affairs, 176, 177, 180, 190
provincial bureau for zemstvo affairs, 237, 238, 242
provincial chambers, 2, 18
provincial commissions on taxes and duties, 18
provincial directorate, 2, 5
Pskov, province and zemstvo, 66, 75n, 85, 230t, 231n
publicity (*glasnost'*), 11–12, 19, 39, 125, 132
public (all-estate) self-government, 120, 134, 175, 194–5; village, 84, 125–9, 135–9, 142, 143, 146–8, 194, 198, 209, 249; *volost'*, 64, 102, 125, 130, 135–9, 142, 143, 148, 152, 249, 253; *see also* decentralization; Kakhanov Commission; self-government

Rechtsstaat (rule of law), xiii, 11, 132n, 184
redemption payments, 66, 67, 103, 109, 115, 126, 245
Reglamentsstaat, xiii, 58n
Reutern, M. Kh., 31, 33, 35–6, 38, 41–2, 44, 45n, 46, 47, 48, 49, 51, 53, 54, 55–7, 68, 115
revolutionary unrest, 25, 32, 34, 36, 56, 61–3, 69, 70–1, 73–5, 79, 104, 105, 108, 110–11, 117, 251
Riazan', province and zemstvo, 52, 64, 65, 66, 94, 230t
Rieber, Alfred J., 17
Riggs, Fred W., 12
Rikhter, O. B., 144
Robbins, Richard G., Jr., 206, 240
Rokasovski, V. P., 242
Rostovtsev, Ia. I., 22
Russian Herald, 149
Russian News, 239
Russo-Turkish War (1877–78), 58, 67, 70, 75, 104

Saburov, A. A., 105, 113
St. Petersburg, province and zemtvo, 55–6, 66, 147, 230t
Saltykov-Shchedrin, M. E., 1
Samara, province and zemstvo, 52, 66, 67, 68, 75–7, 79, 86, 91–2, 94, 126, 230t
Samarin, F. D., 206
Samarin, Iu. F., 31
samosud, 26
Saratov, province and zemstvo, 66, 75–8, 87, 91–2, 94, 95, 98, 126, 127n, 230t
Schweinitz, H. L. von, 156
self-government: and autocracy, vii–xi, xvi, 2–3, 5–6, 8, 10, 18, 30–1, 39–45, 48–9, 61–3, 89, 96, 98–9, 104, 106, 114–17, 119, 132–4, 141, 145, 160–2, 166–70, 172–5, 179–80, 196, 198–9, 202–3, 205, 220, 235, 244, 246–7, 249–50, 252–3; and bureaucracy, viii–ix, xv–xvi, 11–14, 17, 21–3, 25, 30–1, 39–44, 46–50, 55–6, 57–8, 61–2, 63, 65, 70, 74–5, 79–81, 85, 87, 93, 101–2, 104, 109, 112, 120–1, 124, 128, 131–5, 136, 138, 140–1, 145–6, 149, 151–3, 160, 161,

282